MW00629586

ANNALS OF COMMUNISM

Each volume in the series Annals of Communism will publish selected and previously inaccessible documents from former Soviet state and party archives in a narrative that develops a particular topic in the history of Soviet and international communism. Separate English and Russian editions will be prepared. Russian and Western scholars work together to prepare the documents for each volume. Documents are chosen not for their support of any single interpretation but for their particular historical importance or their general value in deepening understanding and facilitating discussion. The volumes are designed to be useful to students, scholars, and interested general readers.

Secret Cables of the Comintern, 1933–1943

Fridrikh I. Firsov, Harvey Klehr,
and John Earl Haynes

Translated by Lynn Visson

Yale UNIVERSITY PRESS

New Haven and London

Published with assistance from the Louis Stern Memorial Fund.

Yale University Press books may be purchased in quantity for educational, business, or promotional use. For information, please e-mail sales.press@yale.edu (U.S. office) or sales@yaleup.co.uk (U.K. office).

Set in Sabon type by IDS Infotech, Ltd.
Printed in the United States of America.

ISBN: 978-0-300-19822-5 (cloth)

Library of Congress Control Number: 2014001760

A catalogue record for this book is available from the Library of Congress and the British Library.

This paper meets the requirements of ANSI/NISO Z39.48-1992 (Permanence of Paper).

10 9 8 7 6 5 4 3 2 1

Yale University Press gratefully acknowledges the financial support given for this publication by the John M. Olin Foundation, the Lynde and Harry Bradley Foundation, the Historical Research Foundation, Roger Milliken, the Rosentiel Foundation, Lloyd H. Smith, Keith Young, the William H. Donner Foundation, Joseph W. Donner, Jeremiah Milbank, the David Woods Kemper Memorial Foundation, and the Smith Richardson Foundation.

Contents

Acknowledgments ix

Introduction 1

CHAPTER 1. Ciphered Communications and the History of the Communist International 7

CHAPTER 2. Subventions 38

CHAPTER 3. The Popular Front 51

CHAPTER 4. The Spanish Civil War 68

CHAPTER 5. The International Brigades in Spain 85

CHAPTER 6. The Comintern and the Terror 111

CHAPTER 7. The Comintern and the Chinese Communist Party: Divergent Priorities 128

CHAPTER 8. The Nazi-Soviet Pact 140

CHAPTER 9. The Comintern, the Communist Parties, and the Great Patriotic War 184

CHAPTER 10. Dissolution of the Communist International 238

CONCLUSION: The Comintern, 1919–1943 245

Notes 251

Index 295

Acknowledgments

In preparing the English-language edition of this book I was pleased to have the assistance of two American historians experienced in documentary publication in the history of American communism, the Comintern, and Soviet intelligence: Harvey Klehr and John Earl Haynes. In the Russian publication the focus was on technical aspects of the coded international cables, on the Comintern's cipher staff and communications methods, and, finally, on Comintern policy and the actions of the Communist parties in the light of these cables. Klehr and Haynes reoriented the text to put the priority on the latter task by focusing on the role of these ciphered cables in practical activities of the Communist International and Communist parties. They added to the book new facts and arguments that further confirmed the principal conclusions and theses of the original manuscript. In essence a new book appeared, and all three authors have made contributions to it. I very much thank Harvey Klehr and John Haynes for this collaboration.

I am deeply grateful to Jonathan Brent for his leadership of Yale University Press's document series Annals of Communism and for his support for my role in that massive publication project. I am further grateful that he encouraged the preparation of an English-language version of this book on the Comintern's ciphered cable traffic. I thank as well Vadim Staklo for his support in preparing the manuscript. The translation of the manuscript from Russian to English was made by Lynn Visson, and I want to express my thanks to her for this job. Working with the editors and staff at Yale University Press is always a pleasure for me. The role of the editor Christina Tucker, with her colleagues Bojana Ristich and Margaret Otzel, was very important on the final stage of preparing our book. The authors greatly appreciated and are deeply grateful for their work in noting flaws, inconsistencies, and other textual errors needing correction.

This book is fundamentally based on its original Russian-language edition. Consequently I express my sincere thanks to the people who worked with that publication—Gennady A. Bordugov, who created and leads the Association of Researchers of Russian Society (AIRO) together with its publishing house, and Andrei K. Sorokin, director general of the publishing house ROSSPEN and director of the Russian State Archive of Social and Political History (RGASPI).

My daughters, Natasha Soolkin and Olga Firsova assisted in the compilation of reference materials for the footnotes, and in the computer input of the data. As the first readers of the manuscript, together with my friend, the late Vladimir Segal, they made many useful editorial comments and suggestions. Our extended family provided unique and invaluable support, understanding, and contributions to my work, and I am deeply grateful to them.

My international friends and colleagues provided valuable advice, recommendations, and information that were important for me. Work on the cipher correspondence of the Comintern presented a multitude of problems and issues. These were particularly complex because nearly all the individuals mentioned in the book are referred to in the documents under pseudonyms. My colleagues helped me establish their identities. Assistance in deciphering the pseudonyms of German Communists was provided by Bernard Bayerlein and Wladislaw Hedeler, those of the Austrian Communists by Barry McLoughlin, of Polish Communists by Feliks Tych and Ina Jazhborovskaya, of Chinese Communists by Alexander Pantsov, and of Latin American Communists by Lazar Jeifets. The senior author is most grateful to all his colleagues for their assistance in obtaining factual information regarding the real names and fates of a number of personages referred to in the book.

Many friends and colleagues helped by searching for needed documents and providing support and assistance. These include Vladimir Reznikov, Valery Brun-Tsekhovoy, the late Yuri Georgiev, Vladislav Smirnov, Mansur Mukhamedzhanov, Bob Newman, Reinhard Müller, Kevin McDermotte, Alexander Vatlin, Irina Mitelman, Eugenia Sevrugina, the late Valentina Gruzdeva, Valentina Tsyrlina, Maya

Dvorkina, Svetlana Rosenthal, Larisa Rogovaya, and Yuri Tutochkin. Heartfelt thanks go to all of them.

Fridrikh Firsov
Lynn, Massachusetts
August 2013

Introduction

In the fall of 1936 an urgent radiogram from Moscow addressed to Maurice Thorez, head of the French Communist Party, asked him to "Do everything possible to send to Italy primarily works by Engels, since there are absolutely none of them in Rome. The bookseller is telling us that Marx's works cannot be sold without Engels's. Telegraph the results here. Rudolf." Three weeks later came a second message: "Browder reports readiness to send 10 works by Marx, 15 by Engels, but the representative of Italy does not have sufficient funds. Do everything possible through Medina. Rudolf." Eight days later came a request to "Try to see to it through Medina that the Italian representative in the United States gives money to buy Marx and Engels. Rudolf." That same day a response from Spain asked Rudolf to "Tell Browder. We have told the representative in Washington immediately to agree to the purchase . . . of 10 works by Marx and 15 works by Engels."[1]

These radiograms had nothing to do with the situation on the Italian book market or the need to find Marxist books to ship to Mussolini's Italy. A telegram wired to Moscow on 19 November by a Comintern employee sent to New York to assist the leaders of the U.S. Communist Party in rendering assistance to Republican Spain gave a hint to the real meaning of the earlier messages: "I can get 10 twomotors heavy stuff carriers and 15 up to date speedy pursuit planes. Lee."[2]

The ten works of Marx and fifteen works of Engels were, in fact, bombers and fighter planes. These coded dispatches were part of the huge cipher correspondence of the Executive Committee of the Communist International (ECCI) with national Communist parties around the globe. The collection of coded dispatches preserved in the Comintern archives for the 1933–1943 period includes 764 files containing communications with more than thirty countries.[3]

While the bulk of the Comintern archives, housed in the Central Party Archives of the Institute of Marxism-Leninism of the Central Committee of the Communist Party of the Soviet Union (CPSU), were classified and virtually inaccessible to researchers throughout the Soviet period, even the existence of this cipher correspondence was unknown to everyone but the staff of the archives. Although the senior author of this book, Fridrikh Firsov, worked for more than thirty years as a staff member in the Institute, he learned of the existence of these materials only in early 1992.[4]

In carrying out planned projects, he was never provided with any of the cipher correspondence. He could not independently select and order other documents of interest to him but relied on a staff member of the archives section who selected materials for the researchers and bore full responsibility to ensure that the researcher did not receive any document containing information that, in the interests of the CPSU, was not to be made public. Even the researcher's notes containing excerpts from the documents he was allowed to see had to be vetted by the archives staff. Excerpts from documents written by or about Leon Trotsky, Grigory Zinoviev, Nikolai Bukharin, and other "enemies of the people" automatically generated objections. That they had played a leading role in the creation and activity of the Communist International rarely proved persuasive, and such materials were usually removed from the researcher's notebook. Any notebooks containing excerpts were regarded as classified documents. An archive representative conducted periodic and random checks on how the notebooks were maintained, and they had to be returned eventually to the archives for destruction.

After the failed Communist coup against Mikhail Gorbachev in August 1991, the party archive housing the Comintern documents became a state archive and was renamed the Russian Center for the Preservation and Study of Documents of Contemporary History (RTsKhIDNI).[5] Many previously off-limits documents became accessible for study, and plans were formulated to publish materials of prime importance for the history of the twentieth century.

Not everyone was enamored of the new commitment to openness. Accustomed to the old methods of work, in which the most important thing was to display vigilance and keep from the reader a document that might "do harm to the Party," the administration of the Comintern documents section and several of its staff workers tried to impede this activity. Nevertheless, Firsov helped prepare two collections for publication jointly with Yale University Press, "The Letters of Georgi Dimitrov and Stalin" and "The Comintern and the Stalinist Repressions."[6]

Other editions of documents were also produced. One, entitled "The Comintern and the Failure of German October," done jointly with a German researcher, Dr. Bernhard H. Bayerlein, dealt with the attempt of the Central Committee of the Russian Communist Party (as the Soviet party was then titled) and the Comintern to organize a revolution in Germany in 1923. While he was compiling materials for another project on the antiwar policy of the Comintern, Firsov came across the hitherto unknown Comintern cipher correspondence. Both Russian and foreign researchers soon were given limited access to this unique source. Several publications subsequently made use of these Comintern cipher telegrams.[7]

Firsov's efforts to prepare a thorough and comprehensive account of this material, however, soon hit a serious roadblock. The director of the archives, Kyrill Anderson, ordered all these documents returned to the storage facility. He explained that the Federal Security Service (FSB), heir to the Soviet KGB, had reclassified them. The alleged reason was that the addresses and the times the coded dispatches had been sent, indicated at the top of the documents, could assist in the deciphering of Russia's modern secret codes. Since British counterintelligence had long ago deciphered the encryption system used by the Comintern, this excuse had little validity. Some foreign scholars were able to receive photocopies, albeit without the supposedly sensitive upper portion on which the alleged material was located. Firsov was subsequently able to persuade the archives administration to send Yale University Press the materials of the cipher correspondence between the Comintern and the U.S. Communist Party, some of which were used by Harvey Klehr and John Haynes in *The Soviet World of American Communism*.[8]

Other ciphered materials were included in the series VKP(b), Komintern i Kitay, and in a collection: Moscou-Paris-Berlin: Télégrammes chiffrés du Komintern, 1939–1941 (Moscow-Paris-Berlin: Coded Telegrams of the Comintern, 1939–1941). The latter anthology avoided entire topics. Either its researchers were given documents by the archives staff or, more likely, they were forbidden from publishing certain documents. At least one topic—the link between the Comintern and Soviet intelligence—was totally ignored despite abundant documentation in the cipher communications of such ties.[9]

Scholars today no longer face the total secrecy about history enforced by the guardians of Soviet history. Millions of pages of Comintern documents are now available on-line and at libraries around the world. But some key collections, such as the files of the Pyatnitsky Secretariat (f. 495, op. 19), the Dimitrov Secretariat (f. 495, op. 73 and 74), and the Manuilsky Secretariat (f. 495, op. 10a), are no longer being shown to researchers, although they are key to an understanding of the nature of the Comintern. Several sections of the Comintern archives have never been shown to researchers, including the materials of the Personnel Department of the ECCI, the Personnel Commissions of the Communist parties, and the Department of International Communications of the ECCI.[10]

Does it make any significant difference that these closed files and partially open files remain out of the reach of scholars? Given the richness of what has been released, how much would our understanding of the Comintern be changed? Of course, by definition we cannot know how our understanding might be reshaped by materials we have not seen. But the significance of the Comintern in shaping world history is a powerful argument that what we do not know about its operations distorts our knowledge of an important slice of the history of the world from 1919 to the mid-1940s.

The Communist International existed for less than a quarter of a century and disappeared from the political arena in the summer of 1943. Its sections were active in most countries of the globe. In some countries, including much of Europe, Communist parties were key players in national politics. Their decisions had a profound impact on internal stability, foreign policy, and the struggle against fascism. In other places where communism never became a mass movement, like America, Communist parties nonetheless played important roles, sometimes disguised as "progressives" or influencing larger political forces. That so significant a political movement, whose operations were often conducted in secret and in the shadows, can now be described more fully and completely with the aid of these hitherto unknown or unanalyzed cipher communications is an important step in fully understanding our shared political history.

An analysis of these materials reveals the methods of the leadership of the Communist parties by the Comintern, the impact of various levers of influence on the policy of the Communist parties, and the nature and thrust of the political instructions that the ECCI was sending to party leaders. Such an analysis allows for both the identification of the specific instructions and advice the parties were receiving and the determination of the most important principles and directives embodying the political thinking of the Comintern. A comparison of these instructions with the practical activity of the Communist parties is important in pinpointing the reasons for various events in the political life of the 1930s and early 1940s, the Comintern's role, and a more accurate reconstruction of the past. Naturally, the materials of the coded correspondence must be viewed in the context of all of the documents and facts related to the activity of the Comintern and to its fundamental ideological, political, and organizational principles, as well as the role and place of this organization in the Stalinist ideological and political system.

Unfortunately, most of these materials are still not unavailable to researchers. This book is an effort to partially rectify this lacuna. Firsov's detailed notes, along with hundreds of pages of photocopies of the cables upon which this book is based, are now housed in the archives of the Hoover Institution on War, Revolution, and Peace, Stanford University.[11] This book represents an effort to illuminate some of the key episodes in Comintern history in the 1930s through the use of these ciphered cables, located in Opis 184 of the Comintern archives. It is neither a comprehensive history of the Comintern in the 1930s nor a detailed account of each episode, but an explication of important episodes as documented in these cables that gives added depth and color to some of the key moments when decisions made in Moscow reverberated throughout Europe and the United States, helping to determine the political course of the decade. Most of the material deals with the period from 1933 to 1943. The former date marks the earliest cables located in Opis 184. Firsov came across a handful of prior ciphered cables scattered in other files, and there are probably many more of them in other sections of the archives. The latter date marks the formal dissolution of the Communist International.

The Communist International was a worldwide institution. Its agents worked on every inhabited continent, and it maintained direct or indirect links with every Communist party in the world. From the beginning, however, the Comintern was Europe-oriented, and particularly as the international crises of the 1930s intensified, it focused even more on Europe and, secondarily, China, regions of intense security interest to the Soviet Union. This book reflects that focus, with Comintern activities in other regions being dealt with only in regard to their relevance to that focus. In what follows, after describing the ciphering system and its organization, we examine what they tell us about Soviet support for national Communist parties, the evolution and difficulties of the Popular Front policy (particularly in France), Soviet activity in the Spanish Civil War, the Comintern's role in Soviet terror, the Nazi-Soviet Pact period, the Comintern's role in World War II and cooperation with Soviet intelligence, and how the decision was reached to shut down the Comintern's operation.

A Note on Authorship

Few scholars in the world can match Fridrikh Firsov's expertise on the Communist International. However, both the length of his original manuscript and its style, congenial to Russians but unlikely to be familiar to an American audience, were barriers to its publication in English. At the request of Yale University Press, Harvey Klehr and John Earl Haynes, with whom Firsov had collaborated on an earlier book, were asked to work with Firsov to transform his translated Russian manuscript into a book more accessible to historically minded readers in the United States as well as more generally to the English-speaking world.

Although Klehr and Haynes have not themselves examined the cables or Firsov's original notes—relying on Lynn Visson's translation of Firsov's original Russian-language book—in the process of rewriting and reorganizing his original manuscript of more than one thousand pages, they have consulted with him frequently and comprehensively to ensure that they were not misreading, misinterpreting, or taking documents out of context. The result is a book that is likely to be the most thorough glimpse into an important cache of Comintern documents that we will have for many years.

CHAPTER ONE

Ciphered Communications and the History of the Communist International

The ciphered communications of the Comintern form only a part of its history. Often short and technical, frequently concerned with routine administrative matters, these cables also provide a unique window on the ways in which the Soviet Union, through its control of the financing, staffing, and bureaucratic structure of the Comintern, imposed its will on Communist parties around the world.[1]

The Comintern's headquarters were, of course, located in Moscow. Despite its formal status as a collection of independent Communist parties united as a transnational organization dedicated to the overthrow of the capitalist system and the establishment of a worldwide dictatorship of the proletariat, no one involved in its functioning could have been unaware that it was ultimately a Soviet institution. The ostensible aim of the Comintern was the promotion of worldwide proletarian revolution. As the directing body of the forces of revolution around the world, the Communist International provided guidance and support for parties struggling to duplicate the success of the Bolshevik Revolution. The vast bulk of the cipher communications may have dealt with prosaic matters such as financing, personnel, and resources, but the communications also enabled Comintern leaders to monitor and direct the activities of its constituent parties to ensure that they complied with the general political line whose contours were laid out in the documents of the congresses and plenums of the ECCI and in various declarations and appeals. The cipher correspondence also demonstrates in detail how the core of the Comintern's policy was its support for and defense of the USSR.

The theoretical basis for the uniting of ranks of the Communist parties around the Soviet Union was the provision of the Platform of the Comintern, adopted at its first congress in March 1919, concerning the need "to subordinate so-called national interests to the interests of international revolution." Acknowledgment of the priority of the interests of "world revolution" (later identified with the interests of the Soviet state) transformed the Comintern sections into "tools of Moscow."[2]

Everything that served the interests of the USSR was of fundamental importance. The Program of the Comintern, adopted at its sixth congress in August 1928, triumphantly proclaimed that "the international proletariat, which has its sole fatherland in the USSR, the major bastion of its achievements and the major factor in its international liberation, is duty-bound to promote the successes of socialist construction in the USSR and through all possible measures to protect it from attacks by capitalist powers." In practice, this provision was much more important than general principles or the needs of the workers' movement of any country.[3]

One of the episodes in Arthur Koestler's powerful anti-Communist novel, *Darkness at Noon*, spoke directly to that point, portraying the suicide of a Communist militant after a Comintern representative ordered Belgian Communist dockworkers to violate a Soviet-supported boycott in order to unload Soviet goods destined for Italy. Koestler's example was not fictional. Dimitry Manuilsky, a member of the Presidium of the ECCI, sent a coded telegram on June 28, 1936, to the Belgian Communist Party: "The Antwerp dockers' strike has detained 9 Soviet ships. Through your supporters on the board of the Union of Transport Workers and the strikers' committee, raise the issue of the need to unload the Soviet vessels, since the strike is aimed at the capitalists and not at a socialist country. In so doing there is a need to avoid friction among the strikers over this issue." Alexander Lozovsky, head of the Profintern, Comintern's trade union arm, added his endorsement, noting that the issue was to be raised orally, so as not to leave a paper trail.[4]

Acting on the international stage as an advocate for and champion of the Soviet system, encouraging acts of solidarity with Soviet policy, the Comintern played the role of the USSR's foreign policy bulwark. It acted as an integral part of the ideological and political mechanism used by Stalin and his entourage to give a stamp of approval on behalf of the "world proletariat" to the policy conducted by this regime. Such a role was particularly noticeable in the ECCI dispatches every year on the anniversary of the Bolshevik Party's seizure of power in

Russia. Communist parties were ordered to pay particular attention to propaganda touting the achievements of the Soviet Union. A typical message, sent to the Greek CP, instructed: "In carrying out the campaign for the sixteenth anniversary of the October Revolution there is a need to stress the difference between the situation of the broad masses of workers and peasants living under the dictatorship of the bourgeoisie, regardless of its 'democratic' or fascist form, and the dictatorship of the proletariat in the USSR." The Greeks were also advised to contrast the USSR's Five-Year Plan with Hitler's Four-Year Plan and Roosevelt's New Deal and to emphasize the "positive results" of Soviet collectivization. And the peaceful foreign policy of the Soviet Union was to be contrasted with the machinations of all the imperialist powers.[5]

The message of the ECCI to all of the Comintern sections on the occasion of the eleventh anniversary of Lenin's death was more pompously emotional in tone. The instructions read as follows:

> Hold the Leninist days in an atmosphere of acquainting the broad masses with the enormous achievements of socialism achieved in over eleven years under Stalin's leadership on the road to the implementation of Lenin's behests, with the successes of the peaceful policy of Soviet power and the international closing of ranks under the banner of the struggle for the Soviets of all those who are exploited and oppressed worldwide. Publicize and expand awareness of the fundamental issues of Leninism, first and foremost the problems of the seizure of power, the dictatorship of the proletariat, the roles of the Communist Party, the organization of the United Front of the working class and its allies on the basis of the irreconcilable revolutionary struggle against class enemies and opportunism, against the imperialist war, against nationalism and chauvinism, against fascism and the entire capitalist system, for the historic objectives of the working class. Engage in a campaign for the theoretical arming of Party personnel and the strengthening of the Bolshevik Party spirit, vigilance, and the refusal to be reconciled to any and all deviations leading into the camp of the class enemy. Take particular note of Stalin's role as the best and most worthy successor to Lenin, his achievements in the area of further work on problems of Marxism-Leninism, and also of Lenin's and Stalin's role in the working-class movement of the country. Devote the newspaper issues of 21 and 22 January to the campaign.[6]

The ECCI carefully monitored the way the Communist press wrote about Stalin, trying to ensure that all his statements were immediately translated, published in full, and appropriately commented on by foreign Communist parties. All of the parties were sent directives from the Secretariat of the ECCI complaining that a speech by Stalin at the First All-Union Conference of Stakhanovites in 1935 had not been given the attention it deserved:

> In a number of countries Stalin's speech was not sufficiently understood. . . . The Party press provided virtually no explanation of Stalin's speech. . . . Here is a need to hold a discussion with the editorial staffs, editorial conferences, a meeting of the Party activists to provide, on the basis of Stalin's speech, clarity regarding problems of the USSR throughout all of the Party propaganda. Stalin's speech must be the focal point for popularizing the Stakhanovite movement. . . . Insofar as possible there must be organization of open meetings, discussions, conferences on the significance of Stalin's speech and the Stakhanovite movement. . . . There is a need to provide for the urgent publication and mass distribution of Stalin's speech and other mass pamphlets on the Stakhanovite movement.[7]

Paeans to Stalin produced around the world were transmitted to Moscow by cable, and Georgi Dimitrov, the ECCI general secretary, frequently passed them along to Stalin's secretariat as evidence of his role as leader of the world proletariat. The details of a meeting in Damascus on 6 November 1937, were transmitted to the Soviet leader, hailed as the "Great comrade, beloved leader of the world proletariat, the hope of the workers, peasants, and oppressed peoples of the entire world." Syrian CP leaders reported:

> On the victories won by the USSR during the 20 years under Your wise leadership, a leadership of genius, [the meeting] sends You, who laid the first mighty cornerstone in the cause of freeing all the oppressed peoples of the world, heartfelt greetings and their most sincere and warm wishes. [The practice of capitalizing "You" and "Your" in messages to Stalin was common in Comintern communications.] We note with pride that under Your leadership our Soviet fatherland has succeeded in achieving its goal of a socialist life. We note with pride and joy that thanks to You Soviet power has succeeded in crushing the gang of spies and traitors, the agents of world fascism, the Trotskys, Bukharins, and Tukhachevskys. We wish You, our dear and great comrade, long life, so that you may lead the land of the Soviets to Communism and help the working masses of the entire world to free themselves from capitalist exploitation, fascist barbarism, and the imperialist yoke.[8]

The ECCI demanded emphasis on the process of writing and adopting the new Soviet Constitution. In instructions to all sections of the Comintern sent on June 15, 1936, the ECCI Secretariat insisted on the publication in full of the draft Constitution in party newspapers and as a separate published brochure. "There is a need, no matter what, to create a situation in which the Constitution of the socialist state indeed becomes the property of millions of the masses," the message emphasized. "Its distribution and explanation among the Social Democratic working masses is particularly important. There is a need to have it made available for discussion by the mass meetings of workers, other strata of workers, the intelligentsia, all friends of peace and human progress; to systematically publish in the newspapers the resolutions of meetings, letters of workers, responses and comments by noticeable figures, to interview them; to organize appeals from participants in the meetings, individual organizations of workers, and eminent individuals' addresses to the workers of the USSR, etc."[9]

Several coded dispatches contained criticism of the Communist parties for having published only excerpts from the Constitution and for having failed to emphasize it sufficiently. One dispatch, sent on 25 November 1936, insisted that the front pages of party newspapers write about the Congress of Soviets at which the Constitution was adopted, publish daily articles by party leaders with reactions from workers and public figures, and republish *Pravda* articles. "Stalin's report and text Constitution must reach millions through publication of special newspaper supplements, mass pamphlets, utilization of all connections to trade unions and other press. . . . Resolutions adopted at meetings, addresses to toilers of the Soviet Union, to Stalin, initiator and author of the Soviet Constitution, are to be published in press and sent here."[10]

One of the main purposes of the propaganda campaign glorifying the Soviet Constitution, with its long list of democratic guarantees and idealistic assurances, was to counter the ugly reality of Stalinist repression and purges. The ECCI frequently warned in its communications that non-Communist sources that circulated stories about Soviet repression or difficulties were not to be believed. When a Dutch Communist newspaper printed a Reuters story about a murder on a Soviet collective farm, the ECCI sent a message: "Suggest to the editor maximum caution in dealing with information about the Soviet Union coming from bourgeois sources." The barrage of information about the Constitution "must be so widely and ably organized that the wild anti-Soviet campaign of the fascists and their Trotskyist agency be brought to naught."[11]

Unlike most of the governmental bodies through which Soviet power and control were exercised, the Comintern had a public persona that suggested it was truly an international organization. Some of its most powerful figures in the 1930s, ranging from Georgi Dimitrov (Bulgarian) to Wilhelm Pieck (German) were not Soviet citizens. Many of the cadres who worked at its headquarters had been dispatched to Moscow by their respective Communist parties. Others were political exiles from around the world. Even its technical experts, responsible for translation, producing forged passports and other official papers, and setting up means of contact, included a significant number of foreigners. Numerous books and articles about the foreign Communists who were among the most successful and glamorous Soviet intelligence officers have emphasized their facility with languages and their cosmopolitan flair, which enabled them to blend into different European or Asian societies and recruit assets by finding appropriate ways to appeal to those in a position to provide information. The Comintern had its own cadre of world travelers. The traits necessary for a Comintern operative were not dissimilar from those required for intelligence work. Living under false identities, crossing international borders with doctored papers, holding clandestine meetings, avoiding surveillance, and communicating surreptitiously with Moscow were all assets transferrable between seeking to build a world revolution and seeking to steal secrets. Gregory Kheifets is one example of a Comintern operative who moved between the worlds of political subversion and espionage. From 1923 to 1929 Kheifets worked abroad for the Comintern in Latvia, Lithuania, Finland, Poland, Turkey, Greece, Italy, Germany, Austria, Belgium, Switzerland, France, and China. In 1931 he transferred to the NKVD (Russian acronym of the People's Commissariat of Internal Affairs, the main security and foreign intelligence instrument of the regime) and was sent abroad on multi-year intelligence missions to Sweden, Czechoslovakia, Italy, and (twice) the United States.[12]

But most Comintern operatives lived far more prosaic and dull lives than their intelligence counterparts did. This is not to say that they did not face dangers. Comintern operatives could and did face arrest, imprisonment, torture, and even death. Particularly for those tasked to assist local Communist parties involved in armed revolts or uprisings or assigned to countries with few or no legal protections for someone charged with political subversion, a Comintern assignment could be fatal. Most Comintern emissaries, however, were paymasters and conduits for passing along instructions and requests, enabling Communist parties to carry out their activities in accordance with plans developed with the approval of the Soviet Union. They were the eyes and ears of Moscow on the ground in New York, Paris, London,

Prague, and numerous other locales, a constant reminder to American, French, British, or Czech Communists that not only were their political struggles part of an international campaign, but they were also being watched and judged by people beholden to a bureaucracy in Moscow and totally unaccountable and unknown to the vast majority of the local party's members. And for many Comintern workers the most dangerous part of their assignment was that they were very likely to run afoul not of capitalist police or executioners, but the NKVD, the sword and shield of the Soviet state. Far more Comintern employees died in the cellars of the Lubyanka Prison than abroad.

The Comintern, of course, made no secret of its existence. It published a variety of newspapers and magazines, openly distributed and read, containing analyses of events around the world, reporting on the resolutions and decisions of its leading bodies, and periodically reminding bourgeois governments that they were slated for destruction. Although many of the deliberations of its leading bodies, including the Executive Committee, were conducted in secret and key decisions were never reported publicly, others were given wide dissemination and Communists around the world took pride in being members of an international revolutionary body.

For the first decade of its existence, the Comintern also made no secret of its interference in the affairs of its constituent parties. It had published a list of conditions for membership in 1920, and it regularly and openly signaled its approval or disapproval of their policies and leadership. When internal disputes got out of hand or seemed intractable, the Comintern dispatched emissaries from Moscow with orders to mediate among and/or impose solutions on the warring factions. On occasion the decisions were published in the party press with no effort to conceal the key role of the Moscow plenipotentiary.

Behind the scenes, however, an extensive Comintern apparatus, headquartered in Moscow, sent money and instructions to specially selected emissaries around the world through coded communications. Staffed by a diverse group of Communists recruited from exiles and battle-tested militants, as well as veterans of the Bolshevik cause in Russia, the center dispatched men and women with false papers and a variety of pseudonyms to cities where they lived shadowy lives, meeting surreptitiously with Communist party leaders to provide financial resources, advice, and orders about policies, personnel, and plans and to receive reports and news.

Within the ECCI, the Department of International Communications (DIC) was in charge of maintaining contact with foreign Communist parties. (After the Seventh Comintern Congress in 1935, it was renamed the Communications Service [CS] of the Secretariat of the ECCI.) The ciphered materials from 1933–1943 indicate that more than forty people, excluding typists, were involved with the technical details of sending and receiving messages—translation, enciphering and deciphering, and verification.

The work was shrouded in secrecy since they were dealing with documents considered top secret. If one person translated a dispatch, another enciphered it, and a third checked up on their work. Often more than three people worked on one dispatch. Employees took turns at the various tasks, and speed was often of the essence. Items were usually dispatched the same day they were enciphered, although the date of verification was occasionally later. Messages were typically deciphered the same day they were received. The documents were received and sent in many languages but primarily German, English, and French.

The cryptographers and translators were kept busy. The materials for the 1933–1943 period encompass 764 files, organized by country. Many of the largest files deal with the most important Communist parties in the Comintern's purview—there are sixty dealing with China, ninety with France, forty-one with Czechoslovakia, and forty with the United States. But correspondence with the tiny Danish Communist Party filled thirty-eight files because Copenhagen, where the Communist Party was legal, if insignificant, was used as the communications center with illegal parties such as that of Germany.

The individual messages themselves varied in length. Incoming messages were generally brief, often no more than one page. The twenty-one files of ciphered communications from Moscow to New York include 3,005 sheets, suggesting a steady flow of messages. During that same period 4,004 sheets came in from Paris. In just two years, 1935 and 1936, when the French Communist Party was building the Popular Front, the ECCI sent 4,162 sheets of coded dispatches to Paris. This communication system was not an emergency network but a regular means of contact between the ECCI and its constituent parties.

One of the most common means of encryption was to employ copies of the same book. Using either a dictionary, a work of literature, or a Bible, the person preparing the text would indicate the ordinal number of the page, the line, and the letter of the alphabet. In January 1936, for example, Moscow sent a request to Basle: "The book we are using for deciphering is out of date. Buy three copies of a very thin book with an index at the end. Send two copies and keep the third.

We will send a telegram indicating the date on which we will start using it. Please do this quickly."[13]

In some cases text was transformed into a string of numbers. At other times, however, there were prearranged substitutions for the names of political figures or sensitive phrases that might prove revealing. In April 1935 the Department of International Communications sent a directive to several European stations: "For various reasons we remind you that in cipher cables and letters it is categorically forbidden to use the names of Russian comrades. Instead of Manuilsky, use Marmor, instead of Vasiliev—Vase, instead of Dimitrov—Diamant, instead of Abramov—Doctor. If a new name appears unexpectedly, immediately replace it, along with an appropriate note." Another communiqué to Paris in December 1936 demanded that "the words Comintern or Communist Party should be replaced by the letters km or kt."[14]

The same sender often used different code names. Georgi Dimitrov's dispatches to France were sent over the signatures of Daniel, Paul, Jeanette, Pierre, Georges, Karl, Rudolph and Helmut. Corresponding with the United States, he signed as George, Brother, Rudolph, and Dime. He sent orders to Sweden under the names Daniel, Paul Nils, Axel, and Rudolph; to Bulgaria, as Marta; and to Spain, as Citrine and Rith.

Different Comintern representatives had their own codes. A cable sending orders to the leadership of the Brazilian Communist Party included a notation that it was sent via Paris "in the repres[entative's] code." On the original copy of another cable to South America was the note "code of Ewert," referring to the Comintern's emissary Arthur Ewert. Other messages to Brazil sent to Pavel Stuchevsky, head of the DIC center there, used the Stock code. Dispatches to the United States often bore on the original the notation "Browder code" or "Kraft code."[15]

The different codes were often tailored to the assignments of the representatives. Carlo Codevilla, also known as Mario Codevilla (Raul, Moro, Ugo), a one-time secretary to Antonio Gramsci and member of the Italian CP since 1921, used the pseudonym Raul while working in Spain in 1936 as the representative of the Communications Service. The ECCI sent a letter to Paris asking that he be given two lists upon his arrival en route to Spain. The first list, intended for the enciphering and deciphering of texts of a general political nature, contained sixty-nine numbered words. The second, entitled "For Calculations," contained symbols for months of the year, financial terms and currencies, and names of countries.[16]

Codevilla communicated with Moscow in a code separate and independent from the code used by the ECCI's official representative to the Spanish Communist Party. He was the conduit for Comintern funds going to the Spanish CP; an 8 July 1936 message indicated that a courier would arrive the next day with "70,000 French francs." Later instructions detailed how much was to be disbursed to the Comintern representative, Medina. Codevilla's responsibilities went even further, however, as he kept Moscow informed about the potential mistakes of its official representatives. "Raul" wrote in 1937 that Medina and André Marty, a member of the ECCI Secretariat serving as commander of the International Brigades, were violating rules of secrecy: "Medina carries with him many texts of telegrams which we have received and which are dated over several weeks. Once I noted that while dictating to me several telegrams which he had authorized me to send you, and while looking for a memo, he pulled out of his pocket an entire series of old texts he was keeping. I took them and personally destroyed them."

Marty was even more careless: "Despite our instructions he is continuing to write all the telegrams through his secretaries. After I once noted that the text contained typical Anglicisms, and since André's secretary at that time was British, I once again went to see him to remind him of the instructions regarding the sending and keeping of telegrams." Even worse, the Personnel Department had no information about the British woman. The warning letter apparently had little impact, perhaps because it was deciphered on 19 May, just two weeks before its recipient, B. Müller, was arrested.[17]

The various secretaries of the Comintern also had their own codes. Wilhelm Pieck, a German Communist leader elected a member of the ECCI in 1928, joined the Presidium in 1931. In 1935 he was put in charge of the Landersecretariat supervising Communist parties in the Balkans. His codebook consisted of two sheets of numbers ranging from 1 to 175. The first sheet contained the names of a variety of political figures, organizations, and terms. The second page gave each of these numbers a randomly selected combination of letters. Thus, Dimitrov was assigned number 1, and number 1 was designated as Fugo. Presumably, the first sheet was to be used for radiograms, the second for written texts. In this case, however, not a single document in the Comintern archive used this code.[18]

Many of the codes were thinly disguised, purporting to be letters to or from a local branch of a business. The Japanese Communist Party sent one such letter in May 1934, explaining that "despite the prosperity produced by inflation, for the last half-year the financial results of our firm's activity have not improved as compared with the first half. A series of crushing blows for some time have left our firm on the brink of bankruptcy." It noted that "we are still tending to make the same mistake; that of selling better quality goods that the broad masses do not like and that do not take into account the time, the location, and the habits of consumers." The letter went on to lay the blame on leadership, reporting "we have had to dismiss quite a number of bad directors," and asking for guidance on "what will happen if we institute a special organization of controllers." The latter was prelude to the creation of "Special Action Brigades," which drew up a list of ten party functionaries suspected of treachery who were executed.[19]

In other letters, disguised as personal or family correspondence, innocuous names substituted for preassigned cover names. For example, one file for correspondence with the Thälmann Defense Committee, coordinating work on behalf of the imprisoned leader of the German Communist Party, contained a list of code names for all the participants in his forthcoming trial and the Comintern officials tasked with organizing mass protests, raising money, etc. "Baby," Thälmann's wife Rosa, conveyed news that was soon sent to the ECCI in a letter that "Gör," Herman Göring, had visited Thälmann twice in prison and that "Fritz's exam will not take place"—that is, that he would not be tried publicly but sent to prison.[20]

Such codes were unsophisticated and not hard to interpret. At times, the amateur nature of the ciphers raised alarms. An addressee in Japan asked that Moscow "rework the tables of the conventional language for the cipher telegrams, because they have been clumsily compiled. For example 'strike'—'suspension,' 'workers'—'office staff,' etc. In compiling these, stick to one principle or line, i.e. for *trade*, then use commercial terminology throughout; if it is literar[y]—then literar[y]-journalist[ic] terminology. But never the way this is now being done—*total confusion and nonsense.*" Nor was the terminology the only problem: "A lot is missing, for exam[ple]: a delegate, textile workers, transport workers etc. [And] . . . there is a need to keep in mind the specific features of each country, for exam[ple] absolutely no one devil from Moscow is sending 'tea' to Aslanidia since there never was and never will be an order for such a purchase. In a word, the cur[rent] cipher table is very weak and is not fulfilling the function for which it is intended."[21]

The messages were transmitted in several different ways. They might be sent by diplomatic mail to those countries where the Soviet

Union had official diplomatic missions. From there, they would be passed on by officials assigned as Comintern liaisons. Special couriers and sailors were also used to carry messages. Radio messages and telegrams were also used, as was regular mail. In May 1935 a message to Rio de Janeiro warned the Comintern representative: "Correspondence with you will be voluminous and animated. So far we only have one address for you for airmail letters. Get at least two more such addresses. In addition, there is a need to provide for communication by telegram."[22]

Letters sent by mail required special precautions. In addition to being ciphered, they often used invisible ink. Moreover, to avoid attracting unwanted attention packages containing printed materials, newspapers, and magazines had to appear different, with varying return addresses, wrapping paper, and handwritten labels.

Once they had been received and deciphered by a local Communist party, the coded dispatches were supposed to be burned, with only a single clear copy being given to the intended recipient. Once a ciphered communication was sent to Moscow, the radio operator was instructed to destroy the original text.[23]

The ECCI was anxious to prevent copies from falling into the hands of hostile police or counterintelligence services. In addition to compromising the codes, that could severely damage the Communist parties, confirming charges that they were tools of Moscow or unpatriotic. For example, in May 1935 the ECCI instructed the French CP to have its parliamentary members vote in support of the Soviet-French treaty on mutual assistance but, nonetheless, vote against the military budget and conscription. The directives were sent with a warning to those charged with deciphering them from Alexander Abramov, the head of the DIC from June 1926 to October 1936: "The addressees are to study this text thoroughly, but do not leave the document in their hands. Once it has been read, you are personally to destroy it."[24]

The repeated instructions to destroy these dispatches once the addressees had read them, however, were continually ignored. The ECCI sent the secretaries of the Central Committees of the Communist parties in New York, Paris, Madrid, Prague, Stockholm, and Zurich a directive in December 1936 on the handling of the coded materials: "All ciphered material is to be read by the addressee only. If other comrades must be informed on the contents of a dispatch, the secretary himself informs them orally." It insisted that "after reading, the coded dispatches are to be destroyed immediately by the addressee personally." If there was a need to share these directives with the party organizations or to give them to other individuals, they were not to receive exact copies of the documents but paraphrases to avoid reproducing the text of the original. Outgoing coded dispatches were to be typed by the sender personally, only one copy, and any drafts were to be immediately destroyed. Receipt of dispatches was to be acknowledged. All old archives containing coded materials were to be destroyed. The credentials of all individuals serving as conduits between the illegal communications center of the Comintern and the party leadership had to be verified. These instructions "must be applied anywhere where there is a ciphered correspondence."[25]

There were still lapses. In March 1937, Abramov's successor, Boris Melnikov, using the pseudonym Müller, sent a dispatch to Lydia Dübi, who headed the Communication Service in Paris: "In enciphered letters from you secret words and phases are often written openly. I call that to your attention. Please encipher short letters in full. Send the numerical text on a separate sheet, not on the same sheet with the open text."[26]

The Comintern had good reason to worry about the security of its communications. The most serious compromise of its messages, however, did not stem from sloppy tradecraft or carelessness on the part of its employees. Instead, it was a function of underestimating just how vulnerable its radio contacts with its sections were to interception. The British Government Code and Cipher School (GC&CS, today known as GCHQ)—responsible for collecting and trying to break ciphered communications—started intercepting a rash of messages in 1930 that was quickly determined to be between Comintern headquarters in Moscow and clandestine radio stations abroad. Several months were required to trace the British end of the operation to a house in Wimbledon owned by a British Communist, who was promptly put under surveillance in order to learn of the path through which Comintern money and instructions were passed along to the leadership of the Communist Party of Great Britain (CPGB).

GC&CS had managed to largely break the codes by 1933, enabling it to pass on to MI5, responsible for counterintelligence, the identities of secret members of the British CP, the identities of couriers coming from and going to Moscow, the names of British and colonial Communists studying at the Lenin School in the USSR, and details about Soviet subsidies to the CPGB. The "obscurely phrased" traffic hindered full understanding of the messages—even the British Communists often did not fully understand what was communicated and had to ask for clarification. The British decryption project, code-named Mask, collected so many messages that many were not given detailed analysis. By 1937, with messages indicating that the Comintern was seeking to moderate British Communists' revolutionary fervor as part of the Popular Front and facing a severe shortage of staff, MI5 discontinued Mask, thereby missing some obscure clues that, if followed up, would have exposed elements of the Comintern's operations linked to Soviet intelligence.[27]

The Mask material, released by the British government in 1997, is a perfect match for a portion of the Opis 184 ciphered communications, illustrating how vulnerable the Comintern codes were to exposure. The British read 1,571 decrypts. Reflecting the secrecy of the effort, even the United States did not learn of this project until 1946. The Mask decryptions were an invaluable and decisive tool that gave MI5 a virtual window into the clandestine operations of the British CP. By following the radio operators as they passed along the secret messages, it was able to construct a picture of the underground apparatus of the party, headed by a Scotsman, Bob Stewart. The British operation used *Treasure Island* as a codebook. One of its chief radio operators, William Morrison, who deserted from the battlefront in Spain, later cooperated with MI5 and provided copious details about the operation, including the names of dozens of British and American radio operators with whom he had worked at the Lenin School.[28]

Many, if not most, of the DIC employees abroad who received and sent the encrypted messages were veterans of the Lenin School, where they had obtained not only Comintern training designed to ensure the requisite ideological loyalty to the Soviet Union, but also training in methods of propaganda and, in many cases, clandestine operations, including wireless communication. Upon returning to their native lands, they were available for deployment in sensitive positions such as liaisons between Moscow and their local Communist parties. Rudy Baker, for example, who directed the conspiratorial apparatus of the Communist Party of the United States (CPUSA) in the late 1930s and during World War II, had studied at the Lenin School from 1927 to 1930. After his return to the United States, he worked in the Pan-Pacific Trade Union Secretariat on the West Coast, supervising clandestine Comintern operations in China and Japan before succeeding J. Peters, who had briefly supervised American students at the Lenin School, as head of the party's most secret unit.

Access to cipher correspondence was strictly limited at the Moscow end as well. In addition to the technical staff who worked directly with these documents, they were usually read by the overseer of the DIC. Meer Trilliser, code-named Mikhail Moskvin, who supervised the Comintern's Communications Service, also initialed coded dispatches. (Trilliser's name often appears in Western literature as Mikhail Trilisser.) In 1937 the encryption work was removed from the Communications Service and given to a separate part of the ECCI apparatus, which then was made directly subordinate to Georgi Dimitrov.[29]

Dimitrov himself wrote many drafts of these dispatches, signing those sent as an official order with "Secretariat." During his absences Dmitri Manuilsky or Palmiro Togliatti performed this function. In such cases the cipher message was sent either under Togliatti's or Manuilsky's pseudonyms. On 27 October 1935 a dispatch to Spain stipulated: "From now on make the following substitutions in all cipher correspondence (telegrams and letters) in place of real names of leading employees: Dimitrov—Dios, Moskvin—Monaco, Kuusinen—Cupon, Pieck—Piloto, Ercoli—Epoka, Gottwald—Grasia, Manuilsky—Mayor, Abramov—Doctor, Marty—Madras, Wang Ming—Vancouver. We will do the same thing in sending our dispatches." A December 1936 coded directive to Paris went even further, replacing Willi Münzenberg's pseudonym, Herfurt, with Hf, and Maurice Thorez's code name of Maurice with Mc.[30]

The concern about exposing Comintern leaders or using the names of Communist figures in plain text was a rational response to the activities of counterintelligence agencies eager to obtain incriminatory or useful information about Communist activity. The obsession with secrecy, however, even extended into the Soviet Union, particularly once the Stalinist purges began to take their toll among those working in the Communications Service. Osip Pyatnitsky, supervisor of the DIC, was removed from his position in 1935 and replaced by Mikhail Moskvin (Meer Trilliser). Former head of the Foreign Department (i.e., foreign intelligence) of the OGPU (Russian acronym of the United State Political Directorate, which was included in the NKVD in 1934) Trilliser played a key role in purging the Comintern in 1936–1937 as a member of the special commission to investigate employees of the ECCI apparatus, declaring at a party meeting on 22 June 1937 that "both the new and the old communications leadership" had been part of an "intensive infiltration of the enemy."[31]

Moskvin developed a special code to communicate with Dimitrov in 1938 while the Comintern's general secretary was on vacation in Kislovodsk, a vacation and spa city in the North Caucasus. The cipher replaced people's names and some place names with numbers: "Comrade 111 reports that the directives of the Secretariat about 162 were broadly discussed in 195 and began the mobilization of the Party and other forces to carry them out." The only people receiving or sending messages in this cipher were Moskvin, Manuilsky, Kuusinen, and Dimitrov himself, who called this the "Moskvin code."[32]

Dimitrov pestered Moskvin for the code, writing on 18 September, "I am awaiting the promised code," and on 24 September, "I have not yet received your code." Two days later he noted in his diary that it had arrived. An amateurish effort, it contained a relatively small number of names of people, countries, and organizations. Several numbers had the same referent—Czechoslovakia by mistake was both 112 and 201, while the Central Committee of the Czech CP was both 151 and 161. Its simplicity and errors may be connected with the purge that had decimated the ranks of experienced cryptologists and/or the possibility that Moskvin himself had created it.[33]

Since the code contained relatively few cipher keys, the non-encrypted part of a coded telegram sometimes revealed the meaning of the encrypted words. For example, Moskvin sent a cable on 29 October that included the following: "For discussion of question 138 on decision 195 a delegation composed of Linderot, Hagberg, Senander, and Oman must leave." Since all four were leaders of the Communist Party of Sweden, this clearly indicated that 138 was the code for Sweden. Dozens of messages contained similar lapses, enabling even a rank amateur to rebuild the "codebook" with little difficulty.[34]

Even as simple as it was, the code hampered Dimitrov. The fall of 1938 was an especially tense period in Europe, and he was kept busy sending suggestions and orders off to Moscow for Communist leaders scrambling for guidance on how to respond to the worsening situation. The encrypted messages were difficult to work with, and he frequently had to remind himself who or what 105 or 112 were. He copied the entire decrypted correspondence into his diary in order to have the clear texts immediately available. A number of his messages wound up being written without the code or with very minor use of it.

The "Moskvin code" did not survive its developer. Moskvin was arrested on 23 November 1938. The following day, Dimitrov met NKVD chief Nikolai Yezhov at his dacha and was told that Moskvin "was closely linked" to a nest of traitors. Those ties would be investigated, as well as "whether he had not fallen into the trap of some kind of fo[reign] intelligence service." Dimitrov promptly sent a letter to

Stalin and the Soviet Politburo saying that "as of yesterday I have temporarily taken over the functions which would have been carried out by Moskvin, who has been arrested, as a member of the ECCI Secretariat (supervision of the Communications Service, the administration, settlement of financial questions). I will not, however, be able to do this for an extensive period of time." He appealed for a new appointee, especially "since the enemy of the people now under arrest unquestionably undermined a great deal of the ECCI apparatus, and that now will have to be immediately remedied and very quickly restructured." Dimitrov received no answer. Moskvin was convicted on 1 February 1940 and shot the following day. The same day he received Dimitrov, Yezhov was removed as people's commissar for internal affairs. He was arrested in April 1939 and shot two days after Moskvin. The following month Dimitrov received Yezhov's dacha.[35]

The plethora of codes was a recipe for confusion. To maintain some control and consistency, the headquarters copy of every message contained a control section where the intended recipient, the means of communication (telegram, letter, via a third country), and the code being used were noted. The text of the cipher correspondence was typed on special blanks, bearing a warning in the upper left corner, "The making of copies is forbidden," and in the right corner, "Top secret." The upper part of the blanks for the outgoing dispatches had several lines for inserting information on the time of sending, the number of the communication, and the address. The lower part contained columns to be filled in, indicating the means of dispatch; who was paying for it; who had typed the text and in how many copies; and who had translated, encoded, and checked up on the results. In addition to facilitating record keeping, these requirements enabled control over and surveillance of those responsible for every ciphered message.

Many messages from the mid-1930s bore the notation "Given to Berta" on the blanks. Berta was Berta Platten-Zimmerman. In 1936–1937 she headed the courier service within the ECCI. The wife of Fritz Platten, a founder of the Swiss Communist Party and a participant in the founding of the Comintern, Berta was a Swiss Communist, tasked to preserve all materials used by couriers, including copies of the false documents they used to travel around the world. Without careful control of which documents were used at which borders and coordination of fake passports and visas, couriers ran the risk of exciting suspicion or arrest for traveling with false papers.[36]

The work of the Communications Service was considered so sensitive that one high-ranking Comintern official in 1930 even told a meeting of the party unit in the ECCI that "we have categories of employees who, even if they were to be expelled from the Party, would remain on the job. The closed nature of this Department is not a minus but a plus." That pledge turned out to be incorrect. By the end of the decade, expulsion from the party became a death sentence for many of the employees of the section.[37]

Whether because of its secrecy or in spite of it, the Communications Service bore an even heavier brunt of the Stalinist purges of the Comintern than other sections. A meeting of the party organization of the ECCI apparatus in June 1937 heard a report that "the largest number of enemies was arrested there." A September 1939 document with lists of those arrested in the ECCI apparatus included thirty-nine people employed by the Communications Service, dwarfing any other division.[38]

The wave of arrests that battered the ECCI apparatus during the period of the Great Terror struck the Communications Service with particular force. A letter of 10 October 1937 from Dimitrov and Manuilsky to the Central Committee of the VKP(b) (All-Union Communist Party [Bolshevik], the title of the Soviet CP at the time) stated that as a result of the arrests, the ECCI apparatus was no longer able to carry out its work: NKVD "organs have recently exposed a number of enemies of the people, and a wide-ranging espionage organization in the Comintern apparatus has been revealed. The Communications Service, the most important department in the Comintern apparatus, turned out to be the one most saturated. It is now necessary to completely abolish this and to proceed without delay to organize this department anew with fresh, carefully selected and verified workers."[39]

Since the arrests had cut off the ECCI from the various Communist parties by interrupting the flow of communication, Dimitrov and Manuilsky urgently requested the submission of new names for employment. Both the Communications Service and the Cryptography Division were assigned new personnel.[40]

The cryptographers and translators came from various countries and included men and, primarily, women of various ages and backgrounds. Each was carefully vetted by the Soviet secret services. All belonged to the Communist Party unit of the Comintern apparatus, although several people remained members of their own Communist parties. Most had long histories of devoted service to the Communist cause. None of these factors prevented a wholesale purge on grounds ranging from Trotskyism to inappropriate friendships. Penalties ranged from execution down to reprimands. Some people were shot, some were arrested and imprisoned, and others were just fired, their alleged party disloyalty having disqualified them from working in a secret apparatus.[41]

Anna Janson, along with her husband Karl, known in the United States under the pseudonym Charles Scott, had been active in the Lettish (Latvian) Federation of the Socialist Party, one of the mainstays of the early Communist movement in America. When her husband came to Moscow in 1921 to represent one of the several American Communist parties competing for Comintern recognition, she accompanied him. They both remained in the USSR, taking on various Comintern assignments. Anna began work as a cryptographer in 1934 but soon fell under suspicion; she was included on a list compiled in September 1936 "of members of the VKP(b), former members of other Parties with Trotskyist and rightist leanings, and also those reprimanded by the Party." Sent to the leadership of the Comintern, the Personnel Department of the ECCI, and the NKVD, the list precipitated Janson's arrest in October 1937 and expulsion from the Communist Party "as an enemy of the Party and the people."[42]

Rosa Gartman (the pseudonym of Irina Benz), Anna Gennis, and Lore (pseudonym of Berta Daniel) had all been members of the German Communist Party since the mid-1920s and had worked for the Comintern apparatus beginning in the late 1920s or early 1930s, before becoming cryptographers. Gartman and Gennis were ousted from the Communist Party and fired from their jobs in August 1937 and arrested a few weeks later. The former was shot on 1 November, the latter in March 1938. Lore was arrested in April 1937 and sentenced to eight years' imprisonment, with an additional ten years added on in 1942. In June 1957 she was allowed to return to Germany.[43]

The speed with which someone could go from trusted cryptographer to enemy of the people was breathtakingly quick. Eugenia Komarova, a member of the Soviet Communist Party since 1920, was one of the rare cryptographers entrusted with translating and deciphering telegrams on her own. On 12 October 1937 she did both with a message from Togliatti on a meeting of representatives of the Spanish Communist Party with the Spanish leader, Juan Negrín. Dimitrov immediately gave the telegram to Stalin. Two weeks later, on 26 October, a party committee decided to expel Komarova "for ties to enemies of the Party and the people and as not deserving of trust." Although the expulsion was later replaced by a reprimand, she was finally expelled in January 1938.[44]

Reprimands and dismissal from work frequently followed the arrest of someone's relatives, friends, or acquaintances. One cryptographer, Elena Trautenberg-Nikolaeva, was reprimanded and fired for "stubbornly insisting on her anti-Party views, i.e., defending a convicted counter-revolutionary, the saboteur Trautenberg" (her former husband). Nadezhda Smirnova shared the same fate for "failure to render assistance to the Party in unmasking her former husband." So did Praskovia Kochkina-Leenman, who had failed to "report on" an acquaintance now exposed as a counterrevolutionary "in a timely manner."[45]

A handful of cryptographers managed to ride out the storm. One of the most prominent was Sigi Bamatter, a protégé of Willi Münzenberg and a longtime Comintern representative in Europe and the United States. He briefly served as head of the Swiss Communist Party from 1929 to 1931, after which he became a Soviet citizen and moved to the DIC. Although professions of loyalty to the regime were often futile, Bamatter's declaration at one party meeting in early 1936 may have helped him survive: "We must be extraordinarily vigilant toward each other. We must know each other not only at work, regarding our production activity, but also regarding our social and private lives. We cannot pass over anything we hear in the conversations of our comrades and anything that seems dubious to us. . . . Each Party member must be on the alert, at any time and in any post he must be an employee of the NKVD, and we must be proud to help the organs of the dictatorship of the proletariat." In the fall of 1937 he moved to a job in the German-language service of Moscow radio.[46]

Long service on behalf of the Comintern apparatus was no protection from denunciation. In fact, it increased the chances that evidence could be developed to prove guilt. One of the more prominent victims of the purges among those with major responsibility for sending ciphered communications was Grigory Gerish, who headed the Bureau of the Secretariat of the ECCI, with responsibility for implementing the body's work. Along with Abramov, he initialed the ciphered messages sent to Communist parties around the world.

A member of the Socialist Party in the United States, Gerish was among the founders of the Communist movement in America and belonged to it from 1919 to 1923 before returning to Russia. He served on the party committee in the ECCI apparatus and on various commissions that investigated suspicious individuals. In October 1936 he called for increased vigilance: "Above all, we must know our comrades. It is the task of the Party committee and the Party group to study each member of the Party and those who are not Party members. In the past we studied and checked up on our comrades through reports on them. The enemy can reveal himself at work, but outside of the apparatus we are not studying each comrade to see how he is living and with whom he is meeting." He did not realize that he himself was already under investigation for decisions taken within the Comintern in 1923, when Stalin and Trotsky had first been at odds.[47]

In January 1937 Gerish was the third name on a list of members of the party organization with Trotskyist and rightist leanings, a charge repeated in a February memorandum to Manuilsky and Moskvin. A special commission of the ECCI ruled on 27 May that he should be released from work until his loyalty was verified. He was arrested several weeks later and expelled from the Communist Party on 15 July. Sentenced to death on 14 October 1937, Gerish was immediately shot.[48]

Despite this supposed nest of traitors in the heart of the Comintern apparatus in Moscow, with access to all the codes and ciphers used to communicate with foreign parties, there was no evidence that any Comintern secrets were exposed at the Soviet end of the network. For all the precautions taken in Moscow to protect the integrity and secrecy of the correspondence of the ECCI with foreign parties, the security regime abroad was far more problematic. After all, in Moscow all the state's police powers were available to thwart carelessness, infiltrators or saboteurs, or other threats. The recipients of the ciphered communications, however, functioned under wildly differing political conditions.

If a Communist party was illegal, even receiving messages via the postal service carried enormous risks. Clandestine radio stations required elaborate and time-consuming efforts at concealment. Even in those circumstances when a Communist party functioned openly and legally, the messages, containing confidential information—some of which could be politically embarrassing, some of which could lead to prosecution for offenses ranging from using false passports to illegal money transfers—had to be concealed from the prying eyes of counterespionage organizations, countersubversive agencies, and political enemies.

The techniques for receiving and sending ciphered correspondence were specific to each country. In cases where the Communist Party was legal, the DIC, later the CS, sometimes sent its messages by mail or telegram directly to Communist Party offices. Albert Vassart, the former secretary of the Central Committee of the French Communist Party who was responsible for his party's communications with the Comintern, recalled, "From 1931 to 1935 telegram communications between the Comintern and the French Communist Party were conducted through the ordinary post office in the suburb of Saint-Denis, near the Gare du Nord." A cipher cable from Moscow would be delivered to the party residence at 120 rue Lafayette. No French party employee could decipher it. Instead, the original telegram would be handed over to a designated employee of the DIC, who was responsible for deciphering it. When sending a telegram to Moscow, the same procedure was used but in reverse order. "The text from the French Communist Party was given to the DIC section, where it was enciphered, and always sent to Moscow through the post office in Saint-Denis."[49]

In all countries, sometimes even when the Communist party was legal, the Communications Service kept itself isolated from the party apparatus, and contacts with it were carried out in secret. Radio equipment would be located in a rented apartment or house, from which operators would receive and send dispatches. Such centers sometimes acted as conduits for messages intended for parties unable to establish direct communication with Moscow. A specific group of numbers at the beginning of a text would signal the need for further forwarding, and the communication would be passed on but not deciphered. These centers were often rented in well-off neighborhoods to deflect police attention, but they frequently had to be changed. Such centers were staffed by employees of the ECCI, sometimes assisted by trusted people recommended by the leadership of the Communist party.

Pavel Stuchevsky, a member of the Soviet Communist Party since 1918 who had previously worked in the People's Commissariat of Foreign Affairs and in Soviet intelligence, was the head of the DIC center in Brazil. He arrived there in the spring of 1935 using the name Leon-Jules Vallée (his pseudonym in correspondence was René). His staff was responsible for ensuring organizational, technical, and financial support for the planned Communist uprising to be led by Louis Carlos Prestes. The cryptographer was his wife, Sofia Stuchevskaia, who, like her husband, had served in Soviet military intelligence. The radio operator was an American, Victor Allen Barron, known as Raymond. The staff included couriers as well as a specialist on various kinds of sabotage; one of the couriers, Johann de Graaf, known as Richard, was an agent of Soviet military intelligence but also an informer for MI6, the British secret intelligence service.[50]

A steady stream of orders, instructions, and advice from Moscow poured into the DIC's secret radio stations, which included a café in

São Paolo and safe houses. Stuchevsky deciphered the messages and passed them on to Prestes and other plotters after they were retyped and the originals burned. Betrayed by de Graaf and plagued by poor planning and overly optimistic calculations, however, the coup quickly unraveled.[51]

In the wake of the failure, the ECCI sought assurance about the safety of the leaders of the Brazilian party and the Comintern representatives. At first optimistic reports came in from Brazil; in a ciphered communication of 15 December 1935, Stuchevsky confidently wrote that the leadership was safe; "our communications operation is not affected, but right now it is not possible to use our radio." Just two weeks later, however, he informed Moscow that Arthur Ewert, the Comintern's chief liaison in Brazil, and his wife had both been arrested "with compromising documents." The party leaders were also soon arrested; Victor Barron died while in police custody.[52]

The Stuchevskys were arrested in early January 1936 but soon released under police surveillance. They immediately disappeared and hid in illegal apartments before making their way to Argentina. Back in Moscow, an investigatory commission deemed their actions suspicious. Some accounts have them arrested; others note that Pavel later worked for the Radio Committee of the USSR. De Graaf managed to deflect suspicion from himself and continued to work for the Red Army's military intelligence arm for several more years before finally defecting to Great Britain. (The Red Army's [later the Soviet Army's] military intelligence agency is best known in the West by its post-1942 initials, GRU, for Glavnoye Razvedyvatel'noye Upravleniye: Main Intelligence Directorate.)[53]

The Paris communications center of the DIC played an extremely important role in the Comintern network, in particular after Hitler came to power in Germany in January 1933. Several international organizations associated with the Comintern were located in France, along with several others that, while formally independent, were in fact under its sphere of influence. Moreover, many Communist parties illegal in their own countries had both their organizational apparatus and their leadership in Paris. Through Paris the ECCI maintained contacts with the Communist parties in Latin America and Asia. All the various threads of the links with these organizations and parties came together in the apparatus run by the DIC.

From 1932 to 1936 the Comintern communications center in Paris was run by Arthur Khavkin, whose pseudonym was Siegfried Walter. The son of a wealthy manufacturer from Lódź, Walter had become a

Communist before 1920; during that decade he worked in the illegal organization of International Red Aid in Poland. In 1932 he joined the staff of the DIC of the ECCI. He was a focal point for the constant stream of messages dealing with the intricate and complicated negotiations about the French CP's organization of a broad, antifascist Popular Front.

In addition to policy issues relating to France, Walter was a conduit through which representatives of a variety of parties and organizations received money, instructions, and papers. The communications center had a hand in obtaining documents for those in France illegally, arranging their accommodations, and setting up meetings with couriers, as well as collecting information and carrying out other instructions from the ECCI, including the production of double-bottomed suitcases for the illegal transportation of documents and money. One of Walter's tasks was to carry out ECCI instructions on the disbursement of money. In a single month in 1933, for example, Moscow ordered him to distribute more than 225,000 francs ($200,311 in 2012 values) to a variety of Communist parties. These enormous sums had to be handed over in person and outside of the actual communications center or any building housing the French CP. Usually these transfers were made in a Paris café or bistro or in a store or during a meeting on the street. Walter himself sometimes was the courier, but more often a colleague using a party code name met a representative of the committee or party.[54]

Walter was transferred to Moscow early in 1936 and worked in the Communications Service but was accused of Menshevik and Trotskyist sympathies in August. In addition to his friendship with Georgi Pyatakov, one of the main figures in a major purge trial, Walter was accused of having given French Trotskyists empty passport blanks and divulging to them the name of a Soviet intelligence agent. Arrested in December 1936, he was dead by the end of January.[55]

Walter's replacement as head of the Paris communications center was Lydia Dübi, a member of the Swiss Communist Party since 1921 who had joined the Soviet party in 1924, when she moved to Moscow to work for the Comintern. By 1936, using the cover name Pascal, she was in Paris to ensure communication between the ECCI and the leadership of the French Communist Party and to distribute funds to other parties and groups. The disbursements did not always go smoothly.

Shortly before the Spanish parliamentary elections of 1936, Medina, the Comintern representative, sent a ciphered communication to Moscow complaining that "the Party has still not received anything from you for the electoral campaign. . . . If you do not immediately send the promised sum, the publication of *Mundo Obrero* is in danger. . . . I am requesting you to report on the sum you have sent and when it will be received."[56]

In Moscow Moskvin noted on the cable that 200,000 French francs had been sent for the Spanish Communist Party and asked Pascal why they had not been delivered in a timely fashion. She explained that the courier "was not received when he showed up at the secret meeting place, and he returned with the money. 48,000 was handed over in time, as per receipts No 1 and No 94,95. On 13 February a courier is leaving with 80,000 fr., and in the next few days there will be another courier. Because of the lack of funds, we could not send them earlier."[57]

In addition to her other duties, Pascal was required to verify the political loyalties of her staff as the purges gathered steam. In a letter to her boss, Müller, she pleaded ignorance, noting that "I received most of the staff from you, and I know them only from their work here." Her predecessor, Walter, had hired the French employees. One employee, "Arno," about whom she had doubts, was essential "since he is the only one here who speaks French and Spanish" and no one else was "in a position to help in delivering things to addressees and couriers." Removing "one or another individual is not satisfactory, since the work must be continued without endangering it."[58]

Pascal was also tasked early in 1937 with a reorganization of the secret communication work in Paris. Her apparatus, whose jobs included "links to the Communist Parties of France, Spain, and Belgium," as well as "transit communications and transit to the French and Belgium colonies" and "authorization of tasks linked to the British CP," was supplemented by an independent apparatus headed by "Karl" (probably Leo Flieg, a member of the German CP); it was given responsibility for "links with the remaining clients (organizations which do not belong to your functions)" and "transit links and transit not included in the functions of your apparatus." All communication with Moscow was to remain with Pascal, who was instructed to find a special liaison to Karl and to assign a cryptographer to service Karl's unit. She was once again ordered to conduct a review of the staff and recommend who could be retained, to change the location of the center, and to "pay particular attention to see whether you are being monitored by the police. . . . Report to us the results."[59]

Dübi had no time to carry out this assignment. At the beginning of June 1937 she was summoned to Moscow; on 5 August she was arrested, and on 3 November she was shot for alleged "participation in the anti-Soviet Trotskyist organization" and for spying for Japanese, French, and German intelligence. "Karl" was also recalled in June; in March 1938 he was arrested by the NKVD and shot a year later.[60]

Not all DIC foreign representatives fared so poorly. Solomon Mikhelson-Manuilov managed, barely, to escape the purges. A Bolshevik since 1914, he lived for many years in Great Britain and the United States, joining Socialist parties there before returning to Russia in 1918. He joined the DIC in June 1929 along with his wife, Maria Komarova. From 1929 to 1932, using the pseudonyms König and Schäffer, Mikhelson headed the work of the DIC group in Germany. The following year he became the first DIC head in the United States, using the code names Kraft and Spektor, serving as the conduit through which the ECCI communicated with party leader Earl Browder, who had heretofore enjoyed direct cipher contact with Moscow. Mikhelson also was the contact man for communication with Comintern representatives in the United States and other Communist parties in North America and the dispatcher of Comintern funds to selected parties and groups. One mark of his deep cover is that none of the histories of American communism published prior to the opening of the Comintern archive or congressional and FBI investigations of the CPUSA mentions his presence or the role he played.

In an early dispatch to Abramov, Mikhelson reported on the start of his activities in New York:

> The organization period is much longer than expected. Everything moves along slowly because first, conditions here are complicated, and second, Browder is very busy and although he helps me gladly, it takes much time to arrange things; third, many things which I should not do myself are being delayed because I have no experienced man to help me. . . . There is yet very much to be organized, but I . . . was able to organize that necessary minimum which makes it possible to start activity and begin to execute your orders. . . . Have already organized: 1. Address for money. 2. 8 addresses for letters. 3. Money sender. 4. 2 registered addresses for cables from Europe. 5. 4 rooms for work meetings and keeping things. 6. Already have a man recommended by Browder. . . . Later I will write more. Spektor.[61]

One of Mikhelson's major tasks was to parcel out money—both to Latin American Communist parties and to the CPUSA itself. One message in 1934 from Moscow instructed him to provide sums ranging from $60 to the Cuban CP to $2,420 to the Mexican CP. A series of messages between 1934 and 1936 authorized him to give Browder amounts between $1,100 and $3,000 for unspecified purposes, although usually there were detailed instructions that the funds were earmarked for specific tasks.[62]

At least some of the money was carried into the United States by couriers Mikhelson recruited to travel to Moscow. The Communications Service carped about their dedication and suitability. One 1935 cable complained that "Lilienstein declared that he and his wife [will] stay here for work. Colodny categorically wants to borrow foreign currency from us for personal purchases. . . . Besides she is talkative. . . . In the future Kraft must personally examine each courier, explaining the importance and honor of the trust given by our organization. We forbid your sending us bohemians, literary people, etc. or those who came here to find work." Moscow demanded a thorough vetting of couriers to uncover their political histories and reliability.[63]

The ECCI also relied on Mikhelson to keep it informed about not only the activities of the CPUSA, but also its political leadership. He cabled Moscow in 1936 that the party wished to enlarge its Politburo and included the proposed slate. André Marty evaluated the candidates for his ECCI colleagues, accepting most but expressing reservations about several others. Dimitrov soon cabled New York with the Comintern's suggestions and blackballs.[64]

Mikhelson also gathered information and material useful for the clandestine activities of the Comintern. In 1936 Moscow wired him: "Send us first opportunity Canadian passport new model proposed by you with description as follows: medium stature, 30–35 years, dark hair and eyes. Communicate when we can receive same." He also periodically dispatched to Moscow seasonal train, ship, and air schedules for domestic and foreign airlines using American airports.[65]

As the purges gathered steam, Mikhelson also sent Moscow news of suspected Trotskyites who had returned to the Soviet Union from America or suspicious American travelers. In 1936, for example, he told the ECCI that "the American engineer G. Lyman Payne is a Trotskyite. He disappeared and apparently went to Russia." Moskvin and Manuilsky ordered the head of the Personnel Department of the ECCI to immediately inform the NKVD.[66]

Such vigilance did not insulate Mikhelson himself from suspicion. He was ordered to return to Moscow in late December 1937 for verification. A year later the NKVD responded that "we object to further use of Solomon Vladimirovich Michelson-Manuilov in the work of the Communications Service of the Comintern." Though such a conclusion usually presaged an arrest, Mikhelson escaped punishment, perhaps because of confusion following Yezhov's arrest or simple bureaucratic error. Early in February 1939 the new head of the Communications Service, Konstantin Sukharev, sent another memo to the NKVD listing former staff members who had been arrested and had previously worked with Mikhelson. Despite this prompt suggesting that he should be arrested, Mikhelson escaped again. Perhaps concluding that he had protectors, Sukharev soon addressed a letter to the Central Committee of the Soviet CP requesting assistance in getting new jobs for Mikhelson and his wife. Carefully phrasing—"as a result of isolation and a lack of control over their work . . . there is insufficient data to give them an exhaustive and precise recommendation"—he noted that Earl Browder had given them a positive reference. The overall tone, however, was negative, once again recounting Mikhelson's connection with "enemies" and his closeness to "Bukharinist circles." Sukharev concluded that "all of this makes us treat Manuilov with a certain distrust" and that he no longer wanted him or his wife employed in the Communications Service. Mikhelson transferred to the Radio Committee of the USSR and presumably survived the purges. Leaving his cloistered and top-secret job, he was required to sign a pledge never to discuss his work on pain of punishment for treason.[67]

The purge of the Communications Service significantly reduced the ability of the ECCI to maintain communications with its constituent parties. One solution was to rely more heavily on people recruited by the foreign parties. In the United States, following Mikhelson's recall to Moscow in 1938, the ECCI and Earl Browder agreed on a replacement who was more closely connected to the CPUSA but still had the trust of the Comintern.

Rudy Baker, chosen to be the clandestine contact between the ECCI and the CPUSA, had been born Rudolf Blum in Croatia. A charter member of the CPUSA, Baker had worked as a party functionary in Philadelphia and Detroit before studying at the Lenin School from 1927 to 1930. Although he briefly held several appointments in the United States after his return, Baker earned the trust of the Comintern in the early 1930s by undertaking several secret missions on its behalf in China, Canada, and Korea. He worked in Shanghai in 1934–1935 as a representative of the Profintern. In a report on his activities, he explained that he had worked underground: "When leaving my house to go to someone else's house or to a meeting, I always covered my tracks; i.e., I first went to a theater, café, or store and from there to the meeting; I never used my phone for calls to any comrades or to anyone's home; with very rare exceptions I always met with my comrades only on work-related matters. None of my comrades ever visited me at home or knew my address."[68]

After his return to the United States, as noted, Baker headed the American bureau of the Profintern's Pan-Pacific Trade Union Secretariat in San Francisco, using the cover name Betford or Bredford. Mikhelson often received cables ordering the payment of money to Baker for publication of Communist magazines to be smuggled into Japan. While serving on the party's Central Control Commission in 1938, Baker was tapped to replace J. Peters as head of its secret underground apparatus, an assignment known only to Browder and a handful of others. While in Moscow in January 1939, Baker wrote a report for the Personnel Department of the ECCI on his activities. Baker identified several key missions: "At the present time systematic efforts are being applied to improving communications, developing and testing [arrangements for] safeguarding important documents, and conducting of experiments in radio links. Attention is mainly focused now on enlarging the apparatus and training its cadres in proper methods of detecting and exposing the enemy within our own Party and within the workers' movement."[69]

The Comintern had been using ciphered telegrams and couriers to communicate with the CPUSA but recognized the need to establish more direct and secure links. During a visit to Moscow in December 1938 Browder received instructions to acquire a short-wave radio, to which the Comintern could send him coded messages. Baker's report indicated that steps had already begun to accomplish that goal early in 1939. By September 1939, just as World War II erupted in Europe, the new method of communicating came into use. A ciphered message to New York on 3 September from Dimitrov ("Brother") informed Baker ("Son"): "According to the new situation I propose that the automobile man start to work with us from the tenth of this month." ("Automobile work" was code for short-wave radio transmission; "automobile man" referred to the radio operator.)[70]

Communication between Moscow and New York was vital because the American communications station was the conduit for countries throughout North and South America. A cipher communication on 15 September 1939 noted that two letters sent by couriers had been received but that it was imperative "to organize the necessary reserves in the automobile connection. You have to inform us about the situation of our Parties in all countries of America." And couriers were a painfully slow method of communicating. A message from New York sent on 12 September was not received in Moscow until 13 October. It warned that "in the critical situation caused by neutral regulation and by the position of the Party," only vital information would be sent via cable; everything else would be sent through "secret writing" and the use of microdots. Baker sent a ciphered cable on 22 February 1940 seeking assurances that the new method was working: "Please acknowledge receipt invisible micro under stamps. Letters in future examine all envelopes, some of them will have micro under flaps of postage stamps."[71]

While couriers could bring the money necessary to pay for these covert operations, other methods were also necessary. Baker proposed: "You send several 1000 bills every 2 or 3 weeks, skillfully concealed inside cover English edition book published cooperative publishing society and addressed Mr. A. Spritsman, 1709 Boston Road, Bronx, New York. Other address will send next week. Notify us when you will send and name book. This is essential to safeguard and extend our work. Also send new address for mail from us."[72]

The new system was not without problems. While the CPUSA radio could receive transmissions, it was unable to send messages. Dimitrov informed Baker in June 1942:

> It's of great importance in the present situation to organize a two-way automobile work with us. The connection by means of greetings for the last 4–5 months cannot satisfy us. We insist on the necessity of more rapid way of communication. If it is not possible from N.Y.S. [New York Station], then organize automobile work from the West Coast or from Hershey [Cuba] or Gilu [Mexico]. Discuss this question with Father [Browder] and let us know by Mirton [an unknown Soviet intelligence agent] all about your decision you will get with Father and what practical steps you are taking.[73]

Moscow pressed Baker to pursue creating a radio link in Mexico. In December 1939 it had urged: "In the present condition we propose to organize an automobile construction in Gilu repeat Gilu to have the possibility to inform us maybe three four times each month. Please investigate this question, and if you agree then organize it." In mid-February 1940, Dimitrov repeated his orders: "I am waiting you start the automobile work with us from Gilu." But Baker had to report troubles due to issues within the Mexican Communist Party. "Gilu automobile work will be delayed; require aid Gilu Party which is undergoing reorganization due to unreliable elements in leadership," stated a coded dispatch of 22 February 1940.[74]

The Comintern remained insistent on the need to build radio transmitters in Latin America. On 26 November the Americans received another dispatch: "Suppose now very important organize automobile work with us from Gilu or Hershey—for your communications to us. Inform us what is done." In reply Baker warned that the Mexican Communists insisted it would cost $4,000, five times more than the cost in the United States. In addition, wartime restrictions on travel and logistical difficulties limited connections between Mexico and other Latin American nations.[75]

When American lawmakers, angered by the Nazi-Soviet Pact, took punitive action against the CPUSA as an agent of a foreign power, Baker warned Moscow:

> Party and related organizations about to be prosecuted as foreign agents violating law connection Moscow. We send telegram only when absolutely essential. There is a need for more private addresses to write to you; the post office of Lux and the address of the CI [Communist International] are well known officially. Entire attack is political, but charges are technical violation passport registration and income law which will affect majority leading personnel, organizations, and press. Names of all who traveled to SU are studied. Our apparatus already fair by new change name address. Hundreds additional secret police assigned against Party.

He added that incoming mail was being scrutinized as never before and thus recommended that the next courier conceal money in his baggage.[76]

Faced with increased scrutiny of its ties to Moscow and passage of the Voorhis Act, regulating agents of foreign powers, the CPUSA found a solution. By agreement with the ECCI, the CPUSA announced that it was officially withdrawing from the Communist International, thus avoiding potential Voorhis Act jurisdiction. The text of this statement of independence was written in Moscow by Dimitrov; initialed by ECCI members Togliatti, Gottwald, and Marty; and sent to Browder in a ciphered form on 16 November 1940, the same date a special CPUSA convention formally disaffiliated. It was a meaningless gesture; the CPUSA continued to receive funds from Moscow, maintain clandestine contact, and receive instructions for its work, though they were not couched as requests and suggestions. Three years later, after the Soviet government had decided to dissolve the Comintern, Dimitrov was not above requesting that the CPUSA demonstrate its solidarity: he sent a dispatch to Baker in July 1943: "Would you not consider it advisable in connection with the tenth anniversary of the Leipzig trial to send D. a Packard or Cadillac car and use this act politically." There is no indication in the files of an answer.[77]

CHAPTER TWO

Subventions

Very few Communist parties could have survived, much less prospered, without the infusion of large amounts of money from the Comintern. Over the years a steady stream of money enabled small or illegal or resource-poor parties to maintain a paid staff to administer, organize, and agitate. No comparable international network provided such benefits to any other political tendency on the left. Communists may have been unusually dedicated militants, but that alone would not have given Communist parties the kinds of advantages that Moscow gold provided. To transmit these gifts and to ensure that the monies were used for the purposes intended by the Comintern required an elaborate organization and extensive controls. But the process was not foolproof, and the Comintern struggled to regulate and oversee the large gifts it dispersed.

The cipher correspondence of the ECCI makes it possible to track how this money made its way to Communist parties, what demands were made on those who received the funds, who was directly responsible for handing them over to the party leaders, and for what purposes these allocations were made.

The exact size of the Comintern disbursements cannot be determined from the Department of International Communications messages. One dispatch sent to its representative in Vienna in July 1935 noted that the Austrian CP's funds for July had been "given out in a different way." Portions of many parties' budgets were paid by other Comintern bodies. Information about the Comintern budget and the annual payments to the Communist parties are found in the materials of its major organs, the Budget Commission of the ECCI, the Budget

Commission of the Central Committee of the VKP(b), the Politburo of the Central Committee of the VKP(b), and other sources.[1]

The total Comintern budget for 1922, as drawn up by the Politburo of the Central Committee of the Communist Party, was 2,950,600 gold rubles. With a rate of exchange of 10.5 gold rubles the equivalent of $5, the budget was approximately $1.4 million in 1922 dollars ($19.1 million in 2012 values). Allocations to different parties ranged from 500,000 gold rubles to the Germans ($3.3 million in 2012 values), 352,800 ($2.3 million in 2012 values) to the Americans, and 327,600 ($2.1 million in 2012 values) to the Czechoslovaks, down to 196,560 ($1.3 million in 2012 values) to the British and 155,763 ($1 million in 2012 values) to the Italians. The budget rose and fell over the years. In 1925, the Comintern was allocated 4,180,450 gold rubles. In 1938, however, the Politburo approved the ECCI's budget of only 1,342,447 gold rubles.[2]

In the 1930s, the communications center in Paris was one of the main disbursement points for Comintern subsidies. On 27 September 1933, for example, Siegfried Walter received a cable from Moscow ordering him to pay out October subventions of 9,780 French francs ($8,706 in 2012 values) to the Belgian CP, 115,380 ($102,721 in 2012 values) to the Italian CP, 2,625 ($2,336 in 2012 values) to the Luxembourg CP, 94,467 ($84,106 in 2012 values) to the French CP, and an additional 10,731 ($9,555 in 2012 values) for party work in the French colonies. The Comintern was funding a substantial percentage of the annual budgets of a number of parties. In 1935, for example, the monthly subvention for the French Communists, 65,000 francs ($71,506 in 2012 values), was supplemented by special allocations for the municipal elections and for publishing activities; the total from Moscow may have accounted for as much as one-quarter of the French CP's budget.[3]

The allocations from the Comintern probably played a much more significant role for illegal parties. In 1934 the Italian CP received an average of 63,000 francs a month, and in 1935, 90,000, while the German CP got 75,000 each month through the Paris center. Even these sums were dwarfed by the size of the subsidies for publishing activities, as well as for antiwar and antifascist committees, International Red Aid, and committees for the defense of Abyssinia, Thälmann, etc. On instructions from the ECCI, 254,000 francs were paid out on 14 January 1934 and 231,000 more on 3 February in what appears to have been Moscow's subvention for these varied Comintern-backed activities in the first half of 1934. (The two payments were the equivalent of $544,811 in 2012 values.) The subsidy for the second half of 1934 was not documented in the cable traffic. In 1935, again apparently for the first half of the year, payments of 339,000 francs on 1 January 1935, 353,000 more on 3 March, 584,000 on 22 April, and another 600,000 by the end of May ($2,063,649 in 2012 values) were authorized for distribution to these Comintern-supported tasks.[4]

One detailed set of instructions for payments to a variety of parties and organizations was sent in early August 1936. The communications center representative in Paris was ordered to hand out 523,680 French francs for September ($528,170 in 2012 values). Five Communist parties received a monthly stipend ranging from 84,000 francs to the Italians down to 2,100 francs to Luxembourg. *Inprekorr*, a Comintern newspaper, received 174,400 francs ($175,897 in 2012 values), while four other organizations also got subsidies. The Comintern's Communications Service representative in Sweden was told to give 2,420 Swedish krona to the Norwegians ($10,228 in 2012 values) and pay the British 23,750 Dutch guilders ($252,620 in 2012 values). In London Harry Pollitt got detailed instructions to parcel out the money received from Sweden for expenses for work in Ireland and India. The Communications Service representative in Prague distributed 422,388 French francs ($426,010 in 2012 values) to Communist parties in Austria, Bulgaria, Hungary, Germany, Romania, Czechoslovakia, and Yugoslavia.[5]

The distribution of the money occurred in several ways. Couriers carried caches of money from Moscow to Communist parties in any number of countries. In September 1936 Alexander Trachtenberg, head of International Publishers in New York, returned from Moscow with $25,000 in cash ($412,400 in 2012 values), which he gave to Mikhelson-Manuilov, who, in turn, gave it to the CPUSA. In October 1936 the ECCI learned that Clarence Hathaway, a party leader, had handed over $16,000 ($263,937 in 2012 values) he had received in Moscow to CPUSA officials.[6]

In addition to party leaders in Moscow consulting with Comintern leaders or attending meetings, there was a cadre of anonymous couriers who ferried money from Moscow around the globe. Among the names that pop up in the coded cables are a number of obscure figures who have never surfaced in histories but were used to courier money. Among the Americans involved were Evelina Strand, Jenny Feldman, Eisenberg, Louis Oshants, Simon Feldman, Emma Richter, and Isaiah Litvakov. Of all nationalities, these couriers traveled with suitcases, preceded by cables announcing their arrival. On 5 March 1936 a cable to Paris noted that the preceding day "the Swede Peterson departed, will give the small suitcase in which are 15,000 Amer. doll and 40 thousand Swiss francs. Acknowledge receipt immediately. He will receive Sov[iet] visa in Stockholm." (These sums were the 2012 equivalent of $247,000 and $199,190 respectively.) That same day Paris also got a similar message about "the Norwegian Akkerman," following the same route with the same amount of money. At the end of the month it was "the English woman Taylor Evelyn" going through Vienna with 30,000 Swiss francs ($149,405 in 2012 values) and 20,000 Dutch guilders ($212,733 in 2012 values) on her way to Paris.[7]

Sometimes Soviet embassies received the funds and passed them on to representatives of the Comintern's Communications Service through clandestine contacts. In Paris, the Soviet diplomatic mission transferred Comintern funds to the French CP. Gabriel (a pseudonym of Maurice Tréand, the representative of the Communications Service in Paris) cabled in 1939 that he had "received 100,000 newspapers, through friends," a reference to the Soviet embassy. (It is unclear if these funds were dollars or francs.) On 5 February Dimitrov let Tréand know that "We have sent through the friends twice as many magazines as previously. Organize receipt. Acknowledge."[8]

Sometimes the money was transferred via Soviet intelligence agencies. In 1928 the military intelligence arm of the Red Army sent a letter to Osip Pyatnitsky, then a member of the ECCI, reminding him that "in accordance with your instructions . . . our apparatus in Harbin sent to Shanghai for your line two thousand Am. dol." Military intelligence, of course, wanted its money back. When it received no response, military intelligence chief Jan Berzin wrote again, complaining that the head of the DIC in China had received $6,000 in total, which had yet to be repaid. That letter did the trick, and the Comintern reimbursed the sum. In 1933 the DIC representative in China informed Moscow that "neighbors" (a term used to refer to organs of Soviet military intelligence and also to the foreign intelligence service of the NKVD) had provided $20,000 ($354,000 in 2012 values).[9]

The NKVD and Soviet military intelligence were also used to send money to American Communists. One unidentified agent, Mirton, delivered money to Rudy Baker in 1940–1941. A message from Dimitrov told him to "please meet Mirton repeat Mirton known to you at the reserve meeting place. He has to deliver you some goods from me." Another message noted that "we are sending twenty thousand goods—acknowledge receipt. We ask you to help Mirton, by recommending him two-three non-Party members who will be able to help him in his work—but all this has to be done with precaution. He will give you the money in forty days." A later message detailed how to distribute the $45,000 ($698,982 in 2012 values) he was bringing; $25,000 was for Trachtenberg's publishing house, with lesser amounts for the Communist parties of Chile, Mexico, Argentina, and Brazil.[10]

When the money was picked up in Soviet embassies or delivered by intelligence agents working under legal covers, it could be carried in small bundles or wads of cash. When Vasily Zarubin, code-named Cooper, visited Steve Nelson in California in 1943, he handed him a number of bills while American counterintelligence agents listening to a wiretap heard Nelson tell the Soviet diplomat—who was actually the head of the NKVD station in America—"Jesus, you count money like a banker." But many of the couriers, who had to pass through customs examinations, carried their money in suitcases with false bottoms, an old Bolshevik tactic for smuggling newspapers into Tsarist Russia.[11]

The suitcases were manufactured in Paris by a man named Nadelman. After the arrest in Moscow of Walter, the former head of the Communications Service in Paris, the ECCI launched an investigation of his apparatus. A message sent to Moscow explained that to mark the preparation of seventy suitcases, Nadelman had organized a celebratory dinner; shortly afterward he "threatened us that he would betray us to the police if anything happened to the suitcases. After that he was liquidated."[12]

On some occasions the money was transferred without using any couriers at all. Currency was also sent in the covers of books or through regular banking techniques. On 16 March 1937 a letter arrived from Hong Kong with a brief message about the activity of the Communist Party of Indochina. It contained a request for money: "We are asking that 400 dollars be sent us monthly, hidden in the cover of a textbook. It should be sent to the following address: Mister Chou-Sam Jee. The Chinese emigrant middle school. Castleroad. Hong-Kong. China. Sometimes a small sum can be sent by check to: Chou-Sam Jee. The book and the check should be sent registered mail." When the representative of the Communications Service in France was told to transfer $20,000 to Alexander Trachtenberg, he proposed using a bank transfer, but the ECCI rejected that option, suggesting instead "sending for this purpose a messenger, possibly from Holland." In November 1939 Rudy Baker cabled proposing "you again send additional 500 d. or 1,000 bill skillfully concealed in cover book published in USSR and to: Mrs. V. Steinberg 326 Beach N66 street Arwerne New York."[13]

In the early years of the Soviet regime, hard currency reserves were in very short supply. As a result, the Comintern used couriers to send valuables and gold and silver items obtained from the State Depository of Valuables of the Soviet Republic. In October 1919, for example, the ECCI sent a courier to Germany with "valuables worth 2,000,000 rubles for the German Party and for publishing." His receipt noted that he had received "a total of seven diamonds at a sum of one million four hundred twenty thousand rub. (1,420,000) and one pearl necklace for No. 757 consisting of 261 pearls valued at 600,000 rub. In all, for two million twenty thousand (2,020,000) [and] a gold ring with two diamonds and [illegible] at a cost of two thousand four hundred rub. (2,400)." Around the same time another receipt noted that the ECCI had arranged for a number of diamonds worth 1,011,000 rubles to be sent to the United States.[14]

By the early 1920s money had replaced jewels and precious metals. Allocations, however, were often irregular and in response to particular pleas from party leaders facing budgetary shortages or some kind of emergency. By the 1930s the process had become regularized. Instead of a series of isolated and random transfers of large sums of money to the leaders of the parties in answer to their requests, a more systematic kind of financing was put in place, so Communist parties typically received part of their budget monthly. In addition, specific allocations were made for various purposes and for publishing.

The Comintern's own funds, in turn, were allocated by the Central Committee of the Soviet Communist Party. Although it received an annual budget, with funds disbursed periodically throughout the year, the ECCI also occasionally appealed to the Soviet authorities for additional resources. In October 1937, for example, Georgi Dimitrov wrote to the secretary of the Central Committee, Andrei Andreyev, that "at present we have exhausted all resources available to us, and to avoid extremely serious difficulties in the work of our sections and to provide for the publishing activity of the Communist International and the functioning of the organs of the ECCI, we are in urgent need of additional funds to implement the fourth-quarter budget. According to our calculations we require funds on the order of 900,000 (nine hundred thousand) gold rubles until the end of the year. If necessary, Moskvin will provide you with appropriate detailed explanations. I request you to give the necessary instructions to the Narkomfin

[People's Commissariat for Finances] to provide credits for us as per the sum indicated above."[15]

The Comintern did not have a free hand to pay funds to the Communist parties in particular currencies but was dependent on what the ECCI received from Soviet financial institutions. It sent money abroad in dollars, French or Swiss francs, Dutch guilders, or Swedish krona and instructed representatives of the Communications Service not only how much to dole out, but in what currency. Telling the CS representative in France to pay monthly subventions in dollars, one cipher communication warned against converting currencies: "From now on pay . . . only in the currency indicated in our instructions."[16]

Exchange rates sometimes complicated the accounting. The ECCI allocated $300,000 for the Chinese Communist Party in 1940 ($4,899,358 in 2012 values). Part of the subsidy had been paid out in pounds sterling. Because the Comintern had calculated that each pound sterling was worth $4 dollars and it was actually worth only $3 dollars in China, the Chinese CP protested that it had actually received only $213,000. But that was hardly the only problem with receiving British currency. The Chinese Central Committee complained in November 1940 that Zhou Enlai had received $43,287 and 11,500 British pounds. "Since British currency at present is not in use in China, we have therefore sent back to you [via the Soviet ambassador all the pounds we had and] request that instead of the British currency you pay us in American dollars."[17]

The Comintern repeatedly demanded strict accountability for the funds it furnished. From its earliest days Lenin had insisted that accepting Comintern money obliged the recipients to abide by a strict code of accountability, not only to the Comintern, but also to the Soviet Communist Party: "Any person taking money from the C[ommunist] I[nternational] is warned that he is obliged to implement absolutely scrupulously all instructions of the ECCI and especially to implement scrupulously all rules and conditions required for providing unconditionally full, rapid, and correct information to the Central Committee of the Russian Communist Party regarding each kopeck of funds spent."[18]

Giving the Communist parties monthly allocations helped to ensure that funds were not frittered away or spent too quickly on temporary whims. In January 1939 Dimitrov gave instructions for $23,500 to be given to Thomas Bell, leader of MOPR (International Organization for Aid to the Fighters of the Revolution, a.k.a. International Red Aid) to cover arrears and current MOPR expenses, along with $15,000 to

Bruno Köhler to organize the evacuation of German Communists from the Sudetenland, but he warned that "Köhler and Tom should not be given the entire sum at once; rather, it should be doled out depending on real need."[19]

By keeping the parties dependent on month-to-month disbursements, Dimitrov and the ECCI could maintain a tighter leash on their activities. In a telegram to Maurice Tréand in May-June 1939, Dimitrov made the restraints clear: "Warn the recipients of the funds that these sums have been firmly set for this year. All expenditures exceeding these sums can be paid only with our preliminary consent. As a rule, pay out only that sum planned for the m[on]th and only in exceptional cases large sums, but not for more than 2 m[on]ths. Aside from [the German CP] none of the enterprises has submitted a report on the funds spent which were allocated for 1938. Warn that if the reports are not submitted by 15.VI, we shall be forced to terminate the further release of funds." The ECCI gave representatives of the Communications Service instructions to be transmitted to leaders of Communist parties at the end of 1936: "For the year 1937 decisions on subventions will not be taken before we get cash-balance of Party cash for 1936." This order was to be communicated orally, not in writing.[20]

While Lenin considered financial allocations to foreign Communists an act of solidarity, they were also a lever for exerting influence and ensuring subordination. Sometimes the messages specified both the sum of money allocated to one or another party or organization and the smallest details on how the money should be spent. In August 1933, for example, Harry Pollitt, leader of the British Communists, was sent a coded dispatch informing him that he would receive $10,411 ($184,226 in 2012 values) to be distributed among the CPGB, its newspaper, the CP of Ireland, and the Anti-Imperialist League. The latter organization was to get $285 per month, of which "220 dol. for the central apparatus (approximate allocation as follows: the secretary—65 dol., the typist—50, rent—40, messenger—25, telegrams and mail expenses—40) and 65—for the English section of the League."[21]

Established in 1927 to fight against imperialism and colonial oppression, the league's headquarters had been moved to London in 1933. Sending 50,000 French francs ($44,521 in 2012 values) to its leader, Willi Münzenberg, the ECCI warned that the money could be spent only to organize a counter-trial to combat the forthcoming Nazi trial of Communists accused of burning the Reichstag. Münzenberg was informed that the funds "cannot be spent for other purposes. You will be held responsible for accounting for this sum." A directive to the representative of the DIC in Prague was even sharper: "Warn the Communist Party of Romania that these funds must be sent in their entirety as designated and cannot be spent for any other purposes, and that we demand an accounting of the activity of these organizations and financial reporting. If the report is not sent, the subvention will be terminated."[22]

The ECCI compared the information on the sums sent from Moscow with the reports of the CS representatives and parties regarding the receipt and use of those allocations. If there were differences between these figures, it demanded an inquiry. Noting that the Communist Party of Spain "is showing a remaining sum of 25,849 French francs with no indications on what it has been spent," the ECCI demanded an accounting for that sum. A directive to the representative in Copenhagen demanded to know "to whom, how much, and for what month" monies had been paid out for the Communist parties of Poland and Western Belarus. "According to our calculations as of 1 January you did not pay out for November and December 39,552 Swiss francs; for January and February there should have been payments of 77,822. You paid out in January 100,000 French francs, 23,855 Swedish krona, and 19,300 guilders. . . . Consequently, the sum still not paid out to the Communist Party of Poland and to the CPWB as of 1.III is 37,289 Swiss francs. Check on our calculations and inform us of the results."[23]

Even small inaccuracies in the accounting and discrepancies in the figures prompted critical comments from the ECCI. In July 1933 the ECCI learned that a leading American Communist, Max Bedacht, had delivered $1,900 upon his arrival from Moscow. Earl Browder quickly received a query: "Bedacht had from us 3,000 dollars; do not understand why he delivered only 1,900 dollars. Clear up and get remainder from him. Wire." The CPUSA responded that it was all a mistake; it had received the full amount.[24]

While the ECCI required information about the receipt of money, it demanded that both DIC employees and Communist parties ensure that no documentary evidence remained of the receipt of funds from Moscow. If they could not be sent to Moscow, receipts or other materials were supposed to be destroyed in the presence of a reliable witness. One telegram from Mikhelson-Manuilov reported that receipts documenting a variety of subventions "were controlled and destroyed [in the company of] Earl [Browder]."[25]

The ECCI's fear of documentary evidence of monetary allocations prompted immediate inquiries whenever Comintern personnel or local Communists involved in the transfer of money were arrested or recipient organizations came under scrutiny. On learning that the New York police had searched the offices of Intourist, a branch of the Soviet tourist organization, Dimitrov asked Browder "to do all necessary that you can in the question of the goods which [Alexander] Trachtenberg received in thirty-seven (Moscow). It is of great importance that [any] documentation . . . not be utilized by our enemies, and all the necessary measures are to be undertaken by you in this direction." When a high-ranking German Communist was arrested in Sweden, Dimitrov immediately wanted to know whether anyone else had been arrested and how much of the money the German had recently received from Moscow had been found on him.[26]

Scrupulous attention to financial matters was easy to assure in Moscow, where the Communications Service had a full-time bookkeeper and the luxury of keeping detailed records. But its representatives abroad faced more daunting challenges. Illegal parties worked in conditions of stress and danger. Even legal parties were forbidden to retain receipts. Disbursing large amounts of money in clandestine fashion often led to gaps in documentation. Lydia Dübi, head of the Paris office of the Communications Service, defended her staffer Arno, who was unable to account for 2,900 French francs: "Some papers were missing during the accounting because due to his excessive workload and because he worked on all these financial matters on the street and in cafés, it could easily happen that he lost one receipt or another or forgot to ask for or write out a receipt. . . . He worked for 3 1/2 years sometimes in very difficult conditions, had more than 20 meetings a day, and in our work it is impossible to ensure complete order in the cashier's office." She asked that he not be held accountable for the money.[27]

Moscow saw things differently. One week after Dübi's appeal, the ECCI sent the representatives of the Communications Service in Prague, Stockholm, and Paris an identical cipher communication: "The information we have concerning the accuracy in your keeping money and the ways of exchanging it provide a most unfavorable picture. An excessively large sum is being kept at the same time in one place, and excessive sums are also simultaneously being given to one person for exchange. There is a need to have the funds dispersed in several places and not to give out large sums for exchange at one and the same time. There is a need once again to consider ways of keeping the money in your apparatus and to change these so that the Party funds are not in danger of loss or theft. We request that you urgently inform us of your views."[28]

As Europe spiraled toward war at the end of the 1930s, the Comintern recognized that the transfer of money across borders would become even more difficult and dangerous. To prepare for the day when neither couriers nor Soviet representatives would have the ability to travel freely, Dimitrov began to create reserve funds of hard currency in Sweden and France. A cipher cable from Moskvin to Dimitrov on 30 September 1938 stated that Karl Fritjof Lager, a member of the Politburo of the Swedish Communist Party, had left that day for Stockholm, "the first attempt to send with him the reserves so far modest in size." In France Dimitrov made Maurice Tréand, once head of the Personnel Commission of the Central Committee of the French CP and at the same time the representative of the Comintern's Communications Service in Paris, the trustee for the monetary reserves. In his diary Dimitrov noted on 17 December 1938 that he had "established the sums which Tréand will be paying out through our account. Have confirmed the rules for the Communications apparatus in P[aris]; Tréand left with (70,000 dol. [w.] him)." Not even the leadership of the Communist parties knew about the monetary reserves. In a cable sent to Paris in late November 1940, the ECCI gave Tréand permission to inform the French CP leadership about the fund "in case of urgent need." The cipher cable was initialed by Dimitrov and signed by Maurice Thorez, one-time leader of the French CP now working for the Comintern in Moscow after deserting from the French Army rather than fighting against the Nazis.[29]

In wartime conditions money was sent on an uninterrupted basis only to Sweden. Some of this money made its way to officials of the illegal Communist Party of Germany. Funds were not sent regularly to other countries, but until it ceased its activities the Comintern continued to supply money to its sections, albeit at a diminishing rate. In late November 1940 Dolores Ibárruri, an exiled leader of the Spanish Communist Party and the secretary of the ECCI (the cipher cable was initialed by Dimitrov, as usual), warned the leaders of the Spanish Communist Party, themselves in exile in the United States and South America, that "the situation requires a radical decrease in the expenditures of the apparatus. It has been decided that only 2 c[omrades] must be paid. The others must work and help the Party without pay."[30]

With the entrance of the USSR into the war the size of the Comintern's allocations from the Central Committee of the Soviet Communist Party decreased, and that led to the Communist parties receiving less and less money from Moscow. For both 1941 and 1942 the Politburo allocated to the ECCI "for rendering assistance to foreign Parties" $200,000 ($3,106,585 in 2012 values), substantially less than in prior years. One large special allocation of $1,000,000 ($15,532,926 in 2012 values) was made to finance the Communist Party of China. The Politburo's decision severely strained the Comintern budget. Dimitrov appealed to Stalin in May 1942 for an increase in the allocation. It went unheeded; at the end of July he reiterated his plea in a letter to the secretary of the Central Committee, noting that the Comintern had originally requested $355,000 in foreign currencies for 1942, an increase from the $200,000 it had been granted in 1941. It had actually spent $268,414 ($3,760,755 in 2012 values) that year, covering the shortfall by manipulating the budgets of the French and Spanish parties and dipping into reserves. "But these means are already almost completely exhausted, and to cover further expenditures there is an urgent need for new foreign currency allocations. Since it would be damaging in this situation to allow for a breakdown in our work abroad, I request that what is needed be done so that at least part of the requested allocation be allowed us within the next few days."[31]

To justify this request, Dimitrov cited the needs of the illegal Communist parties—$110,000, including $20,000 each for the Communist parties of Spain, France, and Germany; $6,000 each for Bulgaria and Poland; $5,000 for Romania, Finland, and Hungary; and $23,000 for a handful of others. A sum of $50,000 would fund operations in Central and Southern Europe; $70,000 would go for communication centers in Europe, Asia, the Americas, and the Middle East (centers were located not only in Paris and New York, but also in the Mongolian People's Republic, Turkey, Iran, and India); $55,000 for publishing activities; and $70,000 for operation of a telegraph agency.[32]

The Comintern apparently received a portion of what it needed, but the amount did not begin to cover its commitments. In late September 1942 Dimitrov again wrote to Andreyev, begging for more money: "The 30,000 American dollars issued to us as of today have been spent. I request you to give instructions to issue in October an additional advance of 30,000 American dollars to cover expenditures: 1) for operating costs of the communications Centers abroad and for sending Party workers to Germany, Czechoslovakia, Romania, and Poland—12,000. 2) For expenditures for the journal *Die Welt*, published in Sweden for Germany and other countries—4,000. 3) For the payment of telegrams, received from our correspondents in Switzerland, America, England, Sweden, China, and other countries—4,000."[33]

Dimitrov again requested more money on 19 November 1942 as Comintern funds dwindled, asking for another $73,000 before the end of the year. Such monthly allocations of foreign currency for the Comintern continued until the very end of its existence in June 1943. Even after it dissolved itself, the monetary chain that linked Moscow to Communist parties around the globe was maintained, although it took on somewhat different forms.

CHAPTER THREE

The Popular Front

While fiercely opposed to fascism, the Comintern did not regard Adolf Hitler's rise to power as a political setback or a cause for panic. By the logic of the Third Period political evaluation of the world situation, in fact, it presaged an opportunity for the triumph of communism. Laid down in 1928 at the Sixth Comintern Congress, the Third Period line foresaw world capitalism entering a period of revolutionary crisis. A worldwide economic decline would usher in fierce struggles for political power that Communist parties had to be prepared to exploit. This final stage of struggle required Communist militancy. Communists had to scorn coalitions with the leadership of other ostensibly left-wing parties—the United Front from above—in favor of appeals to the rank-and-file of such groups to abandon their leaders and join political and economic struggles under Communist leadership—the United Front from below.

Other political groups on the left—whether the Socialist Party or any of the tiny splinter Communist sects—were, by virtue of their standing as obstacles to Communist hegemony, regarded as objectively aiding fascism and denounced as "social fascists." They were accused of being even greater dangers than the fascists themselves because they misled the working class into believing they served its interests. After 1928, at the Comintern's behest, the Communist Party of Germany occasionally cooperated with the Nazis to weaken and bring down German governments. The prospect of Hitler taking power elicited the slogan, "After Hitler, us," the optimistic belief that a brief taste of fascism in power would pave the way for a Communist revolution.

That illusion persisted throughout 1933 and into 1934 as the Nazi regime consolidated its power and destroyed the once powerful Communist Party of Germany along with its socialist rival. While the Comintern stubbornly held on to the fantasy that democratic or even authoritarian regimes were a greater danger than fascism, several of its constituent parties that faced growing fascist movements and growing fears from their own members began to express uneasiness. Even the Comintern could not ignore the perilous state of its constituent parties after six years of militant revolutionary policies. When the ECCI convened in December 1933, only sixteen of the seventy-two parties represented in the Communist International were legal, with another seven in a semi-legal status. Early in 1934 a revolt by the Austrian working class against Engelbert Dollfuss's imposition of fascist rule was defeated, and a fascist triumph seemed possible in France as well. Nowhere was the pressure to modify the rigid Third Period line greater than in France, where the French Communist Party (Parti Communiste Français *[PCF]*), despite a membership that was lower than it had ever been, was the largest Communist party outside of the USSR.[1]

The Popular Front in France

The combined effects of the Great Depression and a series of political and financial scandals had unsettled French politics since 1930. Hitler's triumph in Germany increased fears that the political ground was shifting. Moderate left-wing parties (chiefly France's Socialist Party [SFIO] and the center-left Radical Party) were particularly shaken by large street demonstrations organized by right-wing forces. The largest, on 6 February 1934, organized by a coalition of royalists, nationalists, and fascists, led to violent riots in the heart of Paris. Édouard Daladier, the Radical premier, resigned the next day and was replaced by a Conservative.

Separate Socialist and Communist demonstrations on 12 February spontaneously merged into a combined rally, sparking hopes that the two fractious left-wing parties could unite. While the brief spasm of unity achieved mythic status, the two parties continued to quarrel, with the Communists attacking the Socialists. They had a sudden change of heart in late June, when the CP asked the Socialist leadership to cooperate after the French CP Politburo received a telegram from the Comintern demanding cooperation. The change in policy no doubt reflected the addition of Georgi Dimitrov to the ECCI following his release from a German prison. A symbol of opposition to fascism, Dimitrov accumulated power throughout 1934, being appointed to head the Central European Landersecretariat in April and quickly becoming a leader of the Comintern and reducing the influence of such exemplars of the Third Period line as Osip Pyatnitsky, Wilhelm Knorin, and Béla Kun.[2]

Comintern representative Eugen Fried mediated relations between the French CP and Moscow. A native of Slovakia, Fried had been a left-wing critic of the Czechoslovak party leadership before being recalled to Moscow in 1931 and assigned to Comintern work. Using the pseudonym "Clément," he served as the permanent representative to the PCF. Although he kept a low profile, he played an extremely powerful role in the PCF from 1931 until the end of 1942. He then worked in Belgium until the Gestapo killed him in 1943.

Fried worked very closely with Maurice Thorez, since 1931 the most important figure in the French Communist movement. At least some of the initiative for the Popular Front alliance of Socialists and Communists came from Thorez, who struggled to decipher in what direction the Comintern wanted him to move. Summoned to Moscow in late April 1934, he was upbraided by the ECCI Presidium in May for his obduracy against an alliance with the Socialists, a position entirely in accord with the strong Third Period line opposing "United Fronts from above." Six weeks after his return to France, the Comintern sent a letter to several national parties emphasizing the need for unity with the Socialists; that same day the PCF started negotiations with the French Socialists. Although the talks quickly fell apart, a telegram from Manuilsky ordering unity caused the PCF to tone down critical remarks about the Socialists. The PCF proposed a unity pact with the Socialists on 25 June, and it was signed a month later, providing for joint demonstrations and the cessation of attacks on each other. The two parties also agreed to withdraw competing candidates in the second round of local elections in October in favor of the more likely winner.

Sensing that the Comintern might be shifting its strategy and emboldened by its suggestion of an approach to the non-Socialist Radicals, Thorez issued a call for a Popular Front in early October 1934. Historians have debated just how much of a departure from Comintern policy Thorez had taken since there is some evidence of Comintern unease with his initiative. The coded cables throw some light on its very cautious endorsement of the developing Popular Front.

The Conservative government in power, led by Pierre Laval, was dependent on the support of the Radicals for survival. A significant segment of the Radicals favored a coalition of the left-wing parties. The French Communists proposed to approach the dissidents and asked the ECCI for permission. The Politcommission of the ECCI Politsecretariat sent a message on 5 October to Fried and ECCI member Palmiro Togliatti, then in France, endorsing a limited appeal to the Radical Party. "We agree with your proposal regarding the involvement in the antifascist front of those Radical groups which disagree with the policy of their Party and are in fact fighting against fascism and the National government." It chastised the PCF for sending Julien Racamond, a member of the PCF Central Committee and a trade union leader, to a secret meeting with Radical Party leader Édouard Daladier, calling it "a wrong step; we advise against a repetition of the negotiations."[3]

That message suggests that the Comintern thought Thorez would appeal only to disaffected Radicals, not the Radical Party mainstream led by Daladier. Such an interpretation is supported by its harsh reaction to the publication of a Thorez speech entitled "At All Costs Defeat Fascism: For a Wide Antifascist Popular Front." A Comintern delegation led by Togliatti met with Thorez on 24 October to try, unsuccessfully, to dissuade him from continuing his initiative at a meeting that day of a Radical Party conference.[4]

That Togliatti spoke not only for himself is confirmed by a dispatch of 31 October addressed to Togliatti, Fried, and the Politburo of the Central Committee of the PCF that warned against the opportunist danger that, in the view of the ECCI, threatened the French party as a result of the Popular Front slogan. The telegram made clear that the coalition it had approved was an "antifascist front of workers": "Any participation by the bourgeois Parties in the antifascist front must be excluded in advance. The groups that have split off from these Parties, however, which are linked to the peasant masses and accept the program of the antifascist front, can be involved in the antifascist front." The message emphasized the traditional ideological principles and political goals of the Communist movement, based on the proletarian revolution and Soviet power, whose propaganda was to be merged with the antifascist struggle: "In fighting for the creation of the antifascist front and its program, the Party must take great care not to sidestep the radical difference between Communism and Social Democracy, between the policy of irreconcilable class struggle and the policy of class cooperation with the bourgeoisie. On the contrary, in the process of that joint struggle the Party must, using specific examples, conduct ongoing educational work on these issues. The Party must step up its propaganda for Soviet power and the dictatorship of the proletariat, for the proletarian revolution as the sole path to truly free the workers from capitalism, from the threat of fascism and war."[5]

At a Comintern Presidium meeting in Moscow on 9 December 1934, Thorez defended the French initiative and won support from Manuilsky and, ultimately, Stalin. Soviet foreign policy also played a role in gaining approval for his action. A reluctant Premier Laval signed a Franco-Soviet pact in May 1935; Stalin may well have calculated that it would not survive without a more left-wing French government in power, and that, in turn, was dependent on detaching the Radicals from their alliance with the Conservatives. Immediately after the signing, the ECCI sent a coded message with orders: "The FCP [French Communist Party] will vote in parliament in support of that treaty." But it added that "since the army is in the hands of the bourgeoisie, the French Party will vote against the budget, military loans, and two-year military service."[6]

On 14 July 1935 a left-wing demonstration united Communists, Socialists, and Radicals, who formally committed to forming a political alliance to oppose the right-wing government of Pierre Laval. The Seventh Comintern Congress, convening at the end of July, formally adopted the Popular Front as its policy and lavished particular praise on Thorez and the PCF for demonstrating that it could succeed. The exact contours of the Popular Front were much narrower, however, than a full-fledged alliance.

Dimitrov's report at the Seventh Comintern Congress had been approved in advance by Stalin. He admitted that France had set an example of "how fascism should be fought." The antifascist Popular Front was to be built on the basis of the United Proletarian Front. Parties and organizations dominated by peasants and the urban petty bourgeoisie could also be brought into the coalition.[7] The congress was not yet ready to subordinate the idea of a Communist revolution to halting the advance of fascism, however. It contemplated the possibility of a United Front government (Communists and Socialists) arising from a collapse of the ruling class. In that case, "The Communists must promote *radical* revolutionary slogans (for example, control of production and of the banks, the disbanding of the police and its replacement by an armed workers' militia), aimed at even further weakening the economic power of the bourgeoisie and reinforcing the strength of the working class, isolating the Parties of compromise and prompting the masses to move immediately toward a revolutionary seizure of power."[8] Such revolutionary fantasies, however, bore no relation to what was actually occurring in France.

On 16 October 1935 the ECCI Secretariat authorized Ernö Gerö and André Marty to draw up a letter "which must contain advice on the question of participation in the Government of the Popular Front, on the question of political unity, work in various trade unions, trade union unity, and the danger of the Party being banned." The letter, approved by Manuilsky, warned the leaders of the PCF not to join any Popular Front government: "The government of the Popular Front, which is not being formed in conditions of political crisis and is not based on a powerful mass movement, would not be able to take real action against the fascists and could not implement a policy in favor of the working masses because it would run up against more powerful and reactionary strata of the bourgeoisie, who through the stock exchanges and the banks could totally weaken and overthrow it. The result would be the disappointment of the working masses, a strengthening of the fascist movement, and a loss of authority of the Communist Party if the latter were to support such a government."[9]

Whether that message reached Thorez is unclear. He made a statement that suggested that the PCF was prepared to take responsibility for a Popular Front government. The ECCI Secretariat quickly authorized Manuilsky to "prepare a telegram for the Central Committee of the French Communist Party on the tactics of the Party regarding the Government of the Popular Front." Sent on 22 October, the telegram put forward an even stronger rejection of participation by the Communists in such a government. It warned against precipitating a "premature" government crisis but accepted that "if the government of Laval is overthrown, the formation of a government with a basic core of Radicals, whom the Popular Front will support since this government will be taking measures to disarm and disband the fascist organizations, will be most advantageous to the Communist Party."[10]

Fried responded just as rapidly, assuring the ECCI that "Maurice's [Thorez] declaration on participation in the government is useless chatter and does not represent the views of either the leadership or Maurice. Confirming previous conversations, the leadership is in agreement with the policy of the 7th Congress regarding participation. The oratory of some of the leaders has run dry. Thanks to my intervention Maurice corrected his position in his final remarks at the CC. Details in person." Dimitrov received the exchange while on vacation and signaled his agreement with the ECCI's position. He emphasized that the most pressing objective of the PCF was to increase its influence in the army and demand the organization of a mass self-defense movement for the antifascist front. There was no question about the French Communists joining a Popular Front government.[11]

The Radicals, Communists, and Socialists reached a formal agreement in January 1936; in the ensuing parliamentary elections in April and May, the Communists tempered their militancy, advised by the ECCI Secretariat that "at the present time the most important issue is the victory of the antifascist Popular Front, which had set its goal as curbing fascism, preserving peace, and satisfying the vital interests of the workers" and not "the creation of Soviet power, as the reactionaries would have this appear."[12]

The elections were a victory for the three parties that constituted the Popular Front. They collected 5.1 million votes, and the right-wing parties, 4.2 million. To everyone's surprise, however, the Socialist Party and not the Radicals emerged as the largest party; Léon Blum became the first Socialist prime minister of France. The French Communists had premised their support for a Popular Front government on the belief that it would be led by a bourgeois party, and while they would support the government, they would not accept cabinet posts. They had to decide whether to change their minds after Blum asked them to join his government. Immediately after the elections Dimitrov told the French Communist leadership that "we are expecting a telegram regarding the Politburo's assessment of the election results, the relationship with the Popular Front after the elections, and of your actions in connection with the existing situation."[13]

On 11 May 1936, at a meeting of the ECCI Secretariat, Dimitrov declared that the victory of the Popular Front had not produced a strong majority for the Socialists and the Communists in the French parliament and that a government could not survive without Radical support; the Communists should assist in the creation of the government but not participate in it. "Our participation in the government would break the back of the Popular Front and joint action, i.e., of that front which existed prior to the elections. The interests of maintaining and reinforcing the continuing struggle against fascism and reaction in France speak against our participation in the government." He also worried that Communist participation in the government would lead to even more opposition to the government but did not exclude the possibility that in the future "a situation might be created in which it would be advisable to participate in the government." That would require further mass mobilization, an increase in Communist influence, and even more intense governmental conflict.[14]

Dimitrov endorsed the position of the PCF that it would decline Blum's invitation to join the government but would support it in the parliament. The concern that it would inspire more hostility to the Popular Front was less important than the Comintern's assessment that since the Radicals held the balance of power, the Communists would have limited influence on the government but would have to compromise their long-term commitment to Soviet power and be responsible for running a bourgeois government beholden to the bourgeoisie. The Comintern's insistence on this point for the next year suggests just how concerned it was that a direct government role for the French Communist Party might cause problems.

Fried reported from Paris that Blum had repeated his plea that Communists join the government and that the National Council of the Socialist Party had reiterated the proposal. While Thorez and Jacques Duclos, a senior member of the PCF Central Committee Politburo, had once again said no, "there is a movement in favor of participation among the masses who voted for us." When the Comintern learned that the leadership of the French Socialists had decided to send a delegation to Moscow to press the issue, Dimitrov sent a telegram to Thorez that he would respond that the Seventh Congress had transferred "operative leadership" to its sections, "and therefore the issue of participation or nonparticipation of the CP in the government and other similar questions are decided in Paris by the leadership of the French CP," the very same party to whom it was sending directives demanding that it not join the government.[15]

The ECCI Secretariat once again discussed the French issue on 19 May. Dimitrov emphasized that the Blum government "is not yet a Government of the Popular Front in the sense that we meant at the Congress. We need to give thought to a more accurate name for it. There is a need to take into account the difference between this government and the government of the left bourgeoisie, between the Social Democratic government and the bourgeois one." But there was no doctrinal reason the Communists had decided to stay outside of power: "The question of participation or nonparticipation in such a government is a question of political expediency." If the Blum government "could turn out to be insufficiently protected, then a movement might be created around the struggle of that government which would lead to a government of the Popular Front with our participation."[16] Similar wording characterized the directive sent to Thorez and to the Politburo of the Central Committee of the French Communist Party:

> The participation of the Communists in the government, resulting in an electoral victory of the Popular Front, in the present situation in France is not a question of principle but a question of political expediency. We consider that the Party's position of nonparticipation in the government is correct, but it should support the government against the rightists in carrying out the program of the Popular Front. . . . The Communists and the Socialists in parliament do not have the majority needed to create a strong government without the Radicals. The participation of the Communists in the government at this time would facilitate exerting pressure on the Radicals to undermine the Popular Front and would lead to their split. Since they do not want to wreck the Popular Front, the Communists are now refusing to participate in the government and will support it from outside. . . . The new government must act to carry out the will and programs of the Popular Front.

The Communists were enjoined to "see to it that the most important posts, in particular the ministries of internal and foreign affairs, are in the hands of the most reliable elements from the point of view of the struggle against fascism and for Franco-Soviet cooperation."[17]

The early days of the Blum government saw the Communists doing what they could to facilitate the new government's flourishing. A wave of paralyzing strikes had broken out between the elections and the date on which Blum was slated to become prime minister, 6 June 1936. Many were led by Communists. On 11 June, Thorez tempered the workers' militancy by warning that "it is necessary to know how to end a strike." A comprehensive labor pact was soon reached, and the government enacted an extensive reform program within its first month in power.

The instructions of the ECCI Secretariat to the leadership of the French Communist Party on 7 July regarding the convening of the party conferences stressed that in determining the tactical policy of the party there was a need to think of the useful potential of "extended maintenance of the Blum government as an antifascist government since at this point neither the degree of unity of the forces of the French proletariat, nor the internal situation in France, nor the international balance of forces favor the creation of a genuine government of the Popular Front, which could serve as a step toward the ultimate victory of the proletariat over the bourgeoisie."[18]

The euphoria about the Popular Front did not last long. Inflation eroded wage gains. Talks with the Soviet Union about strengthening the Franco-Soviet mutual aid pact made little progress, stalled by the resistance of the French general staff. Even more consequentially, the military revolt against the Spanish Republic, begun on 18 July 1936, precipitated a request to France for arms and planes for the government. Although Blum was sympathetic, fierce conservative opposition forced him to announce a non-intervention policy in early August. The Communists were bitterly critical, although their absence from the cabinet had increased the influence of those opposed to shipping arms to the Loyalist government. On 4 December 1936 the Communist Party had its representatives abstain in parliament on a vote of confidence in the government. It is unclear if the party leadership had received a directive from the ECCI sent the day before with instructions "that under the present circumstances it is not advantageous to the French working class to intensify a government crisis and even less so to overthrow the Blum government." Stalin himself had approved the directive.[19]

A week later Dimitrov let Stalin know that there was now a possibility that the Blum government might fall, leading to the creation of a new government, still headed by Blum but no longer dependent on the Communists' support and even hostile to them. The Soviet leader issued ambiguous instructions: "They must continue the present policy; criticize Blum without reaching the point of breakdown." While continuing to criticize Blum, the French Communists did become less strident.[20]

The Popular Front government in France collapsed in the spring of 1937. The economic situation had worsened, police had fired on leftist demonstrators, and Blum resigned in June, replaced by a Radical prime minister. Thorez offered to join the new government but was rebuffed. As the political situation lurched from crisis to crisis, the Comintern remained resolute in insisting that the French party remain outside of the government. Giving instructions to the Spanish Communist Party in February 1938, Stalin explained: "Support for the government, but not participation in the government—that must be our goal at this stage. The same is true for France." In March 1938 the Radical government collapsed, and Blum proposed a National Unity government. The ECCI Secretariat again warned the leaders of the PCF not to accept the invitation to join the government. Its instructions stated: "In connection with the governmental crisis we once again are warning the Party regarding attempts to involve Communists in the government. In the light of the international situation and the situation in France there is a need to fight for the Government of the Popular Front without the Communists."[21]

Thorez cautiously expressed his disagreement in his message to Dimitrov the following day: "The position of the Party regarding possible participation is a specific kind of tactic designed to prevent a move (collapse) of the Popular Front and a slide to the right. At the same time, taking the telegram into account, do everything possible to have a government of the Popular Front without the participation of the Communists. The issue must be discussed very soon." A few days later he was more explicit, explaining the dilemma the Communists faced:

> The political circles in France are rushing to prepare for the formation of a government of National Unity made up of representatives of all the Parties, except for small pro-Hitler groups. The Communist Party will definitely be invited to join the government. This proposal will be made within the next few days, and if the international situation deteriorates still further, the question of the reorganization of the government will be raised much sooner. We believe that cooperation with the Parties is inevitable, without joining the Popular Front, since if only Parties of the Popular Front are in power, this will mean a continuation of the bourgeoisie's policy of sabotaging the economic and political measures of the Popular Front and undermining of its actions to defend the country. We are clearly aware of the danger of the participation by the Communists in the government, but a refusal to engage in such participation will either destroy the national concentration of forces, or else that concentration will take place despite us and against us. We must take into account that if there is a breakdown of the national concentration of forces, the country will be faced by the Hitlerite threat; it will be fragmented, insufficiently armed, and, if war breaks out, will be risking defeat. Acceptance of the proposals regarding the formation of a government of National Concentration, however, will strengthen resistance to Hitler and facilitate the struggle of the Popular Front. We are awaiting an answer. We shall consider the lack of any response as indicating approval of the policy of participation by Communists in the government. If you disapprove of this, inform us of what tactic to take. In that case, should we send you a delegation for joint discussion of the question?[22]

Dimitrov and Manuilsky decided to obtain Stalin's opinion and sent him a translation of Thorez's message, along with the comment that "this telegram was sent by him after we gave instructions to the French Communist Party not to participate in the Blum government and after the Party had carried out those instructions. We are requesting Your advice and instructions." The answer was not long in coming; the Comintern leaders sent a coded dispatch to Thorez on 19 March: "No, to your involvement in any combined government. There is no need for your trip here." A longer dispatch was also sent explaining that "the Secretariat is against the participation by the Communists in the government of national unity" since it would compromise the party. Only if a Popular Front government would agree to "arrest the fascists, crush their organizations as traitors to the nation, seriously improve the situation of the workers, peasants, intelligentsia, not tag along behind the reactionary elements of the British Conservatives, and conduct their own national antifascist policy" would Communists join it. If the government "does not encroach on the existing rights of the working masses, if it renders active assistance to Republican Spain, actively steps up the defense of the country and carries out a consistent policy against external fascist aggression," then Communists would support it while remaining outside of it. Only "in case of war" would Communists join a National Unity government.[23]

Swallowing all the warnings he had previously given, Thorez was obliged to surrender. He sent a message to the ECCI indicating that he had received his instructions and "agreed regarding nonparticipation in the government and shall act accordingly."[24]

The Comintern went even further just a few days later. The ECCI demanded that the party work to "create a government whose axis would be the Popular Front, accompanied by representatives of the anti-Hitlerite groups of the Chamber of Deputies and the Senate, with a clearly determined supporter of assistance to Spain at its head instead of Blum." Despite the fantasy that the Communists could push Blum aside while still remaining outside the government, the proposal took no account of the lack of support for intervention in Spain from either Radicals or Socialists.[25]

By the fall of 1938 the government of Daladier had come under Comintern attack for its support of the Munich agreement dismembering Czechoslovakia. The ECCI supported the French Communist Party, which demanded the resignation of the government. A coded message sent from Moscow agreed that Daladier's policy was not "a policy of the Popular Front," and he was "an accomplice of reaction." It specified, however, only that Daladier himself must be ousted.[26]

Since the Popular Front was predicated on an alliance of Socialists, Communists, and Radicals, the withdrawal of support for the leader of the Radical Party seemed to presage the breakup of the Popular Front—or at least the illusion that it might stand in the way of fascism. A message sent to Thorez on 2 October recognized that "as a consequence of Lenoir's [Daladier's] treachery we predict the emergence of pessimism" about its continuation, but it called for "a struggle" to explain to the masses that Daladier's policy "has nothing in common with" the Popular Front and that only the Popular Front could allow

France to "avoid a disgraceful collapse." Dimitrov echoed that sentiment in a message he sent while on vacation to Manuilsky and Moskvin. He acknowledged that the split with the Radical government was "a dangerous fissure which threatens to undermine Natan [the Popular Front] itself." Only mass pressure from below could save it.[27]

Early in 1939 the Communists "launched a campaign with the slogan, 'No, Mr. Daladier, the Popular Front is not dead.'" In fact, it was. The Politburo of the PCF asked the ECCI in April for advice on what to do. Dimitrov and Manuilsky wrote Stalin, suggesting that the PCF should call for the ouster of the Daladier government and the creation of a government of national defense. They admitted that the Popular Front was in tatters and the best hope was a government committed to collective security and opposition to aggression. When no answer was received, Dimitrov pressed Stalin at a meeting and received the brusque response that he was busy and the Comintern should decide on its own. Early in May, the ECCI Secretariat passed a resolution calling for the replacement of the government with "the creation of a government of national defense, based on all groups of supporters of a firm policy directed against the aggressors and based primarily on the Popular Front and a struggle for restoration, strengthening, and expansion, which the Party will intensify in all possible ways." Even at this late date, the PCF would not openly commit itself to joining such a government; it remained on the sidelines, cheering but unwilling to take responsibility.[28]

The Popular Front and the Munich Crisis

The Munich crisis of 1938 forced urgent discussions about how Communist parties should be ordered to respond to the new international situation. Hitler had annexed Austria into Germany in March 1938 and immediately launched a belligerent campaign to annex Czechoslovakia's Sudetenland, a border region chiefly inhabited by ethnic Germans. Czechoslovakia resisted the demands but had little chance to resist a German invasion unless it was supported by Great Britain and France. British prime minister Neville Chamberlain thought Hitler's aims were limited and, seeking to avoid war at all costs, at a conference in Munich in September and without the presence of Czechoslovak representatives, agreed to German annexation. Unwilling to face Germany without British support, the French government under Daladier also supported the agreement. Abandoned by the

Western powers, Czechoslovakia's resistance collapsed, and it acquiesced to the agreement. Ultimately, of course, this act of appeasement failed to satisfy Hitler. Casually breaking his promise to Chamberlain that the Sudetenland was his last territorial demand in Europe, in March 1939 he occupied the Czech provinces as a German protectorate and sponsored a fascist puppet state in Slovakia.

In the weeks leading up to the Munich Agreement, which was signed on 30 September 1938, Dimitrov fired off messages to Moscow from his vacation retreat imploring Moskvin and Manuilsky to urge various Communist parties to issue statements of solidarity with the Czechs and denunciation of the Germans. Despite the weaknesses of the Popular Front policy, illustrated by the political weakness of the Communists in France, Dimitrov clung to the illusion that resolutions of solidarity might impact the situation. He thought that "widespread publication of such a statement" by the Japanese Communist Party "would help the international campaign and would have a certain impact on the masses" in Japan itself. Just more than a month after the ECCI Presidium had dissolved the Communist Party of Poland, thoroughly purged of most of its leadership as spies and provocateurs, Dimitrov successfully demanded a statement to the press "giving guidelines to Communists and for the worker and peasant movement" in Poland about how to respond to Czech events.[29]

On 18 September Dimitrov proposed launching a campaign for an international workers' conference, composed of all representatives of the working class, to devise a unified policy toward fascism and to coordinate responses. He thought that the initiative for convening the conference "should best be given to the French Confederation of Labor and the English trade unions." He reiterated the need to convene such a conference in another message to the Comintern leadership on 24 September.[30]

The reply from his comrades in Moscow assured Dimitrov that the instructions to take the initiative had been given to the leadership of the French Communist Party, which "was to ensure in advance support for this initiative from the British trade unions." The campaign "was to be conducted under the banner of the mobilization of the masses in defense of Czechoslovakia and the undermining of the Chamberlain-Daladier plan . . . in France under the banner of the struggle to get rid of Daladier and [French foreign minister] Bonnet and in England, of the departure of Chamberlain."[31]

The French Communists quickly punctured the illusion that there was any possibility of a Communist-Socialist mass mobilization.

Maurice Thorez and Marcel Cachin, a member of the PCF Central Committee Politburo, had consulted with the chairman of the Socialist International about joint action on both Czechoslovakia and Spain. Informing Dimitrov that the discussion had "yielded negative results," Manuilsky noted that nonetheless resolutions calling for such a conference would be adopted in France, Great Britain, and the United States and that Spanish and Czechoslovak workers' groups "will be appealing to the international proletariat" and "we will act over the heads" of the Socialist leadership.[32]

Even as the final details of the Munich Agreement were being negotiated, Dimitrov continued to insist that the Communists take the lead in convening a conference of all working class groups. Just hours before its announcement, Dimitrov sent a message to Moskvin and Manuilsky: "Have you received any advice, indications, or comments from 101 [Stalin] and from the comrades from 195 [Communist Party Politburo] regarding our work in the present situation. I hope that you are informing 101 of the most important actions we have undertaken." The response was no doubt discouraging; Moskvin cabled on September 30th that "up to now we have not yet established contact regarding our work in connection with the situation with" either Stalin or the Politburo.[33]

Nevertheless, Dimitrov that day directed his compatriots in Moscow to "turn the meeting that is being convened" in Paris into a "strictly closed conference of representatives" of many of the European Communist parties, which would reaffirm Comintern policy and issue an appeal "to the international proletariat and to workers of all countries with a definition of the position of the working class and an appeal for a united and vigorous struggle against the fascist aggressors and their henchmen" and, if war did break out, "to ensure the ultimate destruction of fascism."[34]

Dimitrov's plan, however, met resistance. Manuilsky informed him that the Czechoslovak Communist Party leadership was reluctant to go ahead, believing that criticism of the Social Democratic Second International, which would emanate from such a gathering, would complicate its political efforts; "Gottwald [an ECCI member and the leading figure in the Czechoslovak CP] answered that in his view it was better to have other Parties from the outside make such a proposal." Dimitrov responded that he thought it was "a serious political error" that the Communists had not pushed the Socialists on the issue: "Criticism of the leaders of the Second International and the opponents and saboteurs of the United Front must be fully utilized, to clearly and compellingly demonstrate their historical responsibility. . . . They must be backed up against the wall as never before and tried in the court of public opinion."[35]

When the representatives of the various Communist parties did meet in Paris in mid-October 1938, they did not issue a call for a broad conference. In a report to Dimitrov, Togliatti noted that there was a fair amount of disarray in the Communist ranks. At the start of the gathering "there was a certain sense of confusion" on "the fundamental problems." Thorez "somewhat painfully reacted" to criticism of the Communist response to Munich in France by José Díaz and Dolores Ibárruri of Spain and ECCI member and Comintern deputy general secretary Palmiro Togliatti himself. Togliatti attacked the French Communists for being "late in exposing to the masses the treason of the French government" and insisted that it "should have earlier and must now more clearly expose capitulation and treason." He chastised the French Communists for not "directly facing the masses with vital problems out of fear of 'damaging unity' or 'complicating the activity of the government.'" (Although denouncing the Munich Agreement, the PCF faced problems since the Socialists had supported it, Blum reluctantly.) Communist parties lacked a "clear understanding of the need for the expansion of the independence of the working class in order to impact on and lead democratic forces, prevent treason, drive out traitors." They needed to reassert their independence, "move to open criticism of capitulators to restore our political ties with democratic elements, pacifists, the intelligentsia, and others."[36]

Dimitrov was undaunted by the inability of Communists to organize a workers' conference. Writing to Moskvin about the proclamation for the anniversary of the October Revolution, he proposed including an appeal to hold the meeting. Considering it as "the most immediate task of the international workers' movement and of the antifascist Popular Front," he insisted on "the need to convene an international conference of workers' organizations and the conduct of a unified policy of the international proletariat." He returned to Moscow on 31 October, and three days later the Secretariat of the Comintern sent a cipher cable to Thorez demanding that the Communist parties of Britain, France, Belgium, and Scandinavia begin preparatory work; they had to conduct the campaign "with ruthless exposure of capitulators, opponents of unity and of the Popular Front as accomplices of fascism."[37]

Even as he continued to pursue the chimera of a worldwide workers' conference, Dimitrov demanded that the Communist Party of the

United States take the lead in organizing a Democratic Front, compelling Franklin Roosevelt to initiate "an active foreign policy against the aggressors and warmongers, against the fascist bloc of Germany-Italy-Japan, against the bandit complicity of Hitler, Mussolini, and Chamberlain." In a telephone conversation with Dimitrov, Moskvin assured him that these instructions had been conveyed to Earl Browder.[38]

Dimitrov continued to push the idea of a workers' conference into 1939. On 27 January he sent a ciphered cable to Thorez, exhorting him to "step up the campaign for the convening of the international workers' conference." He sent a message to Browder on 7 May, urging him "to unleash an international campaign for unity of action of all the Internationals and the convening of an international workers' conference." In June he assigned the Swiss Communists the task of campaigning for its convening.[39] Nothing came of any of the initiatives.

CHAPTER FOUR

The Spanish Civil War

Few issues took as much Comintern attention or resources as the civil war in Spain that broke out in 1936. The developing conflict with fascist Germany, the difficulties of implementing a Popular Front, and the political and logistical difficulties of supervising a large-scale military operation generated a continuous barrage of messages between Moscow and Western Europe.

The political situation in Spain was difficult. Not only was the Republic fighting a civil war against a right-wing Nationalist coalition led by General Franco, but also the Popular Front supporting the Republic was deeply divided. Its leading political formations included the Spanish Socialist Workers' Party (PSOE); the Communist Party of Spain (PCE); the Workers' Party of Marxist Unification (POUM, an independent Marxist party hated by the Communists); the center-left Republican Left (led by Manuel Azaña, president of the Republic); and the centrist Republican Union Party. Galician and Catalan nationalists, the Socialist-aligned General Workers' Union (UGT), and the anarcho-syndicalist trade union, the National Confederation of Labor (CNT), also supported the government.

Complicating the Spanish situation was the shifting view of the Comintern on the question of the entry of the PCE into the Popular Front government in the fall of 1936. Just a week after the outbreak of civil war, the Comintern sent a coded message to the leadership of the PCE warning that "vacillation on the part of the government can destroy the cause of the Republic. Therefore, if the government vacillates, despite the mass support shown it by the Popular Front, the question should be raised of the creation of a government for the defense of the Republic and the salvation of the Spanish people, with the participation of the Parties of the Popular Front, including the Communists and Socialists."[1]

Just four days later, however, new instructions arrived. Among the "urgent recommendations" was the caution that "as long as it is possible to do without the direct participation of the Communists in the government, it is advisable not to join the government, since that way it is easier to preserve the unity of the Popular Front. Participate in the government only in an extreme situation, if this is absolutely necessary to crush the rebellion." Before sending the message, Dimitrov "urgently" asked Stalin for his comments and received approval. PCE leader José Díaz responded that "our tactics consist in the consolidation of the Republican government, and we have rejected the proposal of the Socialists for the formation of a government of the Popular Front . . . with our participation."[2]

The question of Spanish Communist participation in the government arose again in August 1936, when Socialist leader Largo Caballero demanded the resignation of the government led by José Giral, leader of the Republican Party. Caballero was anxious to form a socialist government. Díaz and Vittorio Codovilla, an Argentine Communist of Italian origin and the representative of the ECCI to the PCE, sent Dimitrov a message that Caballero was "insisting on the need for our participation." They had "told him that we consider his position as wrong." Because of the "tense international situation we find it necessary to work together with the Republican government—this one or with another one." If Caballero did form another government, the Communists proposed supporting him only if he included representatives from a variety of other left-wing and regional parties "and that the new government make a clear statement to the effect that it will operate within the framework of a democratic republic"—that is, not attempt to enact a socialist agenda as Caballero wished to do.[3]

The future composition of the Spanish government was discussed at a Soviet Politburo meeting in the Kremlin. In his diary, Dimitrov recorded that with Stalin on the telephone, the leadership agreed to the "transformation of the Giral government into a govern[ment] of Nat[ional] Defense, headed by Giral with a majority of Republicans, with the participation of the Socialists and of two Communists, also rep[resentatives] of the Catalans and Basques." The ECCI Secretariat then sent Díaz his instructions: "We recommend the transformation of the Giral government into a government of National Defense, which will still be headed by Giral and in which the majority would belong to the Republicans. It would be advisable for such a government to include, in addition to the representative[s] of Catalonia and the Basques, two Socialists, for ex[ample] Prieto and Caballero, and two Communists."[4]

Early in September that message was transmitted to the Spanish Communist Party, but the ECCI quickly learned that its orders could not be carried out. Díaz, Jacques Duclos (the French Communist sent to Madrid to help the Spanish party leadership), and Codovilla reported that "despite our efforts, it was not possible to avoid the government of Caballero." They had kept Giral in the government, which now consisted of "four Republicans of all stripes, three Socialists of each type, and two Communists." They had been compelled to make this decision to prevent "major difficulties" and to avoid "creating a very dangerous situation."[5]

At the end of February 1937 André Marty (sent to Spain by the Comintern to organize the International Brigades) returned briefly to Moscow. He met with Stalin, Vyacheslav Molotov (a member of the Politburo of the VKP[b] and chairman of the Soviet government), Kliment Voroshilov (a member of the Politburo of the VKP[b] and the people's commissar for defense of the USSR), Lazar Kaganovich (a member of the Politburo of the VKP[b] and secretary of the party Central Committee), Togliatti, and Dimitrov on 13 March. Stalin spoke in favor of the unification of the Spanish Communist Party and the Socialist Workers' Party into a single party that, if the Socialists insisted, need not be included in the Comintern. Referring to the strained relations between Largo Caballero and the Communist Party, Stalin declared, "No need to overthrow Caballero. (There is no more suitable figure to serve as head of government.) Get Caballero to renounce the post of Minister of Defense (and appoint someone else commander in chief). During a possible reconstruction the Communists can demand greater participation by the Party in government. If there is a decision for foreign forces to leave Spain, the Internat[ional] Brigades are to be disbanded and left in the rear, as production workers, and so forth. Continue the recruitment."[6]

In accordance with Stalin's instructions, a directive was sent to Díaz with advice about how to deal with the Spanish government: "To unite the forces of the working class, strengthen the Popular Front, and establish the required correct relations with Largo Caballero and his supporters, we consider advisable the merger of the Communist and the Socialist Parties into a single Party to be called something, approximately, the United Socialist Workers' Party of Spain. We recommend making the appropriate inquiries and engaging in negotiations with

Largo Caballero on this issue."[7] Talks on the unification of the two parties continued for some time, but no merger followed.

Meanwhile, news was coming in from Spain about the military defeats of the Republicans and the deterioration of relations between Largo Caballero and the Communists. On 23 March Dimitrov sent Stalin a report from Ivan Stepanov, one of the Comintern representatives in Spain, dealing with the difficulties in organizing resistance to the Nationalists, the factional struggle within the government, and its weaknesses. Largo Caballero was described in negative terms, and his conflict with the Spanish Communist Party was explained as due to the fact that "the influence and authority of the Communist Party is increasing." Dimitrov, however, insisted in a directive to Spain on "the need to keep Spaak [Caballero] as the chairman of the government."[8]

The ECCI soon received a new report from Stepanov, which more sharply pressed the question of removing Largo Caballero as minister of defense and even as prime minister. "The present difficulties are the result of the lack of a firm political policy and the lack of a Ministry of Defense which would deal solely with military problems," stated the report. "People from the front are leveling direct accusations against the Minister of Defense, giving a negative political assessment of him. From all sides there is a demand to put an end to sabotage, carelessness, inability and the bureaucratic caprice that dominate the Ministry dealing with military affairs." Recounting the growing influence of the Communist Party in the army and emphasizing that the military apparatus at the front was in the hands of the Communist Party or under its decisive influence, the report stated that the leadership of the party was increasingly moving toward the conclusion that, despite all the conditions working toward a victory, Caballero and his group would lead the Republic to defeat. "The Party is awaiting your advice on these questions. The situation is complex, very complex, and your point of view will be extraordinarily valuable."[9]

In sending the report to Stalin on 14 April, Dimitrov noted that it expressed the mood, view, and position of the Politburo of the Central Committee of the PCE. He reiterated that the ECCI Secretariat in its advice to the Central Committee of the PCE had recommended working in every possible way to achieve viability and authority for the Republican government, the separation of the post of head of the government from minister of defense and commander in chief, and the handing over of the latter post to another reliable individual while not breaking with Largo Caballero or engaging in a policy of eliminating him. In so doing, Dimitrov showed that Stalin's instructions on maintaining Largo Caballero as head of government had been transmitted to the Spanish side. At the same time, making use of Stepanov's report and referring to the view of the Spanish party Politburo, he hinted with great caution that it would hardly be possible to fulfill Stalin's wishes, through a reference to the danger of "further deterioration in the relationship between Caballero and the Communist Party" and in the form of a request to get "advice" from Stalin.[10]

Three days later Dimitrov forwarded to Stalin the actual text of the resolution of the Politburo of the Central Committee of the PCE of 27 March. He once again drew Stalin's attention to the spreading campaign among elements of the Popular Front coalition against the Communist Party: "This campaign and many other things point to the fact that Caballero and his circle, together with the majority of the anarchist leaders, are conducting a policy of pitting the UGT [Socialist trade union federation] and the CNT [anarcho-syndicalist trade union federation] against the Communist Party, are working to undermine the Popular Front and create a Caballero government based on the trade unions and independent of the Communist Party."[11] The letter ended with a request to provide advice to the party and the Comintern. In May, Largo Caballero resigned in the political crisis that followed fighting in Barcelona among various Republican militias and Republican government forces. The new government was headed by the Socialist Juan Negrín, who had previously been the minister of finance and was closer to the Communists than Caballero.

One sign of the importance attached to Spain by the Comintern and its concern about the delicate political situation was its dispatch of Palmiro Togliatti to the war zone to oversee its operations. Next to Dimitrov, Togliatti was the most influential non-Russian in the leadership of the Communist International and, while operating within the bounds of Stalinist orthodoxy, among its most politically realistic and astute figures. One of the founders of the Communist Party of Italy, he became its secretary in 1927 and remained its dominant figure until his death in 1964. While in exile in 1935, he was elected a member of the ECCI and was appointed deputy general secretary of the Comintern. Beginning in the summer of 1937, coded dispatches sent to and from "Ercoli," his pseudonym, bore the notation "in special code."

The idea of sending Togliatti to Spain first came up in November 1936. Dimitrov, who was vacationing in Kislovodsk, received a telegram from Togliatti, Moskvin, and Manuilsky in Moscow: "The situation regarding Madrid has deteriorated due to the attempts at disintegration by the Durutti Column [anarcho-syndicalist militia unit] and the squabbles of the various groups. After discussion we propose to send your deputy there immediately, with Maurice [Thorez] or Duclos, to take urgent measure on site."[12] Dimitrov, however, deemed this inadvisable. He answered: "Under present conditions a trip by my deputy there will not be of much assistance, and there is a very great danger of losing him. I agree that he can go to Paris and contact our people in Spain and together with Maurice and Duclos discuss and take all possible urgent measures. He himself, however, should not go."[13]

As the internal situation in Spain grew more fraught and the Comintern's involvement more extensive, the question of Togliatti's travel to Spain came up again the next summer. Preparations were under way in June 1937 for a meeting of a Comintern delegation with representatives of the Labour and Socialist International (the Social Democratic rival to the Communist International) in order to assist Republican Spain. On 13 June Dimitrov informed Stalin that the ECCI Secretariat was planning "urgently to send com. Ercoli [Togliatti] to Paris to personally instruct and assist the Delegation" and requested "instructions." Travel with a political mission outside the Soviet Union by someone of Togliatti's rank required Stalin's permission; Togliatti's August trip from Paris to Valencia, then the site of the Spanish government and the Central Committee of the Spanish Communist Party, also received Stalin's authorization.[14]

Early in August Dimitrov sent a cipher cable to Bohumir Šmeral, a staff member of the Comintern who was working for the ECCI Secretariat in Paris: "If the Italian friend has not yet left for Val[encia], he should immediately go there. He must stay there for a lengthy period of time, until we summon him."[15] The next day a message from Dimitrov was sent to Valencia to José Díaz (head of the Spanish party) and two other Comintern representatives, Vittorio Codovilla, who had worked in Spain under the pseudonym Luis Medina since 1932, and Ivan Stepanov: "Tell our Italian friend that he must remain with you and help you politically for a longer period of time, until we summon him here. We ask that he also pay particular attention to Edition Blasco. He should keep us regularly informed." Other leading figures and staff members of the Comintern who were in the country had their own specific functions, such as André Marty, supervisor of the International Brigades. Togliatti took over the leadership of the Comintern delegation dealing with the Central Committee of the Spanish Communist Party, but, as the message shows, Dimitrov also wanted him to review the situation at the International Brigades headquarters and base at Albacete (Edition Blasco).[16]

Togliatti Assesses the Situation

Having arrived in Spain unofficially—indeed, covertly—Togliatti found himself in a difficult situation. He reported: "Despite all the precautionary measures and despite the recommendations to comrades not to talk about my presence, it is known that I am here. What is known in the Communist Party is known to the leaders of the Socialist Parties who are in Spain (Pietro Nenni had already mentioned this) and also to the government. A situation has been created which in my view is politically erroneous and dangerous. . . . Inevitably the question arises regarding the reasons for the illegal presence in Spain of one of the leaders of the Comintern, and this is becoming the basis for all kinds of insinuations, chatter, campaigns, etc."[17]

This part of the report was preserved in the Comintern archives in handwritten form and was not included in the text of Togliatti's report that Dimitrov sent to Stalin. Apparently, the issue of Togliatti's status was linked to the relevant instructions from Stalin, who did not consider official legalization of his status advisable. This explains why the typed text of the report did not include the section dealing with his ambiguous situation after he arrived in Spain. Informing him of the need to remain in Spain for a lengthy period of time, Dimitrov did not consider it advisable to officially state his responsibilities, as was done in regard to other Comintern "political advisers."[18]

Togliatti's report went on to say that the situation in the country was very difficult, and the internal struggle within the Republican camp had accelerated. Caballero had become prime minister in September 1936 but had been replaced in May 1937 by Juan Negrín. Segments of the Socialist Party as well as the CNT were deeply suspicious of increasing Communist influence. Togliatti warned that "excessively energetic pressure by our Party to make the government change its attitude, demanding that it adopt necessary measures, can only lead to a split both within the present government and within the Popular Front, which will create a number of complications and will intensify the difficulties." The view within the Spanish Communist Party that it should "openly fight for hegemony in the government and in the country as whole" exacerbated the danger and reflected "a great deal of disorder and improvisation." He attributed part of the responsibility for this undesirable situation to representatives of the

Comintern, particularly Codovilla. Togliatti recommended that the ECCI demand "that he [Codovilla] hand over operative work to the Spanish comrades, that he stop being an individual without whom no one does anything or knows what to do."[19]

Codovilla had returned to Moscow, along with Pedro Checa of the Spanish Communist Party, for consultations; Togliatti and Stepanov asked the ECCI not to allow him to return. They noted that the Spanish party was attempting "to rally together Socialists and all groups of the Popular Front and the working class, in particular the Socialists, against Caballero, his clique, and the Trotskyites." This required persuading local units and the party press "that errors of sectarianism be corrected and that a political line appropriate to the Popular Front be followed. We are making use of Luis's [Codovilla's] absence to convince and assist the leadership of the Party in beginning a radical change in methods and in the political and daily work of the leadership."[20]

Togliatti and Stepanov took advantage of every opportunity to reiterate that Codovilla's return was undesirable. Regarding the discussion in the Politburo of the Central Committee of the PCE on the preparations for a forthcoming political campaign to extend the Popular Front and at the same time isolate such enemies as the Trotskyists (Communists regarded the POUM as Trotskyist), they asked Dimitrov to "do everything possible to have Checa return with your instructions prior to the Central Committee meeting. Regarding Tomas [Codovilla], it is our joint view that he should return only if his presence seems to us absolutely necessary. We consider it preferable for the Ouevre's [Communist Party's] center to work for a period of time without him."[21]

Togliatti was even more definitive in his report of 15 September. He insisted that Comintern representatives "stop thinking of themselves as the Party 'bosses,' that they stop considering the Spanish comrades as people who are totally incapable of doing anything, and that they not act on their behalf on the pretext of doing things better and faster, etc. This criticism refers to L[uis]. If the latter cannot change his methods of work, it would be better for him not to return. Every day I am increasingly convinced that this is correct. . . . His presence is harmful to the Party."[22] The ECCI Secretariat was unwilling to withdraw Codovilla and decided instead to assign him a different mission. It adopted a decree on 3 October assigning him to organize "the recruitment of volunteers and the international campaign to support the Spanish Republic" without interfering in the operative leadership of the party.[23]

Having succeeded in greatly narrowing Codovilla's authority, Togliatti also tried to get rid of Marty. A cipher message from Togliatti,

Stepanov, and Diáz to Manuilsky stated, "Everyone agrees in considering that André's return to the Blasco publishing house [International Brigades base in Albacete] not only would fail to improve the situation, but would create a lot of worse things, compounding objective difficulties with a deterioration of the relationship between the Party and the government." There was no response to this proposal. Marty had Stalin's support; without his direct authorization no one in the ECCI leadership would have dared to deprive Marty of his post.[24]

Searching for a Solution

The extent of Soviet interference in the internal affairs of Spain is starkly illustrated by a series of cables dealing with the issue of elections for a Spanish parliament. On 16 September 1937 Dimitrov wrote Stalin, including a "document on the most important tasks of the Party; it was worked out together with the Spanish comrades after the discussion with You." Four days later the ECCI Presidium declared the need to hold elections in Spain to be among the "most important tasks of the Spanish Communist Party." Communists and Socialists had to reach agreement on the need for elections, the way they were to be held, and the major points of the electoral platform. Even more improbably, all antifascist parties and organizations should agree on a single united program and a single list of candidates.[25]

Pedro Checa and Vittorio Codovilla, in Moscow for consultations, presented a document to the ECCI warning that "given present conditions in Spain, it is not considered possible to hold elections, since the most active part of the population is at the front." Togliatti expressed a similar view in his report of 30 August 1937: "The parliament already represents almost no one in present-day Spain, and on the other hand, in this situation it is now pointless to think about reelecting it." Dimitrov sent Stalin both objections, but neither the views of the Communist Party of Spain nor the Comintern representatives there could trump Soviet desires. The ECCI decree also contained instructions about the internal makeup of the Republican government, particularly the need "to replace the present Minister of Justice Irujo, who is linked to fascistic elements and is an agent of conservative British circles." (Irujo was suspicious of the Communists and unsympathetic with their suppression of the POUM.)[26]

Togliatti informed Moscow on 12 October that Checa and two other Spanish Communists, Dolores Ibárruri and Jesús Hernández, had met twice with Prime Minister Negrín, who "is not rejecting the idea of elections. He thinks it possible to begin with a renewal of the Catalonian parliament and with a more intensive study of the potential for general elections." Negrín also "agrees to get rid of Irujo, but wants to wait until all the members of the old Basque government have returned" to Spain. While he was not opposed to the participation of the CNT in the government, he wanted it "to give guarantees and serious proof of loyalty." Dimitrov forwarded this message to Stalin.[27]

By the beginning of 1938 the Republic was on the brink of disaster. Togliatti reported on a growing struggle within the government between Negrín, on the one hand, and, on the other, President Manuel Azaña, who was increasingly pessimistic about the possibility of victory, and Minister of Defense Indalecio Prieto, who wanted to limit the influence of Communist political commissars in the army. He warned that the situation "at the present time is very dangerous."[28]

A second cipher message from Togliatti described the increasing pessimism of leading Republican figures:

> The situation is becoming more critical: Corona [Azaña] has declared to our Ministers that he does not see the possibility of victory, that the duration of the war means moving toward disaster and that now it is time to seek a way out. . . . He urges to request the Council of Ministers to raise the general problem of the prospects of the war. Blanche [Negrín] says that if Corona raises the question of capitulation there would be a crisis in the printing plant [government]. Blanche says that he agrees with us on all issues, but insists that our Ministers not exacerbate relations with Broukere [Prieto], who is declaring that he also considers an immediate military victory impossible unless he quickly obtains airplanes and weapons. . . . The Socialist leadership is demoralized. Despite the pressure [Blanche] is hesitant to accept our proposal for joint work, mobilization of the Popular Front, trade unions and the masses, to assist the government in quickly creating new reserves, to increase the production of barbed wire, political work at the front and in the rear. . . . The position of the administration [Communist Party] is the following: without making its campaign look as though it is in opposition to the government, ask it to take measures required by the situation, to do everything possible to involve the Socialists and the Popular Front in this campaign, request the inclusion of rint [CNT?] in the Popular Front, not to exacerbate the situation in the government and to act in agreement with Blanche.[29]

The disturbing news from Spain prompted Stalin to summon Dimitrov and Manuilsky to meet with him and Molotov on 17 February.

Stalin had concluded: "The Spanish Communists should leave the government. They have two secondary posts. If they leave the government the disintegration of Franco's front will intensify, and the international position of the Spanish Republic will ease somewhat. Their exit should not be demonstrative, nor the result of the government's displeasure, but in the interests of facilitating the government's tasks. The grounds should be that since the syndicalists are not participating, the Communists find it inexpedient to be in the government. . . . Support the government, but not participate in the government—that should be our stance at this stage."[30]

In the fall of 1936 the Communists had joined the government on Moscow's orders, and now they were being instructed to leave it on the dubious grounds that somehow this would encourage the further "disintegration" of Franco's Nationalists. (In fact, the Nationalists were picking up support as their victory seemed more likely.) Stalin's instructions were conveyed to the delegates of the Spanish Communist Party in the form of a directive from the Comintern, and the delegates then set off for home.

Stalin's suggestions, however, did not appeal to the Spanish Communist Party, which feared that withdrawing from the government would severely weaken its influence and encourage elements of the Republican government to attempt a reconciliation with Franco. Togliatti cabled that the PCE had proposed to Negrín "a concrete plan to put the whole country on a military footing" with him (Negrín) as minister of defense. On 15 March Togliatti wrote that the party had been working to get the agreement of Socialists, their union allies, and the anarchist unions on measures to buttress the Popular Front.[31]

The Spanish Communist Party's proposals were set out in greater detail in another message from Togliatti that Dimitrov forwarded to Stalin in its deciphered form. The message explained that "the situation is extremely tense," but the Popular Front initiative supporting a continued fight had been "supported by a wave of popular enthusiasm." Even though the anarcho-syndicalist CNT had taken a reasonable position, "anarchist provocateur elements" could still cause trouble, and a military defeat in Aragon had been "provoked by the sabotaging work of the Trotskyite scoundrels." The Communist goals included "to fight by all possible means against compromise" and to pressure Negrín's government "to implement an energetic war policy" with him as minister of defense "with a Communist General Commissar of the army." As a last resort the party supported the formation of a new government "from the representatives of the Communist Party and the trade union organizations of all stripes." Togliatti asked Moscow to "inform urgently if you agree with this line," with which he agreed.[32]

Left unsaid, but clearly implied, was that this policy totally diverged from Stalin's recent instructions. Rather than removing themselves from a direct role in the government, the Spanish Communists were proposing a militarized National Unity government with Negrín as a front man but with Communists staffing key executive military agencies. If that initiative failed, they hoped to create a new Communist-dominated government. In forwarding Stalin Togliatti's message, Dimitrov cautiously hinted at the advisability of a change in the Comintern's recent directive: "Since the departure of the Communists from the government in the present situation could be interpreted by the masses as flight from the difficulties of the struggle, and since the bourgeois Republicans are leaning toward capitulation, we are requesting Your advice and instructions regarding Ercoli's [Togliatti's] telegram." He did not, however, receive new instructions from Stalin.[33]

Stalin's directive occasioned continued questioning by the leadership of the Spanish Communist Party. Togliatti inquired whether the Communists should leave the government "only in connection with the present situation" or whether the directive meant a blanket refusal to participate in the government. Despite this foot-dragging by the Spanish party, he later reported that "your advice and directives have been discussed and accepted by the administration [Spanish party CC]."[34]

One Communist goal was reached in late March, when defense minister Indalecio Prieto, a critic of the Communists, was relieved of his duties. One of the two Communist ministers also left the government. At the end of April, Togliatti wrote a lengthy account of the government crisis and once again rationalized the Spanish Communists' not fully carrying out Stalin's instructions: "Your tactical advice, even though it has not been implemented since the present situation does not allow for that, has forced the comrades to understand that more than any kind of judgments, reasonable advice, etc., they were risking losing a correct political orientation, even if they did not eliminate the wrong tendencies of which I spoke to you. In practical terms your advice was of decisive assistance in untying our hands during the maneuvering to speedily resolve the ministerial crisis."[35]

Desperate Measures Considered

As the military and political situation of the Spanish Republic became more and more desperate in 1938, Togliatti persistently reiterated the need "of providing more extensive and effective assistance to Republican Spain. This assistance is essential to increase the combat capacity of the army and, in particular, to strengthen and improve the command." He reported on Negrín's intention to declare martial law. Forwarding his telegram to Stalin, Dimitrov voiced support for the idea: "Regarding the possible proclamation of martial law, we think our friends should not oppose [it] on condition that the necessary freedom for political work and agitation is assured, in order to intensify the struggle against fascism and its agents in Republican Spain. We are asking for your advice." There is no record of Stalin's response, and martial law was only declared on 18 January 1939.[36]

Conditions in the shrinking regions of Spain controlled by Republican forces continued to deteriorate, and on 22 July 1938 Togliatti wrote that drastic food shortages were developing. There was a need "to considerably increase the sending of food supplies," prompting the ECCI Secretariat to send Communist parties directives regarding the organization of food assistance to the Republic.[37]

On 28 August Dimitrov and Manuilsky sent Stalin and Molotov a memorandum requesting that the government of the USSR provide food assistance to the Spanish Republic on favorable credit terms. That same day the ECCI Secretariat adopted a decision on practical goals designed to provide the Spanish population with vital food products. All of the members of the Communist parties were to make special contributions, and monthly contributions were to be disbursed by the trade union organizations; an international loan was to be issued and a campaign begun to have food loans made to the Spanish government by the governments of France, Great Britain, North America, the Social Democratic governments of the Scandinavian countries, and others.[38]

As the Republic's military and economic circumstances weakened, so did its diplomatic situation. The once sympathetic French government quietly opened negotiations with Franco as Republican forces retreated from Catalonia. Togliatti reported that in reaction to that initiative, "there is a need for a major push to strengthen the political campaign in favor of Spain." In response the ECCI Secretariat ordered Communist parties to mobilize public opinion, front groups, and sympathetic figures to "prevent the villainies being perpetrated."[39]

Despite the deteriorating military and political situation in Spain, Togliatti devoted a good deal of attention to the translation into Spanish and publication in Spain of Stalin's *History of the VKP(b): Short Course*. Togliatti proposed to the ECCI Secretariat that this book be retranslated into Spanish "on his responsibility and under his direct control," sent the text for typesetting a pilot copy, and wrote that the book would be published in twenty-five thousand copies.[40]

At the same time Togliatti informed the ECCI that preparations were in progress in Spain for the trial of the leaders of the POUM. While the POUM had supported the Popular Front, it clashed frequently with Communists and their allies in the Republican government, and in May 1937 government forces, pushed by the Communists, suppressed the POUM and arrested its leadership and murdered Andrés Nin, its chief figure. Togliatti sent a copy of the indictment of the POUM's leadership to Moscow and urged that it be published "in all the major languages"; he insisted that antifascist organizations of various countries should address the Spanish court with "demands for inexorable justice and the exposure of the activities of Trotskyites in all countries." Despite the efforts of the Comintern and its representatives, the Spanish Republican court rejected the accusations of treason and espionage against the POUM, although five of its leaders were sentenced to prison terms of varying lengths. Subsequently Togliatti was forced to acknowledge "the scandalous result of the POUM trial, which ended without any significant sentences."[41]

The End Comes

As Republican troops lost control of Barcelona in January 1939, the Comintern continued to demand resistance and offer increasingly untenable and unrealistic suggestions about how to avoid defeat. A message to Maurice Thorez urged him to communicate to Togliatti "our instructions to hold on in the territory of [Catalonia] with all their might." Another cable to Thorez explained that "the entire population" had to "be made to participate in this struggle," new recruits had to be added to the army, "people who have lost their courage must be replaced," and Communists must increase their influence in the government and "capitulators" be pushed out.[42]

Togliatti reported on 28 January that "faced with general demoralization that is threatening disaster, we have decided that the [Spanish Communist] Party shall through its own people directly take over the organization of the last line and last efforts at resistance through draconian, firm, and strict measures and discipline." He was confident that Prime Minister Negrín would agree. Dimitrov cabled his approval of the plan to strengthen "the leading role of the Communists."[43]

With the fall of Barcelona, the Republican government's control was reduced to Madrid and a region stretching south to the Mediterranean.

Togliatti cabled the bleak news to Moscow on 1 February that while the Communists had taken some steps to restore morale and order, the head of the Spanish Republican army no longer thought the situation salvageable. Even Negrín "has shown an indication of serious weakness." The senior Soviet military adviser thought the Republican army could not hold out much longer and was convinced that disaster was inevitable.[44]

Togliatti, still in Catalonia with Republican forces retreating toward France, continued to believe resistance remained an option, although he admitted that reorganizing the government was very hard, "since it is extremely difficult to find employees who are . . . better than the present ones. Our intention is to continue resistance until the stabilization of one front on the territory of Catalonia. We consider this plan as feasible if there is a quick and general restoration of order and discipline." He admitted, however, that with Negrín "demoralized," he was "afraid that the majority of the present Clara [government] will come out in favor of capitulation." This was Togliatti's last message from Catalonia. He crossed the French border and, after a short time in Toulouse, returned to Madrid. At the beginning of February all of Catalonia was occupied by Franco's troops.[45]

Undaunted, the ECCI Secretariat urged continuation of the struggle on the Madrid front, cabling Thorez to inform the Spanish Communists that they needed to replace the elements in the government unwilling to keep fighting. Immediately after arriving in Madrid, Togliatti reported that desertions were increasing and there was "a total lack of energetic leadership within the government and military." The Spanish Communist Party, he reported, was increasingly politically isolated.[46]

After reporting the pessimism with the government and military, Togliatti asked Moscow if the Communist Party and its trade union allies "should take over by force all the agencies of power and the leadership of the war, with the threat of virtually complete political isolation in the future, the possibility of resistance, and the risk of the loss of leadership and personnel? Your views will be needed, insofar as possible."[47]

Even as he and the Spanish Communists contemplated a coup d'etat, Togliatti communicated Negrín's request for additional Soviet military aid. He asked Dimitrov if he, Togliatti, could "serve as an intermediary with him on this question." Even as Negrín was moving toward the Communists, "the danger of a mutiny of military professionals and the collapse of the government" had grown. If that occurred, "do you find it acceptable for us to take all power and the leadership of the war into our hands?" Dimitrov phoned Marshal Voroshilov, whose answer was, "In practical terms, it will hardly be possible to render such assistance." Dimitrov sent Togliatti a message conditioning additional Soviet aid on several demands that were impossible to meet.[48]

On the evening of 6 March the Republican military launched a coup against the Republic, claiming it was aimed at heading off a seizure of the government by the Communists. Togliatti reported that "the situation is catastrophic. I foresee great difficulties in the evacuation of the leadership and the Party personnel." He asked that the French and British Communists organize flotillas to sail to various ports to evacuate Comintern personnel and Spanish Communists. The ECCI Secretariat immediately sent that request to Paris. Dimitrov also sent a telegram on 7 March ordering Togliatti to "leave immediately." Informed that Togliatti and Pedro Checa were trying to organize the new leadership, Dimitrov reiterated his demand on 17 March, telling Thorez, "Take all measures to have personnel depart. First and foremost Alfredo [Togliatti] and Checa." On 24 March Togliatti, together with several leading officials of the Spanish Communist Party, flew from Cartagena to Algiers and then proceeded to France.[49]

The defeat of the Spanish Republic led to a series of recriminations that continued to reverberate in the Communist world for more than a decade. Many of the Soviet and foreign Communists who had served in Spain became victims of the Stalinist purges in the late 1930s and again at the end of the 1940s and early 1950s. On 8 April 1939 Dimitrov gave Stalin a set of documents on the last few days of the Republic and the position of the Spanish Communist Party. It included a "Letter from c. Alfredo [Togliatti] to com. Dolores and other members of the Politburo of 12 March 1939. From Valencia." Recounting the last days of the Republic, Togliatti in this letter accused Negrín of complicity with the Republican military officers who organized the coup. He was forced, however, to acknowledge that "As for the masses, at least during the first days the anti-Communist campaign had some success, as the result of the extreme fatigue of those masses, who long above all for peace and considered the Party as an enemy of peace and to blame for the new Civil War."[50]

In Spain, hopes by backers of the coup that they could negotiate an end to the war came to naught when Franco demanded unconditional surrender. With the Republican army no longer willing to fight, Nationalist forces entered Madrid virtually unopposed on 27 March

1939. While most International Brigades and Comintern personnel, including Togliatti, had been withdrawn, those who remained faced imprisonment and, often, execution at the hands of vengeful Nationalists.

In France Togliatti continued to deal with the problems of the Comintern and Spanish Communist refugees. But after France went to war with Nazi Germany and in the wake of the Hitler-Stalin Pact, French authorities arrested Togliatti for the use of false documents. He was imprisoned for several months, but the USSR was able to win his release in early 1940. Togliatti wanted to remain in Western Europe, working with the exiled Italian CP, but Dimitrov thought his plans to operate underground from Belgium were unsafe and insisted on a return to Moscow, and he reached Moscow by mid-1940.[51]

Despite the Comintern's and Soviet authorities' having worked ardently to get him released and safely to Moscow, Togliatti's position was precarious. On 19 July 1941, just over a year after Togliatti arrived in Moscow, Dimitrov spoke with José Díaz, the exiled head of the Spanish CP with whom Togliatti had worked in Spain. Dimitrov's diary records the following: "Díaz is here. He expresses political mistrust of Ercoli [Togliatti]. He bases his suspicions on his work and behavior in Spain. Dolores [Ibárruri] also states that she has less than full confidence in Ercoli. She feels there is something alien about him, something unlike us, although she cannot substantiate that concretely. (Before, too, there was a signal in that regard from Gramsci's family.) We agreed to use Ercoli for the time being only in radio and other propaganda, not admitting him into especially secret business."[52]

Togliatti, indeed, spent the next several years making propaganda radio broadcasts from Moscow. In 1944 he returned to Italy to take the leadership of the Italian Communist Party in the aftermath of Mussolini's downfall. Under his guidance it became the largest Communist Party in Western Europe.

CHAPTER FIVE

The International Brigades in Spain

No part of the Comintern's activities in Spain has received as much attention as the International Brigades (IB). A multinational force of 30,000–40,000 soldiers credited with a heroic dedication to antifascism, the IB was lauded in literature, song, and the media. Credited with saving Madrid from Nationalist assault in the early days of the civil war, it also became the symbol of the Popular Front. During the civil war, the Comintern and the Communist parties who recruited the great bulk of the fighters played down the Communist theme in favor of propaganda stressing antifascism and humanitarianism. While the Comintern's role in organizing the IB has been extensively documented by historians, the cipher correspondence contains previously unknown information that sheds new light on the Comintern's attitude to the volunteers and on its general attitude to the events in Spain.[1]

Communist volunteers who were either in the country at that time or had come in order to defend the Republic participated in the fighting from the very first days of the military uprising against the Spanish Republican government—18 July 1936—led by Generals José Sanjurjo and Francisco Franco. In addition to giving political instructions to the leadership of the Communist Party of Spain, organizing a propaganda campaign in defense of the Republic, and providing assistance for the purchase of required materials, the Comintern tried to help by sending military experts to the country.

Recruiting Volunteers and Organizing the Brigades

On 11 August 1936 the ECCI Secretariat sent a cipher message to the United States, urging Earl Browder to recruit pilots: "The governmental army in Spain is in a great want of aviators. If you have aviators who sympathize with the Party, necessary urgently to send them to Spain." A week later Browder was asked if he had located any: "Inform us whether you succeeded in sending aviators to Madrid. Hasten; every minute is dear." Browder quickly answered: "6 pilots ready to leave for Spain via Paris, send immediately connection and instruction." Even after the pilots arrived in Spain, the ECCI continued to monitor their deployment, demanding that Vittorio Codovilla "do everything necessary for their use."[2]

Maurice Thorez and André Marty informed Dimitrov that they were sending pilots, machine gunners, and artillerists from France who had been asking to fight. Then Marty wrote that their departure had been delayed: "Two pilots and two machine gunners have not yet left." They had apparently been sent, but the message of Thorez and Marty indicated the appearance of new problems: "The French pilots are complaining that there is no plan for proper use or correct maintenance of the equipment."[3] This complaint was a constant one, and the Communist International soon discovered that a modern army with aircraft, artillery, trucks, and the complex machinery of modern warfare required more than willing volunteers who could do little more than carry a rifle. And with much of the professional Spanish Army in revolt, the Spanish government had only limited ability to provide the organizational and logistical support needed by the inter national volunteers rushing to Spain.

Nonetheless, the Comintern began systematically to organize the dispatch of volunteers following the receipt of instructions from the Politburo of the Soviet Communist Party. Dimitrov's diary of 28 August contains an entry stating that the Politburo meeting that day discussed the "Question of aid to the Spanish (poss[ible] organiz[ation] of an internat[ional] corps)," but he did not indicate whether a decision was taken. The Secretariat gave orders to expand the recruitment of volunteers only on 18 September, calling for "engaging in the recruitment of volunteers with military training among the workers of various countries, in order to send them to Spain." The Comintern then moved swiftly to recruit volunteers via the Communist parties and to organize them in Spain as a Comintern-controlled army, the International Brigades. The directive was sent to Communist parties in early October, along with instructions on the recruitment and transfer of volunteers to Spain.[4]

The Comintern's intervention marked a major step in the internationalization of the civil war. Though both sides in the civil war had been relying on foreign political and material assistance and the Nationalists had received significant assistance from Italy and Germany, the organized dispatch of foreign volunteers raised the stakes. An introduction to published Comintern documents on Spain noted that the Comintern's intervention "became yet one more factor exerting a decisive impact on the internationalization of the Civil War in Spain and strengthening the ideological polarization of the conflict, excluding any possibility for compromise."[5]

The first efforts came even before the formal Comintern request. By 28 September Thorez was writing from Paris: "Have commenced implementation of the task assigned us. The group of volunteers and transportation for the first 1,000 have been provided with necessary personnel and funds." Shortly thereafter he reported: "The first contingent of 350 people crossed the border before 3 October. The necessary things for them, uniforms, weapons, and shells, have been loaded and successfully sent off. But receipt and unloading encountered difficulties because of the anarchists, and also because of the weakness of the local Spanish comrades. We had to suspend travel. . . . We are thinking to send 1,000 people again and how possible materials from 9 October. And that after that will continue [to send] 500 a week. We request you for your part to insist on receipt from the Spanish comrades. . . . Major difficulties in sending the airplanes." In subsequent correspondence with the Comintern, Thorez and Marty informed it about the number of "postcards" or "open letters" (volunteers) the French Communist Party had sent to Spain by either "regular mail" (land) or "air mail" (sea).[6]

Recruiting and sending volunteers and the purchase of airplanes and other equipment required money, and the ECCI often received requests for needed funds. On 21 October Thorez and Clément (Eugen Fried, the Comintern's representative to the French party) reported, "Debts and a lack of funds are forcing us to seek a loan. The situation is critical. We ask you to take the necessary measures in keeping with your promise. The sending of postcards may be disrupted." The Comintern cabled back: "Instructions have been sent to transmit you 100,000 francs."[7]

The pressure on the leaders of the French Communist Party was particularly strong because France was the hub for recruitment and transport of the volunteers to Spain. The French Communist leadership was given the responsibility to coordinate recruitment from other Communist parties. On 27 October Thorez received a message "to take superhuman measures to speed up the sending of postcards. Send immediately trusted persons to Czechoslovakia and Belgium to reach agreement with Gottwald and [Xavier] Relecom [a secretary of the Central Committee of the Belgian Communist Party] about the publication [transport] of postcards in these countries." In early November the ECCI sent another directive to Thorez and Clément that demanded they redouble efforts to recruit volunteers in France and throughout Europe and send reliable people to carry out the task. Former soldiers and war veterans were especially desired due to the lack of trained or experienced fighters in Spain.[8]

These entreaties did produce an upsurge in the number of volunteers sent to Spain. On 5 November Thorez reported that in the prior week "817 postcards [had been sent] by regular mail and 250 by airmail, the total at present numbers 3,663." Three days later he claimed 3,720 men had been sent and estimated that another 1,000 would be on their way within days. The ECCI asked Klement Gottwald to send 2,000 Czechoslovak volunteers by 20 November. The courier chosen to deliver the message was told to "remain in Prague until arrangements have been made." Once that assignment had been completed, he was ordered to "go to Paris to take care of the order from London and other countries.[9]

The ECCI thought the recruitment of volunteers in Britain was not progressing satisfactorily. On 11 November Dmitry Manuilsky sent Thorez and Clément a directive: "Need to receive 1,000 English postcards at any price. The political importance here is enormous. Telegraph whether Harry [Pollitt] agrees to this obligation." Clément answered, "Pollitt has promised 500 postcards, but emphasizes major difficulties." Later he wrote, "Pollitt refuses to follow precisely the advice for sending postcards, promises only to try to find 200."[10]

The Comintern also instructed Earl Browder to organize the supply of volunteers and weapons from the United States and through him exerted pressure on the Communist parties of Latin America. In late October 1936 instructions were sent to the Central Committees of the Communist parties of Mexico, Cuba, Puerto Rico, Colombia, and Venezuela via the United States: "Strengthen all means campaign support Spain. Protest against use Latin American embassies and consulates in Spain for support fascists. Send to Spain highly qualified military specialists and airmen. Strengthen collection of funds, food, and clothes."

Browder was also told to send "to Mexico an energetic comrade to urge . . . [Mexican] Party send a few scores of volunteer officers to help Spanish people." The Central Committee of the Mexican Communist Party received the same demand directly. In mid-December Browder confirmed that recruiters had been dispatched to Cuba and Mexico, where the possibilities were good.[11]

The Comintern sent Leonardo Asnos, an employee of its Communications Service (his pseudonyms were Lee and John Peterson) to assist in recruiting volunteers for Spain. Browder also coordinated his efforts with Fernando de Los Rios Irruti, the Republic's ambassador to the United States. On 19 November Browder reported, "I have connected Los Rios with 3 West Point officers on vacation who offer to take 40 skilled under officers for minimum 6 weeks openly declaring they go to fight for democracy and give fundamental training. Also skilled antiaircraft unit offers service." Later he asserted that the "volunteer officers" had been sent "through Grant [Los Rios]. . . . We are sending 50 to 100 cabins [volunteers] and casks [officers] next week to Paris."[12]

Cooperation with the Spanish ambassador, however, proved difficult. A coded dispatch from Browder on 11 December stated that he was "shipping 100 cabins well qualified in 10 days, set quota 500 more (?) in 30 days. We are very disturbed by methods work Grantmen [Los Rios and his assistants] and if we fail to obtain correction from Grant will telegraph you fully soon."[13]

Despite the difficulties, Moscow repeated its demand that Browder speed up the dispatch of volunteers. On 22 November Manuilsky stressed that "Cans [naval officers] are especially needed at present." Browder quickly responded, "We have possibility to secure many cans skilled underwater work. Necessary that Tampa [Spanish government] instruct to give special attention when we bring them for quick action." The Comintern urged: "Please send immediately cans skilled underwater work to Tampa." That same day a message was sent to José Díaz and Codovilla in Madrid: "Browder sends several naval officers and asks that they be immediately used in this matter."[14]

There was no letup in the Comintern's demands for American recruits in December 1936. Manuilsky sent new instructions to New York: "Necessary at all costs strengthen dispatch of cans to Tampa [Spain], need of which very acute there. Necessary to send there by 1 February not less than 10,000 cabins carefully selected accompanied by casks. You must in advance send someone to Thorez in France in order to arrange for reception of cabins in France and to which port the cabins are to be shipped, because it is impossible for you to send the cabins in large numbers through Hudson [unknown]. We are impatiently waiting for information about fulfillment this most important task. The success of the affaire of Tampa depends upon you and the energy of the whole Party." Just a few days later Browder was again reminded how urgent it was to send American volunteers: "Telegraph how many carefully selected cabins you can send till 1 January. They are absolutely necessary at the utmost shortest time."[15]

On 17 December Browder reported progress, although not as much as Moscow wanted, and noted some of his problems: "100 to 120 cabins on ship 'Normandie' to Havre leaving 26 December. We can bring quota to 5,000 within 3 months, but must have 1,500 papers [dollars] to execute. Grant's representative [Spanish ambassador's aide] says has no authority to help. Arrange everything possible with Minor in Paris." (Robert Minor, a senior CPUSA official, was then in Paris supervising the logistical and financial details for the American soldiers.) Browder's request for money was granted. He was told on 19 December that "Representative of friendly firm will give you according our request 1,000 samples of paper. Confirm receipt." The meaning presumably was that the New York Soviet consulate would deliver $1,000 (over $16,000 in 2012 values) to Browder.[16]

A few days later a new dispatch followed, informing the CPUSA leader that soon "you will receive from us 1,000 dollars. Minor so far received in Paris 800 dollars. In addition the French friends obliged themselves to transport cabins at their expense in ships chartered by them. Inform whether under these conditions this sum will be sufficient for fulfillment your program. If not sufficient how much more will you need? Please hasten shipment because later may be more difficult." Browder, however, continued to insist on the need for additional cash. On 29 December he cabled, "90 cabins shipped 26/XII, arrive Havre 31/XII, 30 more 5/I. For this we borrowed but credit exhausted, no more can go until this problem settled. With enough papers can ship 1,000 jacks [volunteers], 2,500 in February. Urge you send papers immediately."[17]

While the Comintern pressured its constituent parties, particularly the American, to send recruits, it also was scavenging for arms and supplies. In late November 1936 Thorez and Clément reported to Moscow that along with 850 more men, a variety of weapons, including artillery, had arrived in Spain: "Our air mail [sea transport] for our operations has arrived. . . . There are works of Rolland [artillery], reports, pictures, and drawings [other weapons]. Message received on Browder's possibilities and on our future sending things. Telegraph immediately where Browder's publications [weapons] are being bought, to go there to purchase them."[18]

After André Marty arrived in Spain to take command of the International Brigades, he informed the Comintern that he needed a variety of weapons. Manuilsky cabled Thorez on 7 November that there was a need for "44 books-charts [light machine guns], 32 charts [heavy machine guns], 10 large works of Romain Rolland [75-caliber cannons], 12 small works of Romain Rolland [37-caliber cannons]. Send as soon as possible." Forwarding one of Marty's telegrams to Semyon Uritsky, the chief of the IV (Intelligence) Directorate of the General Staff of the Red Army, Manuilsky asked him to "take measures for supplying the 3d and 4th International Brigades with rifles, machine guns, artillery batteries, and means of transportation," and also "to hasten the manning of officers of both Brigades"—that is, to supply Red Army personnel to give the International Brigades a professional officer corps.[19]

On 28 November Manuilsky sent another inquiry to Browder emphasizing the importance of his task and asking "in whose name could be bought Dictionarys [airplanes] French and German? Can this be done by authority of Tampa [Spain], or must the transaction be concluded by authority of Colombia [United States]? . . . How can you guarantee forwarding the Dictionarys to Tampa without running the risk of having them seized by gangsters [Franco forces]?"[20]

On that same day a message was sent to Madrid to Marty and Codovilla with instructions about the need to pressure the Spanish government to ensure the purchase of airplanes: "The government of Italy [Spain] must guarantee to its representative in America subsidies for aid affair." Codovilla immediately responded: "Everything necessary has been done for the American airplanes." Manuilsky informed Browder that the question of paying for the airplanes had been resolved: "Grant [Los Rios] received instructions from Norfolk [Madrid] to purchase the French and German Dictionary you suggest. Payment will be made through a special representative of the Ministry of Finance, who has received the relevant instructions. Telegraph results."[21]

The arrangements, however, went awry. A coded dispatch from Browder of 11 December stated: "We have group best box in America ready to ship on usual condition but representative Tampa [Spain] postpones signing contract although report shows inferior boxes already being sent. Also excellent dictionary [aircraft] is being neglected in favor of inferior stocks. We are extremely limited by complete lack of papers [dollars] and dependence upon people who do not work freely with us."[22]

On the same day, the Comintern's Communications Service agent in the United States sent a more optimistic notice concerning transportation of weapons: "As far as I [k]now camel [freighter] . . . by a certain company here, which should by now be at destination, includes 5,000 books [rifles], 5,000,000 (?) bibles [cartridges], and 5 dictionaries [aircraft]. Another camel of 19 dictionaries now on the way. Concluding deal on 5 big dictionaries. And expect close deals on large number of German dictionaries. All camel[s] are camouflaged and manned with reliable people."[23]

Problems with the International Brigades

Even as the Comintern exhorted its constituent parties to send men and materiel to Spain, its representatives in the country struggled to turn the men into an effective fighting force. It was not easy. André Marty, stationed in Albacete, where the recruits underwent training, reported frankly on the early difficulties. On 31 October 1936 Marty and Mario Nicoletti (pseudonym of Giuseppe Di Vittorio, a member of the CC of the Communist Party of Italy) informed Dimitrov and Manuilsky of the following:

> Despite material difficulties 8,000 men are already enrolled in the International Brigade. 2,000 have been included in the 4th battalion—the Italians, Germans, French, Balkans, and Poles. 80% are Communists and Socialists: a few Frenchmen, and many of those are Italians. . . . The Brigade is a very specific type of Popular Front. The Political Commission was selected in precisely the same spirit. Nicoletti is the political commissar of the Brigade. The morale of the Brigade is improving. The drawbacks: there are no submachine guns, artillery, and one-third is not yet operational. There are very few military personnel and they are insufficiently trained. We have requested the French Communist Party to send only those Frenchmen who have military training. We are asking you for no less than 30 officers, battalion and unit commanders, all French-speaking. We request you to send Mexican officers for our Brigade, since we cannot include 500 Spanish migrants.[24]

Marty later reported rather frequently and in considerable detail to the ECCI on the process of the formation of the Brigades, pointing out the need for various types of military specialists and officer personnel and voicing specific desires for various types of weapons and for reserves of supplies and food, etc. He sometimes dealt with incidents and displays of indiscipline. He complained repeatedly of the quality of recruits and problems of morale: "Get replacements in Paris for two-thirds of the battalion, from which 50 [persons] have deserted and 30 are attempting to demoralize the Brigade during combat. The remaining third of the French soldiers, primarily from Lyons, have been primarily recruited in cafés. We think that any noise [publicity] should be avoided; you will be receiving from us all documents, confirm, study [them]."[25]

One cable from Manuilsky suggested that only one-fourth of the Brigades should actually be foreigners, with the rest being Spanish troops. Moscow had already sent similar instructions to Marty on 29 October 1936, but these had not been immediately carried out. But by the end of the year the International Brigades included both foreign volunteers and Spanish soldiers, with the latter eventually becoming the majority. Despite the Comintern's impulse to use the International Brigades to buttress the Communists' prestige, there were risks involved with too prominent a role for the International Brigades and foreigners in what was a civil war. The controversy over one particular Soviet soldier illustrated the dilemma.[26]

On the advice of Spanish Communist leader José Díaz, Largo Caballero, head of the Spanish Republican government, appointed Emilio Kleber as commander of the International Brigades' First Brigade. (Kleber was the pseudonym of Manfred Stern, a veteran of the military intelligence agency of the Red Army who had worked in the ECCI apparatus from 1935 to 1936. His Comintern pseudonym was Fred.) Kleber had been working for the Spanish Communist Party on the staff of the People's Militia, a Communist-led militia formation that had played an important role in reviving the Spanish Republican army after Franco's revolt. In that position he had a falling out with the Soviet diplomatic representative Marcel Rosenberg. As Kleber wrote after his return from Spain, this appointment "was received by Rosenberg with dissatisfaction and ridicule."[27]

Dimitrov, who clearly had information on the falling out, wrote to Manuilsky and Moskvin regarding his concern that non-Spanish Comintern personnel were taking a high-profile role in the fractious politics of the Spanish Republican government:

> A number of foreign comrades in Spain are behaving inappropriately. In particular, a certain Kleber, working on the Staff, who has arrogated to himself the rank of general, has begun to command instead of assisting with tactical advice. Mije [Antonio Garcio Mije was a member of the Politburo of the CC of the Communist Party of Spain and deputy general commissar of the Republican army] stated that the behavior of

> foreigners could be perceived by some Spaniards as a manifestation of a great-power attitude toward them. It also seems that our Ministers [Tomás Jesús Hernández and Vicente Uribe, senior Spanish Communists and members of Caballero's government] are giving in to negative exhortations from Prieto [Socialist Indalecio Prieto, minister of the navy and air force] directed against Caballero, which is exacerbating their relations with the latter. There is an urgent need to take appropriate measures and once again to recommend the strictest caution to our people.[28]

Dimitrov's concern about Kleber's growing prominence was apparently not passed on to Spain since it would likely have prevented him being appointed the commander of the International Brigades' first operational unit.

Due to the extremely difficult military situation, Kleber's First Brigade was sent on 3 November to defend Madrid, and his unit played a major role in the unexpectedly successful resistance by Republican forces. Since the government had largely evacuated Madrid, anticipating its fall to the Nationalists, the Communist role in saving the capital of Spain for the Republic was a signal achievement. Marty reported the good news to Moscow, and Manuilsky promptly informed Dimitrov, who was then in Kislovodsk, that "the International Brigade, of which eighty per cent are Communists and Socialists, is fighting courageously and is the bastion for the defense of the capital. With the arrival of new volunteers, the Brigade is continuing to swell its ranks. There are reasons to believe that the capital will not be surrendered."[29]

Heartened by this message, Dimitrov decided it was time for the International Brigades to take a higher profile. He replied:

> The time has come when absolutely everything possible must be done to reinforce the International Brigade, to transform it into a shock Brigade of the Republican army and hold Madrid. Now there is nothing to be ashamed of. As widely as possible, popularize the International Brigade, its actions, fighters, and outstanding role as a powerful means for ensuring the active solidarity of the international proletariat with the Spanish people. There is a need also to make use of outstanding historical examples of the behavior of revolutionary volunteers, including the British and the intelligentsia in general, for example Byron in the Greek people's struggle for liberation.[30]

This message was taken as an unequivocal order to reveal the previously secret participation of the Comintern in sending volunteers to Spain.

Around the same time, Germany and Italy, who had been rendering Franco major assistance in weapons and in transporting his troops from Morocco and other locations, became more directly involved in the conflict. On 6 November the Condor Legion, a German unit, nominally manned by Luftwaffe volunteers, landed in Seville and provided the rebels a better-trained air force with equipment superior to the Republicans', although modern Soviet fighter aircraft would later partially restore the balance. The Condor Legion also included small German artillery and tank units. At the end of November larger Italian infantry, tank, artillery, and aviation units, well trained and well equipped, entered Spain, eventually growing to nearly sixty thousand Italian troops. On 18 November Germany and Italy formally recognized the Nationalists as the government of Spain.[31]

After his battlefield success the newspapers began writing extensively about Kleber. In particular, an article by Mario Nicoletti, the political commissar of the International Brigade, emphasized Kleber's key role in the defense of Madrid and distorted or embellished several facts regarding his life. To correct these distortions, Kleber gave an interview to the correspondent of the newspaper *Claridad*. The hullabaloo in the press intensified André Marty's ill will toward Kleber. He sent a denunciation to Moscow, ascribing to Kleber the desire to become the paramount Republican military commander.[32]

Since one of the major propaganda points emphasized by the Nationalists was the lack of patriotism of the Republican leadership, the sudden high profile of Kleber, obviously not Spanish, was a political problem. It also provided justification for Franco's acceptance of German and Italian aid for his forces. A message arrived from Moscow calling Nicoletti's article about Kleber "inadmissible" and demanding that further publications of this type be avoided. The following sharply worded coded message was then dispatched to Marty, Codovilla, Díaz, Ibárruri, and the Spanish party Politburo:

> Fred's [Kleber's] criminal babbling to the journalists, with Nicoletti's complicity and Marty's incomprehensible tolerance, is doing enormous damage to the cause of the Spanish people; it is undermining the prestige of the government, facilitating Germany's and Italy's fascist intervention, and encouraging the capitalist governments to take measures against the flow of Republican volunteers to Spain. Fred's boastful declarations regarding victory are nurturing dangerous illusions regarding the enemy forces. With the assistance of the International Brigade, the Spanish people, its army, and government have stopped the offensive on Madrid. The task of the Brigade is to assist the Spanish people and not to replace the Republican army and its Spanish military commanders and leaders. Put an end to Fred's outrageous self-advertising, which

> is lending itself to provocations by the enemy. Inform us regarding measures taken.[33]

The harshness of this message was not provoked solely by potential political and military consequences in Spain, but also by the fear that Stalin would place the blame for these publications on the leadership of the Comintern, which had briefly urged more publicity for the Brigades' role as the defender of Madrid. Dissatisfaction with Kleber on the part of Caballero and José Asencio, the assistant to the minister of defense, who had repeatedly interfered with Kleber's military orders, was well known. Moscow was trying to preserve good relations with Caballero, who was both head of the Republican government and its minister of defense.

Marty hastened to report that Kleber had been relieved of his duties and accused him of various political and military errors. He wrote that Kleber's strategy had been identical to the poor Spanish strategy of sending units out to places where they came directly under fire, with no awareness of possible results. Kleber allegedly "every evening abandoned his command for trips to Madrid, for behind the scenes maneuvers." The leaders of the Spanish Communist Party, whose support had landed Kleber in his position, hastened to state their agreement:

> We share your point of view regarding the role of the International Brigades. In the future we intend increasingly to unite the International Brigades with the Spanish army, to create a large popular antifascist army. On several occasions we have condemned Fred's [Kleber's] self-advertising and several of his views regarding the Spanish military leaders. Fred's policy is threatening the policy of the Popular Front, and we have therefore decided to remove Fred from the Madrid front and to send him to the Malaga front. We have taken this decision bearing in mind that, despite his shortcomings, Fred is a bold comrade with military capabilities. The Malaga front is in need of an energetic commander, and Fred could render service. Telegraph your agreement.[34]

Moscow approved this decision, emphasizing that it was insisting "on strict control over him [Kleber] in the future." The ultimate result was a directive from the Secretariat of the ECCI on 26 December: "In popularizing the International Brigade as a clear expression of international solidarity with the Spanish people who are fighting against fascism, our press should not show the Brigade as the basic force in the defense of Madrid. That is *inadvisable* and politically harmful. More must be written about the heroism of the *Spanish fighters* and the popular masses of *Spain*, who with unprecedented and dogged zeal are resisting the fascist intervention. The newspapers must also refrain from a popularization of General Kleber and not publish his photo, interviews, etc."[35]

Thus, on orders from Moscow, in November–December 1936 the man who had played such a vital role in the defense of Madrid was deprived of his post and consigned to oblivion. On 1 October 1937 he returned to Moscow and again worked in the ECCI apparatus. But on 23 July 1938 he was arrested and on 14 May 1939 was sentenced to fifteen years' imprisonment. He died in a Gulag labor camp on 20 February 1954.[36]

Kleber was not the only Communist leader who ran afoul of André Marty. Marty's leadership was a constant problem for the International Brigades. An inflexible micro-manager who harshly punished any deviation from his wishes, Marty was given the nickname "the butcher of Albacete" because of his cruelty. The Spanish party Politburo made an attempt to limit Marty's autocratic rule over the International Brigades' headquarters at Albacete and to make fundamental changes in his methods of leadership. A message from Codovilla and Díaz of 17 December 1936 stated the following: "After consideration of the situation in the International Brigades at the front and in Albacete we have come to the conclusion that many of the unexpected recent difficulties were the result of a lack of collective leadership in the command and of a lack of flexibility on André's part. He is personally interfering and is taking decisions on all issues, including the most trivial ones, since there is no body that regulates technical and military issues. After a meeting with André, decisions were taken in order to improve work, and we will communicate these separately."[37]

At a meeting of the PCE's Politburo, a decision was taken to make Marty, Díaz, and Codovilla a collective political leadership over the base in Albacete, with the participation of representatives of the Communist parties of Germany and Italy. The Politburo decided to create a staff in Albacete to deal with all of the technical training of the International Brigades and a special propaganda division in foreign languages, primarily German and Italian, and to organize infiltration into the enemy ranks. Gallo (senior Italian Communist Luigi Longo) was appointed general commissar for the International Brigades. It was proposed to Marty that he focus on political work without the distraction of minor organizational problems (meaning running the International Brigades) and that he maintain contacts with the representatives of the Socialist leaders, Pietro Nenni and Julius Deutsch, "to preserve the international nature and the nature of the Popular

Front in the International Brigades." (Nenni served as political commissar of the Eleventh International Brigade's largely Italian Garibaldi Battalion. Deutsch, an Austrian Social Democrat, served as a senior officer in the Ninth International Brigade.) Marty informed Moscow of the decision of the Politburo, with the omission of what had been said about him—namely, that he should not deal with "minor organizational problems." He reported that the decision provided for the organization and integration of Spanish battalions into International Brigades.[38]

In approving this decision, the ECCI Secretariat underscored the need for close cooperation between the Politburo of the Central Committee of the French Communist Party and the leadership of the International Brigades: "We also insist that the collective leadership you have created provide for the closest possible contact with Maurice [Thorez] and the French Politburo and eliminate anything that may hamper amicable work between Albacete and Paris." The tense relationship between Marty, the leading French Communist in the ECCI as well as overseer of the International Brigades, and Thorez, general secretary of the French CP, had begun to have a substantive impact on cooperation between the leadership of the French Communist Party and the International Brigades. A coded dispatch to Marty bluntly stated: "In the interests of the matter entrusted to you, the Secretariat is insisting on the need for highly amicable contacts on your part with the Politburo of the French Communist Party, and first and foremost with Maurice. Lack of coordination, manifestations of individualism, and the aggravation of personal relationships are damaging to the cause. We are giving the same instructions to the Politburo of the French Communist Party."[39]

The ECCI's message to Thorez and Clément was calmer in tone: "In the interests of the cause there is a need for close and friendly contacts with André, to whom we are indicating that manifestations of individualism are harmful to the cause." Clément, however, wrote that the situation was not improving: "Tensions between Maurice and André are rising. André's actions are indeed working to discredit the French Party. The workers of the French Party who accompanied" volunteers into Spain returned "demoralized and discouraged. Maurice is threatening to demand that he be relieved of this work if André continues." The Marty–Thorez antagonism, however, was never clearly resolved and continued to damage cooperation between Paris and Albacete.[40]

The ECCI Secretariat emphasized the need for careful political selection in its instructions about the volunteers. "We have information that the fascists and spies have infiltrated into recent units and have even tried to foment mutiny," stated one message to Clément and Thorez. "We insist on scrupulous investigation of people being sent. Avoid involving unstable elements who are receptive to counterrevolutionary propaganda and likely to violate discipline. Ensure the improvement of political work in the units."[41]

Many units of the International Brigades did suffer from poor morale, and desertion was a major problem. But it was an ECCI delusion that the cause was infiltration by spies and fascists. The soldiers of the International Brigades, despite their demonstrated bravery, were ill-trained, poorly equipped, and commanded by officers many of whom were as woefully short of training and military experience as the troops were. The casualty rate suffered by the Brigades was extraordinarily high, and the ECCI's insistence that these problems could be overcome by stricter political screening was simply Bolshevik conceit.

Dimitrov and Manuilsky were realistic enough to have some sense of this and on 13 December took up the issue of the military training of the volunteers with Stalin and Voroshilov. They proposed the organization of short-term courses "for the training for 6 months of 500 commanders from among the political emigrants, who have been carefully selected and investigated by the Narkomvnudel [People's Commissariat for Internal Affairs]." They also proposed training two hundred more people in Red Army military schools. The Politburo approved the funds needed for this purpose.[42]

The delicate relationship between the Comintern and the Spanish Republican government forced Moscow to calibrate carefully how many resources it would send to Spain. The decisive voice belonged to Stalin. An entry in Dimitrov's diary of 2 January 1937 noted: "In answer to our proposal regarding volunteers from America: Stal[in's] resol[ution]: "No more volunteers are needed. I propose ending recruitment." On 3 January 1937 the ECCI Secretariat sent coded dispatches to Spain, France, and America suspending the recruitment of volunteers. In the message to the leadership of the Communist Party of Spain and to the representatives of the Comintern in Spain, the decision was primarily justified on the grounds that a further dispatch of volunteers would be used by Germany and Italy to send an occupation army to Spain. In the light of the growing operational capacity of the Spanish Republican army and since the Spanish government itself did not consider further increases in the International Brigades advisable, the Secretariat sent instructions to all parties and to its sections to cease recruiting.[43]

The directives sent to Paris and New York did not contain the sentence regarding the negative attitude of the Spanish government toward a further increase in the size of the International Brigades. They did, however, contain a number of specific orders. Browder was told to suspend all actions connected with recruitment in countries neighboring the United States, as well as the sending of volunteers from the United States to France. He was also told: "From the funds you received for this purpose create under your personal responsibility an inviolable fund so that not a cent is spent without our instructions. About the purpose of this fund you will be informed later. Do not dissolve apparatus you set up for recruitment of volunteers; instead direct it toward work of giving aid to Spanish people in all other ways and forms so that if the need arises this apparatus could in the quickest manner renew its former activities."[44]

The French Communist Party also received some specific instructions, including the following: "Send a strong brigade of responsible workers for political work with the French units of the existing International Brigades. Suspend any payments you are making to brotherly Communist Parties for the recruitment of volunteers and demand a detailed report as soon as possible on the use of the sums you have given out, so that not a single centime is spent for unauthorized purposes. Without making this in any way public, as quickly as possible complete the sending in small groups of those volunteers who have already been recruited and who are already grouped together in France."[45]

Marty's message in reply stated that he understood the instructions as meaning the eventual disappearance of the International Brigades. For the first time, he admitted that the Spanish government and its military command had a negative attitude toward the Brigades, but he argued against their dissolution:

> Very often the enthusiasm of the Brigades is used to destroy them, and we are not in a position to act so as to hamper the implementation of the orders of the General Staff. . . . Under such conditions your decision concerning the cessation of sending volunteers is causing great alarm. . . . The present low numbers do not allow for the existence of the former full 4 Brigades: they will automatically have to be deprived of the good material conditions they have now. . . . In addition to all this, the positive role played by the Brigades from the point of view of the Popular Front and unity, and a good military example, already held up as one to be imitated, will disappear. The enemy is everywhere stronger than we are, militarily speaking. At least 10,000 volunteers and another 4 Brigades are needed to strike a serious blow at the enemy.[46]

In another coded dispatch Marty repeated these arguments, asking the Comintern "to review the question of suspending recruiting and to give the opportunity to recruit up to 10,000 new volunteers." His plea was received just a day after the Comintern had received a directive once again altering course from the Politburo of the Soviet Communist Party. In his diary on 7 January Dimitrov noted a "Communication from P[olit].B[uro]. Recruitment and sending of internationalists is allowed." The Secretariat immediately cabled a message to Spain: "After careful discussion of the situation, and in particular since Germany and Italy are continuing to send troops, the Secretariat has given instructions to its sections to resume work on sending volunteers. It is necessary to achieve a positive attitude toward the volunteer movement on the part of Caballero." Paris and New York were sent instructions to "immediately resume work on the recruitment and sending of volunteers to Spain" and to inform the other Communist parties.[47]

Despite the decision to resume recruiting, the Comintern remained concerned about the attitude of the Spanish government. Manuilsky warned Marty, Díaz, and Codovilla that "without a favorable attitude on Caballero's part the recruiting process is encountering difficulties. Do everything necessary to win Caballero's confidence and to ensure his effective assistance to the Brigades."[48]

On orders from the Politburo of the CC of the Spanish party, Codovilla met with Caballero and managed to smooth over some of their disagreements. Caballero wanted "a better selection, since . . . in the last group there were many kinds of provocateurs and people undermining the cause, who had abandoned the front." In a follow-up message, Caballero was reported to have agreed "to organize new and old units, combining them with the Italians [Spaniards]. Insofar as possible we will give the most visible units to the Italians, to blend the foreigners with natives of the country."[49]

The ECCI Secretariat once again resumed pressure on the Communist parties to step up the dispatch of volunteers. In January 1937 Browder was exhorted to "hasten careful verification and sending of cabins [volunteers]." He continued to complain about lack of funds and was asked to raise his own money by charging a commission on the purchase of military goods he was assisting the Spanish ambassador to obtain in the United States: "Necessary strengthen dispatch cabins [volunteers] and display more initiative in overcoming financial difficulties. First you must cover expenses for dispatch of cabins by charging for deliveries you make to Grant [Ambassador Los Rios]. This is fully permissible because you assure for him the best and cheapest conditions of buying goods and because the charges are used for needs of his country. Second necessary dispatch cabins on ships chartered by French friends. Third necessary strengthen money collections. All this will permit widely develop your business."[50]

Louis Fisher, at one time the quartermaster of the International Brigades, was sent to assist Browder. A message addressed to Preacher [Browder] indicated: "American journalist Louis Fisher will arrive in order to assist you in matter of cabins. He has at his disposal 5,000 papers [dollars]. We recommend you work in close contact with him." While urging Browder to speed up the sending of the volunteers, the ECCI Secretariat also demanded a more thorough screening of the recruits: "You choose the cabins not well. The Frenchmen are reporting that on each arrival three or four cabins are disappearing [deserting]."[51]

Browder, however, continued to cite the lack of funds as a serious obstacle to meeting the Comintern's recruitment goals: "January shipment will total only 600 cabins due to delay caused by temporary halt. If I am advised immediately of special ship available 10 February to 18 February we can have ready 400 USA cabins and hardly possible 200 or more Canada. Important have definite information in advance in order to keep coordinated and avoid unnecessary delay and expense. So far received only 1,000 papers. Your telegram regarding Fisher says he brings 4,900 papers; is this correct? We are still paying here transportation to Paris and equipment, total cost averaging 180 dollars per cabin." The answer was rigid: "Continue affair cabins in . . . limits of money which Fisher disposes."[52]

The coded dispatches to Thorez and Clément in France also repeated rebukes over the slowdown in the rate of sending volunteers and demands for tighter screening. Moscow also suggested that the French party send a group of top officials to Spain for political work with the International Brigades. From Spain, Marty kept up a drumbeat of criticism of the leadership of the French Communist Party, which, as he saw it, was derelict in political work with the French volunteers, who comprised eight thousand of the fourteen thousand International Brigades' fighters in February 1937. One complaint singled out one unit in which "a fifth of the soldiers went off with the anarchists to France or deserted from Spain." Another pleaded with Moscow to intervene to improve the quality of the French recruits: "I hope that you step in for fulfillment *within two months our repeated demand regarding the military and political French personnel*."[53]

Providing secure transportation for volunteers continued to be a major headache. In March 1937, the head of the Yugoslav Communist

Party reported that a ship with five hundred volunteers had been forced by a severe storm to return to port, whereupon everyone on board was arrested by the authorities. Milan Gorkić (the general secretary of the Yugoslav party) lamented that 90 percent of the men had military training and "were to have landed in already formed military units with commanders and commissars." He promised to organize another try in a month but failed to do so.[54]

While at first crossing the French-Spanish border had been a relatively simple matter, later on there were enormous difficulties. A coded dispatch from Paris explained that it was impossible to send men by sea since "neither French ships nor [ships] of other nationalities are sailing there from French ports. . . . Our people do not have a single appropriate fast fishing or sports launch along the shore. The French shore is well guarded." A small fishing boat carrying twenty-five American volunteers had been intercepted. "Only speed boats suitable for sailing" were useful; one was available for 50,000 French francs.[55]

Togliatti sent a report to Moscow on the International Brigades on 29 August 1937. On 11 September Dimitrov forwarded it to Stalin. It painted a bleak picture, admitting that "The general situation in the International Brigades cannot be described as good. There is a need to take a number of measures to improve this situation. Fatigue is making itself felt in the Brigades." He noted that since the war had gone on longer than many of the volunteers had expected, they were extremely concerned over the future and their own affairs. Since many of the volunteers from countries like the United States and Britain had received a six-month vacation from their place of work and were in danger of losing their jobs if they did not return, dissatisfaction had increased. But the question of when they would return was being raised in nearly all the Brigades. Togliatti also pointed to another source for unhappiness: "Another reason for fatigue, in the view of nearly all the comrades with whom I have spoken, is that the Brigades are not always used rationally. And, indeed, they were considered as shock troops; they were sent to the most important operations but were not allowed to rest between two operations and were not allowed to fundamentally reorganize after particularly difficult operations, etc." Moreover, the proportion of foreigners in the International Brigades had dropped to 20 percent, while the Spanish government was insisting that the foreign contingent had to amount to 40–60 percent, meaning that the question of new, widespread recruitment was "a burning one."[56]

The report took note of the shortcomings in the leadership of the Brigades, difficulties in relations with the commanders of the base, the trend toward acting independently of the Republican government, and distrust on the part of the Spanish Republican military command toward the International Brigades. Togliatti also noted the problems caused by the role of the various Communist parties: "The problem of the internal organizations of the Brigades is exacerbated by various kinds of interference in their activities from the fraternal Parties. Each representative of a Party, naturally, is primarily interested in the personnel from his Party and tries to promote and protect them. That is right. But given the lack of centralized leadership that would coordinate all this work, all this is leading to disorder." He also cited information on the membership of the International Brigades. Of the 18,216 foreign volunteers who had arrived in Spain, 2,658 had been killed, 696 had "disappeared," 1,500 had been evacuated, and another 3,287 had been wounded. The total losses amounted to 8,141 people. The personnel of the International Brigades at that point included 3,155 men in deployed units; another 3,657 at the headquarters, supply, and training base in Albacete; and the rest spread among other Republican military units (cavalry, artillery, medical units, etc.). Reinforcements in April had totaled 1,103; in May, 1,203; in June, 1,341; and in July, 895.[57]

Along with Togliatti's report, Dimitrov sent Stalin the report of the visiting delegation of the Spanish Communist Party, which included Pedro Checa and Vittorio Codovilla. While they praised the International Brigades' military accomplishments, they identified "the flaw" as "the lack of ongoing methodical political work." The various party representatives attached to the Brigades "are all insufficiently connected to the leadership of the Spanish CP, insufficiently informed regarding the political and the military situation in the country to carry out the political work needed in the International Brigades to deal with relevant problems."[58]

The delegation submitted a memorandum, "Questions for Solution," covering a wide range of international and domestic problems. The Spanish Communist Party wanted to receive instructions on fundamental political issues from the ECCI. One of these items dealt with the International Brigades:

> The fascist governments of Germany and Italy are waging open war in Spain, making use of troops of their nationalities and from their colonies; under such conditions we think that the International Brigades are playing an enormous role—not only in terms of their political significance, but also in terms of their use from a military point of view.

> We think that the five International Brigades now in Spain must be reinforced with new foreign comrades, and at the same time there is a need to intensify the recruitment of foreign volunteers to create new Brigades.
>
> The system of mixed Brigades, Spanish-foreign, has yielded very positive results in the struggle, and through this system, step by step, we have been able to implant the International Brigades in the Spanish army (at present it could be said that the International Brigades in fact account for part of the Spanish army). To improve the fighting efficiency of the International Brigades they must be given military commanders who are more capable than most of those in command at present. Can the ECCI help us to get such officers?[59]

Dimitrov forwarded this document to Stalin and asked if he could speak personally with the representatives of the Spanish Communist Party. This meeting took place, and on 15 September the Secretariat issued a document, "Most Important Tasks of the Spanish Communist Party," as guidance for the PCE. Dimitrov sent this decree to Stalin on 17 September with a request to communicate "Your remarks and corrections of this document, if any, so that we can promptly forward them to the CC of the Spanish Party." The decree noted the need to "settle the issue of the International Brigades, seeing to their prompt reinforcement and growth through an influx of new volunteers, securing for the volunteers and their families the same rights that the Republic has given the Spanish fighters."[60]

While the Comintern continued to press Communist parties to send volunteers to Spain, it also recommended that they widen the pool of possible recruits beyond Communists. The instructions to Browder, for example, told him to "continue to send 200 Fords [volunteers] monthly. It is necessary without fail to diminish quantity of concrete [Communists]." But despite creating a special commission "to better organize the recruitment campaign for Spain and the political campaign in defense of the Spanish people," the numbers arriving in Spain did not meet the Comintern's ambitious goals. A November report from Spain to Manuilsky warned that "the acquisition of foreign 'cahiers' [volunteers] . . . continues to decline." Togliatti listed the need for 400 German and Austrian volunteers, 400 Italians, 200 Poles, 200 Czechs, 200 from the Balkans, 1,200 from France and Belgium, 200 from Great Britain, and 100 Americans, noting that the Spanish Communist Party believed that recruiting was "insufficient, and if the recruitment does not increase, the question of the existence of the Blasco publishing house [Albacete training base] will be a vital issue."[61]

Withdrawing the International Brigades

By early 1938, the leaders of the Spanish Communist Party began to discourage further use of foreign volunteers. They hoped that deemphasizing the high-profile role of the International Brigades would bring about an international situation that would pressure Germany and Italy to reduce their support for Franco. In a message to Manuilsky, Togliatti warned of the consequences if Germany and Italy did not respond as the Spanish party hoped:

> After discussion of the military and international situation the administration [Central Committee of the Spanish Communist Party] believes it absolutely necessary to deploy a new campaign on a broader international scale to demand the withdrawal from Spain not only of the Italian troops but in particular of the weapons from Italy and Germany, which make up a real army for attacking and destroying the country, and one that is entirely foreign. If the issue of recalling the volunteers is resolved by a concession of the Franco belligerent side without Italy's and Germany's recalling their aviation, the military situation of the Republic will become considerably more serious.

The problem of the further fate of the International Brigades and of the foreign volunteers in general was the subject of discussion not only in Spain. The question of recalling foreign volunteers was raised in the spring of 1938 at the International London Committee on Non-Intervention in the Affairs of Spain.[62]

By late summer the Comintern leadership had also come to a conclusion regarding the advisability of withdrawing the International Brigades, following discussions at several meetings of the ECCI Secretariat after 20 August 1938. An entry in Dimitrov's diary on 27 August concluded, "*International Brigades to be officially relieved.* (Marty and the Central Committee of the Spanish Communist Party to be assigned the organized evacuation and further disposition of volunteers)." Following a hasty vote of the members of the ECCI Secretariat, this decree was framed as an expression of an agreement with the decision of the Central Committee of the Communist Party of Spain. The policy was justified by reference to the international situation, which was asserted to be favorable to stepping up pressure for the withdrawal of German and Italian troops from Spain: "The release of the international volunteers is a means for intensifying such pressure. This release will demonstrate the strength of the government of the Republic. It will help the people and the army in the zone under fascist dictatorship to come forward against the German and Italian interventionist troops." Such reasoning did not reflect the real reason for the withdrawal of the International Brigades and was in fact a veiled admission of the practical necessity for that step.[63]

On 29 August Dimitrov sent a letter to Stalin and Voroshilov "on the liquidation of the Intern[ational] Brigades." Voroshilov expressed his agreement and promised that the USSR would continue to fulfill the Spanish request for assistance with weapons and military supplies. The resolution adopted on 3 September by the ECCI Secretariat stated that the Spanish government "must in the most unequivocal and categorical way emphasize that the question of a truce and of the termination of the war cannot possibly be raised as long as a single foreign soldier still remains on Spanish territory."[64]

Juan Negrín, chief of the Republican government, officially announced the recall of the foreign volunteers from Spain in his 21 September speech at a session of the League of Nations. Hopes that the same recall would take place in the camp of the Republic's enemies, however, were not fulfilled. New military units continued to arrive in Spain from fascist Italy.

It still remained necessary to organize an orderly withdrawal of the volunteers that did not look like a defeat. On 29 September Dimitrov received a telegram from Moskvin that "practical measures have been drawn up" and agreement reached with both the CC of the Spanish party and Marty, covering matters "organizational and technical (equipment of the camp for those released, clothes for them, etc.), the sequence of the evacuation, the order of the evacuation. Opportunities for those who wish to stay in the country to obtain citizenship are being planned, and in individual cases to have specialists remain on a volunteer basis."[65]

A major issue was the fate of volunteers who were political émigrés or who had entered Spain illegally from countries with fascist regimes. Early in 1939 Togliatti asked Moscow "urgently to report to Robert [likely Robert Minor of the CPUSA] that 1,500 of 1,591 former volunteers of the Brigades will be going to Mexico in a few days. These are Germans, Austrians, Italians, etc. Advise the Mexican Party to organize for meeting them and to think about sending them onward. They will be arriving around the 20th in Vera Cruz after passing through Havana." Browder was quickly sent instructions and warned to ensure that no sympathizers of Trotsky should be assisted: "Inform the Mexican Communist Party that they will meet warmly with and organize the help to the German and Austrians volunteers going from Spain to Mexico. It is necessary for you and Laborde [Hernán

Laborde, secretary general of the Mexican CP] to take all measures not to admit any disintegrating corrupt propaganda of Trotsky among them."[66]

Volunteers from Czechoslovakia faced difficulties due to their country's dismemberment, and Togliatti asked for the advice of the ECCI: "Given the new political situation of Metz [Czechoslovakia] we are seriously concerned by the sending of the former volunteers to their country. We wish to receive precise instructions from Guy [Clement Gottwald]. There are about 800 volunteers from Metz. Of them 300 will go to Venice [?], a hundred to the democratic countries of Europe. What should we do with the remaining 400?" In response, Gottwald gave instructions to assist the Sudetens in going to Mexico and the Czechs in returning to their truncated homeland.[67]

A few of the volunteers hoped for a more exotic destination. Togliatti sent one cable noting that "several internationalists are asking to be sent to Manchester. Inform whether this can be done. Rose and I have serious doubts." These men were not hoping to land in Britain. When Moskvin forwarded this to Dimitrov in his own code, he replaced "Manchester" with 164 and "Ercoli "and "Rose" with 111 and 193. "164" was Moskvin's code for China. When Dimitrov copied the decrypted cable in his diary, he indicated that Togliatti and Marty were dubious about the desire of some internationalists to go to China. Dimitrov agreed, telling Moskvin that "In my opinion, only those internationalists particularly qualified for this purpose can, as an exception, be allowed to go to China. It would also be good to consult with comrade Voroshilov on this issue."[68]

The ECCI Secretariat adopted a decree on 17 January, "On Arrangements for Volunteers, Members of the International Brigades Now in France." The Communist parties and the Committee of Assistance to the volunteers were instructed to facilitate the return to democratic countries of those volunteers who had previously been legal residents in those countries. The committee was authorized to commence a campaign for the legalization in France and Belgium of people from the Balkans and fascist countries; for some of the volunteers from the Balkan countries to obtain permission for residence in the Scandinavian countries; and for the remaining volunteers from fascist countries who were unable to remain in France to obtain permission for residence in Canada, Cuba, and Chile. The Communist parties of Britain, the United States, Canada, the Scandinavian countries, France, Belgium, the Netherlands, and Denmark were directed to carry out an effort to raise 600,000 francs for resettlement.[69]

The ECCI Secretariat sent the Communist parties directives demanding that permission be obtained for the entry of former volunteers who could not return to their native countries. ECCI instructions to Thorez and Codovilla stated: "A campaign must be begun to protect the former volunteers in all countries of Europe. The objective of the campaign is to find secure places in democratic countries for former volunteers who are citizens of fascist countries, to raise fifteen million francs to assist the families of the volunteers, and to obtain humane conditions in the concentration camps." The same cipher message was sent to Sven Linderot of the Swedish party. A similar cipher message to Browder listed specifically the United States, Mexico, Chile, Argentina, Cuba, and Uruguay as countries appropriate for settling the former volunteers. Some 2,374 men were sent to democratic countries. A considerable number of internationalists, however, continued to remain in the internment camps in France.[70]

Dimitrov requested the Politburo of the Soviet party on 10 January to allow those volunteers belonging to foreign Communist parties who either had their families in the USSR or were Soviet citizens whom the Comintern had sent to Spain to return to the USSR. A month later he repeated this request in a letter to Stalin:

> In connection with the events in Spain, the ECCI had sent from the USSR 589 members of fraternal Communist Parties, who had previously immigrated to the USSR for political reasons. The majority of them had worked as commanders and political workers of the International Brigades; some perished on the Spanish fronts. There are now 466 surviving volunteers in France. We have taken measures so that all the volunteers who can arrange to stay in other countries do not return to the USSR. There remain, however, some 300 volunteers who are under death sentences or are threatened with long-term prison sentences and therefore cannot return to their countries and cannot remain in other capitalist countries because of the danger that they will be handed over to their fascist governments. Moreover, these are people who have families in the USSR (203 persons) and who are also Soviet citizens (115 persons).
>
> It therefore would be right to allow the return of these volunteers to the USSR. The appropriate lists and materials on this question have been submitted to the Central Committee of the Party.

On 14 February the Politburo of the Central Committee of the VKP(b) resolved "To permit the reentry to the USSR of 300 persons, formerly sent by the ECCI as volunteers to Spain, and now located in France." The Soviet Embassy in France was directed to arrange their travel after appropriate "investigation."[71]

The volunteers who were unable to return home or find refuge elsewhere were interned in France, and by February 1939, 6,400 people were housed in French camps. Some of the volunteers, however, were still on the territory of the Spanish Republic. At the end of January the Republic was on the verge of military collapse. Togliatti sent a message: "Due to the extremely serious military situation the government has decided to send to the front those of the internationalists who are still here and who wish to do so, without making this known in any way. Tomorrow 2,000 will go to the front. The government is also discussing the possibility of summoning a new contingent of international volunteers from abroad." A coded dispatch was immediately sent to Thorez: "To save Geneva [Spain], and in particular Greece [Madrid], we propose immediately, without any fanfare, to send to Greece a significant number of trade union cards [volunteers], with a knowledge of technology, selected from among sportsmen [Communists] and supplied with stamps and envelopes [weapons]. At the same time take measures so that the Company [Confédération Générale du Travail] and the musicians [Socialists] also take similar actions. If your proposal is rejected, this work can be done by the workers' trade unions that are under the influence of the sportsmen. Devote all forces and all energy to this work." A day later the demand for sending volunteers was reiterated. Dimitrov also informed Stalin: "We are also taking a number of measures to intensify the campaign to assist the Spanish Republic, including the quiet resumption of the International Brigades and the sending of new contingents of volunteers." This final initiative, however, fizzled out.[72]

On 26 August Dimitrov and Manuilsky informed Stalin that more than three and a half thousand former volunteers remained in French internment camps, with no prospects whatever for receiving asylum in any other country. "Having exhausted all possibilities for obtaining the release of the volunteers," stated the letter, "we are appealing to You, Comrade Stalin, to discuss whether to allow the admission of three to three and a half thousand former fighters of the International Brigades into the USSR, having subjected them to thorough preliminary investigation."[73]

The leadership of the Comintern also later attempted to assist the former volunteers, but the war that began on 1 September 1939 "resolved" that problem in its own way.

CHAPTER SIX

The Comintern and the Terror

The Comintern waged its harshest political battle against those who criticized the Soviet system and its leader. Information regarding the woes, sufferings, and deprivations endured by individuals and the system of total control of the population and the mass wave of terror sweeping over it were hushed up or labeled as counterrevolutionary slander. With the leadership of the USSR's Communist Party [the VKP(b)] setting the example, all difficulties and setbacks were explained away as a result of intensified resistance to the forward march of socialism by the remnants of the toppled classes of the landowners and the bourgeoisie and as the machinations of international imperialism and its henchmen (the Social Democrats and Socialists) and of the Trotskyites and Bukharinists, who were termed spies, saboteurs, and hired killers. (Leon Trotsky had been second only to Lenin in the leadership of the Bolshevik Revolution, but Stalin defeated him in the struggle for leadership after Lenin's death in 1924. Expelled from the Communist Party in 1927, he was deported in 1929. In 1940 a NKVD assassin killed him at his Mexican exile home. Nikolai Bukharin, also a leading figure in the Bolshevik Revolution, had been allied with Stalin for a time in the mid-1920s but broke with him in 1928 and was quickly driven from power. He was executed in 1938.)

After the December 1934 assassination of Sergey Kirov, a member of the Politburo of the CC of the VKP(b) and chief of the Leningrad Communist Party organization, the NKVD quickly executed more than one hundred former White Guards. But this bloody reprisal against those who had opposed the Bolsheviks more than a decade earlier in the Russian Civil War (none of whom had any association with Kirov's killer) was just the beginning of a massive state-sponsored killing spree that all Communist parties and friends of the USSR were called upon to enthusiastically endorse.

In a coded dispatch of 9 January 1935, the Political Commission of the ECCI Secretariat called for foreign Communist parties to explain that the violence undertaken "in the interests of the protection of millions of workers from a brutal class enemy is in fact an act of 'genuine humanism.' " The Communist parties were told to arrange for the sending "of telegrams of support, resolutions from delegations of reformist organizations, from committees, meetings, from production collectives, etc." On Stalin's order, Trotsky and Grigory Zinoviev (another Bolshevik leader and former chairman of the ECCI who had opposed Stalin's rise to power) were then declared guilty of Kirov's assassination, and the ECCI immediately called upon the Communist parties to intensify the struggle against the Trotskyites, depicting them as terrorists and accomplices of fascism. The cipher communications gave specific instructions regarding the organization of the anti-Trotskyist campaign. Even trivial deviations from the official Soviet version regarding Trotskyite plotters and terrorists were severely criticized.[1]

This bloated campaign was elevated to even greater proportions in connection with the trial of the so-called Anti-Soviet United Trotskyist-Zinovievite Center; the trial began on 19 August 1936. On the eve of its commencement the Communist parties were sent an encrypted message with a demand to step up actions in support of Stalin's policy:

> The campaign around the trial of the Trotskyist-Zinovievite band is developing extremely slowly. There are no responses coming in from your country. And yet in the meantime all the international reactionary forces are howling in an anti-Soviet frenzy. The statement of the leaders of the Second International [Social Democrats] is a vile anti-Soviet act. Once again we repeat that there is a need for statements by the CC of the Party, the Party organizations, mass meetings, in particular the Social Democratic workers, with an expression of fraternal solidarity with the workers of the USSR, the leadership of the VKP [Soviet Communist Party], and the leader of the international proletariat, com. Stalin.[2]

The performances staged in Moscow used the device of forcing the victims of tomorrow to join in with the hounding of the victims of today. On 21 August articles by Karl Radek, Georgi Pyatakov, and Christian Rakovsky appeared in the Soviet press. The three, prominent Bolsheviks in the 1920s who had opposed Stalin's rise to power and been pushed aside, demanded the execution of their former comrades in arms, Zinoviev and Lev Kamenev, now in the dock accused of complicity in an anti-Soviet terrorist group that had murdered Kirov and planned to murder Stalin. The next day, however, Andrei Vyshinsky, the general prosecutor of the USSR, announced that he had already ordered an investigation of the authors of these articles, heralding for them the fate of those individuals whom they had just renounced. The publication of the articles was a clever turn in the preparation for future trials. The ECCI Secretariat, too, participated in preparing these trials. On 25–26 August a cipher message was sent to the Communist parties demanding the immediate publication of these articles "throughout the Communist press." Although the intent to engage in reprisals against these people was absolutely obvious, the damning words wrested from them regarding Zinoviev and Kamenev were used as evidence providing grounds for the death sentences. (Zinoviev and Kamenev were executed in 1936, Pyatakov in 1937, and Rakovsky in 1941. Radek was murdered by criminals while in prison in 1939.)[3]

Critics of the trial, in particular, European Social Democrats, who viewed it as utterly fictitious justice, took due note of the distinguishing feature of this procedure, devoid of real evidence except for the stilted and difficult-to-believe confessions of the accused. The ECCI, on the contrary, emphasized that allegedly documentary proof existed that the Trotskyites had established direct contact with the Nazi Gestapo. It gave orders, however, to use solely the official material distributed by Runag, the Comintern's press agency. The leaders of the Communist parties gave assurances that their parties were actively involved in the campaign. Joseph Jacquemote, the secretary general of the Belgian Communist Party, reported: "We are organizing a campaign (conferences, demonstrations, the press, brochures) to expose the Trotskyite murderers who are in the service of international fascism. . . . We are organizing a protest in the organizations of the BWP [Belgian Workers' Party (Social Democrats)] and the YSG [Young Socialist Guards] against the position of the Work. Soc. International [Social Democratic Second International] and the socialist press. We have received the declaration of [Fernand] Brunfaut, a member of the BWP, in which he declares his solidarity with the death sentence. We are trying to obtain similar statements from other socialist officials."[4]

The ECCI called on the Communist parties to distribute the materials of the trial and paid for the publication of pamphlets about the trial. Among the accused, in addition to Zinoviev, were former staff members of the ECCI apparatus and the Communist Party of Germany: Fritz David, Valentin Olberg, and Moses and Nathan Lurje.

They were accused of preparing an attempt on Stalin's life, to which they naturally "confessed." (All were executed.) The Comintern, demonstrating its total devotion to Stalin, required the leaders of the Communist parties to step up the struggle against Trotskyism and with scrupulous care to investigate the members of their parties to see whether they might not be displaying positions incompatible with the principles of the Comintern.

The directive of 26 August, sent to the Communist Party of Lithuania, stated: "Make use of materials of the trial, expose the Trotskyites as linked to the Hitlerite security services and as sliding toward fascism. Great care must be taken to prevent the Trotskyites from infiltrating the Party and the Komsomol [Young Communists]. Nor can those who directly or indirectly protect the Trotskyites and maintain contact with them be allowed to remain in the Party." A cipher message of 14 September read: "The trial has shown that many Trotskyites come from Lithuania. There is a need to thoroughly investigate whether or not Trotskyites have infiltrated the Lithuanian Communist Party, along with those who over the last few years have revealed Trotskyist leanings. Not only the Trotskyites, but those who have to any extent defended the Trotskyites have no place in the Party." A dispatch of 27 September stated, "In exposing the link between the Trotskyites and the Lith[uanian] security services and the Gestapo, indicate the names of those Trotskyites who are linked to the security services, including Szum. [unknown], who after his arrest behaved like a provocateur." Instructions of 2 October stipulated, "There is a need to carefully investigate the intellectuals who are assisting us, those around them, whether they may not have links to the Trotskyites and the security services."[5]

Finally, a directive of 23 December:

> There is a need to tirelessly pursue the struggle against the counterrevolutionary Trotskyist bandits, setting the task of crushing the Trotskyites in Lithuania as enemies of the workers and as agents of the security services. Make use of the materials of the trials of Zinoviev and the Trotskyist saboteurs in the Kuzbass, which have vividly demonstrated that the Trotskyites are agents of the Gestapo and are trying to bring about a restoration of capitalism. . . . Make use of the counterrevolutionary activity of the Trotskyites in Spain, etc. In Poland the security services are proposing to the [Jewish] Bund members that they speak out in defense of the Trotskyites. This is a fact, at a time when security services are openly taking up the defense of the Trotskyites. Work for a broader exposure of the connection between the Lithuanian

Trotskyites and the security services and their counterrevol[utionary] work, their treacherous activity during the strikes. We are still not sufficiently vigilant. This is facilitating the Trotskyites' penetration into the Communist Party of Lithuania and the Lithuanian Komsomol or at least to contact with our comrades and to conduct their counterrevol[utionary] work. Therefore liberalism toward the Trotskyites must never have a place in the ranks of our Party. Engage in a broader unmasking of the double-dealing devices of the Trotskyites, who are capable of various kinds of vile acts."[6]

The persistence—or, more accurately, the stubborn insistence—behind these directives blended with their hollow and bombastic pronouncements. What remained were calls to refute the "slander directed against Stalin, oppose this slander with a broad popularization of his gigantic revolutionary activity [and with] an explanation of his role as a leader of the international proletariat and the workers of the whole world." The ECCI was specifically warned to "avoid detailed statements containing the counterrevolutionary slander, stuffed with quotations, the propaganda of the Trotskyites, and also other kinds of fascist press." Instead, "it is necessary to give a principled answer and not to turn such fundamental questions of the Communist movement as the struggle against Trotskyism, defense of the USSR, [and the] attitude toward Stalin into sensationalist newspaper fraud and irresponsible journalism." In other words, the arguments put forward could only be taken from the materials sent out by the Comintern.[7]

Despite all of their hollowness, such exhortations produced some specific results. They exacerbated the split and the struggle among various left-wing factions in the European and North American working-class movement and slowed down or even undermined the potential for joint actions against fascism. In Spain, where in the second half of the 1930s the Communist Party had real political power, such orders led to the physical annihilation of those who were proclaimed Trotskyist agents of fascism.

The farcical nature of the trial, with the self-incrimination of the accused, evoked clear distrust in Western democratic circles. Attempts were made to find an eminent and respected figure who would take a pro-Soviet position. Lion Feuchtwanger, an internationally famous German-Jewish novelist and playwright known for his outspoken hostility to Nazism, was selected for this role. On 19 November Dimitrov received a communication from "Herfurt" (Willi Münzenberg) from Paris, stating that Feuchtwanger would soon be going to Moscow. He met with the writer on 18 December.[8]

Both Dimitrov's diary entries and the record of what Feuchtwanger said, taken down by a staff member of the Society for Cultural Ties with Foreign Countries who was assisting the writer during his trip, have been preserved. Dimitrov noted that Feuchtwanger and Maria Osten had met with him. The writer set out the doubts he shared with other left-wing intellectuals: "1. It is incomprehensible why the accused committed such crimes. 2. It is incomprehensible why all the accused are admitting everything, knowing that it will cost them their lives. 3. It is incomprehensible why, apart from the confessions of the acc[used], no sort of evidence has been produced. It is incomprehensible why such severe punishment is being applied to political opponents, when the Soviet regime is so powerful that it has nothing to fear from people sitting in prisons. The records of the trial are carelessly compiled, full of contradictions, unconvincing. The trial is conducted *ungeheur* [German: monstrously]."[9]

The staff member reported that "Dimitrov got very excited while talking about this subject, gave explanations for an hour and a half, but did not succeed in convincing him [Feuchtwanger]. Feuchtwanger told me that this trial was being viewed in a very hostile fashion abroad, and that no one would believe that fifteen ideological revolutionaries, who so many times had laid down their lives at the stake, participating in plots, all together suddenly admitted their guilt and voluntarily confessed." Nevertheless, the campaign to convince him continued.[10]

The responses to the Zinoviev trial had barely died down when the leadership of the Comintern informed the Communist parties of the upcoming trial of the so-called Parallel Anti-Soviet Trotskyist Center. In the light of the experience of the previous campaign, the Secretariat demanded "in the Communist press the widest possible convincing explanation of the defendants' confessions. It is necessary to organize a refutation of the arguments of the bourgeois, Social Democratic press, which will try to discredit the trial." The ECCI gave orders that the Politburo of each party should make one of its members responsible for conducting that work. Staff members of the apparatus of the Comintern who were abroad at the time were ordered to carefully follow the press of the Communist parties. Bohumír Šmeral, a veteran Czech Comintern operative, was assigned to see to it that this campaign was carried out by the press organs of the Communist parties in France, Britain, and Belgium.[11]

Each party was given specific explanations. A cipher communication sent to the Central Committee of the Polish Communist Party stated the following:

> In connection with the new Trotskyist trial we propose: first, independently of the assistance we are providing through materials and articles, given the communications difficulties, organize on your own the immediate translation and sending to the country materials from *Pravda, Rudé pravo* [Czechoslovak CP newspaper], *Humanité* [French CP newspaper]. Second, emphasize the treacherous, espionage-saboteur role of Trotskyism with the goal of the restoration of capitalism in the Soviet Union and link it to the struggle against the Polish Trotskyites. Provide broad information about the role of Radek, whom the Polish press will be especially protecting. Third, exert pressure on the legal leftist press through the broadest possible information about the trial and try to publish your own illegal bulletin in the country. Fourth, we ask that you systematically inform us by telegraph of how the various social strata and particularly those within the Party are reacting to the trial. Fifth, make use of the trial to detect Trotskyist and unstable elements in the Party for purposes of a further Party purge.[12]

Although Polish Communists hastened to comply, soon the Comintern disbanded that Polish party itself on the pretext that it had been infected by Trotskyites, provocateurs, and agents of Polish fascism.

The ECCI added that each Communist party should work to convince people that the trial was taking place not only in the interests of the USSR, but also for the working masses of the given country and that the Trotskyites were acting as agents of fascism and were preparing for war. The dispatch sent to the Communist Party of Greece stated: "Very soon there will be a resumption of radio broadcasts in Greek. The broadcasts of materials on the trials of the Trotskyites will be conducted daily. Take measures so that all the more people will hear them. Make use of the wealth of materials from the trial to once and for all expose the Trotskyist bands among the masses. Try to provide good information to the left bourgeois and intellectual circles going to the Popular Front. Make use of the testimony of the accused, to the effect that Trotsky gave Hitler a free hand for the conquest of Southeast Europe and the Balkans."[13]

Georgi Pyatakov was the first of the accused to be interrogated at this second show trial. In response to the prosecutor's question regarding his contacts with Trotsky, he stated that in December 1935 he had flown to Oslo from Berlin. There, Pyatakov claimed, Trotsky had told him of his negotiations with Hitler's deputy Rudolf Hess, demanded that the Trotskyist organization in the USSR use sabotage and terror to bring about a coup d'état to restore capitalism, and pushed for Trotskyist cooperation with foreign intelligence services.

Vyshinsky also interrogated Karl Radek about this meeting. The latter confirmed what Pyatakov had said. This "confession" by Pyatakov became one of the most vital elements of the trial.

Here, however, there was a repetition of something similar to the events of the first trial. At that event, one of the accused, Edward Holtzman, stated that in 1932 at the Bristol Hotel in Copenhagen he had met with Trotsky's son Lev Sedov, in accordance with the instructions he had received. A week after the end of the trial the Danish newspaper *Sozial Demokraten* published the information that a hotel with that name had been razed back in 1917 and did not exist at the time Holtzman stated. This time, too, the falsification of events through a previously prepared scenario for the trial came to light. The day after Pyatakov's "confession" regarding his conversation with Hess, the Norwegian newspaper *Aftenposten* published a report that at that time not a single German plane had landed at Heller Airport in Oslo. The entire propaganda machine of the Comintern was thus compromised.[14]

The Norwegian party leaders asked the leaders of the Comintern for instructions: "Pyatakov's declaration at the trial, that he had flown to Oslo on a German plane in December 1935, was disputed here. It is asserted that not a single German plane had then landed in Oslo. This is extremely important for us. Report on details of Pyatakov's visit to Oslo." After having read the dispatch, Dimitrov wrote, "Has this been answered? GD." The question related to Palmiro Togliatti (Ercoli), at the time in charge of the propaganda campaign concerning the trial. Dimitrov's secretary, Elena Walter, showed Ercoli the cipher message and wrote down his words: "Communication c[omrade] Ercoli. There will be no answer to this telegram, since they have already received instructions in connection with the trial. The views of the press there divided; part of the press confirms the fact regarding the airplane." In other words, it was impossible to debunk this falsification, and therefore all that remained was to pretend that nothing had occurred.[15]

Later the same tactic was employed when a new inquiry arrived. Julius Alpari, the editor of the Comintern magazine *Rundschau*, published in Paris, sent a cipher communication: "Exact details regarding . . . the flight of the airplane to Oslo are extremely important. But we cannot wait six months." Dimitrov's notes on the blank of the message, "Find out from c. Ercoli, what has been done? GD," reflect the confusion this communication had caused. And once again Walter responded with Togliatti's cynical answer: "Comrade Ercoli says that after the material already sent nothing more will be sent. Julius has been sent a visa and he must come here."[16]

The Comintern once again gave instructions regarding the publication in the Communist Party press of materials on the trial and the court records. On 29 January 1937 the Communist parties were sent a directive from the Secretariat of the ECCI: "Provide for the speedy publication of reports on the trial. The manuscripts are being sent from Moscow. Organize on site the publication of pamphlets in connection with the trial. See to it that these publications are widely distributed. Report on what is being published, in how many copies, and date of publication." In response, dispatches arrived from Communist parties around the world reporting on their propaganda justifying the purge trials.[17]

The leaders of the Communist parties and the publishers of the Comintern press were instructed to use only the official materials of the trial, and they did as they were told. But this was certainly not satisfactory to everyone, as shown by the letters sent to Moscow radio. A listener from London asked, "As a British lawyer, it is hard for me to understand why the accused, who know that if they are found guilty, they will be sentenced to death, so frenziedly accuse themselves in their testimony. Can you provide an explanation?" Similar questions were asked by a radio listener from St. Albans: "I would like to ask you to provide further information in answer to two questions concerning this trial: 1) Why is there a need to keep the accused in prison for many months, until they confess and before they are put on trial? 2) Knowing the fate that awaits them, why do all the accused confess so openly?" A listener from Derby asked a similar question: "We are all amazed as to why these accused do not attempt to defend themselves in any way whatever against the charges made against them, and also as to why do these people openly admit that their activity was counterrevolutionary?"[18]

How such questions resonated was also clear from several dispatches from the parties. The ECCI warned the Communist Party of Lithuania:

> The trial now underway of Pyatakov, Radek, and other Trotskyist bandits, who became fascists and agents of the Gestapo, [confirms that they] were attempting to undermine the military might of the USSR, to accelerate a military attack on the USSR, aided foreign aggressors in seizing territory of the USSR, worked for the overthrow of Sov[iet] po[wer] and the restoration of capitalism. In connection with the trial there is a need to still more widely expose the counterrev[olutionary] activity of the Trotskyites so as to evoke the total contempt of the workers toward them. Increase vigilance and observe how members of

> the Party are reacting to the trial in order to make it easier to identify enemies who have infiltrated the Party. Inform us of the attitude of Party members and the workers toward the trial.[19]

The Lithuanian party's answer reflected the difficulty Communists around the world were having in promoting the Comintern's propaganda line:

> The struggle against Trotskyites, especially after the trials started, has been especially accentuated in the press and in general during the whole six-month period. Yet the issue of the Trotskyites has not been discussed in all the organizations. The explanatory work has also been weak among the non-Party members. Our comrades in the factories frequently lacked courage to repulse the Trotskyist slander. [The effort to draw] concrete lessons is even worse. In Kovno, only Geraite [unknown] has been expelled, and that was done on the sly. Although there is an understanding among Party members that the Trotskyites and rotten liberals cannot be Party members, one notes doubts [among comrades] about how the Trotskyites managed to sink to fascism and why they confessed at the trial the way they did.[20]

A few days later a new communication hinted at some dissension:

> It looks as though not everyone has understood clearly enough that the Trotskyites qualify as agents-provocateurs and as the agents of the fascist *okhranka* [secret police]. We are also emphasizing [the need] to review dubious elements and to unmask the Trotskyist elements that no doubt exist among them. In Pantsy (Kovno workers' suburb), two Party members had earlier defected to the Trotskyites. Wherever we maintain our connections, there is no sympathy toward them, though some sharpness toward them is sensed not everywhere. We think that the Kovno organization is not exposing all those places where the Trotskyites are active. Those expelled from the Party are being driven out of the non-Party organizations.[21]

On the same day a new message arrived: "In the circles of the Jewish and Lithuanian intelligentsia there is serious disbelief that the Trotskyites were able to do [what they were accused of] in the Soviet Union and that they confessed. We are pressuring the local [Party] organizations to consider the struggle against the Trotskyites not as a short campaign but as systematic work." Among the messages of the Communist parties to the Comintern such candid dispatches were rare. More often there were misleading claims of propaganda success or excuse-making references to the insidious work of Social Democratic leaders in undermining the acceptance of Moscow's views on the trials.[22]

Meanwhile, the Comintern had not given up on Lion Feuchtwanger. Stalin himself met with Feuchtwanger on 8 January 1937, and this conversation "helped" Feuchtwanger look at the trials from a different point of view. On 2 February Dimitrov again met with Feuchtwanger. At this meeting the writer stated that the second trial that he attended had eliminated his earlier doubts regarding the guilt of the accused. He continued, however, to have some critical views. Following this conversation Dimitrov wrote down Feuchtwanger's comments:

> On the trial: 1. Diversionary actions, espionage, terror—proved. 2. Also proved: that Trotsky inspired and directed. 3. Trotsky's agreement with Hess and the Japanese is based only on the confessions of the defendants.—No evidence whatsoever! 4. The fact that Radek and [Grigori] Sokolnikov were not sentenced to be shot will be exploited abroad as evidence that they furnished such testimony deliberately in order to save their lives. 5. The abuse hurled at the defendants leaves a disturbing impression. They are enemies, deserving of destruction. But they did not act out of personal interest, and they should not have called them *Schüften* [German: scoundrels], *Feiglinge* [cowards], *Reptilian* [reptiles], etc. 6. Why such a great fuss over the trial. It is incomprehensible. An atmosphere has been created of extreme unrest among the population, mutual suspicion, denunciations, and so forth. Trotskyism has been killed—why such a campaign?[23]

Dimitrov's text indicated that Feuchtwanger also said he would write a pamphlet "with factual material about the achievements in the USSR, without omitting the shortcomings." In the book *Moscow, 1937*, Feuchtwanger acknowledged the existence of some shortcomings in the USSR, such as minor inconveniences that complicated daily life. But its main thrust was his effort to convince readers that the trials had fully proved the guilt of the accused. As for the lack of documented evidence at the trial, he asserted, as though voicing the view of the Soviet people, apparently the materials establishing guilt had been checked out during the investigation and presented to the accused, and at the trial "confirmation of their admissions of guilt was sufficient." Feuchtwanger's book in fact was in essence an apologia for Stalin and his policy.[24]

As it had done following the first trial, on 5 February the ECCI Presidium adopted a decree, "Results of the Trial of the Trotskyites," which asserted that the trial had taken place "in compliance with all possible guarantees of objectivity." It strongly condemned the position of the Social Democratic International, which had spoken out against the brutally harsh and unjust sentence: "Anyone who is in solidarity with Trotsky, who undertakes to protect the Trotskyites, becomes an ally of the darkest forces of reaction, an accomplice of fascism in its work directed against freedom, peace, and the independence of all peoples." The Comintern set the eradication of Trotskyism as the highest priority for the parties.[25]

On 5–7 February the Secretariat sent to the Communist parties a directive, written by Togliatti and initialed by Dimitrov, regarding measures to be taken in connection with the conclusion of the trial:

> Basing on results of trial, mobilize Party, working-class, democratic forces for entire smashing of Trotskyism, agency of German fascism, Japan militarism, most vile enemy of Soviet Union, fighter for restoration of capitalism, provocateur of war, enemy of liberty and independence of nations. Give concrete picture of counterrevolutionary activities of Trotskyism in capitalist countries, of his fight against United Front, for the purpose of splitting workers' movement in interest of fascism especially in France, Spain, in your country. During campaign demand of workers' organizations, popular masses the expulsion of Trotsky from Mexico and to subject himself to a proletarian Soviet tribunal. [Use] pressure of masses effect, that organizations and persons influenced by Trotskyism denounce solidarity with Trotsky and his criminal activities. Organize meeting with reports on trial by comrades who [are] present at trial. Popularize in widest way resolution of Presidium on results of trial, reports of trial, and pamphlets on trial. More exact instruction follows.[26]

Stalin, however, called the Presidium decree "trifling," declaring that "a letter to the Parties would be better." He explained the spirit that should dominate the campaign and the type of letter to be sent, saying to Dimitrov, "All of you there in the Comintern are playing right into the enemy's hands." In essence, Stalin himself played the role of the orchestra conductor of the campaign conducted by the Comintern.[27]

Stalin's objection was quickly met. On 17 February Dimitrov sent him a copy of a proposed letter to the Communist parties that contained a request that Stalin "give comments and instructions." Quotations from the defendants were used to prove that they "had the full right to dispute, before the entire world, the accusations resulting from the preliminary investigation. Given the indisputable evidence, however, all of the defendants, many of whom for months had stubbornly denied the charges, could not disavow their crimes against Soviet power, the country and the people." A large excerpt from Pyatakov's testimony regarding his Oslo meeting with Hess was cited. All kinds of grounds were put forward regarding the notion of the

Trotskyist plans to have the fascist countries go to war against the USSR, achieve its defeat, and restore the power of the bourgeoisie. Stalin's other demand, to have these people falsely portrayed as having been opponents of Lenin, was also scrupulously fulfilled.[28]

On 5 April 1937 the Comintern Presidium issued another decree ordering additional vigor on the campaign against Trotskyism, stating: "The ECCI Presidium notes that many workers of the Communist Parties of capitalist countries, as well as the workers of the Comintern, have failed to demonstrate proper vigilance toward Trotskyism and did not in a timely manner give warning regarding the merger of Trotskyism with fascism. . . . They also failed to notice in a timely manner that the capitalist world and first and foremost the fascist states are adopting new techniques in the struggle against the USSR and the international working-class movement, in particular in building their espionage network of provocateurs by supplementing it with Trotskyist personnel."[29] In orienting the Communist parties toward a "purge of Party organizations of double-dealer Trotskyist elements," the ECCI was also offering an apologia for repression in the USSR. Stalin, however, wanted more and told Dimitrov, "The [ECCI] Secretariat resolution has become obsolete. That's what you get when you have people sitting in offices concocting things! 'Using all available means, intensify the struggle against Trotskyites!' [in the resolution]. That is not enough. Trotskyites must be hunted down, shot, destroyed. These are international provocateurs, fascism's most vicious agents."[30]

For the Comintern this meant participating in the reprisals against those who were not welcome to the regime, including officials of foreign Communist parties. Foremost among these victims were the leaders and officials of the Polish Communist Party. The NKVD had created a fictitious narrative about the "contamination" of the Polish Communist Party by Polish counterintelligence and Józef Piłsudski's Polish Military Organization (POW). (The real POW had been created by Piłsudski as a covert Polish military intelligence agency in 1914 to free Poland from its three-way division among the German, Russian, and Austro-Hungarian empires. It had been disbanded in 1921 after the creation of an independent Polish state and lived on only in the imagination of the NKVD. Piłsudski was a particular bête noir to the Soviets due to his having commanded the Polish forces that defeated the Bolshevik Red Army in the 1920 Battle of Warsaw, thereby turning back not only its invasion of Poland, but also plans to drive into Germany.)[31]

The Communist Party was illegal in Poland at the time, and the Politburo of the Polish Communist Party operated in exile in Paris. On

21 May 1937 the Comintern summoned Julian Leński, general secretary of the Polish Communist Party, from Paris: "To resolve a number of urgent issues we request you to come for a short time. Warn Prague that their centers and addresses are collapsed." On 16 June the summons was repeated: "Urgent, tell Leński that visas have been sent for him and his wife." The application to NKVD head Nikolai Yezhov for Leński's entry to the USSR using a passport in the name of Stanislav Adamen stated, "Urgently summoned by the ECCI Secretariat."[32]

Dimitrov wrote in his diary on 17 June: "Leński has arrived. Rilski [Rylski], Skulski, and Próchniak have also been summoned." (Ignacy Rylski [the pseudonym of Jan Lubienecki] was a Polish Communist and Comintern staffer, Stefan Skulski represented the Polish party to the ECCI, and Edward Próchniak was a senior Polish Communist and member of the ECCI.) A coded dispatch was sent to Paris from Robert (Leński's pseudonym): "Sewer [Próchniak's pseudonym] must come for the meeting." Instructions were also sent to Prague: "For now stop sending people. Stefan [Skulski] and Adam [Rylski] must come immediately. Send data for the visa." What occurred next is clear from Dimitrov's notes: "20.6.37. L[eński] at Yezhov's." "21.6.37. [Henryk] Walecki, too." (Henryk Walecki, a senior figure in the Polish CP in the early 1920s, had joined the Comintern's staff in 1925 and in 1937 was a member of the International Control Commission (ICC) overseeing Comintern disciplinary matters.) On 7 July "Próchniak arrived—is with Yez[hov]." "At" or "with" Yezhov meant arrested and in the hands of the NKVD.[33]

Though Leński had been arrested, his name was used to summon other Polish party leaders. On 8 July a coded dispatch initialed by Moskvin asked: "Sewer [Próchniak] has arrived. When is Stefan [Skulski] leaving? Robert [Leński]." On 23 July an inquiry, now in Stefan's name, was sent to Paris: "Why has Adam [Rylski] not left yet?"[34]

In another step toward destroying the Polish Communist Party, Jan Tadek, a member of Leński's political apparatus in Paris, was sent a message summoning two more Polish leaders, Poraj and Teodor, to Moscow, along with instructions regarding the need to "reduce all expenditures for all of the [Polish CP] apparatus of the region [Poland] and abroad by half."[35] Poraj was the pseudonym of Helena Jezierska (real name Romana Wolf), a member of the Bolshevik Party from 1917, member of the Polish CP from 1924, and a candidate member of the Central Committee of the Polish CP from 1932 to 1937. Teodor was Antoni Lipski, a member of the Polish CP from 1921 and a senior figure in its leadership in the 1930s. On 9 August a coded message to Paris stated, "To Tadek. Because the Bureau [Polish CP leadership] is here [in Moscow], temporarily cease the publication *Przegląd* [theoretical journal of the Polish Communist Party]. We confirm Adam's arrival. We repeat that Teodor must be summoned from the region [Poland]."[36]

Similar summonses directed at Polish Communists and supposedly signed by Robert (Leński) were sent to Spain calling for Polish Communists fighting for the Spanish Republic to go to Moscow. Polish Communist Kazimierz Cichowski headed the Personnel Department for the International Brigades staff, while another Pole, Gustav Rwal, was the political commissar of one of the International Brigades. Dimitrov sent a coded message to the representative of the Comintern in Spain: "We are requesting you urgently to send Cichowski here for a report on his work." Another ordered: "Send the representative of the Polish Party Rwal here. Send the name in the passport for the visa." On 28 July, "Kautsky," the pseudonym of one of the ECCI representatives in Spain, Ivan Stepanov, informed "Manu" (Dmitry Manuilsky, a trusted Stalinist who supervised Comintern cadre after 1935) in Moscow: "Today Cichowski departed. He will be waiting for the visa in Paris. He is traveling on a Czech passport under the name Kliment Brabak." Both men arrived in Moscow, where they met the same fate as their arrested countrymen.[37]

These Polish Communists were not naïve. They knew that the Comintern was in turmoil and many of their fellow Poles were under arrest. Marcin Grżegorżewski (pseudonym of Franciszek Grżelszak), a member of the International Control Commission, wrote to Moskvin about some of their recent private conversations:

> On 13 August of th[is] y[ear] com. Cichowski, who had just returned from a business trip, came to the [Polish CP] mission. In the conversation, at which com. Bielewski was present, Cichowski said that he had been passing through Paris, where he met at Fiedler's apartment [Polish Communist living in Paris] with Com. Karłowski. . . . Karłowski told Cichowski that Leński, Próchniak, Rylski, and Skulski had left for the Comintern. Later on in the conversation Cichowski said that at the Comintern he had learned of Leński's arrest. To my question as to who in the Comintern had told him that, he replied that he had spoken to com. Pieck [who] had referred to Leński's arrest while talking with him about several German questions. Later on in the conversation it turned out that Cichowski already knew about the search carried out at Rylski's wife's place and, knowing that Rylski had left, it was noticeable that he had the impression that Rylski had been arrested. Knowing

> how talkative Cichowski is, com. Bielewski and I advised him not to talk to anyone about these questions. In addition, I am reporting that Cichowski was on very friendly terms with Rylski, Próchniak, Morkowski, and others.[38]

This denunciation saved neither Bielewski (real name Jan Paszyn, a member of the Politburo of the Polish party CC and a candidate member of the ECCI) nor Grżegorżewski and was not decisive for Cichowski's arrest. The conversational references to the arrests of comrades were themselves cause for suspicion, and this in turn gave rise to denunciations and mutual accusations

By the fall of 1937 the Polish Communist Party had been deprived of its leadership. Dimitrov was shown the "materials" of the investigation. Nine leading officials of the Polish CP, including Leński, Rylski, Skulski, and Walecki "confirmed" that they had infiltrated the party in order to "neutralize" it and subject it to control by Piłsudski's POW. These "testimonies" spoke of the existence of an espionage organization within the Comintern.[39]

The self-slander of those arrested and the monstrously absurd nature of their admissions strongly suggested that these "testimonies" were extorted from them under torture. They also determined the fate of the Polish Communist Party, which they had headed. On 23 November 1937 Dimitrov, Manuilsky, Otto Kuusinen (Finish Communist), Moskvin, and Wilhelm Pieck (German Communist) prepared a draft decree of the ECCI on the dissolution of the Polish Communist Party. On 28 November Dimitrov sent it to Stalin. In proposing publication, he asked "regarding this issue, whether this announcement will be expedient before the investigation of the former Polish Party leaders under arrest is completed, or should we wait longer?" The answer was brief: "The dissolution is about two years late. It is necessary to dissolve [the Party], but in my opinion, [this] should not be published in the press."[40]

Not only was the Polish Communist Party eliminated, so too were its various organizations and affiliates disbanded. The actual decree dissolving the Polish Communist Party was signed by Dimitrov, Manuilsky, Moskvin, Kuusinen, Wilhelm Florin (ECCI and ICC member), and Togliatti much later, only on 16 August 1938. Of the Polish Communist leaders noted above, Leński, Rylski, Skulski, Próchniak, Walecki, Tadek, Jezierska, Cichowski, Rwal, Bielewski, and Lipski were shot.[41]

The Comintern also played a supporting role in the mass arrests of the ethnic Poles living in the USSR in 1937–1938 on the orders of the

Politburo of the CC of the VKP(b). One study of the NKVD's "Polish Operation" documented the arrest of 143,810 persons, the execution of 111,091 of these, and the sentencing of another 28,744 to the Gulag labor camps.[42]

While Polish Communists suffered the most, other parties lost leaders and cadre to Stalin's terror as well. For example, on 13 July 1937 Dimitrov summoned the leader of the Yugoslav Communist Party, Milan Gorkić (real name Josip Čižinski), from Paris. The directive stated that he "must come here immediately for several days." Shortly after his arrival Gorkić found himself in the NKVD's cells at the Lubyanka and was executed on 1 November. Also particularly hard hit were foreign Communists living in exile in the USSR to avoid repression in their native countries. No comprehensive accounting has been made, but likely thousands went to the Gulag labor camps and a significant portion died, either executed or perishing from overwork and maltreatment in the camps. A special case was the arrest and execution of nearly a thousand Finnish Americans and Finnish Canadians, largely Communists, who had immigrated to the Soviet Union in response to a Soviet-sponsored recruiting campaign in the early 1930s.[43]

By creating the image of the USSR as a state in which power belonged to the working people and served its interests and by exalting Stalin in every possible way as "the continuer of the work of Marx-Lenin, the genial organizer of the victory of socialism in the USSR, the beloved leader of the international proletariat,"[44] the Comintern and its sections on the international stage were serving as the ideological megaphones of the Stalinist regime. In regard to Stalin's Great Terror, the Comintern not only worked through the Communist parties to provide a defense and justification for the Moscow trials, but also enticed leading foreign Communists to come to Moscow so they could be arrested and executed by the NKVD, thus directly participating in the bloodiest phases of that campaign.

CHAPTER SEVEN

The Comintern and the Chinese Communist Party: Divergent Priorities

Ciphered correspondence between the Comintern and the Communist Party of China (CPCh) in the late 1930s and early 1940s shows a considerable divergence between the Comintern's priorities and those of Mao Zedong and the CPCh. From the mid-1930s onward the Comintern, reflecting Stalin's priorities, emphasized the creation of an anti-Japanese National Front in China. Direct intervention by Japan in China was looming on the horizon, and in Stalin's eyes, such intervention was linked to key foreign policy interests of the USSR. Japan and Tsarist Russia had clashed in the past in Korea and Manchuria, and Stalin was well aware that the rich natural resources of Soviet Siberia were a possible target for the aggressive tendencies of resource-poor Japan. While promoting cooperation with the Chinese government leadership through diplomatic channels, Stalin also used the Comintern to influence the CPCh.[1]

After the overthrow of the Qing imperial dynasty in 1911 and the founding of the Republic of China, nearly two decades of instability and civil war followed. But by the early 1930s the Chinese Nationalist Party, the Kuomintang (KMT), headed by Chiang Kai-shek, had established an uneasy supremacy in most of China. The CPCh, however, had established itself as a civil and military power in a large territory in northern China, called the Special Region, headquartered at Yunan, where it resisted KMT control.

After the direct incursion of Japanese armed forces into China in 1937, it was in the USSR's interest that the KMT and the CPCh put aside their internal rivalry in order to confront the Japanese threat. Thwarting the Japanese invasion would keep the Japanese away from

Soviet territory north of China and tie down Japanese troops that might otherwise threaten Soviet Siberia.

In July 1937 a United Front of the CPCh and the KMT was created with the assistance of the Comintern. The status of the CPCh-dominated Special Region was officially recognized by Chiang Kai-shek's Nationalist government, and the Chinese Communist military forces were renamed the Fourth and Eighth National-Revolutionary Armies. On 11 November Stalin received Dimitrov and the representatives of the CPCh, Wang Ming, Kong Sing, and Wang Jiaxiang. (Jiaxiang had worked in the ECCI apparatus under the pseudonyms of Zheng Li and Communard.) Directives were prepared for the active participation of the Communist Party in the anti-Japanese war. "How the Chinese are to fight with the external enemy—that is the decisive issue," Stalin remarked. "When that is over, then the question will arise of how they are to fight among themselves!" He promised to assist the CPCh with weapons and technology.[2]

After his arrival in China at the end of December, Wang Ming informed the Politburo of the CC of the CPCh of the instructions he had received. On 4 January 1938 Dimitrov forwarded to Stalin a telegram from the CPCh: "The instructions of the ECCI were unanimously adopted at a meeting. The results and lessons learned from conducting the United Front were analyzed and several tendencies [in] practical work were corrected."[3] This message indicated that the CPCh was claiming to change its activities in order to promote specific forms of cooperation with the Kuomintang.

Requests for financial assistance were a recurring theme in the messages from China. On 10 January 1938 Dimitrov reported to Stalin on a telegram from the CPCh that stated: "[At] the present time we are experiencing severe financial difficulties. All of our efforts to find a solution using our own means can only partially resolve the question. We are requesting that as soon as possible the promised funds be sent to Fang Lin, and we have already sent our employee to Urumchi for that purpose."[4] Dimitrov proposed that the promised aid be rendered in separate installments. Stalin agreed to the allocation of $500,000 ($8,119,234 in 2012 values). Dimitrov later continued to forward Stalin information from China, in particular regarding the relationship between the CPCh and the KMT, the military situation, the state of the Eighth and Fourth Armies, the activity of the CPCh, and the requests of its leadership.

However, in their communications, the leaders of the CPCh constantly tried to demonstrate to the Comintern that the KMT and Chiang

Kai-shek were not engaged in the war with Japan but rather with battling the CPCh and its armed forces. Chiang Kai-shek was, the CPCh stated, striving for some form of accommodation with the invading Japanese so as to then be free to crush the Communists. It provided information regarding armed clashes involving the KMT troops and the Eighth and Fourth Armies. On 5 June 1939 Manuilsky sent Stalin a telegram from the CPCh on the tense relationship between it and the KMT. The telegram stated that the Plenum of the Central Executive Committee of the KMT had adopted a secret decision to fight the Communist danger through the liquidation of the Communist Party. There was also mention of armed clashes. "Regarding the Special Region, the Kuomintang decided to encircle it, isolate it from the outside and blow it up from the inside, to liquidate this region as a territorial base of the 8th Army."[5]

Along with military and financial questions, the correspondence also raised problems of an ideological nature. Pursuing one of Stalin's priorities, on 15 July 1939 Dimitrov sent a dispatch to the CC of the CPCh with an inquiry as to how the *Short Course of the History of the VKP(b)* was being disseminated. The book had been translated into Chinese, and ten thousand copies had been sent to China. "The distribution and study of this book marks a turning point and is a powerful tool in raising the ideological level of the Party, and an extremely forceful way of ensuring the penetration of ideas of Marxism-Leninism into the largest possible numbers of the masses," the dispatch stressed. "The dissemination of this book in the fraternal Parties has been extremely successful."[6]

In September Zhou Enlai, a Chinese Politburo member, flew to Moscow for medical treatment. He brought with him three codes captured by the Eighth Army during the hostilities with the Japanese. In a letter to Lavrenty Beria, a member of the Politburo of the VKP[b] and the people's commissar for internal affairs, Dimitrov reported, "On the assumption that these codes may prove of interest to You, I am sending them to You annexed to this letter." Dimitrov informed Stalin that the Presidium of the ECCI had listened to and discussed Zhou Enlai's report. According to Dimitrov, the leadership of the CPCh "needs advice on two major issues: 1) What the line of the Communist Party should be and how it should try to prevent the capitulation of the ruling circles in China to the Japanese imperialists. 2) What the line of the Communist Party should be and what measures it should take to further the struggle under the present circumstances, in particular considering the policy pursued by the leading circles of the Kuomintang of persecuting the Communist Party and liquidating the Special Region and the 8th Army." The letter ended with a request for advice and instructions. Dimitrov asked Stalin several times to receive Zhou Enlai, but Stalin refused to do so on the pretext that he was busy. He also stated to Dimitrov that the ECCI should take an independent decision on the Chinese question and promised to provide $300,000 to aid the CPCh, short of the $350,000 requested by the Comintern.[7]

The document adopted by the ECCI Presidium, "Fundamental Political Directions of the Communist Party of China, Intended for the Forthcoming Party Congress," noted that the war against the Japanese in China, called the National Liberation War, was at a critical turning point. The central objective of the CPCh, stated the document, was "the mobilization of millions of Chinese people to overcome the danger of capitulation." The document noted the need to overcome the friction with the KMT. The CPCh was instructed that it must implement the 1937 agreement with the KMT: "Recognizing the immutable authority of the National government and its head, Chiang Kai-shek, in the continuation of the war against Japanese imperialism and cooperating as closely as possible with all supporters of resistance to Japanese aggression, the Communist Party of China will make all efforts to establish fraternal relations with the troops of the Kuomintang in the struggle for the common cause of national liberation." All demands of a political, economic, and social nature were to be subordinated to the primary objective—organizing a rebuff to the Japanese imperialists and achieving victory in the National Liberation War. In a telegram to the CC of the CPCh, Dimitrov wrote: "Zhou Enlai is informing you personally about everything we discussed and have agreed on regarding Chinese matters. All of this must be given serious consideration, and final decisions must be take completely independently. In case of disagreement with us on some issues, we request that you immediately inform and provide explanations." As it turned out, there was a great deal of explaining to do.[8]

The implementation of these instructions broke down primarily because the CPCh and the KMT did not trust each other, and in the final analysis each side was attempting to liquidate the other. Mao Zedong was doggedly pursuing a policy of exacerbating the struggle with the KMT. Yet his messages to the ECCI attempted to portray Chiang Kai-shek as the culprit in the inevitable split in the United Front. On 12 November a telegram was received from Mao regarding Chiang's intention to capitulate to the Japanese, his demand for the withdrawal of Communist military units from central China, and preparations for carrying out a punitive expedition against the Communist Fourth and Eighth Armies. The message stated that to undermine Chiang's plan there was a need "for defense purposes to mount a counteroffensive against him, rout his punitive troops and fortified zones." Prior to taking a final decision, however, the leadership of the CPCh requested appropriate instructions. Dimitrov ordered copies of the telegram sent to Stalin, Molotov, and Semyon Timoshenko (Soviet defense commissar) and responded with a telegram to Mao: "In view of the extraordinary complexity of the question, we will be able to provide an answer only after study of a number of important elements. You should be prepared, but we request that you wait in regard to a final decision."[9]

In early November Moscow received a copy of a secret directive of the CC of the CPCh. It stated the primary objective of the CPCh in ways that differed from the ECCI Presidium's formulation: "The central task of our Party at this crucial moment must be the struggle against capitulation and civil war. The main thrust of our struggle, which in the past used to be focused on the hard-liners, must now be aimed against the pro-Japanese elements and the instigators of civil war." This meant that the main thrust was to be against the KMT, not the Japanese. Copies of this document were sent to Stalin, Molotov, Timoshenko, and Andrei Zhdanov (a member of the Politburo of the VKP[b] and a secretary of its Central Committee).[10]

On 22 November Dimitrov met with Timoshenko, Kyrill Meretskov (chief of the Red Army General Staff), and Fillip Golikov (chief of military intelligence) to discuss China's military situation. The draft response to the CPCh, prepared by Dimitrov, disputed the view that Chiang Kai-shek intended to capitulate to Japan. It was proposed to the CPCh "to follow a policy [that allows you] to gain time, to maneuver, and to bargain with Chiang Kai-shek in every possible way over the evacuation of your troops from central China and from Shandong Province. It is important to gain as much time as possible. It is essential that you do not initiate military action against the expeditionary forces and do not give Chiang Kai-shek an opportunity to portray you to the Chinese people as the violators of the unity of the anti-Japanese struggle and to use your actions to justify his attempts to sign a compromise peace with the Japanese." If Chiang Kai-shek's troops attacked the Communist armies, instructions were to strike at the attacking troops as hard as possible. Dimitrov, who sent the draft response to Stalin, asked for his views as soon as possible because "our Chinese comrades, being in a very difficult position, may undertake some action without thorough reflection." On 26 November Dimitrov's answer was sent to Mao Zedong.[11]

The leadership of the CPCh continued to send messages that constantly referred to preparations for an attack on the CPCh by KMT forces. "In China Chiang Kai-shek is now actively organizing the United Front to fight against the Chinese Communist Party, and its backbone is the bloc made up of Chiang Kai-shek and the Guangxi group," wrote Mao in a telegram of 30 November. "They are attracting intermediate elements and are engaged in a broad publishing campaign regarding the 'crimes' of our Party, thus attempting to paralyze us. At the same time some 500,000 troops have been moved, and 200,000 of them are deployed close to the border area. In central China some 300,000 are ready to exert pressure on us. This is, in fact, a situation exposing us to a dual thrust from Japan and Chiang Kai-shek."[12] As he had done with many previous telegrams, Dimitrov forwarded this one to Stalin and Timoshenko. (The "Guangxi group," sometimes called the "Guangxi clique," referred to a faction of Chinese Nationalist generals who had opposed Chiang Kai-shek and maintained an independent army but who had reached a unity agreement with the KMT to oppose the Japanese invasion.)

At this time Dimitrov's correspondence with Mao Zedong was discussing the organization of the transportation of Soviet weapons to the Communist-controlled Special Region. This was an issue of concern because territories not under the control of the CPCh lay between the border of the Soviet-controlled Mongolian People's Republic and the Communist Special Region. On 27 November in a cipher cable entitled "Mao Zedong—Personal," Dimitrov wrote, "If you could secure the entire road between our territory and the Mongolian People's Republic, we could send you significantly more weapons using that route. There is a need urgently to deal with this question; report to us on your views and concrete proposals." Mao Zedong's answer proposed several other possibilities for sending the weapons, including through special cavalry detachments that could be sent to the border. Dimitrov ordered that Mao's telegram be forwarded to Stalin and Timoshenko, with whom he discussed the question of assistance in sending weapons to the Eighth Army. In a letter to Stalin of 26 December he explained that this cipher cable was an answer to his inquiry regarding "the state of the road between Yunan [administrative center of the Special Region] and the Mongolian Republic and the possibility for the Chinese comrades to reliably provide for the delivery of this material assistance, if this were later to prove necessary and politically possible." Dimitrov requested Stalin's instructions as to whether it was necessary for the "Chinese comrades" to work on securing such a route and which option was preferable. Subsequently an answer was sent to Mao Zedong: "The options you have proposed are under study. This requires a certain amount of time. You must maintain the strictest secrecy regarding the entire question. Dimitrov." From then on this question did not again arise in Dimitrov's correspondence with Mao Zedong.[13]

On 18 January 1941 Mao Zedong reported on an armed clash of the Communist Fourth Army with the troops of Chiang Kai-shek and capture of the Fourth Army's commander, Ye Ting. In a letter to Stalin, Dimitrov expressed the view that "Chiang Kai-shek evidently considers the present moment ripe for a general blow against the Chinese Comm[unist] Party, and therefore his generals have viciously attacked and routed the Fourth Army and are undertaking further aggressive measures against the Eighth Army and the Special Region." The CPCh could respond to this attack, and then, inevitably, a major fratricidal war would break out. In that connection Dimitrov proposed exerting Soviet pressure on Chiang Kai-shek, as well as a campaign of protest "not to allow the unleashing of internecine war and a schism in the anti-Japanese United Front, not to allow the Japanese to conquer China 'by the hands of the Chinese themselves.' "[14]

A message came from China that Chiang Kai-shek had requested that the conflict be considered as a local incident that should not impact on the relations between the central government and the CPCh. He gave assurances that the commander of the Fourth Army would be set free. On 21 January Dimitrov discussed the Chinese issues with Stalin. Stalin called Ye Ting an undisciplined partisan and said it was necessary to see whether he had provided a pretext for the incident. Dimitrov advised Mao Zedong to do everything possible to avoid civil war and to reconsider his position since a break with Chiang Kai-shek was not inevitable. Dimitrov included the text of the telegram in a 6 February letter to Stalin, with a request for a meeting to obtain "directives regarding any further urgent advice to give to the CC of the Chinese Communist Party."[15]

On the night of 12 February Stalin aide Alexander Poskrebyshev phoned Dimitrov, saying that "instructions for the Chinese comrades could be issued in the spirit of my proposals, which St[alin] considers correct." Dimitrov had, in fact, earlier sent this telegram on 5 February. Mao answered that he agreed with the instructions he had received, but he remarked that "We intend to conduct an uncompromising policy toward Chiang Kai-shek, or else we may lose." Even more significant was his statement that "Never before have we had such a mass of people on our side. Chiang Kai-shek has already found himself in isolation. Two to three months from now, when we create better conditions [for ourselves] it will be possible to close this issue." Having given instructions to send this telegram to the Soviet leadership, Dimitrov added a note stating that this was an answer to his message, and he once again cited the text of his cipher cable of 5 February. In so doing, he apparently set down his position, foreseeing inevitable future conflicts between Chiang Kai-shek and the CPCh. Later, too, Dimitrov sent the same addressees the messages he was receiving on the consequences of the January conflict and the emergence of new conflicts. In its messages to Mao Zedong, the Comintern persistently emphasized a policy of coordination of actions between the KMT and the CPCh in military operations against the Japanese troops.[16]

On 22 June 1941 the ECCI sent a telegram to the CPCh regarding Germany's attack on the USSR. In its response, the CC of the CPCh declared its full agreement with the instructions of the ECCI and that it would "vigorously implement them." The instructions it issued stated: "The tasks of our Party are: 1. To resolutely insist on the continuation of the anti-Japanese National United Front. To resolutely insist on cooperation with the Kuomintang to drive the fascist Japanese imperialists from Chinese soil. 2. To conduct a resolute struggle against any anti-Soviet, anti-Communist activities on behalf of the reactionary elements from among the large bourgeoisie. 3. In foreign policy, to contact all the public figures in England and America who are struggling against the German-Italian-Japanese fascist enthrallers to struggle against the common enemy." Dimitrov sent these documents to Stalin, Molotov, Zhdanov, Voroshilov, Timoshenko, and Beria.[17]

On 2 July Dimitrov requested financial assistance for the CPCh from Molotov and Georgi Malenkov (a CPSU Central Committee secretary). The next day he was informed that his proposal had been approved and that $1 million ($15,532,926 in 2012 values) had been allocated to the CPCh. This was a major increase over the prior allocation and explicable by the perilous war situation the USSR faced in the latter half of 1941. After the Red Army's enormous loses in the early days of the war and with the Wehrmacht driving toward Moscow, nothing would be more perilous to the USSR's survival than a Japanese decision to attack the USSR by striking north into Siberia. On 9 July Dimitrov sent the CC of the CPCh the general directive of the ECCI regarding the expansion of the campaign in support of the Soviet Union. On 18 July a response came from that CC on preparations for destroying the communications network in northern China in order to block the movements of Japanese troops and to expand the partisan war in their rear. It also stated that human and material resources were exhausted and that there was a paucity of ammunition and weapons. "If we receive reinforcements of ammunition, machine guns, tools, and explosive ordinances, then the effectiveness of our actions will be significantly enhanced." Dimitrov sent Stalin and Molotov this message with a request to provide "directive regarding the answer to give to the Chinese comrades, in particular, whether they can count on a certain amount of ammunition to step up broader operations against a possible attack by Japan against the USSR." Molotov replied that there was agreement regarding the line of conduct of the CC of the CPCh but not to make promises regarding ammunition. The answer reflected his caution.[18]

On 25 July Dimitrov forwarded to the Soviet leaders the political information the CPCh leadership had sent to the local party organizations. It noted that some elements of the KMT were eager for a Japanese-Soviet war, reckoning that this would decrease the pressure from Japan on China. Mao Zedong's telegram placed particular emphasis on this argument regarding the anti-Soviet orientation of the KMT: "Pro-Japanese and pro-German elements, the organs of the special service and of the Party organization of the Kuomintang consider that the USSR is certain to be defeated, Germany will unquestionably win, and Japan will definitely attack the USSR; they are therefore preparing anti-Communist public opinion in advance, so that once there is a clash between Japan and the USSR a military offensive against us will begin immediately and liquidate our Party on an all-Chinese scale." This was how Mao Zedong explained the reasons for the new deterioration of relations between the CPCh and the KMT. He wrote that in the future the CPCh would rebuff any "attack on us by the Kuomintang." Dimitrov made a note on this document that he sent to the Soviet leadership: "This telegram of c. Mao Zedong is an answer to the following question of c. Dimitrov of 20 July: 'Inform us immediately as to the basis for the reports from Chungking on new clashes between your troops and the troops of the central government and what measures you are taking to counter the possible aggravation of your relations with the Chinese government.' "[19]

The telegrams that followed from Mao contained statements on preparations by the KMT for a strike at the CPCh. They also spoke to the urgent need for funds. Dimitrov immediately forwarded these telegrams to the Soviet leadership. He also wanted the CPCh to assist Soviet intelligence. After Dimitrov received information from Major General Kalganov that Soviet representatives in Yunan were complaining of difficulties in their relationships with the leadership of the CPCh, an inquiry was sent to Mao Zedong: "In the present situation the work of the group of Soviet comrades who are in your country is of the greatest importance, as is the correct coordination of their work with yours. We request you to inform us whether you have provided the necessary assistance, communications et[c]. for the successful implementation of these special assignments. How do you personally view the possibility for their further work?"[20]

Clearly dissatisfied with the activity of the Soviet military intelligence agents in Yunan, however, Mao Zedong responded: "We understand the great importance of the work being done here by the Soviet comrades. We have helped them in every possible way and will continue to do so. They are working very hard, but their work suffers from great shortcomings. Comrade Kar. is a devoted comrade but his work methods are unsuitable; moreover, he does not wish to take account of our opinion. Our representative will give you a report on the details of this matter on arrival [at the ECCI]."[21] Dimitrov forwarded the text of this message to Stalin and to the military intelligence chiefs Fillip Golikov and Aleksei Panfilov.

This was not the first time that Dimitrov had heard about these problems. Back on 12 June he had received a warning from Golikov: the Chinese leaders were not to know that the Comintern received information from Yunan not only from the CC of the CPCh. Golikov wrote in a letter: "An employee of the Directorate in the Special Region, colonel com[rade] Kislenko has requested that when you give instructions to the leadership of the CPCh on the basis of the information sent by com[rade] Kislenko, the source of information should remain unknown to com[rade] Mao Zedong. Otherwise com[rade] Kislenko may be deprived of information from the Central Committee of the Chinese Communist Party and Zhou Enlai."[22]

As is clear from the discussion above, the central topic of the cipher correspondence of those years was the relationship between the CPCh and the KMT. In a letter to Stalin and Molotov of 13 December, in connection with the start of the Pacific Ocean war, Dimitrov "recommend[ed] that Mao Zedong contact Chiang Kai-shek directly in order to quickly eliminate existing misunderstandings between the Communist Party and the Kuomintang, to strengthen the unity of the

Chinese people, to unite its armed forces, and to organize a bold offensive against the Japanese armies in China. In doing so the Communist Party must demonstrate maximum reasonable willingness to reach agreement."[23] In the correspondence with the leadership of the CPCh, Dimitrov persistently emphasized this policy.

On 17 March 1942 a message was received from Soviet intelligence in Yunan stating that the Chinese Communist Eighth and Fourth Armies for a long time had not been engaged in either active or passive actions against the Japanese: "The line of the leadership of the CPCh on breaking with the Kuomintang is continuing, despite all the damage this is doing here to the cause of a war of liberation. Such actions are only playing into the hands of the Japanese, and this situation is giving rise to very serious doubt. . . . It must be taken into account that for us the situation in the F[ar] E[ast] is extremely critical. . . . I believe that Moscow must through all available means force the leadership of the CPCh to change its policy regarding Chiang Kai-shek."[24]

On 16 June a cipher cable was sent to Mao Zedong demanding an improvement in the relations between the CPCh and Chiang Kai-shek and the KMT: "The present situation imperatively dictates that the Chinese Communist Party do all in its power for the possible improvement of relations with Chiang Kai-shek and for the strengthening of the United Front of China in the struggle against the Japanese. We know that Chiang Kai-shek and the Kuomintang leaders are in all possible ways provoking the Communist Party to discredit and isolate it, but we cannot consider this correct policy if people are falling for these provocations instead of reacting to them intelligently."[25]

Mao Zedong replied that the armies functioning under the leadership of the CPCh faced nearly half of the entire contingent of Japanese troops located in China and the three-hundred-thousand-strong army of Wang Jingwei acting in concert with the Japanese troops. (Wang Jingwei, a rival of Chiang Kai-shek, broke with the KMT in 1938 and organized a collaborationist regime operating in Japanese-occupied China.) Mao's messages were filled with information on the hostile activity of the KMT. He kept giving reassurances, however, that "we are continuing to be cautious in all possible ways; we continually remind and order the local Party committees to avoid friction with the Kuomintang. All of the numerous past instances of friction were begun by the Kuomintang." Dimitrov sent all these telegrams to Stalin.[26]

On 11 December 1944 Mao Zedong sent a letter to Dimitrov. It concerned the breakdown in the agreement signed by Mao Zedong and the representative of President Roosevelt, General Patrick Hurley, on the creation of a coalition government in China: "If during the last several years the strength of the Kuomintang outweighed that of our forces, at the present time the situation is changing in our favor, and the balance of forces is moving toward parity (in reference to the operational capacity and quality of the CPCh and the KMT, the confidence of the masses of the people in the CPCh and the KMT). . . . Events are moving toward a situation in which the operational capacity of our Party will gradually exceed that of the Kuomintang. At present our Party has become the active, decisive factor in the anti-Japanese war and the salvation of the state."[27]

These confrontations foreshadowed the subsequent outbreak of a new civil war that developed as soon as the Japanese surrendered in September 1945. The Chinese Communists under Mao Zedong defeated the KMT, and in 1949 Chiang Kai-shek, several million KMT supporters, and the KMT's remaining troops withdrew to Taiwan, leaving all of mainland China to Communist rule. But the subtle but stubborn Chinese Communist resistance toward accepting Soviet directives also foreshadowed the tense relationship that eventually led to the Sino-Soviet split.

CHAPTER EIGHT

The Nazi-Soviet Pact

The Comintern Blindsided and Confused

On 22 August 1939 Moscow newspapers reported on the forthcoming visit to the Soviet capital of Hitler's minister of foreign affairs, Joachim von Ribbentrop, to sign a nonaggression treaty between the USSR and Germany. On the same day, the ECCI Secretariat adopted a decree, sent to the Communist parties as a directive. It instructed the parties to go on the offensive against the bourgeois and Socialist press based on the argument that the conclusion of a nonaggression pact between the USSR and Germany emphatically *did not* exclude the possibility or the need for an agreement among Britain, France, and the USSR to jointly rebuff the fascist aggressors. Since the mid-1930s the Comintern and Communist parties around the world had called for Britain, France, and other democratic states to join with the Soviet Union in a defensive alliance against potential aggression by Nazi Germany and fascist Italy. This support for collective security against aggression had been a key part of the Popular Front policies of that period.

The Comintern decree of 22 August assured Communist parties that the Soviet signing of a nonaggression treaty with Germany was not a repudiation of that collective security policy. The USSR was, the Comintern explained, conducting an independent policy, "based on the interests of socialism and the cause of peace," and through its "readiness to conclude a Nonaggression Pact with Germany the USSR was assisting the small neighboring Baltic countries and was effectively promoting the strengthening of universal peace." The ECCI explained that the British and French governments were engaged in protracted negotiations with the Soviet Union on joint action against the aggressors and were attempting to use these negotiations "as a means to reach a compromise with Germany at the expense of the USSR." British and French influence was also blamed for Poland's rejection of possible Soviet assistance. By signing a nonaggression pact the USSR was undermining the plans of the reactionary bourgeois circles and the leaders of the Socialist International to direct aggression against the USSR, thereby splitting the aggressors and obtaining a free hand to work to assist the Chinese people in their struggle against Japanese aggression. The Soviet-German negotiations, according to the Comintern, were a means "to force the British and French governments to conclude a pact with the USSR. Simultaneously it is necessary to show the Parties the need to continue with ever greater energy the antifascist struggle against the aggressors, in particular against German fascism."[1]

This Comintern decree shows that the ECCI leadership had not been warned of Stalin's intentions and had not grasped the meaning of Stalin's sharp shift toward a rapprochement with Hitler's Germany, and through inertia it continued to repeat the previous formulae regarding the struggle against German fascism. Stalin was perfectly well aware that the Nazi-Soviet Pact gave Hitler a free hand to attack Poland. Moscow was receiving such information from various sources, including Soviet intelligence. A message to Moscow of 23 May 1939 from a Soviet intelligence agent stated, "The Soviet Union is a factor slowing down the unquestionably aggressive intentions of Germany in regard to Poland. In the view of influential Berlin circles, at the present time the position of the Soviet Union is in fact the most important issue." A report from another intelligence agent on 2 May, based on a conversation with Ribbentrop's closest aide, stated, "The conclusion of Germany's preparations for war against Poland are timed for July–August. . . . This entire project is encountering only one reservation in Berlin. That is the potential reaction of the Soviet Union." Stalin also had other information regarding Hitler's military plans.[2]

The secret protocol to the Nazi-Soviet Pact contained the delimitation of "spheres of interests of both countries" and declared the admissibility of "territorial-political restructuring," which meant the forthcoming division of the territory of Poland between Germany and the USSR. Finland, Estonia, and Latvia were included in the "sphere of interests" of the USSR, as well as Bessarabia (then part of Romania) and much of eastern Poland. Stalin thus created favorable conditions for Hitler to attack Poland and was also planning to participate in this invasion. Germany attacked Poland from the west and north on 1 September. The USSR's invasion from the east came on 17 September, when Soviet troops embarked on the so-called liberation march into what the USSR defined as Western Ukraine and Western Byelorussia, territories then part of eastern Poland.[3]

The leaders of the ECCI could not have known about any of this, but in the situation preceding the direct outbreak of war their directives served to cover up Stalin's complicity with Hitler and promote the disorientation of the Communist parties. On 27 August Dimitrov sent Stalin, Molotov, and Zhdanov a set of materials on the responses of the Communist parties to the signing of the pact. The letter of transmittal to Stalin stated, "We are sending You the material we have as of today, showing the position of the Communist Parties of France, the United Kingdom, the U.S., Italy, Sweden, Denmark, Belgium, Switzerland, and Holland concerning the nonaggression treaty between Germany and the USSR." These materials did not include even a reference to any kind of negative reaction among Communists to this action by Moscow. The only documents sent were those that unequivocally showed support for and approval of this action, presumably considered as a success of the Soviet Union's in strengthening the cause of peace.[4]

On that same day, Dimitrov and Manuilsky asked Stalin for advice on the position the French Communist Party should take in this situation. They wrote that the Communist parties, above all the French and British ones, "have taken the correct position on the Soviet-German Nonaggression Pact, which foils the plans of anti-USSR warmongers. The Communist Parties have reacted appropriately to the rabid anti-Soviet campaign in the bourgeois and Social-Democratic press." In France the Communist Party was being harassed, its press closed down, and meetings of Communists banned. Dimitrov and Manuilsky stated:

> It is obvious that despite the persecution, the Communist Party will continue to defend, with all means possible, the Soviet-German Pact as an act of peace, an act that corresponds to the interests of the international working class and the French people. However, in the complex current situation a question arises about the position of the Communist Party on the measures taken by the [French Prime Minister] Daladier government in the cause of the so-called national defense of the country. We think that the Communist Party must maintain its position of resistance to the aggression of fascist Germany. It must support the measures aimed at strengthening the defensive capacity of France but, at the same time, condition its support of those measures by

> demanding that the Party be allowed to express its views openly and to promote its activities. Simultaneously, the Party must indicate that the current government of Daladier-Bonnet does not enjoy the confidence of the people and does not provide guarantees of either a sound policy that matches the interests of the French people or the proper defense of the country.

The leaders of the Comintern requested Stalin to reply, "whether such a position is correct."[5]

Dimitrov's letter did not receive an immediate answer. The letter's reiteration of the argument regarding acts of aggression by Nazi Germany shows that the leadership of the Comintern had not been able to quickly restructure its thinking and to fully grasp all the consequences of the Ribbentrop-Molotov Pact. This confusion continued even in the first few days after Hitler attacked Poland and after France and Great Britain had declared war on Germany. On 5 September the ECCI leadership began working on a draft of the conceptual framework regarding the war and the objectives of the Communists.[6]

The initial drafts described the war as unjust and imperialist, aimed "on the one hand (the British-French-Polish side) at maintaining the borders of the forcibly imposed Versailles peace agreement, and on the other (the German side) at redistribution of the borders of Europe and the colonies." The conclusion was that in no case whatever could the Communist parties of these countries back the policy of their countries' ruling classes, which had plunged people into a new imperialist bloodbath. "The Communist Parties must expose this policy in all of the belligerent countries."[7]

Under the illusion that Stalin's antifascist policies of the pre-pact period were still in place, the draft went on to assert that "the victory of German fascism in the war presents the greatest danger for the international working-class movement. It is therefore the duty of Communists of all countries, and above all the German Communists, to assist in defeating fascism." The watchwords of the defeat of German fascism and of national liberation were to be used in the countries enslaved by Hitler's Germany. It was acknowledged that in the event of the overthrow of the Polish government, which had brought the country to this disastrous situation, and the establishment of a government of workers and peasants, the Polish people would engage in a struggle for the national independence of the country. Demands were made for the resignation of the present government of the United Kingdom and its replacement by a leftist government of trade union leaders and for the replacement of the French Daladier government by one that would unite the people, organize the defense of the country, and "be able through its policy to inspire confidence in all the antifascists of the world." This, in substance, meant that the new policy was to attempt to transform the war into a genuinely antifascist one. These Comintern assessments, however, badly failed to take into account Stalin's view of how the pact fitted with Soviet foreign policy.[8]

The initial attempt of the Comintern leadership to reconcile the pact with the antifascist policies of the Popular Front period was echoed by other Communist parties. The Central Committee of the Bulgarian Communist Party (BCP) reported:

> The Soviet-German Pact was received by all of us with joy and hope. The democratic leaders are embarrassed and discouraged. Some of us think that there is a need to change the attitude to fascism in general and to Germany in particular. We believe that in this situation there is a need to put forward the banner of neutrality and friendly relations with all the Balkan neighbors, relying on the peace-loving powers and above all on the USSR. The Palace [Bulgarian monarchy] and the fascist government are agents of Germany and Italy. Their neutrality is insincere. They represent a danger to the national and state independence of Bulgaria. Our goal is to organize the National Front to overthrow the fascist government, restore democratic rights and freedoms of the Bulgarian people, and provide for peace and for our independence from the fascist onslaught.[9]

Thus the Bulgarian party continued to advocate antifascist slogans and to treat Germany as a threat to the independence of Bulgaria. The Communist parties of France and Britain, as well as that of still neutral Belgium, took a similar position and continued to condemn fascist aggression. The Communist parties demanded the organization of an effective defense against Hitler's aggression and the transformation of the war into a genuinely antifascist war. This demonstrated the impact of the antifascist movement of the preceding years, and, above all, a realistic assessment of the actual situation. At the same time the Communist parties had no doubts regarding the advisability of the Nazi-Soviet Pact; they just did not as yet understand Stalin's intent.

Stalin Instructs the Comintern

On 5 September Dimitrov wrote a letter to Zhdanov, enclosing a copy of his and Manuilsky's joint appeal to Stalin of 27 August, noting that it "was sent before the outbreak of the war, and the question raised in it is still facing the French comrades today, but now, of course, in connection with their position regarding the war." Then he wrote that the ECCI was preparing a document on the war and the fundamental policy and tactical positions of the Communist parties: "I must note, that in drawing up this policy and, in particular, the tactical positions and political tasks of the Communist Parties in new conditions, we are encountering extraordinary difficulties, and to overcome them and to take a correct decision we are more than ever in need of direct help and advice from comrade Stalin." On the copy of the letter to Zhdanov, Dimitrov later noted, "Conversation with com. Stalin, in the presence of c[omrades] Molotov and Zhdanov took place on 7.9.39."[10]

Dimitrov's diary reveals the nature of the instruction contained in the answer he received: "A war is on between two groups of capitalist countries—(poor and rich as regards colonies, raw materials, and so forth)—for the redistribution of the world, for the domination of the world!—We see nothing wrong in their having a good hard fight and weakening each other. It would be fine if at the hands of Germany the position of the richest capitalist countries (especially England) were shaken. Hitler, without understanding it or desiring it, is shaking and undermining the capitalist system." Stalin added, "To the same degree the Nonaggression Pact helps Germany. The next step is to nudge the other side forward." He then said the Communist parties "should be speaking out boldly against their governments and against the war. Before the war, opposing a democratic regime to fascism was entirely correct. During war between the imperialist powers that is now incorrect. The division of capitalist states into fascist and democratic ones has lost its previous meaning." The slogan of the Popular Front, said Stalin, had to be done away with. There was a need to expose the neutrality of the bourgeois neutral countries, which were supporting the war in order to obtain profits. During the conversation Stalin used the word "fascism" *only* in reference to Poland. And he let slip the plan for its dismemberment, noting, "The annihilation of that state under current conditions would mean one fewer bourgeois fascist state to contend with! What would be the harm if as a result of the rout of Poland we were to extend the socialist system onto new territories and populations?"[11]

Stalin's words signaled the need for a radical change in the policy guidelines for the Communist parties. The line of struggling to defend democracy and counter fascism as the major threat and source of aggression, proclaimed at the Seventh Congress of the Comintern, was dropped. The Communist parties were to direct the leading edge of propaganda against imperialism in general, do away with the slogan of the Popular Front, and reject cooperation with Social Democrats, Socialists, and others of the liberal left. The slogans advocated the struggle against war and its perpetrators, but the point of criticism was directed against the opponents of Germany, and nothing was said of the need to fight fascism and Nazism. Stalin was in fact ordering the Comintern and the Communist parties to turn the front line of the struggle against the democratic states of the West.

Stalin's formula that the distinction between democratic and fascist states had lost its meaning in wartime did not, of course, take into account the national interests of those peoples who were actually resisting fascism. By unleashing war, Hitler's Germany had made its goal the establishment of a "new" order throughout the world, the enslavement and actual physical destruction of some peoples and nations. Regardless of the goals pursued by the ruling factions in countries at war with Germany, the war was a matter of national and ethnic survival in many countries. The Soviet Union's policies fractured the forces resisting Nazi Germany, weakening national resistance and leading to the increasing political isolation of the Communist parties.

Now that Dimitrov understood what Stalin intended, the Comintern on 8 September prepared a directive reflecting the spirit of Stalin's new instructions as guidance for the Communist parties. The war now under way was defined as an imperialist and unjust one, for which the bourgeoisie of all the belligerent states was equally to blame. The war could not be supported in any country, nor by the working class, let alone by the Communist parties. "The bourgeoisie is fighting the war, but not against fascism as Chamberlain and the leaders of Social Democracy claim. The war is being fought between two groups of capitalist countries for control of the world. The international working class can certainly not defend fascist Poland, which has rejected the help of the Soviet Union and suppressed other nationalities." It was noted that the Communist parties wished to create a genuinely antifascist front with the participation of the USSR, "but the bourgeoisies of England and France have repudiated the Soviet Union in order to pursue a predatory war." The war radically changed the situation, and the broad antifascist liberal/left alliances of the Popular Front era were no longer acceptable: "The division of the capitalist countries into fascist and democratic [camps] has lost its former significance. Tactic of the Communist Parties in all warring lands at this stage of war is to oppose the war, to expose its imperialist character. . . . Everywhere Communist Parties must undertake a decisive offensive against the treacherous policy of Social Democracy." The Comintern insisted that the Communist parties of France, Britain, the United States, and Belgium "must immediately correct their political line."[12]

The ECCI Secretariat saw to it that all the Communist parties received this directive, demanded immediate confirmation, and worked to ensure its implementation. The ECCI's lack of immediate communications with the leadership of the French Communist Party prompted it to try to make contact through the Belgian Communist Party. A coded dispatch to the Comintern's Dutch contact, Daan Goulooze, stated: "We are requesting the leadership of our branch in Belgrade [Brussels] to find out everything about the family of our Mayer [Paris], where they are, what they are doing, and through you to provide information about themselves. We are also asking you to urgently transmit to the English branch the directive received yesterday and to keep in constant contact with it. I request you immediately to confirm when you have carried out these instructions."[13]

On 15 September Goulooze reported that communications with "Mayer [Paris] have been established through Belgrade [Brussels]. Clément is there. The Party is legal. The press is banned. Thorez . . . Légros [Tréand] have been mobilized. Duclos is the secretary. Neither Thorez nor the Central Committee are correcting the policy of the faction in the parliament."[14]

A message came through Holland, too, from Xavier Relecom, the secretary of the Central Committee of the Belgian Communist Party, stating that the party's line had been corrected in accordance with the directive. Goulooze also replied that he had sent the directive on to London. Reports also came in from Sweden that "Communications have been established with Paris. Political directives have been sent to Norway, Denmark, Paris, Brussels, Amsterdam, Latvia, and Finland." A message also arrived from New York confirming receipt of the directive and voicing full agreement with it.[15]

The leadership of the British Communist Party (CPGB), however, did not immediately obey the ECCI's demand. Consequently, Douglas Springhall, the British Communist Party's representative to the ECCI, immediately set off for London to put things right. Springhall returned to Britain via Stockholm, and Dimitrov directed the Comintern's Swedish party contact, Karl Lager, to meet with Springhall. The outbreak of the war had considerably disrupted established Comintern communications channels, and Dimitrov wanted to arrange better communications links from London to Moscow through Sweden. Directives were also sent to Communist leaders in Stockholm and Amsterdam: "By any and all means whatever try to urgently inform the

British friend about the directive on the war. That is extremely important and indispensable."[16]

Following the intervention by the Comintern, the leadership of the British Communist Party changed its position. The CPGB general secretary, Harry Pollitt, who had disagreed with the directives from Moscow, was relieved of his post and replaced by Rajani Palme Dutt, who had vigorously supported complying with the Comintern's directive. Dimitrov also sent a coded dispatch to London: "We suggest Harry and Johnny [John Campbell, editor of the *Daily Worker*, who also had resisted the directive] should not be in Politbureau but should remain in Central Committee." Dutt replied: "I received your message [regarding] Harry and John after the Central Committee had elected Harry to the Politburo. . . . While we understand the importance of your message, we still recommend that Harry remain in the Politburo subject to your confirmation." Dimitrov relented, replying, "Harry could remain member of Political Bureau." (Campbell was also replaced as editor of the *Daily Worker.*)[17]

Creation of a European Communications Center

Concerned with ensuring reliable links with Communist parties scrambling to figure out how to behave and what to say in a chaotic new situation, Dimitrov sent instructions on a new organizational structure for the Comintern in Europe. In coded language that barely disguised its meaning he issued an order: "Alfredo [Togliatti], Clément [Fried], and Luis (Codovilla) must go to a neutral country and establish a commercial center of our firm there. This center must immediately get in contact with the main directorate, establish contacts with branches of the firm, engage in the greatest possible amount of commercial activity, and prevent our competitors from making use of the present situation against the interests of our firm."[18]

The order was fleshed out on 17 September when Dimitrov sent a directive to Amsterdam:

> We authorize Clément and Luis together with the Dutch friend [Goulooze] to create a temporary communications center of the European Parties. That center together with [Sven] Linderot [a leader of the Sweden Communist Party] must care about: 1) establishing connections to the Parties; 2) quickly correcting the Party line of the Parties, in particular the French and the English, in the spirit of this directive; 3) ensuring further publication of our organs; 4) rendering necessary assistance for sending on our Spanish and other leading foreign friends; 5) organizing

> information for us on the present situation and activity of the Parties. After the establishment of this center Luis can leave with the task of establishing such a center for the American countries, which can have a link to your center. The required funds must be given by the Dutch friend. Confirm receipt of these instructions and report on measures taken in this area.[19]

The triumvirate entrusted with oversight of Comintern operations had to change, however. Togliatti had been interned by the French government and was not released until 1940, whereupon he returned to the Soviet Union. Clément (Eugen Fried), for much of the 1930s the Comintern's key link to the French Communist Party, had moved his base of operations to Belgium. Maurice Thorez, mobilized into the French Army, deserted on 4 October and fled, first to Belgium and then to Moscow. Maurice Tréand, who controlled the Comintern's money in the late 1930s, was not mentioned in the coded cable. He had also deserted from the French Army and gone into hiding in Belgium, his whereabouts unknown to the ECCI. When he did reestablish contact in a cable on 11 October, Tréand petulantly reminded his bosses that he was responsible for the available funds and asked whether he was supposed to hand over his functions to Clément: "There is an opportunity to give out the journals [money] for September, October, November, and December, but give instructions. Very urgently . . . I am asking you whether I should transfer the entire organization and give everything over to Clément."[20]

In late October Dimitrov asked Clément to "report on the present situation of the apparatus, who is there now, who are the employees, but only their functions, not their last names. Also with whom you are in contact from our Parties." Clément responded that Tréand was not in France but that "communication has been established between the apparatus and the French Party" through Gabriel Péri, a member of the Central Committee of the French Communist Party and the editor of *L'Humanité*, and "between the apparatus and Gabriel [Gabriel Péri]. . . . Communication has been established with the Italian, Romanian, and Czech Communist Parties."[21]

In his coded cable in response, Dimitrov restored Tréand to his functions as leader of the communications apparatus in France: "We are assuming that as soon as you resume direct contact with us, Gabriel [Tréand] will take on leadership of the Communications apparatus. Your apparatus must have ties with the remaining countries, Parties and organizations, with England, Switzerland, and Belgium. The Dutch apparatus remains in reserve."[22]

Two weeks later Dimitrov sent Clément, Tréand, and Goulooze a directive naming them the leadership of the European communications center and delineating their responsibilities. Clément was entrusted with issues of the political work of the parties and the party press, the conduct of international campaigns, and providing for the publication of the organs of the Comintern. Tréand was assigned organizational questions of communications with the parties, communication with the Comintern, financial issues, and the implementation of instructions from the Comintern regarding assistance to parties and to leading functionaries. Goulooze was responsible for the publication activity and communications between the Communist Party of Holland and the Comintern. His apparatus was to become the reserve apparatus. He was also instructed to create a reserve communications center. The European center was also to organize a courier service, using for this purpose the Belgian, Dutch, and other Communist parties.[23]

Although Clément's supervision of political work seemed to give him pride of place, Tréand's control of the Comintern's communications in Europe led to frequent conflicts between the two men. Thorez acknowledged in a conversation with an employee of the ECCI Personnel Department, Stella Blagoeva, at the end of November that Clément had accused Tréand "of being too slow in establishing communications." While Clément "said there are no grounds for not trusting Tréand . . . he considers that in these difficult times there are weaknesses in Tréand's work; he reprimanded him, and Tréand is angry."[24]

Tréand's reports to the Comintern were even harsher. One message included accusations that Clément "had worked for a long time in Paris. . . . Moreover, the police did not bother him." He blamed Clément "for the legalistic and opportunistic orientation that had begun to manifest itself in the leadership of the French Communist Party toward the end of August, and that then already contained the seeds of the mistakes made later in September." And, he complained, Clément intended "to eliminate him from the leadership working on international communications and intends to concentrate this work in his own . . . hands." Tréand suggested that Clément be summoned to Moscow and another comrade be sent to replace him. Dimitrov ignored the suggestions.[25]

Giving Substance to the New Line

On 28 September, during Ribbentrop's second visit to Moscow, the German-Soviet Treaty of Friendship, Cooperation, and Demarcation was signed. Among other measures, secret protocols in this treaty formally ceded to Germany some Polish territory that it had already occupied but that had been assigned to the USSR under the first Molotov-Ribbentrop agreement. In return, the new treaty assigned most of Lithuania to the "sphere of interests" of the USSR. In a joint public statement, both sides favored the immediate cessation of the war.[26]

At first, the Soviet leadership toyed with the idea of allowing the Baltic nations a modicum of independence. With the possibility of aid from the West cut off by the Nazi-Soviet Pact and the outbreak of World War II, all three—Lithuania, Latvia, and Estonia—signed pacts of mutual assistance with the USSR, which Stalin believed was "the right form to allow us to bring [them] into the Soviet Union's sphere of influence." He told Dimitrov in late October 1939 that "we need to be vigilant, to strictly watch over their internal regimes and autonomy. We will not attempt to Sovietize them. When the time comes, they will do that themselves!"[27]

The period of limited autonomy for the Baltic states was short-lived, however. Acquiescence to Soviet influence was coerced and widely resented by the Baltic peoples, and Baltic diplomats quietly approached Western states and Nazi Germany seeking counterweights to Soviet pressure. Slightly more than eight months later, the USSR presented an ultimatum to all three countries, demanding the formation of new governments and acceptance of occupation by Soviet troops. The Comintern's instructions to the Lithuanian Communist Party were typical: "The main task at this stage is the organization of the masses under our leadership in the cities and in the countryside. Publish legal newspapers. Organize legal trade unions and factory councils at the enterprises and peasant committees in the villages. Have political prisoners released immediately. Cleanse the army and the state apparatus of anti-Soviet elements. Confiscate the property of reactionaries who have fled. Put forward a program of action that for now does not go beyond the popular-democratic framework. The Democratic Popular government should consist of honest representatives of the people. For now the direct participation of the Communists is not advisable." Emissaries from Moscow directed the process of Sovietization. In Lithuania Vladimir Dekanozov, the deputy people's commissar for international affairs of the USSR, played this role. Dimitrov wrote to the leaders of the Communist Party: "We recommend that Dekan's [Dekanozov's] advice be taken into account in resolving important Party questions. He has precise instructions." Following legislative elections on 21 June, Lithuania asked to join the USSR.[28]

The second agreement between Germany and the USSR immediately resulted in changes to the Comintern's political directives to the Communist parties. Although the war was described as imperialist from both sides, it was now emphasized that the problem of fascism had begun to play a tertiary role, that the primary issue was the struggle against capitalism and, above all, against the regime of bourgeois dictatorship and reaction in each country—that is, those countries at war with Germany and states that had declared their neutrality. Stress was also placed on intensification of the struggle against Social Democrats and Socialists, whose leaders were branded as vile enemies of the Soviet Union, preparing to go to war against it. Germany and Hitler's National Socialism were no longer regarded as the primary or even secondary enemy.

France had declared war on Germany on 3 September and several weeks later proscribed the French Communist Party due to its support for the Nazi-Soviet Pact. But while the French party supported the pact, it did not immediately embrace, and likely did not yet fully understand, all that Stalin's new policy required. And on 22 September the Comintern sent Clément (Eugen Fried), its chief agent in France, a demand to take the measures necessary to implement the ECCI directives in France.[29] On 28 September the ECCI sent an additional directive to the PCF:

> After the ban on the Party it has become clear that there is a need for a decisive break with the policy of sacred unity [French patriotism] and for the exposure of the two-faced attitude of the French bourgeoisie regarding an allegedly antifascist war. This is not a war of democracy against fascism; this is an imperialist, reactionary war on the part of both France and Germany. In this war a position of national defense is not a correct one for the French Communists. The struggle against the imperialist war is the best form of protection of the vital interests and the entire future of the French people. Today the question of fascism is playing a secondary role; the primary issue is the struggle against capitalism—the source of all wars—against the regime of bourgeois dictatorship in all its forms, and above all in your own country. The tactic of the United and Popular Front is no longer applicable in the light of the shift of Socialists and Radicals to the camp of the war and of imperialist reaction; this is also because the war has created a new situation, in other words, a profound and drastic crisis of capitalism.

The ECCI Presidium expressed its confidence that the Central Committee of the party "would correct the errors committed."[30]

A coded dispatch to the British party leadership via Clément further explained how Communist parties should understand the Nazi-Soviet Pact:

> The English Party's position in support of the imperialist war is wrong. This is in fact support for Chamberlain. In the war each Communist must fight against reaction in his own country, not against fascist reaction in a foreign country. It is not fascist Germany, which concluded an agreement with the USSR, but reactionary anti-Soviet England, with its enormous colonial empire, which is the bulwark of capitalism. Therefore the tactic of antifascist struggle is also not applicable here. By reiterating formulas about the antifascist war, the British Communists are helping the bourgeoisie drag the workers into the war. The slogan of Communists of all the belligerent capit[alist] states is: the struggle against the imperialist war.[31]

On 7 and 8 October similar directives were sent to Amsterdam for forwarding to the Communist parties of Belgium, Switzerland, and Sweden and for dissemination in the other Scandinavian countries; they were also to be sent to New York to American party leader Earl Browder for dissemination to the Communist parties of Latin America:

> The provocateurs of anti-Soviet war are raging because the USSR has sabotaged their true intent, strengthened the positions of the socialist countries, wrested 14 million people from capitalist hell [a reference to the USSR's occupation and later annexation of eastern Poland on 17 September]. Their anti-Soviet and anti-Communist campaign is tantamount to preparation for war against the USSR. . . .
>
> It is necessary to conduct yourself in the way taught by Lenin and Stalin in the period of war 1914–1918, the way Liebknecht behaved. Selflessly defend the French Communists from brutal French reactionary forces. Struggle vigorously against the offensive launched by reactionary forces in your country.[32]

While the Communist parties of France and Britain had to swallow adopting policies that opened them to accusations of treason, those in neutral countries faced other pressures. One of the more interesting cases involved Bulgaria, about whose policies Dimitrov took an especially keen interest and of whose Communist Party he was a long-time leader.

Immediately after the pact was signed, the Central Committee of the Bulgarian Communist Party sent a message to the Comintern proclaiming that the Bulgarian monarchy "and the fascist government are agents of Germany and Italy. Their neutrality is insincere. They represent a danger to the national and state independence of Bulgaria. Our goal is to organize the National Front to overthrow the fascist government, restore democratic rights and freedoms of the Bulgarian people, and provide for peace and for our independence from the fascist onslaught."

The main danger, in other words, remained fascism and German pressure on the government.[33]

The ECCI Secretariat sent a coded dispatch to the Bulgarian Communist Party in October 1939 that emphasized how Communists in a neutral country like Bulgaria should understand the war situation: "The neutrality of the bourgeoisie of the nonbelligerent countries is hypocritical. The bourgeoisie is attempting to enrich itself through the war. The United States is supplying Japan with weapons and, together with England, they are setting their dogs on the USSR. . . . The USSR has a unique, independent position. It has made colossal efforts to preserve peace. Having concluded a Pact with Germany, it remained outside the military conflagration and today serves as a powerful bulwark for all peace-loving forces. The USSR is serving the interests of the workers, humanity, and socialism. It has fulfilled its liberating role in Western Byelorussia and Wes[tern] Ukraine." Describing the war as an imperialist one for the parties to the conflict, the message repeated the claim that the "the distinction between democracy and fascism has disappeared."[34]

In another directive to the Communist Party of Bulgaria in November 1939 the ECCI Secretariat instructed it to campaign for a pact of friendship and mutual assistance with the Soviet Union. The message stood reality on its head:

> The German-Soviet Pact and the firm position of the USSR in East European affairs weakened German expansion in the Balkans and strengthened Soviet influence. Today, the Soviet Union is the sole pillar of support for the neutrality of Bulgaria. In striving for domination, the British and French imperialists are organizing an assault on the rulers of the Bulgarian people in an attempt to make them their vassals and, insofar as possible, to plunge them into the war with Germany. They are preparing to make Bulgaria a springboard against the Soviet Union. Our major objective today is the mobilization of the masses against the involvement of Bulgaria in the war on any side whatever; moreover, the major thrust must be against British and French imperialism.[35]

In the face of the ECCI's strange notion that the Nazi-Soviet Pact had weakened German influence and the chief threat in the Balkans was British and French imperialism, the leaders of the Bulgarian Communist Party did point out to the ECCI that ruling circles in their country had understood the Nazi-Soviet Pact as indicating a need to rely more on Germany. Once again, however, Bulgarian Communists received instructions from the ECCI to vigorously attack the British plan to create a Balkan defensive bloc as serving only the interests of Britain and France and to step up the campaign against the anti-Soviet intrigues of these powers. A directive of 11 December 1939 warned the Bulgarian Communists that negotiations with the leaders of the bourgeois opposition parties and the Social Democrats were not permitted. The ECCI reminded them: "The most reliable criterion is unconditional friendship with the USSR and opposition to the attempts of England and France to include Bulgaria in their front against Germany, and thus, in fact, against the USSR."[36]

Over the next year and a half, the Comintern persistently pressured the Bulgarian Communists to focus their attacks on elements in the Bulgarian government sympathetic to Great Britain and France. One message warned: "There are signs that in the very near future British-French pressure will be exerted to involve the Balkans in the blockade and in the war with Germany. . . . We demand of the government, first of all, the rejection of participation in the economic blockade of Germany, as contravening neutrality. Second, a firm policy defending peace, neutrality, and independence against attempts to force a violation of our neutrality." Bulgarian Communists enthusiastically endorsed the message, commenting in a reply to Moscow that their deputies in parliament would "demand guarantees that neutrality will be firmly and unswervingly championed." They would expose "the capitulatory tactics" of the pro-Ally forces and "demand the arrest of the British-French agents. We warn that in the event of the capitulation of Bulgaria to the British-French bloc, the people will have a free hand regarding traitors and betrayers."[37]

Such fervor did not please the ECCI Secretariat, which considered the demand for the arrest of the British-French agents as premature: "First of all, the goals and methods of these agents must be exposed, in order to paralyze their activity. We also consider the holding of negotiations with the government as premature. There is a need to step up popularization of our independent position among the people and not to make any particular proposals to the government, which we continue to distrust." After receiving that warning, the party leaders decided to protect themselves by obtaining more specific instructions. In a message from Sofia they asked, "In our propaganda we have been insistently raising the issue of the conclusion of a Pact on Mutual Assistance with the USSR as the most important condition for the preservation of the independence of the Bulgarian people. Are we acting correctly, and is this position of ours in keeping with the policy of the USSR?"[38]

To protect himself, Dimitrov sent the Bulgarians' query to Stalin, summarizing what the party had done. While he thought the policy was "correct" inasmuch as it not only voiced "the genuine attitudes and wishes of the overwhelming majority of the people," Dimitrov also believed the policy was "a blow to the Anglo-French agents who are working ever more intensively in the circles around Tsar Boris and in the ranks of the government, and to the political and military officials of the country, who are attempting through any and all means to make Bulgaria into a tool of the Anglo-French bloc." He was "eager for Your advice on this question." Dimitrov also pleaded with Soviet foreign minister Molotov: "For us to give an answer to the inquiry from our Bulgarian comrades, we badly need to know, from the point of view of the Balkan policy of the Soviet government, whether it is possible and advisable at the present moment to raise the question of the conclusion of the Mutual Assistance Pact between Bulgaria and the USSR, as is being done by the Bulgarian Communist Party."[39]

Even as the Bulgarian Communist Party faced increasing pressure inside Bulgaria from advocates of an alliance with Nazi Germany, the Comintern resisted any effort to align it with pro-British elements in the country. In late June 1940 the Bulgarians sent a warning to Dimitrov:

> German successes in the West and Italy's forthcoming entrance into the war are stirring up irresponsible nationalist elements, which openly favor moving Bulgaria toward the countries of the Axis. This surge of activity and the numerous German visitors are raising concerns in Party circles regarding a possible heightening of the German-Italian danger in the Balkans. In our struggle for peace and against the war there is obviously a need to emphasize that we are not only opposing the Anglo-French warmongers, but also firmly oppose any military adventure on the part of Germany and Italy. We are in favor of remaining outside the war, and we are for friendship with the USSR.

The Comintern acknowledged that the military defeat of France meant that "the imperialist objectives of Germany and Italy should not be passed over in silence." Communists should "express our solidarity with the French people, who have been betrayed by their bourgeoisie," and "persistently" work "for the conclusion of the Pact of friendship and mutual assistance with the USSR."[40]

Although the messages from Sofia contained more and more information on the growing influence of Nazi Germany on Bulgarian foreign policy, the ECCI's assessments remained unchanged. On 21 September it approved the general line of the Bulgarian Central Committee but noted some "serious errors," most notably "the depiction of the German danger as the main one, while the danger from British imperialism is relegated to second place." The Communist Party was warned against contact with supporters of the Anglophile opposition since "the major enemy today is British imperialism, and the major blow should be aimed at British agents." The key issue was the conclusion of a Mutual Assistance Pact with the USSR.[41]

Although the BCP quickly and succinctly informed the Comintern that its directive was "superb, we shall make use of it immediately," less than two weeks later it had to acknowledge that there had been "individual digressions from this line" due to the fact that "German imperialism in recent times has been on the rise in Bulgaria, and examples of this are so numerous and so significant that inevitably there is an emphasis on the struggle against them [the Germans]." The Bulgarian party leadership nevertheless gave assurances that "as a whole our line does not differ from yours." But again a mid-October 1940 message from Bulgaria acknowledged that while the general line was correct, "in the practical work of the Party a certain degree of underestimation of the British danger has recently been manifest. The Party has above all focused the attention of the masses on the danger of German imperialism, and the struggle against this danger was conducted much more intensively."[42]

While Dimitrov sent a cipher communication to Sofia in mid-November expressing satisfaction that "the Central Committee is correcting the shortcomings we had criticized in its political line," he also asked for information about who had participated in discussion of these questions in the Central Committee, what views had been expressed during the discussion, and by whom, and "whether the Central Committee is accepting all our concrete proposals or is continuing to protest against some of them."[43]

At a meeting with Stalin and Molotov on 25 November 1940 Dimitrov learned that a formal proposal had been made to the government of Bulgaria for the conclusion of a mutual assistance pact with the USSR. He then recorded in his diary an extraordinary statement from Stalin. If Bulgaria signed, Stalin emphasized, "we not only have no objections to Bulgaria's joining the Tripartite Pact, but we ourselves in that event will also join that Pact. If the Bulgarians decline our offer, they will fall entirely into the clutches of the Germans and the Italians and so perish." Stalin added that "it is important for that proposal to be widely known in Bulgarian circles."[44] The Tripartite Pact, signed by Nazi Germany, fascist Italy, and imperial Japan on 27 September

1940, was an expansion of the 1939 Axis pact between Germany and Italy. Stalin, then, was stating that under certain circumstances the Soviet Union would become one of the Axis powers.[45]

Dimitrov immediately sent a message to Sofia reporting the Soviet government's proposal about the mutual assistance pact and the possibility of both Bulgaria and the USSR joining the Tripartite Pact. The Communist Party was authorized to "take immediate and vigorous action to publicize this proposal inside parliament and outside it, in the press and among the masses." He also informed Stalin that the Bulgarian CP had been notified.[46]

The Central Committee of the BCP sent a cipher communication expressing its support: "We have received particularly joyful news. We shall make use of all means and efforts to make it known in the most remote corners of the country, to mobilize the entire Bulgarian people for the implementation of the proposal by the Soviet government." Dimitrov sent the Russian translation to Stalin and Molotov. Subsequent dispatches from Bulgaria reported widespread distribution of the news and preparation for a mass demonstration to pressure the government to agree to the Soviet proposal. One report did mention some popular puzzlement about why the USSR needed to join the Tripartite Pact.[47]

The Soviet government reaction was not positive. On the evening of 28 November Molotov called Dimitrov from Stalin's office and expressed dissatisfaction that in Sofia the Communists were distributing leaflets about the Soviet proposal. A new message had to be sent, in which such actions were termed a mistake and instructions were given to halt them: "This proposal must be made public through the deputies and other appropriate persons but not through printed documents and in no case on behalf of our organs." In response the perplexed Bulgarians complained that they had no idea that propaganda was to be conducted entirely orally and requested to be informed "how it was necessary to conduct the campaign." Dimitrov reported to Stalin and Molotov that the Central Committee of the BCP had acknowledged its error.[48]

While the Soviet Union was anxious to conclude the pact with Bulgaria, it was also wary of offending its German allies or providing them with a pretext for conflict. Dimitrov emphasized to his Bulgarian comrades that the purpose of the proposed pact was simply to prevent war. The campaign for the alliance, therefore, had to be conducted not on a class but a national basis. In no case could it be given an "anti-bourgeois, anti-dynastic, or anti-German character." To bring about a Soviet-Bulgarian pact, "the popular masses are not enough. The majority of the intelligentsia, officers, bourgeois and other circles must support the Pact. Therefore there is a need to refrain from any action that might bolster the arguments of the enemy that the Pact represents a danger to the bourgeois system, the government, and Tsar Boris. In connection with the Pact, the Party must conduct all its work solely as a propaganda and ideological struggle. In no case give in to those acts of provocation, to which opponents will resort, in order to stage an alleged Communist threat."[49]

Molotov informed Dimitrov on 20 December that the government of Bulgaria had rejected the Soviet proposal. Dimitrov sent Stalin a letter on 11 January 1941, asking what the policy of the Bulgarian Communist Party should be in the event of German troops entering Bulgaria; he recommended that it condemn such a violation of neutrality and blame the government of Tsar Boris for precipitating the situation by rejecting the pact with the USSR. He proposed the development of "a mass movement against the creation of an occupation regime in the country and the seizure of its economic and food resources, avoiding careless statements, provocative actions, and armed clashes." Stalin agreed, warning against provocations that "would only make it easier for the Germans to occupy the country. . . . The Party should act on its own behalf, not as the Soviet Union's auxiliary."[50]

The complex and intricate maneuvers by the USSR to conclude an alliance with the Bulgarian government and use the Bulgarian CP as a tool put Dimitrov in a very uncomfortable situation. At the end of January 1941, Dmitry Manuilsky complained to Dimitrov that by communicating directly with the Central Committee of the VKP(b), Dimitrov had created the impression that Manuilsky himself was not taking part in decisions. Dimitrov, sensing trouble, wrote in his diary: "Need to be prepared for any kind of unpleasant surprises." In fact, on 30 January, Manuilsky denounced Dimitrov to Molotov, complaining that at a training session for Comintern lecturers, many of them foreigners, Dimitrov discussed the Soviet offer of a pact and the Bulgarian refusal. After Manuilsky had whispered that this information had not been mentioned in the Soviet press, Dimitrov "then made a correction, saying that the Soviet proposal for a Mutual Assistance Pact with Bulgaria should not be talked about. . . . Since I consider it wrong to make public those issues that are the subject of unpublished official negotiations of the Soviet government, I would ask you to advise Comrade Dimitrov to avoid revealing such communications."[51]

Bulgaria formally signed the Tripartite Pact on 1 March 1941 and allowed German troops to pass through Bulgarian territory en route to attacks on Yugoslavia and Greece. After the Wehrmacht conquered both countries, Bulgarian troops joined the war, occupying territory in Thrace and eastern Macedonia that had Bulgarian ethnic populations and to which there were Bulgarian historical ties. While some elements in the Bulgarian party grumbled that "the atmosphere of chauvinist intoxication" over these territorial conquests had "partially affected the working masses" and asked for Comintern guidance about how to navigate between Soviet condemnation of the action and popular support for it, Dimitrov used NKVD radio facilities to tell his comrades in Sofia that the major goal of the party was "to explain to the people the danger of utter national enslavement and to rally the healthy forces of the nation to the struggle for national independence. An authentic national policy must be opposed to the traitorous policy of the bourgeoisie: the Bulgarian army must be the defender of national independence, and not a gendarme detachment for Germany; against involving Bulgaria in the war; defense of the state against foreign intervention and the withdrawal of German troops from the country; defense of the economic independence of the country and the future of its people as an independent and full-fledged nation; friendship with the Soviet Union."[52] That goal, however, had ended in ignominious failure.

Czechoslovak Communists faced even more unpalatable orders following the pact. The Czechoslovak Republic, already weakened by the Munich Agreement of September 1938, capitulated without resistance to a Nazi invasion in March 1939. Hitler then dissolved Czechoslovakia, declaring roughly two-thirds—the Czech regions of Bohemia and Moravia—to be a protectorate of the German Reich and began a harsh program of Germanizing the regions and eradicating Czech national identity. Slovakia became an independent puppet state under a quasi-fascist government allied with Nazi Germany.

The British and French declarations of war against Germany in September 1939 stirred the Czech people's hopes of eventual freedom from Nazi rule and the regaining of national independence. On 13 September 1939 a message from Prague arrived in Moscow concerning an appeal prepared by the underground Communist Party, a statement in which Czech Communists reflected and attempted to appeal to this understandable view of most Czechs that the outbreak of the war offered hope for eventual Czechoslovak liberation: "The aggressor is Hitler's Germany. For us this means a stepping up of the struggle against the major enemy, supporting the war against Hitler, and at the same time sharply distancing ourselves from Western reactionary forces. For Slov[akia]—cutting ourselves off from the Western imperialists, supporting the liberation struggle of the Czech people. We perceive the policy of the USSR as an instrument for the independent policy of the interna[tional] prolet[ariat], for the liberation of all peoples. The most important principle is that of doing everything possible to defeat the fasc[ist] aggressor."[53]

The statement of the underground Czechoslovak Communists ran counter to the new directives of the ECCI and Stalin's new policy. The Comintern's answer was signed by Klema, the code name for Klement Gottwald, a senior Czechoslovak Communist Party official but also a member of the ECCI in Moscow. Gottwald explained the correct line:

> The Czechoslovak Communist Party is using this war to expand the struggle for the national liberation of the Czechoslovak people. In so doing it opposes the use of this liberation struggle in the interests of the imperialists of the British-French military bloc, as is being done by the Beneš supporters. [Edvard Beneš had resigned as president of Czechoslovakia after the Munich Agreement, left Czechoslovakia, and would in 1940 become the chief organizer and president of the Czechoslovak government-in-exile aligned with the anti-Nazi Allies.] Beneš's foreign policy activity is now designed to serve the imperialists and the enemies of the Soviets. Therefore the national liberation movement in the country cannot be subjected to these foreign activities and cannot support them. It is not the Chamberlain-Daladier imperialists, who a year ago handed Czechoslovakia over to Hitler and betrayed the Spanish Republic, who will free us from foreign domination; together with the German and Austrian working class, the Czech people will overthrow Hitler and free[Czechoslovakia] as a nation and as a social entity. The Soviet Union continues to remain the sole loyal friend of all oppressed peoples, and therefore also a friend of the peoples of Czechoslovakia.[54]

For people in a country under Nazi occupation, such instructions must have looked extremely odd. Not a single word was said about fascism and Nazi aggression; instead there was a condemnation of those countries fighting a war against the occupiers. Nonetheless, Communists in Prague hastened to assure Moscow that the directive was in keeping with their own views but candidly acknowledged, "At the present time among the petty bourgeois and to some extent among the workers there is disorientation regarding the nature of the war and the policy of the Soviet Union." The Central Committee of the Communist Party of Czechoslovakia informed the ECCI of the popular protests against forced Germanization in Prague and other cities in the fall of that year and in particular on 28 October, the anniversary of the independence of Czechoslovakia, proclaimed in 1918. There were also reports of harsh acts of repression carried out by Nazi authorities against those resisting German rule.[55]

The Comintern was unmoved and continued to demand the exposure of Beneš as an enemy of the USSR and flunky of Western imperialism and insisted on the establishment of solidarity with the German workers: "The revolutionary perspective requires close ties with the German working class within the ranks of international proletarian solidarity, along with friendship with the Soviet Union. Therefore anti-German chauvinism is incompatible with the development of the Czech liberation struggle." Further, Czechoslovak Communists were told to downplay Czech nationalism: "Make use of all forces to paralyze the influence of chauvinist elements. Speak out openly against Beneš as an agent of Chamberlain. Beneš is facilitating the arrests of our people in France and England." Gottwald warned that the Czechoslovak party should *not* allow itself to become involved in protests or actions that could develop into an armed struggle against Nazi occupation authorities and demanded vigilance in regard to provocations by the "agents of Chamberlain," a reference to those who supported the exiled Beneš. On 19 December a message was received from the Central Committee of the Czechoslovak Communist Party stating that the party leadership had fully accepted the policy expressed in the ECCI directives. It spoke to the need to expose Beneš and to fight for the creation of a United and Popular Front from below on the basis of the protection of the vital interests of the workers.[56]

If the Comintern's demands of Czechoslovak Communists seem perverse, those imposed on German Communists were, if anything, even more bizarre. On 25 September Wilhelm Pieck, an ECCI member and the chairman of the German Communist Party, submitted to Dimitrov a draft appeal from the Central Committee of the German Communist Party. Declaring that Hitler's fascism was the fiercest enemy of the German people, it called for the overthrow of German imperialist financial capital, on whose orders Hitler's fascism had plunged the German people into war. After discussion of this draft, the ECCI Secretariat ordered that it be radically rewritten and published on behalf of the Communist parties of Germany, Austria, and Czechoslovakia. The statement of these parties, entitled "Against Imperialist War—For the Social and National Liberation of Peoples," spoke of the brutal dictatorship of German large-scale capital, of a regime "that had shed rivers of its people's blood to establish and maintain its domination," rather than of Hitler's fascism. While it called for a lethal blow against German imperialism, it insisted that this could be accomplished "only if it is possible to unite the National Socialist, Social Democratic, Catholic, and Communist workers for the struggle against imperialism and war, for peace and socialism." It is not clear whether the Comintern authors of this appeal and those who received it considered the involvement of National Socialist (i.e., Nazi) workers in a joint struggle for socialism with the Communists and workers of other political inclinations as a realistic possibility or merely an ideological cliché inserted to have the appearance of offering a strategy for the overthrow of Hitler's regime.[57]

Though the war was described as imperialist and unjust from both warring sides, the statement asserted that British imperialism had attempted to set Germany on a course of war against the USSR: "German imperialism was afraid to go to war against this great socialist power, which is so closely linked to the popular masses in the capitalist countries; it rejected the proposal of the British imperialists to buy the subjection of Poland at the price of war against the USSR and also concluded the Nonaggression Pact with the Soviet Union. When the failure of plans for war between Germany and the Soviet Union became evident, the British imperialists howled that Hitler had gone back on his word; they embarked upon a course of war with imperialist Germany and sent their Polish vassal on ahead." The major blame for unleashing the war was placed on the Western powers: "The armies of the British and French imperialists come bearing on their bayonets not national freedom and democracy, but capitalist bondage and irreconcilable hostility toward the Soviet Union and socialism."[58]

The document was sent to the Communist parties, but then on 5 December, someone in the Comintern had second thoughts about how this statement would be read. The Secretariat of the ECCI sent the parties further instructions: "It would be better not to publish the joint statement of the Communist Parties of Germany, Czechoslovakia, and Austria. If already published, it should not be widely publicized."[59]

Following the banning of the French Communist Party, the Communist deputies in the French parliament united to form the "workers-peasants group." The Soviet-German statement of 28 September that both countries "by mutual agreement" intended to work for the end of the war served as an impetus for the initiative of the Communist deputies. In a letter to Édouard Herriot, a leader of France's Party of Radicals and Radical Socialists (a centrist party despite the name), they stated their preference for the conclusion of a "just and lasting peace." As a result of this letter, the deputies were arrested and put on trial for opposing France's participation in the war against Nazi Germany.[60]

The Comintern saw this action by the Communist deputies as an error because it supported a peace leaving Germany, France, and Britain undefeated. A coded dispatch on 3 October from the ECCI Secretariat to the leaders of the French party indicated: "We consider the letter to Herriot a mistake. In present circumstances the French Communists cannot take the initiative and shoulder responsibility for the conclusion of peace among the bourgeois governments of France, England, and Germany, because such a peace would be an imperialist peace, inevitably spawning new wars. In fighting against the imperialist war, the Communists are trying to end it through the defeat of the bourgeois government and the victory of the working class, which would eliminate the sources of war." At the same time the party leadership was ordered to make use of the forthcoming trial of the deputies for propagating "a line of principle against imperialist war and the capitalist regime." The Comintern carefully followed the party's preparations for the trial and demanded a campaign of protest against the trial in France and in other countries.[61]

On 17 October Dimitrov sent Stalin the text of his article "War and the Working Class of Capitalist Countries." The letter of transmittal stated: "Although the Communist Parties have, in the main, rectified their position in regard to the war, there is still some confusion in their ranks regarding the new tasks of the working class and the necessary changes in the tactics of the Communist Parties that emerge now. Considering this, we would deem it necessary to publish the enclosed article in the magazine "Communist International" and in the Communist press abroad. Since this action acquires great importance under present conditions, I request Your advice." Another copy of the draft article was sent to Andrei Zhdanov, a close associate of Stalin and often a point man on ideological matters.[62]

Stalin personally made corrections to Dimitrov's article. On 25 October he summoned the leader of the Comintern and in Zhdanov's presence made a number of comments on the text of the article. The major point was that the text should not "run ahead" of events and "slogans must be used that are in keeping with this particular stage of the war." Stalin considered as correct such slogans as "Down with the imperialist war! End the war, end the bloodshed!" Stalin reminded Dimitrov that "We will not come out against governments that favor peace!" (a reference to the Soviet-German statement of 28 September that both countries "by mutual agreement" intended to work to end the war. Germany, therefore, was a government that favored peace and should not be specifically targeted.) He also noted, "Raising the issue of peace now, on the basis of the destruction of capitalism, means helping Chamberlain and the warmongers, means isolating oneself from the masses!"[63]

The sense of these comments was the need for a struggle to defeat the governments of Britain and France. In Stalin's interpretation, they were the aggressors, while Nazi Germany was for peace. At this time *Pravda* published Ribbentrop's discussion with a Japanese correspondent. Hitler's minister stated that "Germany has always wanted peace, not war. War with Poland was imposed on us despite the Führer's reasonable proposals. In the West as well, it was not Germany but England and France who declared war. If Germany is nevertheless still ready to conclude peace that is nothing new."[64] The same newspaper published Stalin's answer regarding the statement by the French Havas news agency. Stalin echoed Ribbentrop's points: "a) It was not Germany that attacked France and England, but France and England that attacked Germany and bore the responsibility for the current war; b) after the onset of hostilities Germany made peace proposals to France and England, and the Soviet Union openly supported Germany's peace proposals, since it continues to consider that a speedy end to the war would radically ease the situation of all countries and peoples; c) the ruling circles in England and France crudely rejected Germany's peace proposals as well as the attempts of the Soviet Union to end the war as soon as possible."[65]

Rewritten in accordance with Stalin's instructions, Dimitrov's article was published and sent to the Communist parties for use as a directive of the ECCI. Though the article cited the previous assessments of the nature of the war, the emphasis was nevertheless that the imperialists of Britain and France, who had miscalculated in terms of their hopes of a clash between Germany and the Soviet Union, were responsible for the carnage. Nothing was said to disparage Hitler or attack fascism. The need for comprehensive support of the Soviet Union's policy was persistently reiterated.[66]

The Comintern also demanded that the Communist parties immediately distribute two of Molotov's speeches. The first denounced "the ruling circles of Poland" and called the country "this ugly offspring of the Versailles treaty, which had been staying alive by oppressing the non-Polish nationalities." Mocking the British government's statement that its goal was "the destruction of Hitlerism," Molotov insisted that "ideology cannot be destroyed by force and cannot be terminated by war," labeling the British goal "both senseless and criminal." The relationship between the USSR and Germany "was built on the basis of friendly relations, on readiness to support Germany's aspirations for peace." Molotov's tenets, the Comintern declared, were fundamental to the Communist parties' understanding of the war.[67]

In early November 1939 Stalin went even further, suggesting that "in Germany, the petty-bourgeois nationalists are capable of a sharp turn—they are flexible—not tied to capitalist traditions, unlike bourgeois leaders like Chamberlain and his ilk." Old ways of looking at ideological issues needed to be changed: "Bureaucracy means holding to established rules, routines, not thinking independently, contributing nothing new that might be dictated by changed circumstances," implying that the Nazis might adopt anti-capitalist positions.[68]

The political platform of the German Communist Party, approved by the ECCI Secretariat on 30 December, stated that the aggressive British-French imperialist bloc was gravely endangering the national freedom and independence of the German people. The document emphasized that there should be no letup of the campaign against the oppressive policy of the ruling regime in Germany. The Communist Party of Germany did not support the war of German imperialism. Its emphasis, however, was elsewhere. The center of gravity of the struggle, the document stressed, "had to be shifted to undermining the military plan of British and French imperialism and to the destruction of the enemies of the German people, who want to undermine the Soviet-German Friendship Pact, support the British-French war plans against the German people, and plunge the people of Germany into the greatest catastrophe, which could be a war with the great Soviet people."[69] The aggressive British-French imperialist bloc was the chief enemy of German Communists, not the Nazi regime.

The Comintern's illusions concerning the potential for cooperation with the Nazis were also evident in instructions to German Communists on the need to transform mass Nazi organizations into bastions of support for the interests of the German masses. As the German Communists put it, "The goal of friendship with the Soviet Union, which also emerged among the National Socialist working masses as a result of the Soviet-German Pacts on Nonaggression and Friendship, opens up broad opportunities to win them over and include them with the Communist and Social Democratic workers in the ranks of the common fighting front to counter the rapacious plans of British and French imperialism and the rich capitalist traitors to the fatherland in

Germany, in order to create a solid guarantee for maintaining and strengthening the friendship between the Soviet Union and Germany."

The leadership of the German Communist Party was trying to implement this policy as late as January 1941, suggesting to the Communists inside Germany that they "create responsible leadership in the country itself, consisting of comrades living there legally." The guidelines for work in Germany, where the Communist Party was banned and severely repressed, included such delusional suggestions as: "In the public awareness campaign among National Socialist workers and officials, focus on the nature of the war. Carry out in the DAF [German Labor Front, the Nazi substitute for the abolished trade unions] a campaign for better working conditions, air defense, food, genuine peace without the oppression of other peoples, and so on. Conduct open mass propaganda in favor of the Soviet Union." Whether any Communists inside the German Reich attempted to carry out this policy is unknown, but certainly nothing was accomplished. On 7 January 1940 Dimitrov and Manuilsky told Stalin that they agreed with the German Communists' line.[70]

Some foreign Communists occasionally departed from the ECCI's playbook. On the same day that the ECCI Secretariat approved the political platform of the German Communist Party, a manifesto from the Communist parties of Britain, France, and Germany, prepared by some officials of those three parties without Comintern supervision, was published in London, calling on the workers of these countries to speak out in favor of ending the war. Each party called for resistance to the government of its own country. There was a statement on behalf of the German Communist Party that "the working class of Germany must wage a struggle against Hitler using all possible means."[71]

The publication of the London manifesto threw the leadership of the ECCI into a panic. Dimitrov gave instructions to find out the reason for the appearance of this document. He sent an inquiry to Douglas Springhall, the Comintern's agent in the British party: "Communicate who has published proclamation of German, French, and English Parties. Take measures that in future such publications do not appear without our agreement." Wilhelm Pieck, the leading German Communist in the ECCI, explained to Dimitrov that the manifesto had been printed without the knowledge of the Central Committee of the German Communist Party, with authorization by Wilhelm Könen, a leading German Communist then in exile in London. Pieck assured Dimitrov that the German Communist Party did not endorse it. Walter

Ulbricht, a leading German Communist in exile in Moscow, wanted the British Communist Party told that "it is not admissible for a fraternal Party with one member of the German Communist Party to sign on behalf of the Central Committee of the German Communist Party, since the comrades in emigration do not have any such right to do so." In his zeal to distance himself from the issue, he had obviously forgotten that *all* the senior leaders of the German Communist Party were émigrés, including himself.[72]

The London manifesto violated Stalin's ban on "speaking out against governments that are for peace" that is, Nazi Germany. The sharply negative reaction of the Comintern leaders showed the extent of confusion in their own arguments due to the zigzags of Stalin's policy and how fearful they were of the slightest digression from it. Even a mere reference to previous instructions was seen as a manifestation of disloyalty. In February 1940, an issue of the *Communist International* containing prewar articles and documents appeared in Britain, circulated by the CPGB. The ECCI Secretariat reprimanded the leadership of the British Communist Party: "We consider as a big political mistake publication and circulation in February [1940] of the September [issue] containing materials that had been written before outbreak of war in Europe." The Secretariat proposed withdrawing the issue from circulation and suggested it was necessary "to make an inquiry in order to know who is responsible for this act that indirectly runs counter to the Party's policy and that measures be taken so that such outrageous incidents are not repeated." Springhall apologized for the error and assured the Comintern that measures had been taken to avoid a recurrence of similar blunders. The publication of Comintern materials propagandizing the antifascist struggle and formulations that laid the blame for the outbreak of the future war on Hitler's Germany were harmful. The main fire was supposed to be "directed against British and French imperialism."[73]

In the spring and summer of 1940 Germany struck a series of consecutive blows at neutral countries and then at the British and French troops. On 9 April the Wehrmacht invaded Denmark and Norway; on 10 May, Belgium, the Netherlands, and Luxemburg; and on 14 May, attacked France. Unmoved by these developments, the Comintern continued to castigate Britain and France as the aggressors.

In justification of the invasion of Denmark, Ribbentrop authorized the German ambassador to the USSR to report to Molotov that the German authorities "had received totally reliable reports on an inevitable strike from the British-French armed forces on the coastline of

Denmark and Norway, and therefore had to act immediately." Molotov responded that "The Soviet government understands that Germany was forced to resort to such measures. The British, unquestionably, have gone too far. They totally fail to take into account the rights of neutral countries." In conclusion Molotov added, "We wish Germany a total victory in its defensive undertakings."[74]

The directives of the Comintern reflected a similar assessment. On 10 April the ECCI Secretariat sent a statement to Stockholm, signed by Dimitrov, to be passed along to the Danish Communists. They were instructed to publish it: "The British-French aggressive imperialist policy of war in Scandinavia has resulted in imperialist countermeasures from Germany. The major culprits are the warmongers in London, Paris, and their agents in the Second International. The governments of Scandinavia are equally to blame, since they are pandering to the unleashing of an imperialist war and have supported military preparations against the Soviet Union." The Danish party was allowed to protest against the occupation of its country and attempts to impose German domination on the peoples of Scandinavia. But, the Comintern reminded it, "The peoples of Scandinavia speak out in favor of the end of the imperialist war, must speak out for peace. They cannot in any way allow themselves to be used by British imperialism in order to expand the war in Scandinavia."[75]

Exactly how this was to be done was not clear, and specific tasks the Comintern set the Danish Communist Party reflected this confusion. Another directive sent on the same day contained instructions to "to seek any opportunity to maintain any legal position, to avoid any kind of bravado in order to prevent the occupying powers from taking measures against the Party, to warn the workers to be vigilant in regard to the agents-provocateurs." But while Danish Communists were to avoid irritating German occupation authorities, at the same time the Comintern instructed the party to prepare for underground activity. Later the ECCI Secretariat was forced to provide a special warning to the party regarding the danger that demagogic maneuvers by the occupiers might create the impression that the Danish Communist Party was on their side. "Avoiding giving deference to the occupation," stated the ECCI Secretariat's directive of 28 June, "the Party must prepare the masses politically for the struggle for national liberation." The confused nature of such instructions is perfectly obvious since it was hardly possible to raise the question of the restoration of independence while passing over in silence the question of against whom this struggle should be directed.[76]

Through Stockholm Nils (Dimitrov) sent a similar warning to the Norwegian Communist Party: "Inform immediately our friends in Oslo that it is not admissible to take a pro-German position. The Communists must in any and all circumstances have their own position, strictly distance themselves from both warring sides, and in present circumstances not take on any responsibility for the actions of the occupiers." A copy of this message was simultaneously sent to the leaders of the French Communist Party. Warning a party, operating in conditions of the occupation of its country, against any kind of cooperation with those resisting the occupiers meant weakening the potential for resistance to the invaders. At the same time the reference in the instructions to the Communist parties of the occupied countries concerning the inadmissibility of any cooperation with the occupiers was significant; there was a limit to how far the Comintern would accommodate the Nazi regime.[77]

In this situation, the Comintern in its instructions to the Communist parties of these countries unceasingly placed responsibility for the loss of independence on both of the warring sides and on the bourgeoisie of each country. "The line must be the following: To explain to the Dutch people who bears responsibility for the present disaster. . . . The blame for this lies with British and German imperialism and with the policy of the Dutch bourgeoisie and Social Democracy." Once again, the Comintern was assigning the blame for the seizure of the Netherlands first and foremost to "British imperialism" and only then to the other culprits. The objectives of the party were also set forth:

> To fight against the plundering of the country by the occupiers, against shifting the consequences of the occupation onto the masses, to fight for the demands of the masses in the social and economic spheres, against political reaction and depriving the people of their rights, for the restoration of the political independence of the country. No cooperation with the Dutch elements cooperating with the occupiers, and simultaneously a firm separation from the Dutch government and dynasty. In all areas an independent policy of the Party. . . . Make full use of all legal possibilities, but it is necessary to combine these with illegal work. In legal statements avoid anything that could be interpreted as solidarity with the occupiers. Intensive propaganda of the principles of communism and the popularization of socialist construction and a policy of peace of the Soviet Union.

The Comintern warned the party that it would have to take into account an extremely brutal campaign of terror directed at it and that therefore it should take all possible measures to protect personnel, "so that the Party remains functional in all circumstances." The ECCI Secretariat demanded that necessary measures be taken so that leading officials could remain in the country and continue their party work.[78]

The Comintern continued, however, to be wary of giving its instructions an antifascist slant. In preserving the traditional demands of propagandizing the principles of communism and popularizing the role of the USSR, it could not sidestep the question of the occupiers, though it categorically opposed cooperation with them and stressed the need to prepare for harsh assaults on the party. These warnings, however, were not always heeded by those to whom they were sent. For example, in Belgium, Norway, and France the Communists tried to obtain the agreement of the occupying powers to publish their printed materials. This was not as preposterous as it sounds. "Officially the Party is not banned, although its activities and political publications are illegal," reported Clément on 21 March 1941, describing the situation of the Belgian Communist Party. "In many cases, comrades are continuing to carry out their duties in local government."[79]

The Secretariat of the ECCI found out that in France the leaders of the Communist Party engaged in negotiations with the Nazi occupiers. It was scandalous news. Dimitrov was infuriated. Duclos wrote on 6 July that since the Belgian Communist Party had obtained permission from the Germans to publish a Communist newspaper in Flemish, "we would like to obtain from the German authorities permission for the legal publication of *L'Humanité*." The French police, however, had arrested the Communist negotiator, along with Tréand, in June. The party had immediately retained a lawyer who appealed to the Germans, and on 24 June the two Communists were released. Otto Abetz, an official of the German Ministry of Foreign Affairs serving in the office of the German occupation forces, then requested a meeting with Tréand and several other Communists to discuss the publication of *L'Humanité*. The party leadership acquiesced and sent Tréand with another candidate member of the party CC, Jean Catelas, and the lawyer to the meeting with Abetz. This meeting took place but produced no results. The actions of the party leaders illustrated the disorientation caused by the Nazi-Soviet Pact. The ties between the ECCI and the Communist Party were threatened because of Tréand, who was illegal and was one of the major figures in this matter. In a letter to Stalin of 3 August 1940 Dimitrov reported on the instructions of the ECCI Secretariat sent to Duclos on 19 July. He told Stalin that for the most part the French party line was acknowledged as correct. The party was called on to step up its vigilance against the maneuvers of the occupiers. It had been correct to try to obtain the right of its press to legal publication, but the meeting with Abetz, Dimitrov noted, was a serious mistake, threatening to compromise the party and its leadership: "We consider it appropriate to encourage passive resistance by the broad masses to the occupiers in every form, but it is imperative to do so carefully, using illegal means, without overt propaganda, and not involving the Party formally. While avoiding any premature action that might play into the hands of the occupiers, it is important to support open manifestations of popular discontent, provided such a movement is well prepared and organized and will be joined by broad masses, especially women." Later the ECCI Secretariat prepared a directive for the French Communist Party containing much stronger wording of the demand that the party categorically reject and condemn "as treason any manifestation of solidarity with the occupiers." The draft of the directive was sent to Stalin, and following his approval the ECCI Secretariat adopted it on 5 August. Dimitrov wrote on the text of the document that has been preserved in the archive, "Received from c. Stalin 5.8.40 GD."[80]

Dimitrov and Maurice Thorez (the French party leader in exile in Moscow) stressed in a cipher communication to Clément that the materials received from him "reaffirm our concern, caused by information from other sources, regarding the extreme danger to the Party caused by the maneuvers of the occupiers. We categorically insist that you immediately break off negotiations with Abetz and his agents." On 21 August Communist leaders in Paris sent an explanation for what had happened to Moscow: "Following the previous communications all negotiations have been broken off. We are taking measures to step up vigilance. . . . The Party is fighting against the French authorities and against the occupiers. Some 150 comrades have been arrested as a result of the demonstrations and of distributing literature. The maneuvers of the occupiers have been followed daily. We are taking your instructions seriously and will be guided by them. We are surprised that it could have been thought that we could have become toys in the hands of the occupiers." Blame for the negotiations with Abetz was placed on the lawyer, Robert Foissin, who was quickly expelled from the Party.[81]

Duclos wrote reassuringly, "We will do everything possible to ensure that, through its political firmness, vigilance, and mass work, the Party shows itself worthy of the confidence of the French people and the confidence of the Communist International." When sending Stalin Duclos's letters and other materials from the French Communist Party, Dimitrov reported that "From these documents as well as from other sources of information, it is clear that the leadership of the French Communist Party is carrying out the directive sent to it."[82]

While Hitler's troops were finishing off their crushing military rout of France, the Comintern and, therefore, the Communist Party of Germany continued to avoid direct criticism of the Nazi regime and direct ire at British and French "imperialists." The declaration written by the leaders of the German party, adopted by the ECCI Secretariat on 29 May, stated that German imperialism was seeking to dominate European peoples and colonies and expressed sympathy for "the victims of violence and imperialist war in Denmark, Norway, Holland, Belgium, and Luxembourg, and for the enslaved Czech, Polish, and Austrian peoples." It was noted that the regime ruling the country "is keeping imprisoned many thousands of the best fighters for peace, freedom, and bread." Simultaneously, it emphasized that "The assertion that the victory of the British-French imperialists brings the German workers and toilers freedom is blatantly deceptive." The authors of the document limited themselves to noting that the workers of all countries were equally interested in putting an end as soon as possible to this slaughter of peoples and punishing the perpetrators of the war. Dimitrov in a coded communication to Swedish Communist Party leaders ordered that the German party's declaration be published in the Swedish party newspaper *Ny Dag* and that everything be done to ensure "the broadest possible discussion of the document in our press."[83]

The leaders of the Comintern also requested Stalin's views "on the policy of conduct of the German Communists in regard to the policy of conquest of the German ruling classes." With that goal in mind, Dimitrov and Manuilsky sent him the draft declaration of the French Communist Party and the declaration of the German Communist Party. In regard to the latter, the letter states:

> The German Communists have produced a document, published in the foreign Communist press, in which they expose the imperialist plans of their bourgeoisie and put forward the banner of peace, peace without territorial seizures and war indemnities, without the enslavement of some peoples by others, a peace based on the free expression of the will of peoples in determining their own fates. C[omrades] Pieck and Florin are raising with us the question as to whether it might be advisable that the German Communist Party put forward the demand of the confiscation of war profits, nationalization of the banks, major trusts, and concerns in order to shift the burdens of the war onto the propertied classes and ease the difficult situation of the workers and peasants.

While voicing their view that the position of the French and German Communists "is not erroneous," they nevertheless deemed it necessary to give them advice and instructions in regard to these documents. They explained their request by the fact that "the present international situation is so complex and the times are so momentous, that any political error of ours can have a negative impact on the interests of the USSR." There was no answer to it.[84]

The lack of criticism of the Hitler regime in the Comintern's documents did not remain unnoticed in Germany. A survey of events compiled by the Gestapo on 20 June 1940 observed:

> The Russian government is taking a favorable position in regard to Germany and has on numerous occasions shown that it considers the measures taken by Germany in the war—the taking of Norway, Denmark and the entrance into Holland and Belgium—as necessary and proper. The Comintern, too, is avoiding any open attacks on Germany. In its press the Comintern is adapting to the present foreign policy of the Soviet Union and recognizes that Germany is waging a just war. This present position of the Comintern is only a declaration that its resistance to the Reich has remained unchanged and that it has only changed its method of work. In its organs it does not openly call for its supporters to struggle against National Socialism, but does so primarily in veiled form.[85]

Although the remark that the Comintern was recognizing "that Germany is waging a just war" was inaccurate, the fact that, following Molotov's statements, the ECCI declared that the German Army's takeover of Denmark was allegedly provoked by Britain and France gave certain grounds for such an exaggerated view.

The Winter War of 1939–1940

The Soviet-Finnish war provided a special demonstration of the Comintern's servile deference to Stalin's foreign policy. In late 1939 the USSR demanded territorial concessions from the Republic of Finland, including the right to establish a military base on Finnish soil. The Finns rejected the demands, although offering a few minor border adjustments. The war began on 30 November with a massive Soviet attack on Finland.

As the Red Army crossed the border, Soviet radio announced the establishment of the "Finnish Democratic Republic," with which the Soviet Union immediately concluded a Treaty of Friendship and

Mutual Assistance. In the treaty the Finnish Democratic Republic, among other points, accepted all of the USSR's border demands. The USSR was the only nation that diplomatically recognized the Finnish Democratic Republic. The chairman of this puppet republic was Finnish Communist Otto Kuusinen, for many years a member of the Comintern leadership. On 4 December the ECCI Secretariat sent the Communist parties a cipher communication written by Dimitrov with instructions to organize a vigorous campaign of solidarity with this newly created Finnish Democratic Republic and to publish declarations and resolutions of meetings, organizations, and individuals in support of Kuusinen's government. Greetings were to be sent "to the Finnish People's Government and the Red Army, emphasizing its mission of liberation." The next directive, which also spoke to the need for solidarity with the government of this republic, specifically underscored the objective of paralyzing "anti-Soviet propaganda. Explain and popularize the policy of the Soviet Union. Vigorously oppose the warmongers. Ruthlessly expose the counterrevolutionary plans of the British and French imperialists and their Social Democratic lackeys, and struggle against them."[86]

In fulfillment of these instructions, the Central Committee of the underground Communist Party of Czechoslovakia sent greetings from Prague: "We are convinced that in a short period of time, with the assistance of the glorious Red Army, the great task of liberation will be fulfilled, the Finnish people will be provided with an open road to a happy future, and the Soviet Union under the leadership of Stalin will continue its mission of liberation and of rendering assistance to peoples groaning under the imperialist yoke and struggling for their liberation."[87]

The Communist parties, however, were about the only entities to support the Soviet invasion of Finland. The USSR's attack set off a strong wave of support for Finland, particularly in the Scandinavian countries, for their small neighbor that had fallen victim to unprovoked aggression. Sympathy for Finland extended beyond Scandinavia as well, and the USSR was expelled from the League of Nations. Britain and France considered providing military aid to Finland or even intervention, and the possibility of the establishment of a military coalition against the USSR was looming. In this situation the Comintern attempted through the Communist parties to weaken the rise in anti-Soviet feeling, depicting this as a reflection of war plans against the USSR. A directive to the Swedish Communist Party from the ECCI noted, "The national interests of the Swedish people require a struggle against attempts by the English imperialists to plunge Scandinavia into a war with the Soviet Union. Through material assistance and the sending of volunteers and military materiel to Finnish White Guards [Finns and Finnish immigrants who supported resistance to the Soviet invasion] the Swedish reactionary forces are trying to make the country be at war with the Soviet Union without a declaration of war." The Communist Party was called on to campaign for the neutrality of Sweden and to oppose providing assistance to Finland.[88]

The Comintern did not limit itself to declarations of solidarity with the actions of the Red Army. Its directives to the Communist parties contained a demand to prevent assistance to Finland. "It is necessary to intensify the campaign against White Finns in America, Canada, and in countries in Latin America. To the reactionary campaign to help the White Finns it is necessary to counterpose the widest campaign for help to China with demand that America stop the war supplies [to] Japan in the war against China." The ECCI Secretariat gave instructions to the U.S. Communist Party to assist Mirton (Merton), an unidentified Soviet intelligence operative, in selecting Finnish American Communists to be sent to Finland to assist Soviet intelligence. The cipher communication from George (Dimitrov) to "Dad and Son" (party chief Earl Browder and Rudy Baker, head of the CPUSA's covert arm), stated: "We beg you to help comrade Mirton, who will bring you that letter and inform you in detail in fulfilling the task of sending a group of Finnish people to Finland for special work. This task is of great political importance, and it has to be carried out very carefully by the Finnish comrades Karl Paivio or Onni Kaartinen or another whom you will find better for this work but under your control. Please connect comrade Mirton with the Finnish comrade who will be authorized for that." (Karl Paivio and Onni Kaartinen were veteran leaders of the Finnish ethnic section of the American Communist Party.)[89]

The hostilities continued until the spring of 1940. While the Finns made the Red Army pay a very high price, eventually the sheer weight of Soviet numbers prevailed, and a peace treaty was concluded between the USSR and Finland. The Finns made painful territorial concessions to the USSR but retained their national independence and, in fact, renewed the war in 1941 in an unsuccessful attempt to retake what had been lost. As for the government of the Finnish Democratic Republic, launched with much acclaim by the USSR and the Communist International in 1939 and slated to rule all of Finland, it disappeared, nominally merging into the Karelian Autonomous Soviet Socialist Republic, part of the USSR's Russian Federation, to create the Karelo-Finnish

Soviet Socialist Republic of the USSR. In its directives to the Communist parties, however, the Comintern continued to reiterate that the conclusion of peace meant "a new victory of the S.U. peace policy" and that this had undermined the attempts of the British and French imperialists "to drag Scandinavia into the war and to unleash the conflagration of a world war."[90]

Given the USSR's attack on Finland, which had prompted vigorous condemnation of such an act of aggression, all these appeals contributed to discredit the Comintern and the Communist parties. The Soviet-Finnish war also caused many Finnish Communists to reconsider their allegiance. Arvo Tuominen was a founding member of the Finnish Communist Party in 1918 and became its chief (general secretary) in 1935. Finnish Communists faced legal suppression in Finland, and he spent most of the 1930s either in Moscow or in Sweden. He was in Sweden at the time of the Soviet attack on Finland in late 1939 and remained there, not taking part in the government of the new Finnish Democratic Republic created by the Comintern and Stalin. When the war ended in March 1940, Tuominen broke with the Communist movement. In a bitter message to Dimitrov in June, 1940, he wrote:

> In the same way that Hitler forgot to ask the peoples of Austria, Czechoslovakia, and Poland whether they wanted a liberator in the form of Hitler's army, the Soviet government forgot or arrogantly did not deem it necessary to ask the people of Finland regarding the views of that segment of the population whose maintenance [support] was counted on at the outset of the offensive, and to ask whether they wanted such a "People's Government" and the Red Army for their liberation. . . . It should now be the duty of the Comintern and its Parties to declare that Moscow peace is not peace, but rather the typical diktat of an imperialist aggressor whose hands have stripped the people of Finland of more than 10% of their lands and national property.[91]

His ties with the Comintern ended, Tuominen began to write anti-Communist pamphlets that received much attention in Finland. He remained underground in Sweden, however, until after World War II. He returned to Finland in 1956, became a Social Democrat, and was elected to parliament.

Fascist Italy: A Different Approach

The pact of 1939 was strictly between the USSR and Nazi Germany, and Stalin's solicitude for the latter did not extend to Hitler's fascist ally, Italy. Consequently the leadership of the Comintern took a different position regarding Italy, which had entered the war on 10 June 1940. On 28 June the ECCI Secretariat approved the declaration of the Communist Party of Italy. Dimitrov cabled Swedish party leaders that "You will very soon be receiving from us the Declaration of the Italian Party. It must be published immediately in *Ny Dag*. Send it by telegram to London and Geneva. Inform us immediately as to when publication in *Ny Dag* will take place." A query followed later: "Urgently confirm the receipt of the Italian Declaration and inform of date of publication in *Ny Dag*. Nils [Dimitrov]." The answer read, "The Italian Declaration came on the sixth. Will be published on the eighth in *Ny Dag*. Gustav [Lager]."[92]

The coded dispatch sent to the Communist Party of Yugoslavia contained a detailed description of this document. It emphasized that "the fascist clique is assisting German imperialism in establishing hegemony [over] the capitalist world [in] the hope of strengthening its terrorist regime. . . . The Communist Party of Italy is stating in the name of the Italian people that: it does not wish to be either the slave of its fascist bourgeoisie, or a vassal of foreign imperialism, or the jailor of the fraternal French people. . . . The Declaration calls on the Italian workers, peasants, toilers, and soldiers not to lay down their arms until they expel the fascist plutocracy." In addition to the slogan of immediate cessation of hostilities and peace without territorial seizures or the enslavement of foreign peoples and indemnities, it cited the Communist Party's demands for democratic, antifascist transformations in the country. Messages with a similar content were sent to Prague, Amsterdam, Brussels, and Sofia. Neither the coded dispatch nor the full text of the declaration itself contained a single word of abuse toward Socialists and international Social Democracy. It was noted, however, that only a worker and peasant government could put an end to capitalist exploitation and imperialist military adventures and ensure the total liberation of the Italian workers. At the same time the Communist Party expressed its "readiness to cooperate [with] all Parties and groups fighting [for] the above-cited measures."[93]

For the first time since the beginning of the war, a document approved by the ECCI Secretariat had expressed the readiness of the Communist Party, in certain conditions, to cooperate with other parties and groups in the antiwar and antifascist struggle. This was a kind of blunder or slip since all other such documents had always contained a negative assessment of the role of Social Democracy. This is reaffirmed by the fact that in a coded dispatch to Silvati (Antonio Roasio, member of the Foreign Bureau of the Italian Communist Party in France), Ercoli (Palmiro Togliatti, the Italian party leader and a high-ranking Comintern official) later gave a special warning that readiness to cooperate "does not change our present policy of struggle against Social Democracy." At that time the Comintern also began to emphasize that Communists in those countries that had lost their independence during the war had to act as defenders of the interests of the working class, the toilers, and also national interests. It was emphasized, however, that this goal could be achieved only under the leadership of the Communist Party and through the struggle for socialism.[94]

As the flames of war kept spreading, the problems of defending national independence and resisting the enslavement of countries by the Nazi aggressors became ever more pressing and vital. In its instructions to the Communist parties, however, the Comintern often seemed oblivious to the war in this period. For example, directives to the parties dealt with the need for dissemination of the short biography of Stalin and yet another edition of his anthology on *Questions of Leninism*. Directives were sent to Sweden requesting the provision of assistance to the German Communists in distributing this biography. Pieck, on behalf of the ECCI, asked to be informed "how many copies could be sent to the country [Germany] directly from Sweden." Instructions for the publication and propaganda of these editions were sent to the Communist parties of the United States, Yugoslavia, and other countries.[95]

Early 1941: A Change in Tone

As the Nazi occupation of Western Europe solidified, underground Communists provided the Comintern with a rising volume of reports on the campaign of terror conducted by the Hitlerite occupiers. On 4 January 1941 Goulooze reported on Dutch protests against the anti-Semitic actions of the German authorities: "For two weeks there was persecution of the Jews in Amsterdam. The fascists encountered resistance from the population. On 22 January the Gestapo began arresting many Jews. Today there was a general strike in Amsterdam and mass demonstrations in protest against the persecution of the Jews. Nearly the entire population participated in these. Report this to Clément." Dimitrov added to the text the phrase "The Dutch friend is informing us" and forwarded the message to France.[96]

This information prompted the Comintern to take action. The instructions of Maurice Thorez and André Marty to the underground

Central Committee of the Communist Party of France stated, "Conduct the campaign against anti-Semitism more vigorously, striking at the reactionary regime and racial theory of the occupiers." They stressed that "while directing the main fire of the campaigns against all agents of the occupiers and all channels for a policy of compliance, and criticizing the antidemocratic tenets of the de Gaulle movement, there is still a need objectively to take into account the positive role of this movement at the present stage." On the text of this message Dimitrov noted, "Agreed."[97]

Dimitrov's "Agreed" annotation meant that the text of the directive had received the approval of the Soviet leadership, and it represented a shift in Soviet attitudes. General Charles de Gaulle had refused to recognize France's surrender in 1940 and had gone into exile in Britain to organize the "Free French" movement. The Free French were aligned with Great Britain and received British aid, and Free French troops fought alongside British formations. De Gaulle's movement also provided assistance and aid to the anti-Nazi resistance in occupied France and contested the authority of the collaborationist Vichy government that ruled the portion of southern France not occupied by German troops. Initially the Soviets were hostile to de Gaulle because of his alignment with Britain and continued belligerency toward Nazi Germany, so this grudging recognition in early 1941 of the "positive role" of the Gaullists represented a shift. This change in the Comintern's approach was not, of course, a Dimitrov initiative. Every shift in the Comintern's line reflected Dimitrov's understanding of Stalin's attitude. Possibly Hitler's decision to ignore Stalin's proposal of late November 1940 that the Soviet Union become a full partner in the Axis alliance caused Stalin to reconsider his hitherto unalloyed hostility to the anti-Nazi Western alliance and begin to hedge his bets. Whatever the reason, while the general line of the Nazi-Soviet Pact period continued, starting in early 1941 one can read in the cables a change of tone and a slow shift toward directing the Communist parties to a renewal of antifascist activities.

The leadership of the underground French Communist Party, however, was slow to realize that Moscow's policies were shifting. Duclos wrote in answer, "We are fighting against all agents of the occupiers, all protectors of collaboration, and have also shown the reactionary nature of the de Gaulle movement." The ECCI Secretariat once again had to point out to the leaders of the French Communist Party the need to change their attitude. In a directive of 26 April, Dimitrov, Thorez, and Marty called the struggle for national liberation the most important task of the party, which meant the creation of a broad National Front to fight for independence: "In fighting for the creation of this broad Front of National Liberation . . . the Party is ready to support any French government, any organization and all people in the country whose efforts are aimed at waging a genuine struggle against the invaders and traitors. On this basis, the Party is not taking a hostile position in regard to the supporters of de Gaulle, though it is providing appropriate criticism of his reactionary colonialist positions." In his answer Duclos, then the ranking member of the PCF in France, indicated that the party was planning to create a National Front but that French Communists were continuing to take a negative attitude to the Gaullist movement, calling it "a reactionary and colonialist movement, created on the model of and in imitation of British imperialism," an unusual display of French party reluctance to accept Moscow's directive.[98]

The veiled anti-Hitler thrust of the Comintern's shifting stand during this period is particularly visible in the ECCI Secretariat's instructions to American party leader Earl Browder: "Consider absolutely necessary in present situation publication of German popular democratic paper as well for Germans living in America as for influencing Germans in countries occupied by Germany, as for Germany itself." It was suggested to Browder that German writers come up with a letter addressed to German soldiers: "Letter should be in simple popular language and explain to German soldiers that war of Germany is not against English plutocracy, not for luck and prosperity of German people but in interest of German plutocrats, to put down working-class movement of other countries. Necessary to prove that there is neither power of people nor socialism in Germany. One of most important preliminary conditions for restoration of peace is complete national independence of all people oppressed by Germany. Give to understand that German soldiers should fraternize with people of occupied countries. Letter should be published first in non-Communist American paper and only then sent to Scandinavian telegraph agency."[99]

Such directives revealed the impact of many factors. Traditional ideological patterns were intertwined with harsh Stalinist precepts, reflecting the lines of Stalinist foreign policy. These precepts could not be abandoned; they had to be presented as the peaceful policy of a socialist power that was defending the interests of all of the workers and small peoples. The Comintern conducted this line steadily. At the same time, it tried to take into account the objective realities of a situation in which the German Army had seized nearly all of Europe. This produced both naïvely dogmatic notions of the inviolability of the class solidarity of workers of various countries, including soldiers of the German Wehrmacht, and growing and more evident tensions between Germany and the USSR. This assessment was backed by the record of a conversation between Dimitrov and Molotov after the latter's return in November 1940 from his trip to Berlin for negotiations with Hitler and Ribbentrop. "We are following a course of demoralizing the German occupation troops in the various countries, and without shouting about it, we mean to intensify those operations still further. Will that not interfere with Soviet policy?" asked Dimitrov. Molotov responded that Dimitrov should not worry: "That is of course what we must do. We would not be Communists if we were not following such a course. Only it must be done quietly."[100] Times were changing.

After Germany attacked Greece and Yugoslavia on the night of 5 April 1941 Dimitrov stated the following at a meeting of the ECCI Secretariat: "Yugoslavia is waging a just war, a defensive war, despite the fact that it is linked to British imperialism and is receiving assistance from England. The Yugoslav people are protecting themselves against aggression from German imperialism, and the Communists of Yugoslavia must take the position that this war is a defensive one, that there is a need to participate in it and to mobilize the masses against the aggressor. But the Communists are not forgetting that the Yugoslav bourgeoisie bears the responsibility for this, and is not fully in solidarity with the policy of the government, and must not cover up the errors of the national policy of the Yugoslav bourgeoisie." Dimitrov emphasized that in the process of development of the present imperialist war there would be some countries, some peoples, who would be waging not an imperialist war but a war in defense of their own independence. However, the assessment of the European war as a whole as an imperialist one remained unchanged.[101]

Dimitrov's statement was not an improvisation. On 9 April during his meeting with Zhdanov he heard, "The events in the Balkans do not alter the overall stance we have taken as regards the imperialist war and both of the combatant capitalist alignments. We do not approve of German expansion in the Balkans. But that does not mean that we are deviating from the Pact with Germany and veering toward England."[102]

In accordance with these instructions, the Secretariat of the ECCI prepared a directive to the parties. On 17 April Dimitrov sent a draft to Stalin and Zhdanov. The letter of transmittal to Stalin stated, "If there are no other instructions from You on this matter, the directive will be sent off in the appropriate form during the next few days." Though the draft contained the traditional assessments of the war, new wording also appeared. The Communist parties of the occupied countries were given the task of "mobilizing the masses against the bourgeoisie and the occupation regime, directing the major blow at those groups of the bourgeoisie who are the henchmen of the occupiers." In regard to the countries that had defended their independence, the directive stated, "Those peoples who have been subjected to attack, such as, for example, the Yugoslav and Greek peoples, are waging a just, defensive war." Solidarity was proclaimed "with the just war of the Yugoslav and Greek peoples, who fell victims to imperialist aggression." The next day Zhdanov reported to Dimitrov by phone on Stalin's comment. The wording regarding the just war of the Greek and Yugoslav people received Stalin's approval.[103]

CHAPTER NINE

The Comintern, the Communist Parties, and the Great Patriotic War

The Soviet Union's status as a non-belligerent ally of Hitler's Germany abruptly ended on 22 June 1941, when more than 3 million German and allied Axis soldiers crossed the western Soviet border in the most massive invasion in history. The Comintern's policies, built around neutrality but giving priority to opposition to the British-led anti-Nazi coalition, immediately lost all meaning.

On 22 June Dimitrov was summoned to the Kremlin, where Stalin complained, "They attacked us without declaring any grievances, without demanding any negotiations; they attacked us viciously, like gangsters." He told Dimitrov: "For now the Comintern is not to take any overt action. The [Communist] Parties in the localities are mounting a movement in defense of the USSR. The issue of socialist revolution is not to be raised. The Sov[iet] people are waging a patriotic war against fascist Germany. It is a matter of routing fascism, which has enslaved a number of peoples and is bent on enslaving still more." The imperialist war had been transformed into an antifascist liberation war. Comprehensive support of the Soviet Union, not the spreading of the proletarian revolution, was the most important activity of the Comintern and the Communist parties. As Dimitrov emphasized at the meeting of the ECCI Secretariat held that same day, "Everything that can assist the Soviet Union and speed up the rout of fascism is decisive for our actions."[1]

In the next few days, the secretary general of the ECCI devoted his time and actions to mobilizing Communist parties around the world to carry out the new orders. Directives were sent to the parties. The specific circumstances in which each individual party was working determined its particular tasks, but each message ended with the sentence, "Keep in mind that at the given stage the question is about defense of peoples against fascist enslavement and not about socialist revolution." (The messages to Yugoslavia and France varied slightly, reading: "of the liberation from fascist enslavement.")[2]

Entrenched ideological attitudes, however, caused some of the Communist parties to have difficulty articulating the new policy, and they did not immediately carry out the turn in their policy in full compliance with the instructions of the ECCI. There was a tendency to keep on emphasizing the traditional Communist slogans, which treated war as a manifestation of international class struggle and an opportunity to advance socialism. The ECCI Secretariat immediately sent these parties appropriate explanations, sternly warning them against seeing the war between Germany and the USSR as a war "between the capitalist and socialist systems," and emphasizing that a repetition of such an appraisal "meant assisting Hitler in uniting the anti-Soviet elements of the capitalist countries around him." In a directive to the leadership of the French Communist Party regarding the need for cooperation with the Free French movement headed by General Charles de Gaulle, the ECCI Secretariat warned: "We once again are insisting on the absolute need to avoid having your propaganda represent the war of Germany against the Soviet Union as a war between the capitalist and socialist systems. For the Soviet Union, this is a defensive war against fascist barbarism. Chatter about world revolution is rendering a service to Hitler and is hampering the international consolidation of all anti-Hitlerite forces."[3]

Such a sharp depreciation of the slogan of world revolution had been foreshadowed by prior Soviet and Comintern policies that had downplayed Communist militancy when it interfered with the foreign policy needs of the USSR. During the era of the Popular Front, Communist parties had been urged to build alliances not only with Socialists but with bourgeois forces as well and to place the need for social revolution on the back burner. Now, with the Soviet Union under attack and its survival in jeopardy, the Comintern demanded that its constituent parties avoid any activities that might complicate building the widest possible coalition against Nazi Germany.

The demands of the war meant that Dimitrov rarely had direct contact with Stalin. He continued to send him the most substantive information received by the Comintern, in particular the operational information and materials of major political significance. He attempted to reach agreement with him on the directives. But such questions would increasingly frequently be decided on with Vyacheslav Molotov (foreign minister), the CPSU Central Committee secretaries Alexander Shcherbakov, Andrei Andreyev, and Georgi Malenkov, and other people in Stalin's inner circle.

On 30 June Dimitrov received instructions from Molotov: "Communists everywhere should take the most decisive steps to aid the Soviet people. The main thing is to disorganize the enemy's rear and demoralize his army."[4] The appropriate directives were sent out to the Communist parties. The dispatch to Josip Tito, general secretary of the Central Committee of the Communist Party of Yugoslavia, stated: "The time has come when the Communists must make the people rise up and engage in active struggle against the occupiers. Without the slightest further delay . . . organize partisan detachments and launch the partisan warfare in the enemy's rear. Burn down the military factories, warehouses, oil storage tanks, airfields; destroy the railroads, telephone and telegraph communications network; do not let through the transportation of troops and ammunition. Organize the peasants to bury grain supplies and drive the cattle off into the forests. The enemy must be terrorized through all possible means, to make him feel he is in a fortress under siege."[5]

Daan Goulooze in Holland and Clément (Eugen Fried) in France received cipher communications instructing Communists in Western Europe to "use all ways and means to make the people rise up and fight the occupiers." They should organize demonstrations of the population demanding bread; organize strikes at enterprises working for the Germans; undermine arms production through all possible means; create small groups to destroy military enterprises, oil supplies, bridges, railroads, the telegraph and telephone network; and block the transport of troops and weapons.[6]

The leadership of the Communist Party of the United States was given instructions to drop its agitation for American neutrality and opposition to American rearmament: "We suggest to develop immediately in all towns antifascist demonstrations of many thousands of people under slogan all-out aid to Soviet people struggling for defense of their country and simultaneously for security of American people against Hitler-barbarism." These actions should avoid a "narrow Communist character" by having non-Communist groups take the initiative in organizing. The Communist Party of Canada and the parties of the Latin American countries received similar orders.[7]

At a 1 July meeting the ECCI Presidium approved a directive ordering Communist parties in occupied countries to organize National

Fronts and establish contacts with all forces fighting against fascist Germany: "The objective of such a Front must be to rouse all strata of the population of the given country to active battle against the Hitlerite yoke." In Britain and the United States Communists were to raise the idea of forming such groups, and "Communists were not to raise the question of their hegemony in the National Front." After Molotov approved its wording, the directive was sent to the Communist parties.[8]

The Comintern and Soviet Intelligence in the Great Patriotic War

The Comintern began cooperating with Soviet intelligence from the time of its creation, but this collaboration grew closer than ever during World War II. While they technically had different aims and occasionally stumbled up against each other, the Communist International and the major Soviet intelligence agencies—the NKVD's Foreign Department and the Red Army's Intelligence Directorate of the General Staff (changed to Main Intelligence Directorate [GRU] in February 1942)—often had overlapping missions and used similar techniques. The Comintern, organizationally a representative body composed of Communist parties that were local sections of this organization dedicated to fomenting revolution in their respective countries, was thoroughly controlled by the Soviet Union. Not only was it headquartered in Moscow, but also virtually all its funding came from the USSR. While its most prominent leader in the 1930s, Georgi Dimitrov, was a Bulgarian and other powerful Comintern figures were not Russians, none of them were independent. Believing that the Soviet Union was the shining hope of world revolution, Comintern personnel, including its foreign leaders, were dedicated to defending and advancing the Soviet cause, identifying it with the success of their own local Communist parties.

Soviet intelligence agencies, dedicated to protecting and promoting the interests of the Soviet state, meanwhile understood that Communists abroad were a valuable resource to assist Soviet interests. Since defending the Soviet Union was one of the chief tasks of foreign Communist parties, persuading Communists to provide useful information about their own country's plans, military resources, or industrial secrets offered a novel way to commit espionage. The ideologically motivated spy was often easier to find, cheaper to supervise, and less prone to second thoughts than the more traditional disgruntled malcontent or flawed individual blackmailed or pressured to reveal secrets. During the 1920s and 1930s a number of Soviet intelligence recruits thought they were actually working for the Comintern, an illusion that may have eased their concerns that they were betraying secrets to a foreign state.

Moreover, both the Comintern and Soviet intelligence agencies operated in secrecy. They both relied on operatives traveling on false papers, capable of operating in a clandestine fashion, using safe houses, and avoiding surveillance. Both set up illegal radio networks and relied on encrypted communications. Several high-ranking Comintern officials had close ties to Soviet intelligence. Meer Trilliser, an important figure in the OGPU, serving as chief of the Foreign Department in the late 1920s, became a member of an illegal commission of the ECCI and the chief of the Far Eastern Department of the ECCI earlier in the 1920s. Trilliser replaced Osip Pyatnitsky as head of its secret arm, the OMS, and supervisor of the Communications Service in 1935 and became a member of the Presidium of the ECCI under the name Mikhail Moskvin. Several of the USSR's most successful espionage rings in the 1930s were staffed by Communists recruited through Comintern and Communist Party–related networks. Whittaker Chambers worked for Red Army foreign intelligence in the early 1930s, recruited by CPUSA officials J. Peters and Max Bedacht.

Once World War II began, the need for closer coordination between the Comintern and Soviet intelligence became more urgent. While Soviet intelligence agencies earlier had made use of foreign Communists and Communist parties, they had also limited the extent of their exploitation of the Communist parties because of concern that the parties, with their many thousands of members and high rates of membership turnover, were vulnerable to infiltration by foreign security services. But the immediate needs of the war effort caused these concerns to be put aside. Dimitrov reached an agreement with Pavel Fitin, head of the NKVD Foreign Department, and Fillip Golikov, head of the the Red Army's Intelligence Directorate, on ways to cooperate, and his entries in his diary from 20 August to 24 September 1941 reflect this shift. The first entry said: "Fitin to see me. We agreed concerning contact and mutual cooperation in the area of liaison with foreign countries in the interests of intensifying operations in all spheres. Commissioned Fit[in] and Sorkin to work up the concrete issues and make a report." The second noted: "Gener(al) Golikov (Intelligence Dir[ecorate]) on sending activists abroad, on the coordination of work between the Intelligence Dir[ectorate], the NKVD, and the Communist International on these issues, on China and Manchuria and so on. We agreed on specific formalities." Directives were sent out to networks of Soviet intelligence agents through Comintern communications channels. ECCI radio stations and communications centers passed information from intelligence agents to the Center, as their Moscow headquarters was called, and received instructions from the "Director" (the chief of military intelligence) to his people. Intelligence officials in return provided Dimitrov with information regarding the Communist parties.[9]

Dimitrov warned his Comintern comrades that they were not to interfere with military intelligence operations. Despite the cooperation, he did not want the Comintern emissaries to get deeply involved with intelligence gathering or the intelligence personnel to exert any control over political activities, including Partisan operations. In a message sent to Yugoslavia on 23 August 1941 he explained:

> Military intelligence workers have their own special tasks. The nature of their work and the methods they use are unique. It is inadvisable and harmful for the Party to inform you of these tasks and who is carrying them out. Work within military intelligence must be conducted completely separately from work within the Party. Also bear in mind that, by its very nature, the intelligence agency uses, and must use, all kinds of elements. It must recruit its operators on its own. Senior Party workers are the only ones the intelligence service cannot hire for its work without your approval. For your part, do your utmost to facilitate the work of the agents and prevent any unhealthy rivalry in this area. With respect to the Partisan movement, its organization and leadership must be in your hands exclusively. Take all of this into account and handle your relationships in this spirit.[10]

The Comintern became a prime source of recruitment for the intelligence services during World War II. On 5 February 1942, Dimitrov received an inquiry from a high-ranking staff member of the NKVD about selecting people suitable for the role of "illegal residents, who have the capability to build independent groups to obtain political and military information, who can give an objective analysis of the internal political situation of a country," and those who could be used to carry out "individual special assignments in the country and in the enemy's rear." (An "illegal resident" was an agent-handler operating under false identity who managed one or more espionage networks as well as single agents.) Dimitrov was warned that "work to select the necessary people must be carefully concealed; for instance, people should be chosen on the pretext of the creation of partisan groups, and the real goals of the selection should not be mentioned. A very small number of people should be aware of this activity. The work must be kept strictly secret from those around you."[11]

Some requests from the NKVD asked for assistance in a particular country; other times they asked about particular people. On 19 July 1942, for example, Dimitrov was asked to select "for use for our purposes, 2–3 people for Romania and 2–3 for Hungary, from among the people being trained at your school." Just months before Fitin sent Dimitrov a note: "I request your authorization to use for our purposes an Italian, Macciaci, Filippo (a.k.a. Andrea), who is available to the ECCI." Within two weeks Dimitrov's Secretariat sent instructions to the ECCI Personnel Department making Macciaci available to Fitin.[12]

Numerous requests from Fitin and responses from Dimitrov about the suitability of specific people for Soviet intelligence have been preserved in the archives. Fitin sometimes asked for the password to establish contact with individuals active in Comintern operations. On 12 March 1942, for example, Sorkin notified Dimitrov of Fitin's request for a password to make contact in London with a German Communist emigrant, Jürgen Kuczynski: "I have the password. I am requesting your authorization." Later, Sorkin also informed Dimitrov that Fitin was requesting that the response concerning Kuczynski be expedited. Kuczynski cooperated with Soviet intelligence during the war.[13]

One request from Fitin about a famous Soviet spy is dramatic confirmation of the compartmentalization of Soviet intelligence agencies. Following the Japanese arrest of Richard Sorge as a Soviet spy in Japan, Fitin notified Dimitrov that "a certain Sorge testified that he has been a member of the Communist Party since 1919; he joined the Party in Hamburg. In 1925 he was a delegate to the Comintern Congress in Moscow, and afterward worked in the ECCI Information Bureau. In 1930 he was dispatched to China. From China he went to Germany, and to cover his activity on the line of the Comintern, he became a member of the National Socialist Party." Fitin concluded: "I am asking how plausible this information is." The response confirmed Sorge's work in the ECCI apparatus but noted that he had ceased work for the Comintern at the end of the 1920s. Neither Fitin nor Dimitrov was aware that after leaving Comintern service, Sorge had directed a large and successful Soviet military espionage apparatus that had infiltrated the highest circles of Japanese society.[14]

While the intelligence services made use of Comintern resources, the Comintern, in turn, used intelligence channels when its contacts had been cut off. Faced with the inability to establish communications with the Austrian Communists, Dimitrov asked GRU in August 1942 to ask its "man in Vienna" what party organizations he had contact with, what their activities were, and whether they were able to hear a clandestine radio station. The response made no mention of any organized party center but did report a handful of resistance groups of Communists. The Comintern's radio broadcasts were rarely audible because of jamming.[15]

Comintern contact with the leadership of the British Communist Party was, to a great extent, maintained through intelligence channels. Fitin sent Dimitrov party leader Harry Pollitt's extensive messages about the situation in the country, the position of various social circles and political figures, and the Communist Party's interactions with the Labour Party. Pollitt often requested instructions from Dimitrov regarding various issues in political life and received them through Fitin's intelligence network. Not all his reports were accepted at face value by the intelligence service. When Pollitt reported in February 1943 that "the campaign for the Communist Party to join the Labour Party is proceeding with great success," Fitin commented that "according to our resident [NKVD station chief] in England, the assertion that this campaign is proceeding 'with great success' does not, for the moment, correspond to reality." Despite efforts to establish direct radio contact with the Comintern, Pollitt had to report "so far no signs of your activity have been detected."[16]

The Comintern, Tito, and Yugoslavia

The implementation by the Communist parties of Comintern instructions after the Nazi invasion of the USSR that they take an aggressive antifascist stance and join the anti-Nazi resistance in occupied countries depended primarily on the specific conditions prevailing in each country and on the possibilities available to the various Communist parties. The most rapid response to this appeal came from the Communist Party of Yugoslavia, where the liberation struggle quickly overflowed the bounds of a covert resistance movement and was transformed into an open war against the occupiers and their collaborators.

On 4 July 1941 the Politburo of the Central Committee of the Yugoslav Communist Party called for an armed uprising. On 7 July Serbian Communist Partisans entered the fray, and on 13 July an uprising began in Montenegro. (Yugoslav Communists, under Josip Tito's leadership, had organized the People's Liberation Army and Partisan Detachments of Yugoslavia, called more simply the Partisans.) On

31 July Dimitrov sent Stalin, Molotov, Malenkov, Beria, and Georgy Zhukov (chief of the General Staff) two radiograms. The first one, from Iosip Kopinić in Yugoslavia, stated: "According to information from the Croatian General Staff there is an uprising in Montenegro. There are 25,000 rebels; the Communists are leading it. Walter [Tito] reported that an uprising is being prepared in Montenegro." Kopinić, known as Vokshin in this cipher traffic, ran a Comintern communications center operating from Zagreb in Croatia. A veteran of the International Brigades, he belonged to the Yugoslav Communist Party but worked for the Comintern. The second cable was from Tito, known as Walter in Comintern traffic: "We request you to respond whether you can send by plane from the USSR to Serbia weapons, ammunition, and several military specialists. If you agree, we will inform you of the place and ensure landing for the plane." Dimitrov replied: "The question of the possibility of sending what you request is now being explored. As soon as that is done, you will receive an answer."[17]

In August Tito reported on the increased military aggressiveness of the Communist-led Partisan forces, detailing their attacks on airfields, gasoline depots, ammunition storage facilities, and bridges and roads. One account explained: "Numerous Partisan detachments are active in the country in accordance with the plan of the Yugoslav CP. The major objective is the destruction of the communications network, military objects, and ammunition, and to sow panic among the enemy. The railroads, telegraph and telephone communications continue to be destroyed. The Partisan detachments have destroyed two battalions of Croatian troops and shot down three German planes. The Party successfully organized an uprising in Montenegro. All of the cities are in our hands." The radiograms were immediately sent to Stalin.[18]

The Partisan movement, however, did not uniformly cover all of Yugoslavia with its complex mix of ethnicities with often competing national aspirations. Strong sentiment for Croatian independence from Serbian-dominated Yugoslavia had produced the Ustashe, a fascistic nationalist militia that became the military arm of the independent Croatian puppet state created by the German and Italian occupation forces and fought under German direction. Kopinić informed Moscow that the Croatian Communist leaders were showing signs of sympathy for Croatian national ambitions and thwarting resistance to the fascists in a radiogram of 30 June: "The CC of Croatia is slowing down the masses in the struggle, threatening expulsion from the Party. The CC has forbidden the wrecking of communications or the destruction of radio stations. The CC in fact is against inflicting damage on rail[roads] or burning down storehouses. The Party masses are against the CC, calling members of the CC traitors. I urgently request your intervention."[19] The Comintern reacted angrily: "The position of the Croatian CC is cowardly and treacherous. The liberation of the peoples of Yugoslavia is linked to the defeat of Germany and the victory of the Soviet Union. The United Front of the peoples of Yugoslavia against the fascist enslavers must be combined with Partisan actions in the rear of the enemy. There can be no wavering or dawdling. Make c[omrade] Stalin's statement known to the masses of the people."[20] Kopinić was given instructions: "We authorize you to create another Center to carry out our line. Break off immediately any contact with the treacherous CC. Take urgent action to secure yourselves and the apparatus from treachery. What is Walter [Tito] doing? Send information on the Partisan movement in Serbia, Montenegro, and Bosnia and Herzegovina."[21]

Tito and the Central Committee of the Yugoslav Communist Party set up an investigatory commission; it concluded that Kopinić's accusation was unjustified. Kopinić radioded this conclusion to Moscow but added his rebuttal. Tito's investigation concluded that "Vokshin [Kopinić] falsely accused the leadership of Croatia of treachery, provocations, and a sabotage of action. On the basis of these false accusations he demanded a mandate from you for a change of leadership, without communicating this to the CC of the CPYu [Communist Party of Yugoslavia], though he had the possibility to do so." Referring to a disastrously botched escape of some interned Communists, the report also accused Kopinić of being "the initiator of the criminally planned and accomplished flight of 90 comrades from Kerestinec, of whom three are alive. All of this was done without the knowledge of the leadership of Croatia and the country, although he was informed that this flight was being planned" and "[his] having acknowledged these gross errors in a statement to the CC of the country." The Yugoslav party found "it necessary to replace Vokshin and leave his assignments up to our Party, since we do not trust him with the work he is now doing."[22]

Kopinić emphatically rejected these conclusions, telling Moscow that he had delivered Moscow's orders to the Croatian party leadership but "during the first month of the war in Croatia your line was not carried out. The secretary of the leadership [Tito] stated that he did not believe in and does not accept the materials I have received from you." He repeated the charges he had made earlier of the party leadership's refusal to engage in sabotage and angrily refuted charges that he had been responsible for the deaths of the Partisans who had been interned at Kerestinec, insisting that the escape, even though it had led to many deaths, had raised morale. He complained that Tito and the Communist Party were asserting that "I am to blame for everything, but nothing is said as to why the leadership of Croatia was punished." He closed by noting that he and his wife, both Serbs, were in Zagreb: "Serbs are being shot here, and the same fate awaits us. We have decided to work until the end. We continually asked Walter [Tito] for help, but to no avail. We have no reserve Center, no apartment or valid documents (Rosa has been without documents for a whole year now), and no funds. Walter has a lot of money but is not giving us any. We have constructed a stronger two-way radio for reliable communications and Walter wrecked that. Walter's proposal also means the liquidation of our Center, for if I leave, Rosa will be shot as the wife of a Serb who left without permission."[23]

Unhappy with the rift, Dimitrov sent Tito a directive to put an end to the feud and assist Kopinić: "We know Vokshin well and trust both him and you. We propose to once and for all put an end to this misunderstanding. Vokshin must stay and continue to be the head of the communications Center. Give full assistance to Vokshin in carrying out his work—material help, documents for Rosa, etc. The times are too critical now to resolve such issues in haste and under the influence of subjective notions."[24] That ended the conflict.

Dimitrov made numerous efforts to organize the supply of weapons to the Yugoslav Partisans, even interceding with Stalin after being rebuffed by Molotov. Dimitrov later wrote to Tito: "Iosif Vissarionovich [Stalin] and I have personally discussed on numerous occasions the ways and means for rendering you assistance. Unfortunately, up to now it has not been possible to provide a positive solution because of the insurmountable technical and transportation difficulties. We shall continue unceasingly our efforts to find real possibilities for sending assistance. As soon as these possibilities are realized, we will do everything possible." Soviet military assistance to the Partisans was finally provided at the end of 1943.[25]

Dimitrov was also concerned about the growing antagonism between the Communist-led Partisans and the Chetniks, a nationalist Serbian resistance movement loyal to the Yugoslav monarchist government in exile and led by Draža Mihailović, a colonel in the Royal Yugoslav Army. Dimitrov asked Tito "to urgently inform us who are the military Chetniks, who is leading them, and what the relationship is between the Partisan headquarters and the military Chetniks." The Comintern also wanted to know, "What measures are you taking to create a unified leadership as a movement against the occupiers?"[26]

On 6 December in a letter to Stalin and Molotov, Dimitrov explained that unity was impossible because Mihailović was fighting against the Partisans: Tito accused him of "stabbing us in the back." Another Tito message stated that "our attempts to get him on our side in the struggle against the Germans have failed. When he stabbed us in the back, we smashed his detachments. He was left with only gendarmes and policemen, who are terrorizing the Partisans and their families horrendously." He linked the warfare between Partisans and Mihailović to the arrival in Montenegro of the British military mission, whose leader unconditionally demanded to be put under Mihailović's command.[27]

In his coded dispatches to Tito and the Yugoslav CP, Dimitrov explained that the Partisan movement could not afford to be perceived as Communist or bent on the Sovietization of Yugoslavia. He sent Stalin a copy of his dispatch to Tito, in which he objected to calling a Partisan unit a "proletarian brigade," and recommended cooperation with the government in exile in London. In a coded dispatch of 8 August Dimitrov again called for a rejection of the name "proletarian brigades": "Quit playing right into the hands of the enemies of the people, who will always make vicious use of any such lapses on your part." In another cable, he advised Tito to conduct a more cautious policy regarding the émigré government and in exposing the actions of the Chetniks, "but not to attack the government directly." Dimitrov nonetheless frequently urged the Soviet government to assist the Partisans and to denounce the Chetniks and attempt to weaken their support from the Yugoslav government in exile.[28]

The British Mission to Yugoslavia That Disappeared

Several coded messages between Tito and the Comintern dealt with the case of a British military mission to Yugoslavia in 1942 whose fate has long been a mystery. It included a British major, a British sergeant, and a Royal Yugoslav lieutenant sent by the government in exile to assess the Yugoslav resistance. Tito radioed Moscow with the news of its arrival in the Partisan-held town of Foča. After a conversation with Molotov, Dimitrov responded on March 1: "Nothing is known here about a British military mission. A meeting with Tito at Supreme headquarters is advisable. There is a need, however, to display extreme caution in discussions. Not to give away any of our secrets. Try to find out the true objectives and tasks of the mission. Keep us informed of developments." Tito wrote that he had attempted to convince the British that the Chetniks were cooperating with the Nazis and that by continuing to support Mihailović, the Yugoslav government in exile, headquartered in London, "has totally compromised itself in the eyes of the peoples of Yugoslavia." He relayed his belief that a new government had to be formed, "which would issue an appeal to the peoples of Yugoslavia to fight against the occupiers and would openly stigmatize all traitors and collaborators with the occupiers. We informed the mission of this, and they agreed to inform London of this."[29]

Tito's arguments, however, did not convince the mission. In mid-April he informed Moscow that on 14 April, its members "disappeared without a trace," along with a defector from the Chetnik forces, General Ljubo Novaković, "whose life we had saved three times since he had been condemned to death by Mihailović" and who "left a most outrageous letter with our general staff. We believe that this vile act was the work of the [British] Intelligence Service, revealing to us the shady work and the objectives of its agents. We will do everything possible to catch these bastards who enjoyed our hospitality, since we considered them our allies." Novaković's letter threatened to raise a force of Bosnian Serbs to fight the Partisans. In a later report Tito explained that Novaković had been plotting to murder Communists in a Partisan detachment and had fled after one of his co-conspirators had been arrested, fearing exposure.[30]

The fate of the British mission has never been resolved; its members were never heard from again. Exactly what happened has never been very clear. Novaković, who left with them, later claimed he had become separated from them. He himself was killed in 1943 by Chetnik forces loyal to Draža Mihailović.

The Uneasy Relationship of Yugoslav Communists and the Comintern

Dimitrov informed Stalin that in late December 1942 the Yugoslav Communists had created the Antifascist Assembly for the People's Liberation of Yugoslavia (AVNOYu) and elected an executive committee. Dimitrov had previously advised Tito not to try to replace the London-based government: "Bear in mind that the Soviet Union has treaty relations with the Yugoslav king and the government and that an open attack on the latter will create additional difficulties for joint military efforts and in relations between the Soviet Union, on the one hand, and England and America, on the other." Tito initially paid lip service to this wish: "Although we do not consider this Executive Committee as representing any kind of government, it will nevertheless deal with all questions of public life and the front; moreover, Popular Liberation Committees will help it, and these have been created in virtually all areas on the liberated and on the not yet liberated territory," he reported. "We have no other civilian authority aside from these Committees." A year later AVNOYu was proclaimed the supreme legislative and executive body of Yugoslavia, essentially pushing aside the claims of the exile government.[31]

The relationship with the Yugoslav leadership was no simple matter. Moscow did not want to acknowledge that Tito and his movement were attempting to act independently. On 2 April 1943 Dimitrov sent Tito a coded dispatch: "We are troubled by the fact that you are engaging in an exchange of prisoners with the Germans, and also by the fact that the German ambassador in Zagreb has expressed a desire to meet with you personally. What is this about? The people are involved in a brutal war with the occupiers, and suddenly there are such relationships between you and the Germans. Is not all of this linked to the German policy of using our people to foment internecine struggle among the Yugoslavs themselves and thus to achieve the rout of the People's Liberation Army? I am requesting your explanations on this question."[32]

In his radiogram in response, Tito protested against the "mistrust and doubts" expressed in the inquiry. He explained that the issue was an exchange of groups of civilians and also of a group of Croatian and Serbian officers who did not want to join the ranks of the Liberation Army:

> We have no food for them, and eliminating them [killing them] would be very much the wrong thing to do politically, since this could have major consequences. . . . There are still hundreds of patriots and our leading comrades in the concentration camps of Pavelić and in others. Such an exchange to save these comrades is of great political significance. The broad masses of Croatia, Bosnia, Dalmatia, and others approve of this, not to mention our People's Army, which sees in this our concern for people. . . . You must also know that we are responsible for the lives of several million inhabitants, who trust us and our struggle, and we must act to ensure that this trust remains unshaken. I

> repeat that we have not merited your criticism and that your reproaches are very painful for us.[33]

Dimitrov ordered that Tito's answer be sent to Stalin and others. (The phrase "the concentration camps of Pavelić" referred to the prisons of Ante Pavelić, the Ustashe leader who headed the Croatian collaborationist regime.)

On other issues there was no disagreement. Tito sent news in September 1942 that among the prisoners held by the Partisans were "seven Russian soldiers of General Vlasov. We request you to inform us immediately what to do with them. We think to shoot." (Andrei Vlasov, a Red Army general captured in 1942, collaborated with the Nazis and recruited Soviet POWs for the "Russian Liberation Army" that fought the USSR under Wehrmacht command.) On the cipher message Manuilsky wrote "Shoot." The next day Dimitrov cabled: "We agree with your decision regarding the Russian captives, soldiers of General Vlasov—to shoot them."[34]

The Comintern, the Partisans, and Soviet Intelligence

The Comintern also sought to facilitate cooperation between Soviet intelligence and Tito's Partisans. This was particularly important in July 1941, when the Intelligence Directorate's contacts with its resident agents had been cut off and needed to be reestablished. In late July 1941, Ivan Ilyichev, head of the Political Department of the Red Army's Intelligence Directorate (he became chief of the GRU in 1942), sent the text of radiograms for its agents in Yugoslavia to G. Z. Sorkin, Dimitrov's aide, who (with Dimitrov's consent) dispatched them on to Iosip Kopinić, with a postscript: "Promptly forward this telegram and inform us of the response." The messages were addressed to the Red Army's military intelligence operatives such as Ivan Srebrenjak, who headed an intelligence network in Zagreb. He was ordered to send reports about the German occupation forces and what transmitters were available to resistance forces. When he did not respond, another message to Kopinić asked whether the earlier communiqué had been passed on and "why are they not reporting about their work through you."[35]

The coded messages also illustrate the tensions that existed between the Communist Party apparatus and the intelligence service. Tito had complained in 1940 to Dimitrov that Srebrenjak had been arrested in Bulgaria and turned over to the Yugoslav police. Claiming to be a

Soviet citizen, he had tried to get the Communist Party of Yugoslavia to facilitate his release. Tito had been suspicious, telling the Comintern it was a "dubious story" and Srebrenjak's behavior was "provocative." Dimitrov had immediately conveyed this denunciation to the NKVD. In August 1941, Tito reiterated that the Communist Party of Yugoslavia did not trust Srebrenjak. Representatives of Soviet military intelligence, however, confirmed to Dimitrov that there was nothing suspicious about Srebrenjak's behavior. Dimitrov reassured Tito: "The information about Anton [Srebrenjak] here is positive and rules out any grounds for not trusting him. If you have specific facts that are cause for mistrust, you should report them to us immediately." He added that Tito needed to facilitate the activities of the Soviet intelligence agents in Yugoslavia in every way and not try to gain control over them himself.[36]

The Red Army's Intelligence Directorate also reprimanded Srebrenjak: "Stop competing with Walter [Tito], establish businesslike contact with the Party through a communications worker, and subordinate all of our work to the interests of the common cause," a radiogram from the Director demanded. He also reproached Srebrenjak because his messages were incomprehensible due to poor cipher work; he was ordered to encrypt them the way he had been taught. Things had not improved a few months later. Tito received a message to pass on to Srebrenjak ordering him to "Report in a telegram the name of the book, the page selected for work, how you compose and disguise the sample groups, and their location in the telegram. Tell us whether the receiver has been assembled and why the music [radio communications] is not working yet. We are listening to you on the program." It was a futile plea; Srebrenjak was captured by the Croatian Ustashe and executed in 1942.[37]

Dimitrov also ordered Tito to cooperate with the Soviet intelligence agencies. He asked him to select two men "for work through the NKVD" and give them a two-way radio and a radio operator: "These comrades' task will be to carry out special intelligence tasks on the territory occupied by the Germans and in neighboring countries, and in particular to make contact with people there from the above-mentioned agency. The permanent location of the comrades and the two-way radio is in one of the regions controlled by the Partisans. Submit the candidates to us for confirmation. Also, report the technical information about the two-way radio and desirable conditions for contact. Here, we will work out a way to transmit a code for this two-way radio."[38]

Tito also kept Moscow informed about people potentially useful for espionage work. He reported that Colonel Fyodor Makhin, a

Russian emigrant, had been actively involved in Partisan activity. He had been taken prisoner by Mihajlović's Chetniks in Montenegro but had been freed. Tito asked the Comintern to check on him with the NKVD. When it was determined that he had previously cooperated with Soviet intelligence, Tito was assigned to contact him via a cutout, to ascertain whether he had any information for "the neighbors"—that is, Soviet intelligence—whether he could "go back to Mihajlović or stay in the occupied territory and work on the neighbors' assignments and carry out communications from there." Makhin was given the code name "Mars." One of his assignments was to demoralize Mihajlović's supporters, even organize the kidnapping of one of his closest colleagues. A subsequent coded communication noted: "It will be necessary to hand Mars over to work with comrades who will be assigned to you for special work. For now, stay in contact with him. If you cannot select suitable comrades, give the two-way radio and radio operator to him for communication with the neighbors. Keep in mind that, although Mars has been tested in his work by the neighbors, he is, nonetheless, not one of their regular personnel representatives, so he must be monitored in a way that cannot offend him. Code for him will be sent through you."[39]

Intelligence information did not go only to Moscow. Sometimes information obtained by Soviet intelligence was sent from Fitin to Dimitrov, who in turn gave it to Tito. One bit of news was that the German intelligence service had its own agent at the main headquarters of the People's Liberation Army of Yugoslavia. Contact with him was maintained by the German intelligence resident agent Ott, director of the aluminum company Hanse Leichtmetall in Mostar. Tito gave a reassuring reply: "Regarding German intelligence agent Ott, we know everything. There is no agent of his at our headquarters." A loyal Communist had been used to contact Ott and pretend to provide information. "The issue is clear to us, and there is no need to be concerned about this."[40]

Tito and Kopinić also transmitted information of interest to Soviet intelligence. Dimitrov asked them to gather information on German and Italian troop movements and deployments, numbering and numerical strength, and airports and industrial-military facilities, without limiting this to the territory of Yugoslavia. One of the dispatches received contained information about a motor plant in the region of Graz in Austria; another one dealt with a factory producing synthetic gasoline near Leipzig in Germany itself. Such dispatches were then sent to Stalin and to the Red Army General Staff.[41]

The Comintern and Italian Communists after the German Attack on the USSR

Radio contact between Moscow and Yugoslavia was also used for contacts with the Communists in other countries. In July 1941 Tito had been instructed to pass on orders to the Italian Communists on the need for stepping up activity among the workers in military industry to sabotage production, organize resistance among the peasants against requisitioning, etc. Another objective was to foment trouble in Slovenia and Croatia, "to organize through all possible means the decay of the Italian army, desertion of Italian soldiers, refusal dispatching to war against the Soviet Union, and armed clashes between soldiers and the fascist militia. And in particular to encourage hostile relations between the Italian and German fascists to the point of open conflicts."[42] ("[R]efusal dispatching to war against Russia," an addition to the message inserted in Dimitrov's own hand, was a directive that Italian Communists should discourage Italian troops from serving with the Italian Army units Mussolini was sending to the Eastern Front to assist the Nazi invasion of the USSR.)

In July 1942 Kopinić reported to Dimitrov that "We have regular contact with Italy through the leadership of the [CP] of Slovenia, and through the CP of Italy with the CP of France and have the possibility of contact with the CP of Switzerland. We shall clarify possibilities for contact with the CP of Bulgaria." Through Tito a request was sent to Umberto Massola (Quinto), organizer of the covert internal apparatus of the Communist Party of Italy in 1941–1943, asking for detailed information about the status of the Italian Communist organization, its activities, success in building coalitions, and labor unrest.[43]

On 10 February 1943, a radiogram from Dimitrov instructed Edvard Kardelj (Birk), a leader of the Communists of Slovenia, to convey to the Italian Communist Party a request to provide information about antifascist activities, troop movements, and military production. In another dispatch Kardelj and Massola were told to maintain constant communications for joint work with both parties. "Point out to Quinto," wrote Dimitrov, "that he must have full confidence in you and Walter [Tito]. For your part, you must take into account that Quinto enjoys the full confidence of the leadership of the Italian Communist Party, and of Ercoli [Togliatti] personally." Kardelj sent a radiogram to Moscow: "Quinto reported that he has summoned from Fr[ance] se[veral] c[omrad]es and has established an interim leadership of the Italian Communist Party. Party organizations have been established in Milan, Turin, and Genoa. The Party is becoming a mass movement."[44]

Kardelj also informed Dimitrov in 1943 that Massola had been asked to carry out intelligence tasks for the GRU. "He replied that he would do this only when you require it of him." Dimitrov authorized Kardelj to tell Massola "that, through a thoroughly verified comrade, he should transmit all the information he has now and will have in the future for the Director [GRU]."[45]

The Comintern and the Military Crisis of Tito's Partisan Army in 1943

In mid–1943 Tito's Partisan forces faced a difficult situation. "I must inform you that our situation is very difficult," wrote Tito. "We are surrounded on all sides by the superior forces of the Germans, Ustachis, and Italians, whose goal is to annihilate us. It will be very hard for us to break through the enemy's encirclement, but we will fight to the last drop of blood." The Communist People's Liberation Army, straining every nerve, broke the encirclement ring. On 23 June Tito [under his Walter code name] sent a radiogram about the breakthrough of the encirclement:

> The last attack by the Germans, Ustachis, and Italians on our troops in Montenegro, Herzegovina, and Sandjak, with the goal of the total annihilation of the People's Liberation Army of Yugoslavia, lasted precisely 40 days. The offensive was prepared with great care. 8 of the enemy's divisions participated in it. Despite the adversary's technical and human superiority, this offensive ended in failure. . . . The enemy suffered enormous losses. . . . The 369th, 118th, and the SS "Prince Eugene" divisions lost 50 percent of their personnel. This time we also suffered very large casualties—up to 2,000 killed and wounded. The enemy organized a triple system of encirclement, but we broke up this entire blockade. . . . A great deal of military materiel was seized. Our units are now attacking in the direction of Herzegovina and Eastern Bosnia. Now fighting is going on in the cities of Vlasenica and Sokolać.[46]

On the text of this coded dispatch, as on the previous ones, Dimitrov wrote, "Send to c[omrade] Stalin and the oth[ers]." He congratulated Tito and made a proposal regarding further action by the Partisan army: "It would be desirable for you to think about whether it might not be advisable to keep the limited liberated territory as a base for the People's Liberation Army and send most of the battleworthy forces of the army to destroy as fully as possible the communications of the Germans and Italians, until Yugoslavia is totally separated from the West and the Balkans. At this stage it would seem that such a tactic would yield more effective results in the struggle against the occupiers and also be the more rational use of your armed forces, to some extent keeping them in better condition for the further decisive struggles in Yugoslavia. Please inform us of your views on this issue."[47] This clearly was not Dimitrov's personal opinion.

Creating the Polish Workers' Party

In accordance with Stalin's diktat, the leadership of the ECCI had abolished the Polish Communist Party in the fall of 1937. Poland itself had been abolished in the aftermath of the Nazi-Soviet Pact, with the USSR annexing the eastern half while Nazi Germany occupied western Poland. Most of the senior leadership of the Polish party had been executed during the Terror of the late 1930s; the few who survived were those fortunate enough to be in Polish prisons or operating covertly in Poland rather than living in exile in Moscow. But the entrance of the USSR into the war as an ally of Great Britain and the United States required Moscow to rethink its position on Poland. A Polish government in exile existed in London, and significant Polish military formations fought under Anglo-American command in North Africa and Western Europe. Given the diplomatic situation, the defeat of Nazi Germany would mean the reestablishment of an independent Poland, at least on the Polish territory that had been annexed by Germany. Consequently, the Soviet government concluded an agreement with the émigré Polish government headed by Władysław Sikorski that restored diplomatic relations and called for mutual assistance.

Stalin and the Comintern began to create a new party to replace the one dissolved in 1937. On 4 July 1941 a group of surviving Polish Communists living in the USSR was selected to be sent to Poland. On 27 August Dimitrov received Stalin's instructions: "It would be better to create the Workers' Party of Poland with a Communist program. The Commun[ist] Party frightens off not only alien elements, but even some of our own as well. At the present stage, the struggle is one of national liberation." A day later Dimitrov spoke with a group of Communists scheduled to be infiltrated into Polish territory by air. The interim leadership included Marceli Nowotko, Paweł Finder, and Bolesław Mołojec. The flight, however, did not take off because of an accident at the airport, and it was only possible to send the group in December.[48]

The Polish Workers' Party (PWP) was founded on 5 January 1942 at a clandestine meeting in Warsaw with Nowotko as leader. Although the PWP formally was not a part of the Comintern, Moscow determined its policies and it was de facto a Communist party. The PWP set about organizing Partisan detachments, later known as the People's Guard. Dimitrov kept himself informed about its activities and deflected its pleas for weapons. One message from the Central Committee of the PWP urgently demanded aid, asking that its request for help be conveyed to Stalin, and explained why it needed these weapons so badly: "Counting on the assistance that You promised us, we have created a large fighting organization of several thousand people here. We have done everything possible to obtain weapons on our own, but the quantity that we received this way is totally insufficient for arming even a small part of those people who could be sent out to fight. We do not see any possibility for resolving this problem by relying solely on our own means."[49]

On 17 July Dimitrov sent Nowotko a coded dispatch in which he approved the tactic being used by the Partisans aimed at destroying the communications of the German troops. "Make extraordinary efforts to better protect the leading Centers of the Party and the military organization from the enemy's strikes," he emphasized in his message. "And do not get distracted, watch your step, do not go after quick victories of expedience. Think this through carefully, be sure your work is thorough, gather your Party forces, and work on your communications with the masses." Soon Nowotko wrote of the growth of the influence of the party: "We are standing on our own feet firmly, and all the efforts of the bourgeois Parties to present us as agents of the USSR are not dangerous for us; in fact, they are helping us to win enormous sympathy of the masses in the USSR. . . . The greatest difficulty is to break down the sectarian attitudes, particularly among the former members of the Polish CP, for whom anyone who is not a Communist is an enemy."[50]

The instructions from Moscow emphasized the gathering of intelligence data. "You need to organize a special intelligence service attached to the CC," stated a directive of 19 August. Specifically, the Comintern directed:

> For that purpose identify an appropriate leader of that service; select the most cultured and strongest Communists, who understand the international situation and who know Poland. Assign each of them individually a specific region of the country, where, with the assistance of

> Party comrades and patriots who are sympathizers and through other means, they should organize the gathering of reliable military and political information. In addition to accumulation of such information through the secret agents, make it your business to get information through other means; for example: organize the kidnapping of an important staff officer, a major Gestapo officer, and force them to talk. This can provide you with the means for further expansion of work and for obtaining better specific information. The entire intelligence service must be under your tight control.

In addition to gathering intelligence information, orders were given to engage in active acts of sabotage. "At present the destruction of military storehouses, military trains going to the east, airports, and planes are of particular importance," states one of the directives. "Pay extremely close attention to the destruction of railroad tracks and to routes going eastward. Anything that is being sent or that will be sent to the east should be targeted for destruction using all possible ways and means."[51]

Following his instructions, Nowotko sent Dimitrov a detailed description of military facilities and of the deployment of German troops in the three major centers around Warsaw. This dispatch provided a detailed list of the locations of the barracks, military storehouses, centers of military technology, enterprises, and workshops working for the German Army. It also gave precise information to guide airplanes to these sites: "Rembertov. There is the triangle of the training ground. To the north of the triangle is the station Zelenka of the narrow-gauge railroad, to the west of this station is General Olbricht Street, from there up until Piłsudski Boulevard at a distance of about 400 meters from the military church there are barracks and military schools. There are approximately two battalions of soldiers in the barracks and schools. 150 meters northwest of the military church is the tank and armored car center—about 100 units." Dimitrov ordered that this dispatch be sent to Stalin, Molotov, Voroshilov, Beria, Alexander Vasilevsky (the chief of the General Staff of the Red Army), and Ivan Ilyichev.[52]

Moscow attached particular importance to the communications on Soviet-Polish relations. Nowotko reported that all of the Polish bourgeois parties were writing about the Soviet Union "as enemy No 2. Not a single one of the bourgeois Parties is calling for war with the occupiers. It is the Soviet Union, with the help of England and the U.S., that must crush the Germans, and assistance should not be given before the Soviet Union has exhausted all its forces in the struggle against Germany. This assistance might be rendered when the Germans have gotten to the Volga. Their major watchword is 'a buildup of forces to fight for the borders of a future Poland; advocating a struggle at present is against the interests of the Polish people.'"[53] Such information was of substantive importance for the formation of the Soviet leadership's policy regarding Polish political organizations and the émigré Polish government.

In the fall of 1942, in response to a PWP report of a large-scale action in Warsaw, when bunches of grenades were thrown into German restaurants and into the editorial offices of newspapers published by the Germans, Dimitrov congratulated the party leaders: "We are very pleased with the intensification of your combat activity. We believe that the line of your work and struggle is correct." He described the information sent as extremely valuable and requested that this work be continued in every possible way. The cipher communication expressed concern for the safety of the party center and of Nowotko: "I have no doubt that you are taking serious measures. But I request you once more to review the steps taken so far and think about additional measures to secure the Center against collapse and ensure continuous leadership of the Party and the fighting organization."[54]

Dimitrov's fears were well founded. The leaders of the PWP were being hunted, both by the Gestapo and by the underground organizations of other political movements fighting for hegemony in the liberation struggle and in the future government of a restored Poland. Nowotko reported that a person by the name of Obest had appeared in Warsaw. Some comrades knew him as a former activist in the dissolved Polish Communist Party. He was trying to persuade them to establish contact with members of the disbanded Communist Party and the new Polish Workers' Party in order to convene a conference. Nowotko explained:

> To find out what this was all about, two of our comrades were allowed to take part in this conference. At the conference, Obest presented himself as someone who had come to Poland with a special mission: there was a need for them to have their own trusted individuals at all factories, people who could provide information about what was being done at the factories and so on. When asked what he knew about the new PWP, he replied that the PWP was being led by people the Comintern trusted and that he did not intend to interfere in this work; on the contrary, people from his organization would have to be sent to the PWP to find out what was being done there. In private conversations with our comrades, this Obest said that before the dissolution of

> the Communist Party, he had worked in the Comintern's Passport Department with Krajewski. According to him, Manuilsky is now heading this department. Although Obest does not explicitly mention Manuilsky, he speaks in such a way that listeners themselves conclude that he is someone the Comintern trusts and that it was Manuilsky who sent him. During the conference, at Obest's suggestion, a committee of three people was selected, consisting of three of our comrades. A few days ago our comrades received blank form number one, which asks them to fill in the family names of reliable people from the PWP at factories and to provide their home addresses. These forms clearly show that we are dealing with a Gestapo agent-provocateur. Our special group was assigned to find his apartment, take all of his papers, and kill him.[55]

Dimitrov gave orders to immediately establish Obest's identity and to report the results to him. "We have not sent anyone from here bypassing you," stated his reply to Nowotko. "Manuilsky is not the head of any department. He is not even working right now at the ECCI on a permanent basis. This Obest is obviously a provocateur. You should have sent us an inquiry at once, as soon as you found out that he was convening a conference."[56]

The Murder of Marceli Nowotko

Dimitrov received a coded dispatch in early December informing him that a week earlier Nowotko had been caught in the street by the Nazis: "We knew nothing about Nowotko for several days. But later the police reported that he had been killed on the spot," Mołojec reported.[57] Dimitrov immediately asked for a detailed report on the circumstances surrounding the death of the man the Comintern had picked to head the new Polish party. The reply from Mołojec talked about "the major carelessness" of Nowotko and hinted that he had violated the rules of secrecy. In another dispatch, the murder was blamed not on the Nazi Gestapo but on the so-called "Second Department (Sikorski's people)"—that is, the intelligence section of those who backed the émigré government in London.[58]

On 7 January 1943, however, new information was received. A cipher communication from four PWP leaders—Paweł Finder (one of the original three sent to Poland in December 1941), Małgorzata Fornalska (a PWP Central Committee member sent to Warsaw in May 1942), Władysław Gomułka (who reached Warsaw in July 1942), and Franciszek Jòźwiak (who joined the PWP leadership in May 1942)—

stated that Bolesław Mołojec's conduct seemed suspicious. He had been with Nowotko when the latter was killed and had concealed this information. He had tried to take control over communications with the Comintern, made arbitrary changes in dispatches that he and Finder had jointly written to the Comintern, and had concealed from other members of the leadership some messages that had been received from Moscow. On their own, the radio operators had begun to transmit copies of all telegrams to Finder for verification, and that was how it came to light that Mołojec was falsifying dispatches. At meetings of the leadership he made confusing comments and lied:

> In these circumstances, in light of all these facts, we, the undersigned members of the interim Central Committee at a meeting (without Mołojec and Kowalski) and, after a thorough discussion of the issue, took the following decision: since we and a number of other activists are firmly convinced that Nowotko's murder was directly or indirectly the work of Mołojec, that his attempts to take full control of the Party leadership at any cost are leading to the elimination of the best activists and represent an ongoing threat for the Party, that his behavior and his practice of "double-entry bookkeeping" in relations with the Comintern and with us have generated profound mistrust in him at a time when, following Nowotko's murder and in the context of the war and Hitler's terror, the need for trust in the leadership is vitally important. Taking into account his anti-moral behavior and the fact that it was impossible to remove him, even temporarily, from the leadership until the murder has been thoroughly investigated, we have decided: 1) To eliminate Mołojec. 2) To create a special commission made up of Duracz, Fornalska, and Kowalski to carry out a definitive and full investigation into the circumstances of the murder. 3) To send you a full report on the events that had taken place. 4) To consider ourselves the interim leadership and to continue our work, placing our mandates in your hands while we await your ultimate decision and to obey it unconditionally, whatever it may be. Our decision was carried out. Mołojec was killed at 4:40 on the 29th. Everything in his pockets was removed. In these actions, we were guided exclusively by our Bolshevik conscience and by the good of the Party, believing that in wartime it is necessary to act in a military fashion.[59]

Dimitrov forwarded this document to Stalin, Molotov, Beria, and Ivan Ilyichev.

On 10 January the Comintern sent instructions to the Polish party leadership "to urgently take all necessary steps to continue the work of the Party begun under Nowotko's leadership and to fully ensure reliable and uninterrupted contact with us. It is necessary to preserve the combat solidarity of the Party's core group at any cost." It also suggested that other means should have been used to remove Mołojec from the leadership and neutralize him. The Comintern, however, did not suggest any change in the composition of the new leadership. The response from Finder asserted that there had been no other way to "neutralize" Mołojec and that party unity had been fully preserved, and he included the findings of the investigative commission, with a confession by Zygmunt Mołojec, Bolesław's brother. He indicated that on his brother's orders, he had obtained a revolver and shot someone whom he later learned "was a member of the Secretariat." The commission concluded that "the motive for the murder is the desire to head the Party at a 'historic moment.' "[60]

Ironically, leaders of a party that had suffered losses at the hands of the German occupiers and its own political rivals were killing each other. Nor was the murder of Mołojec the only example of the elimination of Communists by other Communists.

The three Lipski brothers, Ludwik, Antoni, and Leon, were among the active officials of the prewar Communist Party of Poland. Ludwik was arrested by the NKVD and executed on 13 December 1937. Antoni headed Poland's party leadership in 1937. On 16 February 1938, he arrived in Moscow. He was soon arrested and disappeared. Leon, who was also a member of the party leadership, had stayed in Poland and published a leaflet opposing the dissolution of the Communist Party. After the German invasion in September 1939 he fled east and was arrested by the NKVD in 1940 and imprisoned in Minsk. He got out of prison in the turmoil that followed the German attack on the USSR in June 1941 and covertly returned to Poland, where he joined the anti-German resistance and also agitated for the creation of a Polish Communist Party independent of Moscow. On 12 June 1943, the PWP leadership sent Dimitrov a coded dispatch stating that Leon Lipski (Łukasz) was engaged in spreading propaganda and would have to be eliminated. On 5 July Finder reported: "Given that Lipski Łukasz, through both his subversive activities among members of the Party and his public declarations against the Party in the press and at meetings, was once again unmasked as a fascist agent who was extremely dangerous for us, the CC has decided to eliminate him. The decision has already been carried out. For the moment we consider advisable not to promulgate this fact." Dimitrov forwarded the letter on to Stalin, Molotov, Shcherbakov, and Vsevolod Merkulov (commissar for state security), adding that the other Lipski brothers had been arrested by the NKVD and also that "during the time Lipski Łukasz had worked in Poland before 1939, he was known as a drunk and a morally rotten person, and a number of members of the Communist Party of Poland suspected him of acts of provocation."[61]

PWP Relations with the Polish Government in Exile

Finder, who headed the PWP leadership after Nowotko's death, informed Dimitrov in February 1943 of contacts with representatives of Sikorski's London-based government in exile and asked: "Are we ready to recognize their right to run the country after the occupiers are expelled? So far, our representatives have not given a definite answer. Our impression is that they are ready to make major concessions, provided that we do not hinder Sikorski from taking power in the country. We consider it advisable to obtain the largest possible number of concessions from them, while we get away with making promises."[62]

Subsequently, new dispatches arrived that spoke of both sides testing the waters regarding the future government of Poland and its eastern borders. (The government in exile demanded a return to prewar borders while Stalin intended to keep the half of Poland that the USSR had annexed after the Nazi-Soviet Pact.) The PWP leaders sent a message indicating their desire to "establish a rule of the workers and peasants." Dimitrov responded that this was a political error at the current moment: "Avoid such language in your political campaign. The main slogans of your struggle should be: 1) Expelling the occupiers from Poland; 2) Achieving national liberation; 3) Establishing a genuine People's Democratic government, but not the power of the workers and peasants. I request you to keep this in mind."[63]

A coded dispatch to Finder contained detailed explanations and guidance on the nature of power and the social transformations in the new Polish state. It emphasized that the new state would require "a new foreign policy, based on a true alliance with the USSR, and socio-economic changes carried out in a democratic spirit." Dimitrov insisted that the party had to talk about a democratic, not Soviet, system; about the nationalization (not socialization) of banks and large-scale industry; and that the party would announce that not only small, but also medium-sized industrial and commercial enterprises would be returned to their former owners, who would receive appropriate state assistance. "At this stage," he noted, "we are not providing the platform for a socialist order." At the same time he thought they should "point out that the Party, while setting out a program for the structure of postwar Poland, is not limiting its aspirations to the implementation of this program" and should "cite the Party's ultimate goal in the formulation previously used in the Party platform." On the issue of borders, there was a need to explicitly take "a position recognizing the will of the Ukrainian, Byelorussian, and Lithuanian peoples, expressed in 1939," and thereby endorse the actions and annexations by the USSR in September of that year.[64]

The Katyn Massacre

Through the PWP an attempt was made to influence Polish society in connection with the discovery in the Smolensk region of the mass graves of Polish officers who had been murdered in 1940 by the NKVD, an event known in the West as the Katyn Massacre. Nazi occupation forces uncovered the graves in 1943 and displayed them to delegations of Poles and foreign observers, in hopes of heightening tensions between the USSR and the Polish government in exile. The USSR, for its part, denied responsibility and blamed the murders on the Nazis. On 19 April 1943 Dimitrov sent Finder an inquiry: "How are you, the masses, and other political organizations reacting to the anti-Soviet campaign regarding Smolensk?" He requested that the PWP issue a declaration disassociating itself from the statement by the Polish government in exile that accused the government of the USSR of murdering the captured officers, "as well as [producing] resolutions of protest by workers, peasants, and the intelligentsia on this issue and comments in our favor in the press of other Parties."[65]

Finder's dispatches cited quotations from the Polish press that unequivocally laid the blame for these executions on the Soviet authorities and also listed the Poles in the delegation that had visited the sites of the mass graves. On 28 April a new directive was sent to Poland. It repeated Soviet statements blaming the Germans for the executions and announced a break in relations with the government in exile in London, which "not only did not rebuff German-fascist slander against the USSR (the Smolensk provocation), but did not even consider it necessary to ask the Soviet government any questions or engage in any explanations on this issue and appealed to the International Red Cross." Instructions were given "to launch the most active kind of exposure campaign on this subject and call on all Polish patriots, regardless of their political affiliation, to vigorously condemn the provocative conduct of the Polish government and to advocate strengthening the friendship of the Polish and Russian peoples in fighting against the German aggressors and their Polish henchmen."

It is quite unlikely that the Comintern leadership knew that this massacre had been carried out pursuant to a decision of the Politburo of the CC of the VKP(b) of 5 March 1940.[66]

Dimitrov forwarded to Stalin and others the coded dispatches Finder sent in response; these claimed "the Sikorski government's virulent anti-Soviet campaign" was using the Katyn provocation "to realize territorial claims to lands that, in terms of ethnography, are not Polish" and was aiding "Hitler in his intention to break up the unity of the Allied camp."[67]

The Soviet government continued to deny any responsibility for the massacre of the Polish prisoners of war. Not until 14 October 1992 did a representative of the president of the Russian Federation, Boris Yeltsin, hand over to the president of the Polish Republic, Lech Wałęsa, photocopies of documents confirming that Stalin and the Soviet Politburo had approved the execution of more than twenty thousand Polish prisoners of war.[68]

The Warsaw Ghetto

In the fall of 1942 Nowotko reported to Moscow on the systematic annihilation of Warsaw's Jewish population. His dispatch of 20 October stated: "In July the Germans started to liquidate the ghetto. Liquidation meant that the Germans took away all the Jews who were not working at factories producing war materiel (shoemakers, tailors, etc.) and gassed them. Within one month the Germans had liquidated all the ghettos in the Warsaw region. In Warsaw itself only 50,000 of 400,000 survived; the rest were murdered." Nowotko claimed that the Workers' Party had organized a meeting of representatives of various Jewish parties and proposed resistance and an effort to break through German lines and join partisan units but that no agreement could be reached.[69]

By April 1943 Finder was reporting "the liquidation of the Warsaw ghetto." He noted:

> The Jews are showing armed resistance. For three days and three nights now real battles have been going on. Detachments of the SS, police, Shaulis [Lithuanian fascist armed detachments], and Ukrainians are conducting a siege using mortars, artillery, tanks, and armored vehicles. Yesterday cluster and incendiary bombs were dropped. The Jews are defending themselves heroically as best they can and with the arms available (grenades, machine guns, and pistols). The reserves of ammunition are exhausted. There are hundreds of casualties among the

> Germans and Shaulis. Our Polish groups are carrying out diversionary attacks from outside on the gendarmes and the SS, and several Germans have been killed.

He reported that the rebels had hung Soviet, Polish, and British flags on the highest building. "It would be very useful now to carry out a raid on the German sector of Warsaw, simultaneously throwing weapons into the ghetto." Dimitrov sent these reports to Stalin and others. But Finder's proposals were ignored. On 14 May he wrote, "The fighting in the Warsaw ghetto has weakened but has been going on for the fourth week now. Yesterday the Germans again dropped cluster and incendiary bombs. Huge fires are raging. The number of German casualties exceeds one thousand. 500 armed Jews broke out and with our assistance went off into the forests."[70]

The Comintern and the French Communists after the German Attack on the USSR

In line with the new policy of cooperation with all resistance forces, Thorez and Marty sent a message from Moscow to Duclos (the underground leader of the French Communist Party) declaring that the next objective for the underground Communists was to establish direct contact with the Gaullist resistance movement and formulate the platform for such cooperation—a joint struggle for national liberation and joint efforts against German fascists and collaborators. It pointed out that "It is superfluous to ask questions about the future, but it is essential to ensure the independence of the Party."[71]

Thorez, Marty, and Dimitrov also issued directives to French Communists to engage in large-scale acts of sabotage and diversions "to rattle the Nazis' rearward base and give them no respite"; the directives also demanded "the organization of armed groups and armed operations." Duclos reported that the occupiers were threatening the death penalty for sabotage. This caused "some fear among the masses, who are unanimously against the aggressors but fear the consequences of active operations." On 21 December Stalin and others were forwarded Duclos's coded dispatch about the execution of hostages in Nantes and then a message about German reprisals in the departments of Nord and Pas-de-Calais. "There is a growing certainty among the masses that the Nazis will fail," wrote Duclos."[72]

Underground Communists in occupied France reported on the state of German soldiers arriving from the Eastern Front on furlough: "The soldiers are very despondent and describe the horrors of the Eastern Front. Many say that they would rather commit suicide than go back to the Eastern Front. A dozen suicide victims have been found in the district. There are quite a few cases of desertion, which forces the German army police to conduct searches of farms. There are more and more signs of demoralization of the German army. We are taking measures to intensify this process."[73]

Directives to the French Communist Party leadership emphasized maximum assistance for the Soviet Union in its war with Germany. Instructions were given to impede "the operation of factories working for the Germans. It [the party] needs to blow up factories, power units, and power stations. Carrying out such missions requires the organization of suitable groups outside of the factories. The terror and joblessness that would follow the blowing up of factories should not be allowed to frighten people. It must be explained to workers that better a few months of hardship and several hundred victims than years of torment, hunger, and hundreds of thousands of victims in fascist slavery." The goals were to obtain weapons, create partisan detachments, and prepare the party and the people for mass armed activities. The use of people who knew German to spread propaganda among German soldiers was recommended: "Regardless of any kind of risk or danger, it is absolutely essential to develop as extensively as possible our activities aimed at demoralization of the German soldiers, who are already quite shaken and demoralized. Strive to undermine military discipline, make German soldiers unfit for actions against the masses of the French people, and urge them to refuse to go to fight the Soviet people."[74]

Duclos reported (and his coded dispatch was immediately forwarded to Stalin) his complete agreement with the directives and his intention to organize strikes in the most important branches of industry, to increase the number of partisan groups in the provinces, to muster people who spoke German, to expand weapons production, and so on. Several days later he informed them about numerous acts of resistance, ranging from killing German soldiers to the sabotage of facilities.[75]

The correspondence with Duclos dealt with many issues of interest to Soviet intelligence. There were requests for information needed to send intelligence agents to France. "We request you to report what documents French people must have in Paris and in the occupied territory of Vichy. What innovations the Germans have introduced recently in the occupied territory. What money is in use in Paris and in the south of France. Whether there are food ration cards and for what products," asked Dimitrov. "What the rules are for travel on the r[ail]roads and highways and for entry into cities. What sort of system exists for examination of documents. The rules for registration and residence in cities. What the value of an Am[erican] doll[ar] is in unofficial exchanges. Whether one can live without ration cards if one has money. What the rules of residence in France for citizens of Axis countries are now." Very often questions were asked about German troops and the names of their officers, at the request of Soviet military intelligence.[76]

Radiograms were reliably protected by special codes. Nevertheless, various methods of verification were also used. In one radiogram Thorez asked Duclos: "In order to verify who is communicating with us, tell me who we both dropped in on for a visit one evening in the hope of having dinner and returned with empty stomachs." Duclos replied that it was Paul Langevin, thus dispelling doubts that he was the author of the message Moscow had received.[77]

Numerous reports detailed the toll that German police and counterespionage organizations were inflicting on French Communists. On 15 March 1942, Duclos reported a failure in the underground network that resulted in the arrest of Félix Cadras, a member of the CC of the French Communist Party who ran the party's organizational work, as well as a staff member of the leadership apparat, Arthur Dallidet. "We have discovered the source of this provocation, aimed at destroying the entire leadership. We are taking steps to eliminate any opportunity for a provocateur to harm us and to safeguard the work of the Party." Duclos reported the shooting of Gabriel Péri and Pierre Semard by the Germans and the torture of Cadras and Georges Politzer, the editor of *L'Humanité*. He also reported on acts of retribution: "The second of our operators to be arrested has gone over to serve the Gestapo. We are trying to find him, in order to settle a score with him. We have taken measures to ensure the security of the transmitting equipment and to create new backup equipment," read one of the coded dispatches.[78]

There was anxiety in Moscow over a press report that the Communist Party veteran Marcel Cachin had made a statement that condemned terrorist attempts to murder German occupiers. The Comintern learned from Duclos that after being released from prison, Cachin had said: "I have been asked if I approve of attempts on the lives of German army soldiers. My answer is that individual attempts run counter to the goals pursued by those who carry them out. I never praised such acts or instigated them. I have always tried to dissuade my comrades from them." Duclos explained that after resisting efforts to go underground or retract his comments for several months, "Cachin has at last agreed to go into hiding. We are preparing a strong statement for him to sign, which we will communicate to you in a timely fashion for use on the radio." Dimitrov forwarded to Stalin and others the statement, in which Cachin called on every Frenchman to "take his place in the struggle to cast off the yoke."[79]

French Communists and Charles de Gaulle's Free French Movement

The relationship between the French Communist Party and the Gaullist Free French movement figured prominently in the correspondence. Duclos reported that the party had been invited to send its delegate to London "to discuss with de Gaulle the issue of delivering weapons and questions concerning the postwar period." He asked for Dimitrov's opinion. The French Communist Party leadership believed that it should insist on the delivery of weapons and the maintenance of regular communications within the country, emphasizing that the main objective was to expel the invaders, but it was reluctant to hold a meeting in London. The dispatch was forwarded to Stalin, and in May 1942 Dimitrov radioed: "Regarding the proposal by the representatives of Free France, we consider the position you have taken to be correct."[80]

In early December, Dimitrov submitted to Stalin and Molotov directives to the Communist parties of France and Italy that had been drawn up together with Thorez, Togliatti, Manuilsky, and Marty. The French Communist Party would strive to unite all national forces in a National Front, cooperate with de Gaulle and his supporters, and back all the other elements in France and northern Africa that were actively involved in the struggle against Hitler. The Communist Party of Italy was given the task of strengthening the bloc of leftist antifascist forces, preparing for the creation of a National Front to lead the people in an active struggle against the Mussolini regime, and organizing "an uprising to overthrow the fascist government." On 9 December Dimitrov reported to Togliatti: "The French and Italian documents have been approved by comrade Stalin."[81]

With Moscow's agreement, Duclos was now prepared to send a delegate to meet with de Gaulle. Dimitrov cautioned him that the representative would have to work closely with the Soviet envoy to London, Alexander Bogomolov: "Almost all of de Gaulle's military and civilian entourage is highly suspicious in various ways, including of some ties with the enemy and Vichy. Therefore we advise the delegate you send to de Gaulle to be extremely cautious in all respects: political, organizational, personal, and in contacts with you. Choose an intelligent, firm delegate. Upon arrival your delegate must see the Soviet representative to de Gaulle, Bogomolov, who will give him useful advice." The delegate was a member of the Central Committee of the French Communist Party, Fernand Grenier. Dimitrov immediately forwarded to Stalin and others Duclos's coded dispatches on Grenier's activity and on the plans of de Gaulle's entourage for postwar France.[82]

The Comintern and the Red Orchestra

The Comintern's coded correspondence throws some new light on one of the most famous Soviet intelligence operations of World War II, the legendary Rote Kappelle, or Red Orchestra. With tentacles throughout Western Europe, including Germany, the Red Orchestra was the object of one of German counterintelligence's largest operations. Its postwar notoriety was burnished by an outpouring of books chronicling its exploits and the compelling story of its "Big Chief," Leopold Trepper, imprisoned by the Soviet Union after the war and later persecuted by Communist Poland when he tried to emigrate to Israel.

Born in Poland in 1904, Leopold Trepper joined a left-wing Zionist youth group and left in 1924 for Palestine, where he quickly joined the Communist Party. A founder of Unity, dedicated to Jewish-Arab cooperation, he honed skills working underground while evading British police. Facing arrest, he moved to France in 1929 and then Moscow in 1932 to study at a school designed for promising young Communists. While working as a journalist on a Jewish newspaper, he was recruited by Soviet intelligence to return to Paris to investigate the collapse of an espionage ring in 1932. Trepper developed proof that the initial suspect was innocent and that Robert Gordon Switz, an American expatriate working for Soviet intelligence, had been the traitor.

Trepper's success led to his enlistment by Soviet military intelligence; he was dispatched to Brussels in 1938 as Adam Mikler, an industrialist. Using old comrades from Palestine, he developed a front company exporting raincoats throughout Europe and built an espionage network. Relatively quiet even after the Nazi conquest of Western Europe, the Red Orchestra sprang into action following the attack on the Soviet Union. Between 1940 and its demise in 1943 it sent some fifteen hundred dispatches to Moscow with information on German war materials, weapons, and plans.

With excellent sources scattered throughout Western Europe, the Red Orchestra's biggest problem was how to communicate its harvest of secret information to Moscow. Prior to June 1941, Trepper's ring had nine radio transmitters, three each in Belgium, Berlin, and the Netherlands. The transmitters, however, were vulnerable to detection, particularly when they were on the air for long stretches. Much of the information coming out of France was smuggled into Vichy and turned over to the Soviet military attaché stationed there. Once the Soviet Union and Nazi Germany went to war, however, that passageway closed.

Plagued by inexperienced radio operators and damaged equipment, the Berlin branch of the spy ring struggled to communicate its information. Desperate to obtain intelligence in the face of a relentless German offensive, the head of the Red Army Intelligence Directorate ordered one of Trepper's lieutenants to travel to Berlin to "determine causes [of] failures [of] radio links." The coded message, however, included the addresses where the transmitters could be found. Nine months later, German cryptanalysts decoded this telegram. This catastrophic error led to the arrest of more than 130 people involved in both intelligence and resistance operations within Germany.

Aware that he lacked enough transmitters and experienced "pianists," as the radio operators were called, Trepper asked Moscow for contact with the French Communist Party, which operated its own clandestine links to Moscow and the Comintern. By the end of 1940 Fernand Pauriol, the French CP's radio expert, had agreed to train several operators for Trepper and provided a transmitter that, although not powerful enough to broadcast to Moscow, could send messages to the Soviet Embassy in London.

The Germans, however, seized one of the Belgian transmitters, along with two radio operators and a Soviet intelligence officer, Mikhail Makarov, on 12 December 1941. Trepper hastily relocated to Paris, from where he reestablished contact with Red Army military intelligence headquarters using the Comintern's radio communications with the French Communist Party. Several messages to Dimitrov and Sorkin in February–March 1942 have been preserved in the Comintern archives, as have Dimitrov's instructions after passing the material to the Red Army Intelligence Directorate: "Send a cipher telegram on your two-way radio to Otto's [Trepper's] address in Paris."[83]

The archives files contain neither messages to Trepper nor his reports, with the exception of one "Message from Otto to the Director." All that has survived are letters of transmittal to Soviet military intelligence and dispatches from Jacques Duclos, such as: "Below we are transmitting a message from Otto, known to us as Leo. We request that you urgently forward it to the leadership of the Intelligence Directorate." Another communiqué from Duclos noted: "Messages [for] Otto have been sent to their destination. He would like to be kept informed."[84]

The Comintern's agent Clément (Eugen Fried), then living in Belgium, was given a task related to the Red Orchestra. On 14 December 1941 Dimitrov asked the following of him:

> Establish contact with our friends' person, either through your person or, if possible, directly. A meeting place has been set for the 19th and a backup for 21 December near the "Agora" movie theater, at the main entrance from the square, at 16:00. Our friends' man will be smoking a pipe and holding the magazine *Berlin-Rome-Tokyo*. He will be holding a brown briefcase and will be dressed entirely in brown; a brown cane, hat, suit, and gloves. Your person coming to the meeting should be holding the same magazine, *Berlin-Rome-Tokyo*, and should have in his mouth a pipe that he is not smoking. Your person will ask for a match from our friends' person; he will first take out a lighter that has no gasoline and then matches. Our friends' man will ask your man if he knows what film is playing at the "Metropol" movie theater. He will get the answer: "La femme."[85]

The same day Dimitrov also instructed Duclos to make contact with Trepper: "We agree to have comrade Leo [Trepper] contact with our friends to provide them the necessary assistance." But on 28 December, Dimitrov informed military intelligence officials that Fried had reported a failure: "I personally went to the backup meeting place and rigorously followed all of your instructions. No one came." The meeting was aborted because on 13 December the Gestapo had seized the Red Orchestra's radio station in Brussels and Trepper had fled to Paris.[86]

Makarov's successor as head of the Belgian network, Konstantin Yefremov, another Red Army military intelligence officer, was also arrested at the end of July 1942, along with Johann Wenzel, a veteran German Communist code-named "Professor" who had served as the Comintern's chief radio operator in Western Europe. Wenzel supervised Rote Kappelle's radio operations. Yefremov betrayed not only several Belgian agents, but much of the Dutch network of the Red Orchestra as well.[87]

Trepper's warnings that his networks had been compromised were resisted in Moscow. At the beginning of September he received an order from the Director to go to Brussels and meet with Yefremov. Military intelligence asked the Comintern to send the message: "I am herewith transmitting one coded dispatch, which I request you to transmit to Paris on your radio station with the postscript, 'For Leo's service.' The telegram is extremely urgent and is intended for our employee, Otto." Just days later came another request to the Comintern: "I am herein sending three cipher communications, which I request to transmit to Paris through your radio station with the postscript, 'For Leo. [Trepper]' " After surveillance confirmed that the Gestapo was watching the meeting place, Trepper stayed away.[88]

Trepper was arrested on 24 November in Paris. German counterintelligence was anxious to use him and the remnants of his network to penetrate and destroy the French Communist underground, with which he had contact, and to continue to feed false information back to Moscow. To do so, it needed to keep his detention a secret. In his autobiography, Trepper insisted that he had concluded the Germans' ultimate goal was to weaken Allied unity and, eventually, conclude a separate peace with Great Britain and the United States. As a result, he decided to feign cooperation with them, hoping to find a way to alert Moscow.

Moscow, however, knew about the multiple blows suffered by its prime espionage network. The head of the Dutch Comintern communications center, Goulooze, reported the Netherlands' arrests in a dispatch to Dimitrov in October 1942. He warned that "the Gestapo has certainly found out something about us." In November, shortly before Trepper's arrest, Goulooze reported that one member of the network had turned up in Amsterdam, but "we have the impression that the Gestapo is behind this." Dimitrov asked an aide to "urgently clear this up with the neighbors and prepare a response." That response was unequivocal: "The person who has come to you . . . is a provocateur. Cut off all contact with people . . . [he] used to visit. . . . Be careful. If need be, change your apartment, meeting places, and communication links."[89]

In addition to knowing that both the Belgian and Dutch cells of the Rote Kappelle had been taken over by the Gestapo, Moscow was also aware that Trepper himself had been arrested. Dimitrov received word from France in late December that "Leo disappeared about 12 days ago, and along with him, his backup and a woman working with them. Leo's communications agent, who met with one of our comrades, informed us of these facts, and according to him, the apparatus has not been affected. He talked about a parallel sector of work that has been affected." Dimitrov immediately ordered the message sent to Ilyichev, head of the GRU.[90]

In his memoirs Trepper insisted that by January 1943 he had persuaded his captors that only a personal meeting by him with a French Communist Party contact could ensure that Moscow would accept that he was still free; when he did meet with that contact, Juliette Moussier, he managed to give her a long message he had secretly composed while in custody, laying out who had been arrested and the deception the Germans were practicing. He asked that Moscow send a radio message on 23 February with greetings on the anniversary of the Red Army as a signal that his message had been received and understood. When it arrived, he exulted that "the initiative for the Great Game was passing into the hands of the Red Army. The hour of revenge had come!"[91]

The ciphered telegrams in the Comintern archives tell a somewhat different story. The Center received Trepper's first coded dispatch controlled by the Germans on 25 December. Amazingly, it ignored the warnings and red flags sent out from the Comintern radio transmitters. On 29 December a radiogram expressing Trepper's desire to meet with a representative of the French CP went to Moscow. A day later Duclos informed Dimitrov: "It has come to our knowledge that Leo, who had disappeared, has shown signs of life and is to have a meeting on 2 January."[92]

More than a month passed before the Center radioed Duclos on 18 February 1943 to organize a meeting between Trepper and "Michel," the communications link between him and the Communist Party leadership: "Leo requests that Michel be told to come for a meeting on Sunday the 21st at the agreed time and place. If the meeting on the 21st does not take place, come to the same place at the same time on the 28th." Because Trepper had previously arranged with Michel that their meetings be held at a designated time and place different from those ordered by the Center, the rendezvous fell through.[93]

A. I. Galagan, the author of the introduction to the Russian edition of Trepper's biography, writes that he worked in the GRU archives and they contain no copy of the supposed 23 February message indicating Moscow had received Trepper's smuggled message. Moreover, French Communist Party officials continued to receive directives for a meeting between Michel and Trepper. A coded dispatch of 5 March read: "Tell Michel that on the next Sunday, 7 or 14 March, he should come to the known place at the designated time for a meeting with Leo." On 12 April, the ECCI received a letter from the GRU: "I request you to inform com. Duclos that we will provide Leo's instructions on going to meet Michel at the agreed time and the established place on 18 and 25 April."[94]

The Center clearly interpreted Trepper's dispatches as requests for a meeting and not as part of a deception operation carried out at the Germans' dictation. The willingness of the GRU to have Dimitrov give the Communist Party directions on the meeting indicates it did not believe its network had been compromised—or that it was willing to sacrifice key French party figures. One odd communication from Duclos, received on 26 May, demonstrated that despite its earlier report that Trepper had been arrested, the French Communist Party underground also still believed in the integrity of his network. The message began with Duclos claiming: "I received the message regarding a meeting that took place between Leo and Michel." In fact, that was a Comintern Communications Service mistranslation of the original French that actually read, "I received the message regarding the meeting Leo has set up with Michel." The message went on to report: "Unfortunately, the latter has disappeared and has doubtless been arrested. If Leo so desires, there is the possibility of making arrangements, according to his instructions, for him to meet with Duval [Ferdinand Pauriol, the French CP's radio expert], whom he knows." Since the Germans were even more anxious to capture Pauriol, who could give them access to the French Communist communications systems, it is difficult to believe that Duclos really believed Trepper had been arrested by the Germans. Dimitrov gave orders for this dispatch to be sent to Ilyichev.[95]

The coded messages convincingly demonstrate that Trepper passed his message exposing his network's collapse and the radio game the Germans were playing to Juliette Moussier in early June 1943, more than five months later than Trepper or historians have claimed. The first sentence of the message from Otto to the Director, received in Moscow in July 1943, said that Trepper and his comrades "have been in prison for five months." They had all been arrested between late November and late December 1942. Thus, Trepper had not transmitted his message until May or early June, a dating confirmed by Duclos's sending a dispatch to Moscow confirming Trepper's arrest on 5 June, presumably just days after the latter had passed his information to Moussier: "It has come to our attention that Leo has been in Gestapo hands since November and that they know the codes used by his service and are corresponding with his superiors. It is the Gestapo who transmitted Leo's secret meeting places for Michel, and they were then transmitted to us.

The Gestapo probably has the codes of all the services in the occupied countries and is carrying out correspondence as if the services were operating normally. We will soon give you the details of this matter." On 7 June Dimitrov gave the order to send this dispatch to Ilyichev. Its first sentence explained that "as a result of a terrible conspiracy by the German 'Kontra,' we—Otto, André, René, and Harry–and some of our people have been in prison for five months."[96]

Duclos sent a follow-up radio message on 12 June that "Otto, who is being held by the Gestapo and pretending to have betrayed his convictions, transmitted this message through the representative of a commercial establishment, who is in contact with one of our services. I asked Clément [Eugen Fried] to expedite the sending of the text of the message, in spite of its length, because it contains important information." He added that Trepper's contact, Moussier, had gone into hiding and the underground would "eliminate provocateurs who are trying to make contact with our organizations, supposedly in the name of various services."[97]

On the same day, Fried notified Dimitrov that he had received a message from Otto for the Director of the GRU via Duclos. Since it numbered about two hundred lines of typewritten text and contained a large number of names, preparing it to be radioed in code would take two to three weeks. The text would be sent in its entirety. The first portion arrived in Moscow on 7 July; the second, on 10 July; both were immediately sent to Ilyichev. The "Message from Otto to the Director" makes no mention of a radiogram of congratulations for 23 February, nor does it recommend a temporary pause in communications, as Trepper had claimed. Instead, "In order to take all precautionary measures and organize my rescue, you must be sure to continue the music [communications] along all lines without interruption, as has been the case until now."[98]

Trepper explained that some of the members of the intelligence network had turned traitor and were cooperating with the Germans. Through treachery and torture the Germans had obtained the codes and radio frequencies; "So far, Harry [Henry Robinson] is the only one who has not given his code." Kent (Victor Sukulov) and Pascal (Yefremov) had been drawn "into the game by various maneuvers," and counterintelligence "is threatening to extend the conspiracy to Switzerland, Italy, and other countries."[99]

After receiving this message, Dimitrov warned Duclos of the need for the utmost caution. "Halt all of your communications with the representatives of the 'friends' [Soviet intelligence] in Paris. Send word of this to Belgium. Do not meet with anyone without our recommendation; no matter what the request or whom it is from, ignore it. It is possible that there are comrades of yours in this whole affair with the 'Kontra' who must be isolated—immediately. Be careful. If you have the slightest suspicion, cut everyone off from your contacts. Take another look at those around you, and reassess the trustworthiness of your radio operators." Duclos reported that the instructions had been received and forwarded to Fried in Belgium.[100]

Despite Trepper's claim that he had alerted Moscow to what was happening in January 1943, the impact of his June 1943 warning was to generate suspicions about his own loyalty. When Duclos conveyed the decoded text of Trepper's message, he had added that "no one knows the details or the conditions in which Otto could have transmitted this document in such a way that the guard did not notice." Duclos was quickly instructed to "report how Otto conveyed his message for the Director, which you have sent us through Clément." These suspicions were reinforced when Trepper escaped from German custody. Learning at the beginning of September that Pauriol, the French radio expert, had been arrested and a Communist Party radio transmitter confiscated along with copies of radiograms, Trepper feared that his smuggled message to the Director of the GRU would be discovered. He contrived to escape and remained hidden until Paris was liberated.[101]

Duclos was wary about Trepper's escape. He radioed Dimitrov: "We have found out . . . that Otto has supposedly escaped. This escape seems suspicious to us, and we have taken safety precautions." Dimitrov notified Ilyichev, who asked him to inquire: "Did Otto go to see one of com. Duclos's people and seek refuge with them, or did com. Duclos receive this news through his informers in some other way and Otto's location is unknown to him?" Dimitrov sent the message to Duclos. No answer was in the archives. When Trepper returned to Moscow in 1945, he was arrested as a traitor and held in prison until May 1954.[102]

The evidence indicates that many of the legends that have been disseminated about the exploits of the Rote Kappelle are grossly exaggerated. Far from providing war-changing information, it sent a steady stream of useful but not spectacular material to Moscow. Despite Trepper's boasts about how he and his chief lieutenants outwitted the Gestapo and prevented it from achieving its goal of splitting the Allied coalition or promoting a separate peace, it appears more likely that Moscow remained clueless about the destruction of its West European networks for months, and its immediate reaction to Trepper's warnings was to conclude that he had gone to work for the Germans.

The Comintern and the Belgian Party after the German Attack on the USSR

Coded dispatches arrived from Belgium via Eugen Fried (Clément), who had physically moved from France to Belgium. He put the ECCI in contact with the Communist Party of Belgium and other West European Communist parties. Through his help these parties learned of the directives sent after Dimitrov's conversation with Stalin on 22 June 1941. Fried responded, "The directives have been passed on to the Belgian, French, Italian, and Swiss parties. All immediately reacted along the lines indicated." He assured Dimitrov that public opinion among all segments of the population in Belgium and northern France was against Hitler and was firmly on the side of the Soviet Union. In sending Fried the directive of 30 June, Dimitrov emphasized: "Use every means available to speed up the rapid implementation of our directives. Fateful times call for decisive and effective military hostilities, regardless of the difficulties and casualties. Give us specific information about such actions. What are Ives [Duclos] and his friends doing?" Later an inquiry was sent asking why there were no reports about the resistance movement in Belgium and what had been done to implement the directives. The cipher communication ended on an extremely harsh note: "Right now there is very little difference between any sort of passivity and crime and treason."[103]

On 22 February 1942 Dimitrov sent Stalin and others Fried's information about the activity of the Communist Party of Belgium. It dealt with the organization of sabotage by the party, supporting the economic demands of workers, and antifascist propaganda. The total circulation of all illegal newspapers published by the party amounted to seventy-five thousand copies a month, and local and factory newspapers were also being distributed. The Communist Party of Belgium numbered more than seven thousand members. "The Party is completely illegal. 800 Party members have been arrested. Many have been shot. The deputy Cordier was murdered in prison." Moscow was dissatisfied with Fried's information, as shown by the harsh tone of a radiogram sent him: "Your behavior is utterly incomprehensible to me. You keep on sending telegrams about technical issues, but you do not provide any information about what is happening in your country—about the activity of the occupiers, the anti-Hitler movement, the mood and movements of the masses, the activity of the Communist Party and other Parties and organizations, etc. You do not raise any political issues. What is the problem? We request that you respond promptly and take steps to eliminate this serious oversight in your work."[104]

Dimitrov forwarded to Stalin the coded dispatches that arrived following this message; they contained more detail about resistance operations and efforts to build coalitions of the various political tendencies. One report noted that of the thirty-five members and candidate members of the Central Committee, fifteen were still active, many had been arrested, and five people had been expelled, one of them for treason. "More than a thousand of the Party members have been arrested, 71 have been executed by shooting, and 80 have died in concentration camps built by the Germans."[105]

Fried reported information he had received alleging that Britain and the United States were in secret negotiations with the Germans. A source reported that fearing the Soviet military advances, "the German generals and financiers, allegedly, seem to favor a compromise peace and are ready at any moment to part with Hitler." This dispatch was communicated to Stalin, and Fried was tasked to report: "1. Who exactly is conducting negotiations with the Germans. 2. Where are these negotiations being held. 3. What is the specific content of these negotiations." Fried's response has not been located, and the source for his information remains unclear.[106]

Fried also reported on conditions in prisoner of war camps; he forwarded one letter asking for help in escaping and asked "whether the Party should respond to such appeals. I report also that there are escaped Soviet prisoners in all regions of Belgium. Some have joined the ranks of the partisans. We wait for your instructions." He was told that "it is necessary to provide every form of assistance and aid to Soviet prisoners and, at the same time, to observe extreme caution, so as not to harm honest prisoners of war and so that the Party does not swallow the bait of potential provocateurs."[107]

The Belgian party came under fierce German attack in mid-1943. Fried reported the disruption of the party apparatus and the arrest of many of its leaders in late July, adding: "I am not directly in danger, because I am isolated from the Communist Party. But because of the situation in the apparatus regarding apartments, I am having increasing difficulties. I am trying to get to France without my apparatus." Later he reported that starting on 10 August he would have to break off communications and proposed that contact be maintained through Duclos. Dimitrov agreed but at the same time warned Duclos: "Report what kind of ties you have with Belgium and with whom personally. Since arrests are taking place there that can influence your connections, be cautious. Send your messengers who used to travel back and forth to Belgium to live in another region. Liquidate the sec[ret] apartments that your messengers from Belgium knew about. Only as a last resort, assign one of your experienced people to maintain contact with Belgium." On 27 September Moscow sent an inquiry to Fried: "Why are you not communicating informational material to us?" There was no direct answer but Duclos responded: "The recent failures disorganized the transmitting apparatus: Clément's apparatus was disrupted. Clément himself fell victim to a provocation and was killed by the Gestapo."[108]

The Comintern and Dutch Communists after the German Attack on the USSR

In Holland the Comintern's communications center was run by Daan Goulooze (code name Bernard). Assignments for the Communist Party of the Netherlands contained instructions on the struggle against the German occupiers and on the need to try to unite patriotic antifascist forces but to prevent the Dutch government in exile in London from "using the Party as its instrument." Goulooze was set tasks to gather and communicate information on the number and location of German troops in the country, military sites, transportation of troops and munitions, the mood of the occupying forces, and relations between the occupiers and the urban and rural populations of Holland. Dimitrov warned that information should be carefully verified "so as not to fall victim to hostile disinformation."[109]

The Comintern also instructed Goulooze to assist Soviet foreign intelligence. When an agent code-named "Hermann" (Jan Kruyt) was parachuted into Holland, he was unable to establish radio contact with Moscow. Pavel Fitin asked Dimitrov to transfer "to us the standby radio operator you have in Holland for use there." Goulooze assigned a radio operator. Dimitrov later used Goulooze's network to facilitate the parachuting of an NKVD agent into Holland but only if Goulooze thought such an operation would not be dangerous: "We repeat, if it is risky for you, we will cancel this action." Fitin relied on the Comintern network to shelter the agent, Peter Kousnetsov, and escort him into Germany. When Goulooze radioed that such a mission was hopeless, Fitin acquiesced and allowed Kousnetsov to work with "Hermann." Although several parachute drops brought equipment to the pair, they were captured by the Gestapo in late July 1943.[110]

The Comintern's Attempt to Create an Anti-Nazi Resistance Inside Germany

The information the Comintern received from its contacts in Western Europe about Germany sometimes exaggerated the German public's discontent. In December 1941, Goulooze sent a message about western Germany, which Dimitrov transmitted to Stalin:

> With each day the masses' mood to fight against Hitler increased. After Hitler's speech of 3 October about the victories of his army, there was noticeable despondency among the workers. News of the defeat near Rostov had spread by Sunday, 30 November. The myth about the invincibility of Hitler's army has been dispelled once and for all. At factories workers are openly holding discussions and saying: "We will never win this war, so why continue to make sacrifices in vain?" In general, successes by the Soviet Union are very heartening to everyone. Workers' confidence in their own strength has already grown, which is being reflected in increasingly conscious speeches at factories. They are already beginning to compare today's situation with the situation in 1918, not only because of shortages of goods, but also because of the mounting war fatigue among the population and the soldiers and because of the growing revolutionary mood. Letters from the Eastern Front are full of demands for peace.[111]

In part on the basis of these reports of German civilian discontent with Hitler, German-speaking Belgian and Dutch Communists, as well as German Communists living covertly in Belgium, Holland, and France, were ordered to enter Germany to foment an internal anti-Nazi resistance inside the Reich. Instructions were sent to Fried in Belgium: "We request that you entrust the leadership of the Belgian Party to find a German instructor who is now in Belgium and notify him that he and other comrades, especially the head of the border crossing point, should go to the country for Party work. Make arrangements with them for continuous contact with Belgian comrades to receive information. All this should be carried out by the Belgian comrades under your control. Notify us of what has been done." The directive proceeded from an assumption that it was possible for former émigrés to work illegally in Germany. Such attempts inevitably resulted in failure and arrest.[112]

The Comintern ordered Goulooze to transmit a directive to Wilhelm Knöchel, a member of the Central Committee of the Communist Party of Germany and its clandestine agent in the Netherlands, Belgium, and Switzerland since 1940. Knöchel was told to send "all of the verified German comrades to the country [Germany] to organize direct actions in support of the Red Army and the struggle to overthrow Hitler. Leading comrades in the country should organize groups as soon as possible for special operations and subversive activity in the country."[113]

At the beginning of 1942 Knöchel crossed into Germany to steer the party's covert work. His departure was preceded by an inquiry that Dimitrov sent through Soviet intelligence channels to Arthur Illner, a Stockholm-based member of the illegal leadership of the Communist Party of Germany: "Alfred [Knöchel] from Amsterdam has been prepared for a trip to the country. It is necessary to know if the Berlin secret meeting place is in order and what the password is. Reply promptly." Knöchel's dispatches were forwarded through Goulooze and optimistically reported increasing numbers of protests and discontent and calls for "the creation of committees to fight against the war. A rapid and general worsening in supplies of food and raw materials is to be seen."[114]

Knöchel was given instructions to create fighting groups of antifascists inside Germany, to spread propaganda among soldiers, and to establish illegal committees at factories and in villages that included former members of trade unions, Catholics, Social Democrats, and Nazis. In May 1942, however, Dimitrov instructed Goulooze to notify Knöchel that Herbert Wehner, a candidate member of the German party's Politburo who had been sent to Sweden to work among exiled German Communists and as a link to the underground party in Germany, had been arrested and was cooperating with Swedish security, placing other German Communists in Sweden and in Germany itself in danger.[115]

Despite the warning, Knöchel continued to work. Several radio operators traveled from Holland to Germany in December and met with him. But on 19 January 1943 Goulooze reported that he had not been heard from for six weeks. Dimitrov "urgently" asked for news and complained to his replacement in Holland, Elly Hansmann: "Why are you not sending regular communications about events in Germany?" Goulooze was puzzled because he had a report that Knöchel "is still in good health." In January Hansmann had gone to Germany to meet with him, but due to several arrests of contacts, the rendezvous had not taken place. "We do not understand what is going on there." Goulooze radioed on 25 February that "we cannot say definitively whether Alfred has been arrested, but for several weeks there have been no messages from him." The Comintern issued contradictory instructions to Goulooze on the same day in March, in one ordering a radio operator to return to Germany to work with Knöchel, the other cutting off all contact with him.[116]

In fact Knöchel had been captured by the Gestapo on 30 January 1943. Under torture, he provided information that led to other arrests of underground Communists in Germany. From then onward no organizational leadership of the Communist Party of Germany existed, and the thin hopes for an active anti-Hitler resistance evaporated. The Comintern, however, remained oblivious to reality. In mid-April it asked Goulooze to forward a message to the German underground to launch a new campaign against the war on May Day, to establish organizations of antifascist activists at factories and in military units, to step up sabotage, to eliminate Gestapo agents, and to hang red flags.[117]

The Dutch Communist Party Is Crippled

The destruction of the German Communist underground also doomed that of the Netherlands. Knöchel had worked there before infiltrating into Germany, and after his arrest, the Gestapo used information it had extracted from him to begin rolling up members of the Dutch party. Goulooze notified Dimitrov that contact with the Central Committee of the Communist Party of Holland had broken off. He explained that in late January "the Gestapo attacked the central board of the party's central organ, and from there they got to the leadership as well. The head of all internal communications was arrested and revealed a great deal of information. This created complications for the S[ecretaria]t. Subsequently, new arrests took place, which completely severed all ties." He still maintained contact with the Amsterdam organization of the party but was reluctant to reestablish "communications with new friends—we think that right now this is hardly advisable." Dimitrov warned Goulooze against exposing his apparatus by meeting with any new people: "Your work is very important and such contacts could threaten your Center." Instead, he proposed that three leaders of the Amsterdam organization of the party act as intermediaries with other groups, "but every measure should be taken to ensure the security of your Center."[118]

Goulooze continued to send messages to Moscow about resistance activities throughout Holland and Nazi roundups of Dutch Jews. But in mid-July 1943 Dimitrov asked Fried to find out what had happened to Goulooze: "For unknown reasons we have not had any contact with Bernard [Goulooze] since 1 July. Try to find out immediately what is the matter and notify us." While out of communication, however, Goulooze was not arrested until November 1943. Only on 13 October 1944 did Dimitrov learn what had happened to him from Pavel Fitin, who explained that "we received a message from Holland from our worker there that Goulooze (Goulos) and several other technical staff members have been arrested." He survived the war in the Oranienburg concentration camp.[119]

The Comintern and the Bulgarian Communists after the German Attack on the USSR

Bulgaria had formally declared neutrality but in fact was cooperating with Hitler. After Germany's attack on the USSR the Communist Party leadership assured the Comintern that the Bulgarian people were ready to enter the war on the side of the USSR:

> In spite of the mass arrests, war leaflets against fascist Germany's attack on the Soviet Union are being distributed in Sofia. These slogans are visible on the walls of houses: "Down with Hitler, long live the Soviet Union." The general mood is: "we do not want to and we will not fight against the Russian people—our liberator." Many say—let the Soviet Union occupy Bulgarian ports, landing troops and helping us arm ourselves for the struggle against our common enemy. Comrade Stalin's speech is well known in Bulgarian Communist Party circles and among the left-wing strata of the population and the intelligentsia. Measures have been taken for the broadest possible dissemination of this historic speech.[120]

Believing its own propaganda, the Bulgarian Communist Party began preparations for an armed uprising. Dimitrov wrote to Stalin on 2 August with information from the party leadership that Germany was urging Bulgaria to enter the war. Tsar Boris and the government, though still wavering, were inclined to do so, but the overwhelming majority of the people and soldiers were opposed. A group of officers with "a significant influence within the army and particularly among officers in the reserves" had "made a proposal to our Party to engage in joint action. Negotiations on this issue are under way. . . . In this connection, the CC of the Party is inquiring as to how and to what extent the USSR can provide assistance in the event of an uprising in Bulgaria." Dimitrov requested urgent instructions.[121]

Stalin was far more realistic. He told Dimitrov: "No uprising now. The workers would be smashed. For now we can render no assistance. An attempt at an uprising would be a provocation." The Comintern sent instructions to Bulgaria that an uprising was premature and doomed to a crushing defeat: "Proceed with an uprising only when it is possible to combine actions within and outside the country, which at this point is still impossible. Now we must replenish our strength, do our utmost to prepare and reinforce positions in the army and at key points." The Bulgarian party agreed: "We will comprehensively prepare for an uprising of the army and people at a suitable moment, to be agreed upon with external forces; this will require the appropriate organizational restructuring and military-technical preparation of the Party and the masses." It added: "We will combine this preparation with the deployment of a struggle and with disrupting rear positions of thc fascists."[122]

The Comintern maintained contact with the Bulgarian Communist Party through the Soviet diplomatic mission still operating in Sofia. On 3 January 1942 Dimitrov wrote to Pavel Fitin, asking his apparatus to assist in arranging meetings and setting up communications. Although Fitin agreed, he expressed concern that several of the Bulgarian Communists were police agents. Dimitrov and the Bulgarian party disagreed with that assessment.[123]

Dimitrov gave the Bulgarian party leadership assignments of interest to Soviet military intelligence. In November 1941 Ivan Ilyichev requested detailed information on the Bulgarian Army and "the number of German troops in Bulgaria, their deployment, the distribution of various sorts of weapons among them, and the numbering of the German units."[124]

By April 1942 the party was focused "mainly on using any means whatever to prevent Hitler's troops from involving Bulgaria in the war against the USSR and preventing even a partial deployment of Bulgarian troops to the Soviet-German front." Dimitrov sent Stalin and Molotov a dispatch he had received reporting that "combat groups have been organized in the army to lead this struggle." Sentiment in the army was overwhelmingly opposed to fighting the Soviet Union. "The situation in the country is extremely tense. Mass arrests and raging terror cannot suppress the growing opposition among the people and the army to the pro-Hitler policy of Tsar Boris. We can expect major internal convulsions and violent incidents. The Party is making strenuous efforts to carry out its duty in a worthy manner."[125]

Dimitrov told the Communist Party that if Bulgaria entered the war, it was "to prepare revolts in the army, a popular uprising, and a partis[an] war against Hitlerites and their Bulgarian servants." Bulgarian troops, however, never did attack the USSR. The party leadership was arrested in April 1942 and tried in July; some were executed and others imprisoned.[126]

The Comintern and the Scandinavian Communists after the German Attack on the USSR

The Comintern's communications liaisons in neutral Sweden were carried out by Sven Linderot, the party leader since 1929, and Karl Lager, a member of the Politburo of the Swedish party. The ECCI transmitted instructions through them to the Communist parties in occupied Norway and Denmark and to German Communists who maintained contact with the Communist underground in Germany. After the Nazi invasion of the USSR, Dimitrov sent ECCI directives through Linderot ordering active support for the USSR. He also cautioned that the Communist Party of Sweden should be ready for a ban on the party and possible arrests. He emphasized that Linderot "must be in a position to remain in the country, in order to address the working class and the people as a popular leader from the underground." The party was to explain that the Swedish policy of concessions to Hitler would lead to the country's loss of its independence.[127]

Contacts with Linderot were carried out through staff members of Soviet intelligence agencies working in the Soviet diplomatic mission in Stockholm. On 30 December 1941 Fitin informed Dimitrov: "The money has been given to 'Paul' ['CP of Sweden' was written above this word] and 'Nikolai' ['CP of Germany' was written above this word]. Paul [Linderot] has reported that he recently established contact, hears well, and is receiving everything."

In addition to using Soviet intelligence channels for communications, the Comintern also called on the leaders of the Communist Party of Sweden to collect information of interest to Soviet intelligence. Instructions were given in a coded dispatch to Lager for Linderot to select "the most devoted and suitable comrades" among the party activists and form a group to be assigned to "gather military-political information in your country. This special service must be kept strictly confidential and organized in various regions in the country." The news to be sent to Moscow included information on what military cargo was being sent to Germany and Finland, on which ships and from which ports, how the Germans were making use of Swedish ports and railroads, which German Army units were headed to Finland, what anti-Soviet work was being conducted by the pro-fascist group of the Swedish military, and what was taking place in the Swedish Army and Navy. "If you find people who can be sent to Norway and Finland," read the coded dispatch, "notify us, and we will give you an assignment for them." Instructions were also given for the party to create a special intelligence service reporting directly to the Comintern: "In organizing this service, do not in any case whatever link the comrades working on this matter with our neighbors' service [Soviet intelligence]. Your inf[ormation] service must be under Paul's [Linderot's] direct control. It must not be dependent on anyone and must not be connected with any of the neighbors' representatives that you know. Send directly to us all material received by your inf[ormation] service."[128]

This directive was apparently carried out in an unsatisfactory manner because Dimitrov sent a harsh reproach to Linderot, again transmitted via Soviet intelligence channels:

> Your behavior is incomprehensible to me. In spite of the repeated requests, you still have not reestablished regular direct contact with us. What is the matter? Do you really not understand that this contact is of extraordinary importance right now? Are you not aware that it is your Party's duty right now to help us provide for communication with Norway, Finland, and Denmark? For a number of years we have helped you and given you substantial loans. Do you really not consider it necessary now, in a decisive struggle against the fascist enemy, to make every effort and use all of your own material resources in order, at the very least, to establish the necessary contacts and thus contribute to successfully deploying the struggle in countries neighboring on yours? Where, in reality, should your internationalism be expressed, if not, above all, in this area? I most strongly request that you urgently take the necessary measures to put an end to this abnormal situation.[129]

While the ECCI leadership cooperated closely with the Soviet intelligence services, fulfilling their requests and wishes and instructing Communist Party leaders to do the same, at the same time, it insisted that its sections keep the British and American intelligence services at arm's length. Two coded dispatches sent by Dimitrov to Axel Larsen, the leader of the Danish Communist Party, are illustrative. After receiving news from Sweden that Larsen had ties to British intelligence, Dimitrov asked him, "We request you to report what kind of help the English are giving you and what assistance you are giving them. What made you enter into contact with the English, through whom did you establish contact with 'Intelligence,' and through whom do you maintain it?"[130]

While allowing Larsen to receive assistance from the British, Dimitrov warned him to be extremely cautious:

> We recommend the utmost caution in your dealings with the English. You should maintain contact with them through intermediaries. Do not use any leading comrades for such communications. Do not reveal any of your internal affairs or intentions. You may receive material assistance from them, but do not undertake any obligations toward them. Your newspaper, and its orientation and content, should in no way depend on the English. Be independent in everything, and do not let your hands be tied. Be careful that English intelligence agents do not infiltrate any branches of the Party or recruit people from the Party. Remember—they could create dangerous demoralization within your ranks.[131]

The Comintern, the CPUSA, and the OSS

The Comintern leaders became particularly alarmed after they discovered that the American Office of Strategic Services (OSS) was recruiting former members of the International Brigades in Spain for covert assignments in the German-occupied countries of Europe. Even though the CPUSA had formally disaffiliated from the Comintern in November 1940 in response to punitive legislation, on 3 April 1942, Dimitrov sent an inquiry to William Foster, a leading American Communist, and Robert Minor: "We have information that Woulf repeat Woulf from Abraham Lincoln Brigade is recruiting comrades from this Brigade for special work. He has selected till now from the Brigade comrades a dozen Jugoslavs and five Greeks. He is acting in the name of Minor. . . . Please examine carefully this question and inform us urgently."[132] "Woulf" was Milton Wolff, last commander of the Abraham Lincoln Battalion of the Fifteenth International Brigade during the Spanish Civil War. A member of the American Young Communist League when he went to Spain, he became a member of the Communist Party of Spain while there. After his return to the United States, he headed the Veterans of the Abraham Lincoln Brigade.

Dimitrov's information seemingly came from Fitin because the Comintern head immediately forwarded him the reply, signed by Tim Ryan, the Comintern pseudonym of Eugene Dennis, a veteran CPUSA leader who had been the party's representative to the ECCI in the late 1930s. Dennis assured Dimitrov: "Wolff has our approval working for government . . . now recruiting Americans as commandos for U.S. army also recruiting training non-citizens as commandos guerrillas saboteurs especially for Balkan countries." He added that Spanish Civil War veterans in Mexico and Canada were also available.[133]

Fitin was not appeased, sending Dimitrov a memorandum categorically warning against such cooperation: "For our part, we regard this entire matter as a political mistake by the leadership of the U.S. Comparty, thanks to which the American and British intelligence services have been given the opportunity to infiltrate not only American Comparty channel but also the Comparty organizations of other countries."[134] Dimitrov promptly repeated these words in a directive to leaders of the CPUSA: "We consider as a political mistake the permission to Wolff to recruit people for English and American Intelligence. This makes it possible for the Intelligence to penetrate into the American and other Communist Parties. We suggest discuss seriously the most reasonable measures and forms for ceasing this recruiting and all kind of connections with the above-mentioned Intelligence. Warn about it also the Spanish and Italian comrades."[135]

Faced with an order from the Comintern to stop cooperating with the OSS in fighting Nazi Germany, the CPUSA leadership swiftly capitulated. Dennis conveyed its complete agreement with "proposals regarding the activities of *Wolff*" and pledged that the necessary measures to put an end to them were being taken. He conveyed the request of leaders of the Spanish Communist Party in exile in Cuba that they be allowed to work with American intelligence to infiltrate their men into Spain. He did think that information the CPUSA developed about the activity of Nazi agents in the United States should be conveyed to American authorities and asked for permission to continue working with the authorities in radio propaganda targeting Germany, "if, of course, you are in agreement."[136]

Dimitrov's response was to reiterate that the ban on cooperation with the OSS also extended to the "Spanish comrades"—that is, Spanish Communist exiles living in the United States or Mexico. He did grant the CPUSA permission to transmit information about "Fifth Column" activity "to the government organs" and to cooperate in broadcasting propaganda (this referred to Communists working in government agencies).[137]

Given the Comintern's long-time existence as an appendage of Soviet foreign policy, it is hardly surprising that it functioned as an adjunct to Soviet intelligence during World War II, while the very survival of the USSR was in danger. By 1940 no experienced Comintern operative anywhere in the world had any view other than that the route to world revolution required obedience to the needs of the Soviet Union. In countries under the thumb of Nazi Germany, the requirements of survival could lead to local initiative. Those more fortunate Communist parties functioning in democratic societies occasionally had to be reminded that helping their own countries defeat fascism was not as important as protecting and insulating Communist intelligence networks.

CHAPTER TEN

Dissolution of the Communist International

Although the final decision to dissolve the Comintern was made hurriedly and with little consultation, the possibility of jettisoning the organization, or at least fundamentally altering it, had been raised earlier. On the evening of 20 April 1941, after a concert of Tajik performers at the Bolshoi Theater, members of the Soviet leadership, including Dimitrov, had enjoyed dinner and drinks. When a toast was proposed to Dimitrov's health, Stalin suddenly remarked: "Comm[unist] Parties ought to be made independent, instead of sections of the CI." He added that they had to take root in their own countries and focus on their own specific objectives, goals hampered by their existence as sections of the Comintern. His concern was likely driven by his desire to maintain friendly relations with Germany and his belief that the Comintern had become an embarrassing obstacle to Soviet foreign policy. It also may have been sparked by the decision of the Communist Party of the United States to withdraw from the Comintern in response to an American law.[1]

Dimitrov took Stalin's suggestion as an unequivocal order. The very next day he talked with Togliatti and Thorez about "discontinuing the activities of the ECCI as a leadership body for Com[munist] Parties, converting them into authentic national Parties of Communists in their respective countries, guided by a Communist program, but resolving their own concrete problems in their own manner, in accordance with the conditions in their countries, and themselves bearing responsibility for their decisions and actions." A body in charge of information and ideological and political assistance to the Communist parties was to replace the ECCI, meaning that Moscow would maintain its ties with them, but in a different form. On 12 May Dimitrov discussed a proposed resolution with Manuilsky and Zhdanov. The latter warned that dissolving the Comintern meant "we will have some serious explaining to do abroad as well as among our own Soviet Communists." They would have to "evoke enthusiasm" and avoid creating "a funereal mood and dismay" by emphasizing the maturity of national parties and combining proletarian internationalism with a healthy nationalism (Zhdanov specifically condemned "rootless cosmopolitanism," which "paves the way for the recruitment of spies, enemy agents"). He recommended that so important a decision was best taken at the initiative of the Communist parties themselves and should not be rushed.[2]

The Nazi invasion of the Soviet Union in June 1941 brought a halt to immediate discussions of abolishing or altering the Comintern. Instead, it turned its attention to closely coordinating its activities with Soviet intelligence agencies and consulting with its Communist affiliates around the world about how best to promote the Soviet war effort. In February 1943 a letter to Stalin from employees of the ECCI apparatus was published in *Pravda*, leading Dimitrov to crow in his diary that "the fact that it was published is significant, a public confirmation of the existence and activity of the Comintern under conditions of the Patriotic War."[3]

Just ten weeks later, however, on the evening of 8 May Dimitrov and Manuilsky were summoned to meet with Molotov. In his diary Dimitrov noted that they "reached the conclusion that the Comintern as a direct[ing] center for Com[munist] Parties in the current conditions is an impediment to the Com[munist] Parties' independent development and the accomplishment of their particular tasks. Work up a document for dissolving that center."[4]

Suffering from influenza, Dimitrov nevertheless met at home with Manuilsky on the evening of 10 May and discussed a document to dissolve the Comintern. The following day they completed a draft for the ECCI and sent it to Molotov and Stalin. That evening the four men met, and Stalin approved the draft. It was decided to "consider the draft in a meeting of the Presidium and adopt it as a proposal for the sections . . . distribute it to the sections and request their consent . . . upon receiving consent of the sections, publish it." Dimitrov and Malenkov were authorized to discuss and prepare a proposal for how a new coordinating body would work. Stalin announced that "experience has shown that one cannot have an interna[tional] directing center for all countries." He mused that "there should be perhaps a transition to regional associations, for example, of South America, of the Uni[ted] States and Canada, of certain Europ[ean] countries, etc., but even this must not be rushed."[5]

Within days, Dimitrov finally met with the foreign Communist leaders in Moscow—Marty and Thorez of France, Spain's Ibárruri, Pieck and Ulbricht of Germany, Hungary's Mátyás Rákosi, Ana Pauker of Romania, and others. Since this was unmistakably a Stalin directive, unsurprisingly, "all consider the proposal to CI sections to dissolve the Comintern . . . to be correctly formulated, both politically and on principle." At a restricted meeting of the ECCI Presidium on 13 May the proposed draft was unanimously approved. A message from Stalin received before the meeting suggested that the issue should not be rushed; members should have "two or three days" for discussion or amendments. Obediently, the Presidium reconvened on 17 May to receive a few minor changes to the wording. It was decided to publish the resolution with the Presidium members' signatures "as a proposal to the sections for their approval" rather than send it out for discussion.[6]

An editorial commission cleaned up the language on 18 May, and Dimitrov sent everything to Stalin and Molotov. On 19 May the Presidium decided to retain in the USSR the foreign bureaus of the Communist parties of Germany, Spain, France, Austria, Czechoslovakia, Italy, Bulgaria, Hungary, Finland, and Romania. The archives of the Comintern and the individual parties were transferred "for preservation" to the Central Committee of the Soviet party, "with the possibility for the Foreign Bureaus of the various Communist Parties to access their Party archives." That evening Beria, Anastas Mikoyan (a member of the VKP[b] Politburo), and Dimitrov discussed the decree once again in Stalin's office. They agreed to warn sections of the impending resolution, to issue it in ten days, and, after receiving approval from the sections, to "publish a communiqué from the Presidium signaling final dissolution."[7]

The very next day, however, Stalin phoned Dimitrov asking, "Couldn't the Presidium resolution be submitted to the press today? Publication should be hurried along." Dimitrov answered that a coded dispatch was being sent to the parties, and that the decree could not be published until they received it.[8]

The cipher cable sent to the Communist parties by Dimitrov on 20 May stated, "On 22 May the Presidium of the ECCI will publish a proposal to the sections on the dissolution of the Comintern as the leading center of the international workers' movement. The primary reason is that this centralized organizational form of international union no longer meets the development needs of the Communist Parties of individual countries or national Workers' Parties and in fact is even an obstacle to that. You are urgently requested to discuss this proposal in the Central Committee and to report on your decision."[9]

The formality of having notified the affected parties met, the Politburo of the Soviet party convened on 21 May in Stalin's office with Dimitrov and Manuilsky present. Molotov read out the text of the decree of the ECCI Presidium on the dissolution of the Comintern. Mikhail Kalinin, a member of the VKP(b) Politburo and chairman of the Presidium of the Supreme Soviet of the USSR, favored moving the center of the Comintern to another place, such as London. This suggestion was received with laughter. Stalin explained:

> Experience has shown that in Marx's time, in Lenin's time, and now, it is impossible to direct the working-class movement of all countries of the world from a single international center. Especially now, in wartime conditions, when Com[munist] Parties in Germany, Italy, and other countries have the tasks of overthrowing their governments and carrying out defeatist tactics, while Com[munist] Parties in the USSR, England, America, and other [countries], on the contrary, have the task of supporting their governments to the fullest for the immediate destruction of the enemy. We had overestimated our forces when we created the CI and believed that we would be able to direct the movement in all countries. That was our error. The further existence of the CI would discredit the idea of the International, which we do not desire.

The Soviet dictator offered one additional reason for dissolving the Comintern, which he admitted "is not mentioned in the resolution. That is the fact that the Com[munist] Parties making up the CI are being falsely accused of supposedly being agents of a foreign state, and this is impeding their work in the broad masses. Dissolving the CI knocks this trump card out of the enemy's hands. The step now being taken will undoubtedly strengthen the Com[munist] Parties as nat[ional] working-class Parties and will at the same time reinforce the internationalism of the popular masses, [an internationalism] whose base is the Soviet Union." The resolution was then unanimously adopted and published in *Pravda* the following day.[10]

Over the next few weeks Dimitrov held frequent meetings with foreign Communists, Comintern cadre, and Soviet officials to deal with the logistics of formally closing the Comintern's offices. Communists from Germany, Hungary, Romania, and Italy discussed how to create antifascist committees to coordinate the struggle in their homelands;

newspaper editors talked about creating or converting newspapers for prisoners of war into general antifascist organs. Comintern employees discussed transferring responsibility for radio broadcasts to foreign bureaus of Communist parties, what to do with the library and archives, and transferring publishing responsibilities and "registration of foreign cadres" to the Soviet Communist Party.[11]

Some key aspects of the Comintern's structure remained intact. The clandestine operations, in particular, were not abandoned. Dimitrov wrote in his diary that it was decided "to preserve the liaison service (radio communications, passport technology, and so on), meanwhile leaving open the question of where and how it is to be conducted." He met with Pavel Fitin, head of Soviet foreign intelligence, to discuss how to use "our radio communications and their technical base" in the future for the needs of the intelligence agency. At a meeting with Merkulov, the people's commissar of state security, he "clarified matters concerning transfer of a variety of our establishments" to Merkulov's people's commissariat for state security (NKGB), of which Fitin's foreign intelligence directorate was a part, and its "servicing of the Foreign Bureaus of the different Parties in transporting their cadres to their [respective] countries." (The NKGB was split from the NKVD in 1943.) Dimitrov also consulted Lieutenant-General Ilyichev and Colonel Ivan Bolshakov of the GRU and "settled questions of the further cooperation of our correspondents and communications Centers abroad." At another meeting with Stalin "it was decided to form a special Department of International information" within the Central Committee of the Soviet party "to be entrusted with directing" all the activities—publishing, radio broadcasting, creation of antifascist committees, liaison with foreign Communists, etc.—being spun off. Concerned that critics might point to this new body as simply a continuation of the Comintern under a new name, Stalin decreed that Dimitrov and Manuilsky would formally be deputies under Alexander Shcherbakov, the secretary and candidate member of the VKP(b) Politburo, and that their appointments would not be publically announced.[12]

Even though the Communist parties were being given less than a month to respond to the dissolution of the organization that had directed their policies, determined their leadership, and financed many of their activities for more than twenty years, none dissented. Messages expressing approval of the Presidium's proposal immediately began arriving from the Communist parties. Some were short and others fairly extensive. In addition to a message on the unanimous approval of the Presidium's proposal by the Central Committee of the

French party, it appended an expression of "the deepest thanks to the Comintern and love for the USSR." Dimitrov forwarded all the messages to Stalin and Molotov.[13]

Stalin was impatient to be formally done with the Comintern. He again pressed Dimitrov, calling him on 2 June to ask: "Must we wait for reports from all Parties and then publish the communiqué?" Dimitrov responded that a few Communist parties were scheduled to meet either on 7 or 8 June, and he thought it would be more seemly to wait. On 8 June the final meeting of the Presidium of the Communist International heard that all existing parties had unanimously approved and all the organs of the CI were henceforth abolished.[14]

After receiving the messages from the Communist parties approving the Presidium proposal, Dimitrov sent them another request. He wanted to know how it had been received by the active members of the party, whether any particular views had been expressed during the discussion, and "whether elements have appeared in the Party that are trying to make use of the dissolution for factional and disorganizing activity, and if so, who are these people and what kind of people are they?"[15]

The only signal of dissent came in a message from Paweł Finder of the Polish Workers' Party. Along with a report that the proposal had been unanimously approved by the Central Committee, he noted that "some of the Party activists" had "incorrectly understood the proposal of the ECCI, considering this as an interim maneuver, or rather, as a regrettable need to make concessions to Soviet diplomacy." While no one within the party supported such factionalism, he identified one former Polish Communist who had been campaigning against the dissolution of the Polish CP, Leon Lipski. As noted in chapter 9, the decision had been made to eliminate Lipski, and he had been executed.[16]

Stalin's motive in shutting down the Comintern clearly had little to do with the ostensible reason given in the official communiqué. World War II had not changed in any fundamental way the ability of national Communist parties to operate independently or the need to use different tactics in different countries depending on their relationship to the Soviet Union. None would behave independently after the dissolution of the Comintern. When Earl Browder interpreted the end of the Comintern and the joint British, American, and Soviet Tehran Declaration as signaling the need for American Communists to alter fundamentally the way they operated in America, he was denounced by Jacques Duclos in an article prepared in Moscow, and he was swiftly expelled from the Communist movement when he refused to recant.[17]

Stalin was frank in answer to a Reuter's correspondent's question about why the Comintern had been dissolved. He emphasized that it debunked the lie that Moscow interfered in the affairs of other states and facilitated a union of antifascist progressive forces. As to why he picked May 1943 to act, it may well be that the timing was linked to the arrival in Moscow of the American diplomat and former ambassador to the Soviet Union Joseph Davies. Davies's defense of the Soviet Purge Trials, *Mission to Moscow*, had just been released as a motion picture, and Davies had been tasked by Franklin Roosevelt to arrange a private meeting for him with Stalin. The Soviet leader, in turn, pressed Davies for massive amounts of new Lend-Lease aid.[18]

Molotov and Stalin received Davies in Moscow on 20 May, the same day that, in a conversation with Dimitrov, Stalin inquired whether it was not possible to publish immediately the decree on dissolution. While the published reports of the Davies-Stalin meeting do not explicitly refer to the Comintern, it is possible that the Soviet leader, anxious to gain FDR's support for territorial annexations in Poland and the Baltics, concluded that abandonment of the symbol of world revolution would make his government appear more reasonable.

The decision to eliminate the Comintern, however, in no way meant that the bond between Moscow and the Communist parties—and its impact on their policy—had been broken. On 19 June 1943 the Communist parties were sent a coded dispatch. Dimitrov ordered it dispatched to party leaders ranging from Finder, Tito, and Duclos to Mao and Browder. They were requested to "continue to send information in the same way as heretofore."[19]

Conclusion: The Comintern, 1919–1943

Founded under the spell of the victorious Bolshevik Revolution, flush with the conviction that the worldwide triumph of the proletariat was imminent, and filled with the hubris of revolutionaries secure in their belief that Marxist-Leninist theory gave them the key to understanding the future shape of the world, the Comintern set out to shape the formation and development of revolutionary parties in Europe, the Americas, Asia, and Africa. It molded disparate revolutionaries and rebels into disciplined Communist parties. It expelled troublesome or disobedient leaders. And it dispatched organizers and overseers to the far corners of the earth to enforce its dictates and supervise its branches.

By the end of its first decade, the Comintern had solidified its control over its constituent parties. It had become clear to all but the most obtuse that its stated mission of worldwide revolution took a back seat to the need to support and strengthen Soviet foreign policy. Belief in the scientific wisdom of Marxism-Leninism had been sorely tested by a series of disastrous failures in countries ranging from China to Germany. The Nazi triumph in 1933, substantially aided by flawed and destructive Comintern demands placed on the German party, allowed the Comintern to revive its fortunes later in the decade, as it trumpeted its status as the most resolute opponent of the scourge of fascism, a stance exposed as a hollow camouflage with the signing of the Nazi-Soviet Pact in 1939. Its remaining years until its dissolution in 1943 only further demonstrated its total subservience to the interests of Joseph Stalin and the Soviet Union.

The Communist International's history spanned less than a quarter of a century. The coded cables that form the core of this book are mostly confined to less than a decade, from 1934 to 1943, during which time the Comintern played an outsized role in the history of Europe. Its leader, Bulgarian Communist Georgi Dimitrov, a heroic symbol of resistance to German Nazism, seemed to embody the international dimension of the Comintern's mission. In fact, he was the conduit for the extension of Soviet control of Communist parties.

The Comintern's cipher correspondence with all of the Communist parties was ongoing, if not equally intense. ECCI directives governed the activity of the Comintern sections. Political instructions, reports on how these instructions were being carried out, information about events of international significance, and information on the situation in one or another country and the internal life of the parties flowed back and forth between Moscow and the national parties. Apart from an emphasis on the defense and support of the USSR, the Comintern commented on and frequently issued orders to ostensibly independent political organizations. Trusted parties and leaders might occasionally be given more leeway, but all ultimately were subject to Comintern direction. Virtually all of this control was exercised sub rosa. Secrecy was mandatory.

Many of the orders and directives came directly from Stalin. Dimitrov often transmitted Stalin's desires; other times he was careful to check with him to make sure that he was not misinterpreting his wishes. In moments of great crisis, Stalin's disdain for the Comintern could become apparent, and he could express frustration with its behavior or annoyance at some inconvenience it had caused.

Comintern propaganda touted Soviet domestic and foreign policy and inculcated the image of Stalin as the brilliant heir to the cause of Marx and Lenin, the leader of the Soviet Union, which was putting into practice the aspirations of the workers of the entire world. No Communist party could ignore the leading role of Stalin or fail to fulsomely praise his accomplishments and wisdom.

The coded correspondence demonstrates just how thoroughly the Comintern controlled the implementation by the parties of general political precepts, the content and orientation of the Communist parties' publications, and statements by their leading officials. Jay Lovestone, chief of the CPUSA in the late 1920s, is said to have wisecracked, "Why is the American Party like the Brooklyn Bridge? Because it is suspended at both ends by cables." There is more than ample documentation to extend his witticism to all of the Communist parties.[1] The financing of the parties by the Comintern also represented a significant aspect of its control.

This did not mean that on various—and sometimes substantive—issues the sections of the Comintern could not occasionally take decisions on their own. While the Comintern could and often did micromanage some of the activities of the Communist parties, it did not micromanage everything, its attention shifted from time to time, and the parties had tactical flexibility in some areas. And one can see in the cable communications of the Comintern with the Yugoslav and Chinese parties a foreshadowing of their later angry rejections of continued Soviet leadership of the Communist bloc. But these hints of independence were as yet faint, and the general political orientation of each party, approved by its leading bodies, had to conform to the basic precepts and orders of the Comintern or be sanctioned by it. Research on the history of the various Communist parties during the era of the Comintern must be closely linked to the history of this organization and to its decisive impact on the policy, ideology, organization, and internal life of these parties. Histories that do not link the evolution of the Communist parties to the evolution of the Comintern are fundamentally flawed.

A reading of these ciphered cables also demonstrates that the policies, ideological justifications, and arguments advanced, and even the stylistic tone of messages, did not depart materially from the Comintern's public discourse in the torrent of press articles, pamphlets, and speeches that poured forth from the Comintern and its agencies in this period. It is a mistake to dismiss these public pronouncements as "typical Communist boilerplate" with the assumption that no one could really believe such things and that they were only said for public consumption and propaganda value. But these cables were not public propaganda pamphlets, broadsides, or CP newspaper passages intended for the rank-and-file party members or a public audience. They are secret operational communications between senior Comintern officials in Moscow and senior officials of the Communist parties around the world, as well as with the Comintern's own senior staff on foreign assignments. The fact that the ideological language, arguments, and tone of these secret communications closely parallel those of public Communist pronouncements demonstrates the deeply ingrained nature of the Stalinist belief system. So deeply ingrained were these ways of thinking that even after the dissolution of the Comintern as an organization, one historian aptly noted that Communists continued to live in a "mental Comintern" where the Soviet press and the speeches of Soviet leaders were scrutinized for signs of what was the proper course.[2]

The coded communications also shed additional light on how the Comintern involved the Communist parties in providing assistance to the Stalinist regime in its fight against the system's opponents, in particular in the campaigns against Trotskyites as betrayers, spies, and agents of fascism. As the coded cables compellingly demonstrate, in its instructions to the parties the Comintern acted as the mouthpiece of the Stalinist system, provided an ideological and political cover-up of the Stalinist policy of savage punishments of its enemies, and was used to deliver future victims to the regime. No episode more directly demonstrates this bloody process than the summoning to Moscow of the leading officials of the Polish Communist Party, who then wound up in Yezhov's torture chambers. The Comintern also made its own contribution to the Great Terror, delivering both employees of the ECCI apparatus and many Comintern officials into the maws of the interrogators.

Some of the most fascinating details about Soviet foreign policy emerge from the coded cables sent after the Nazi-Soviet Pact, as panicked and confused Communist parties struggled to find firm footing in a world turned upside down. Stalin had no problem touting the alliance with Germany as a triumph of Soviet foreign policy, but Communists in countries now at war with Germany had a lot more difficulty. The cables offer rich evidence that for Stalin the alliance was not merely a tactical maneuver, but also the expression of a strategic vision for which he was more than willing to sacrifice his Communist comrades around the world. There is no evidence in the tone or substance of the secret cables between the Comintern and the Communist parties to support the notion that Stalin regarded the Nazi-Soviet Pact as a temporary tactical maneuver to gain time for the USSR to mobilize for war against Nazi Germany. Indeed, so thoroughly had Stalin put aside the antifascist doctrines of the late 1930s that he even secretly pursued negotiations to have the USSR join the Tripartite Pact of Nazi Germany, fascist Italy, and imperial Japan.

The cabled correspondence also provides detailed evidence that once the Soviet Union and Germany became wartime enemies, the task of national Communist parties expanded well beyond full political support for the USSR. In wartime conditions the Comintern insistently demanded that its constituent parties and staff members cooperate fully with Soviet intelligence organs, facilitating not only the collection of military and political information and the organization of sabotage activity and the partisan movement in the countries occupied by Germany, but also the infiltration of the governments of its allies. The intelligence information acquired by the Communist parties and the Comintern's illegal communications centers was sent to Stalin and to the commanders of the Soviet intelligence services.

From the very beginning of its activity, the Comintern was closely linked to Soviet intelligence organs, assisting them in every possible way and providing both information and human resources. Long an important underground organization in many parts of the world, during World War II the Comintern became an essential part of the Soviet intelligence services. In turn, Soviet intelligence supplied the leadership of the Comintern with various kinds of information on subjects relevant to the Comintern and the Communist parties; its representatives sometimes organized contacts between the Comintern and its sections and provided financial subventions to the Communist parties.

During the war, this cooperation and coordination of actions between the Comintern and the leaders of Soviet political and military intelligence was ongoing and permanent. The cabled messages reflect various forms of such interaction. Radio stations and the ECCI communications centers were used for liaison between the Center and the intelligence network and groups of intelligence agents in the countries occupied by Germany. The Comintern cipher communications are therefore of interest both to historians studying this organization and to those focusing on the history of the Soviet intelligence services.

Nothing symbolized the Comintern's life so much as its manner of death. It had long served Soviet foreign policy interests; when those interests dictated that it had become an impediment, Stalin abruptly ordered it eliminated. Even the speeded-up process to close down its organization was not fast enough for Stalin; he demanded immediate action to suit his own schedule. Once Stalin deemed the further existence of the Comintern inadvisable, the organization was disbanded. It left its mark, however, on the history of the twentieth century.

Notes

INTRODUCTION

1. Russian State Archive of Social and Political History (henceforth: RGASPI), f. 495, op. 184, d. 6, special, outgoing 1936 to Paris, ll. 53, 41, 19; ibid., d. 13, special, incoming 1936 from Spain, l. 33 reverse. Rudolf was the pseudonym of the secretary of the Executive Committee of the Communist International (ECCI), Dmitry Manuilsky. Earl Browder was the secretary general of the Communist Party of the United States. Medina was the pseudonym of the representative of the Comintern in Spain, Vittorio Codovilla.

2. RGASPI, f. 495, op. 184, d. 15, special, incoming 1936 from New York, l. 9.

3. All of them are included in Opis 184 of the ECCI files (RGASPI, fond 495).

4. The senior author's publications on the history of the Comintern of those years suffer from the same defect that characterized the Soviet historiography in general and the historiography of the Comintern in particular. The events and facts of the past were considered solely from the point of view of the ideology of the CPSU. No other explanation and analysis were permitted, and diverging from these positions inevitably led, at best, to a ban on professional activity. Only in the second half of the 1980s were these stifling regulations first relaxed, and the opportunity then emerged for the publication of studies that went beyond the permitted framework. In 1987 the author was able to publish his article, written in 1963, "K voprosu o taktike edinogo fronta v 1921–1924 godakh" (*Voprosy istory KPSS*, 1987, no. 10, pp. 113–127). Overcoming the dogmas and stereotypes on which several generations of Soviet citizens had been raised was a complex and peculiarly agonizing process. Here the growing and increasingly intense crisis of the existing system and its collapse in August 1991 were decisive. For the author, the knowledge gained in studying the history of the Comintern played an important role in the process of liberation from ideological fetters.

5. The modern name of this archive—the Russian State Archive of Social and Political History (RGASPI)—appeared considerably later.

6. During work on the collection more than two hundred letters from Dimitrov to Stalin were discovered. At the beginning of the 1980s publication of a collection was planned by the Institute for Dimitrov's ninetieth birthday. The author was asked to write an article, "Georgi Dimitrov—Generalny sekretar' Ispoplkoma Kominterna." The relationship between Dimitrov and the Central Committee of the All-Union Communist Party (Bolshevik) (VKP[b]) was of great importance for this article. A request to the administration of the Central Party Archive of the Institute of Marxism-Leninism (TsPA) to provide any materials whatsoever, attesting to Dimitrov's contacts with the CC of the VKP(b), produced an answer from the then director of the TsPA that there were no such materials in the archives. Firsov's "The Letters of Georgi Dimitrov and Stalin" was published as *Dimitrov and Stalin, 1934–1943: Letters from the Soviet Archives*, ed. Alexander Dallin and F. I. Firsov; Russian documents translated by Vadim A. Staklo (New Haven: Yale University Press, 2000). Materials from the second collection prepared by Firsov, "The Comintern and the Stalinist Repressions," were used in William J. Chase, *Enemies Within the Gates? The Comintern and the Stalinist Repression, 1934–1939*; Russian documents translated by Vadim A. Staklo (New Haven: Yale University Press, 2001).

7. Work on the Russian edition took place in 1994, and the book as finalized by Bayerlein was published in 2003: *Deutscher Oktober 1923: Ein Revolutionsplan und sein Scheitern*, ed. Bernhard H. Bayerlein, Leonid G. Babičenko, Fridrich I. Firsov, and Aleksandr Vatlin; translated from the Russian by Tanja Timofeyeva (Berlin: Aufbau-Verlag, 2003). These additional works included William Waack's book on the Comintern's attempt to organize a revolution in Brazil in 1935 (*Camaradas. Nos arquivos de Moscou. A história secreta da revolução brasiliera de 1935* [São Paulo: Companhia Das Letras, 1993]) and the biography of Eugen Fried, written by the late Annie Kriegel and Stéphane Courtois (*Eugen Fried: Le grand secret du PCF* [Paris: Éditions du Seuil, February 1997]).

8. Harvey Klehr, John Earl Haynes, and Kyrill M. Anderson, *The Soviet World of American Communism* (New Haven: Yale University Press, 1998).

9. *VKP(b), Komintern i Kitay: Dokumenty*, vol. 4: *VKP(b), Komintern i sovetskoe dvizhenie v Kitae, 1931–1937*, in two parts. Editorial board: M. K. Titarenko, M. Leitner (chief editor), K. M. Anderson, V. I. Glunin, A. M. Grigoriev, I. Krüger, R. Velber, K. V. Shevelyov. (Moscow: ROSSPEN, 2003). *Moscou-Paris-Berlin: Télégrammes chiffrés du Komintern, 1939–1941*, ed. Bernhard H. Bayerlein, Mikhail Narinski, Brigitte Studer, and Serge Wolikow (Paris: Tallandier, 2003).

10. The phrase "the Communist parties" will usually refer to the non-Soviet Communist parties. The Comintern supervised the non-Soviet parties. It did not supervise the Soviet party.

11. Fridrikh Igorevich Firsov collection, Hoover Archives, Hoover Institution, Stanford University, Stanford, California.

CHAPTER 1. CIPHERED COMMUNICATIONS AND THE HISTORY OF THE COMMUNIST INTERNATIONAL

1. The initials "CP" for Communist Party will often appear in the text.

2. *Platforma Kommunisticheskogo Internatsionala—Pervy Kongress Kominterna, Mart 1919*, ed. E. Korotky, Béla Kun, and Osip Pyatnitsky (Moscow: Partynoe Izdatel'stvo, 1933), p. 179.

3. *Kommunistichesky Internatsional v dokumentakh: Reshenia, tezisy i vozzvania kongressov Kominterna i plenumov ECCI 1919–1932*, ed. Béla Kun (Moscow: Partynoe Izdatel'stvo, 1933), p. 35.

4. Arthur Koestler, *Darkness at Noon*, translated by Daphne Hardy (New York: Bantam Books, 1968), pp. 56–60; RGASPI, f. 495, op. 184, d. 39, outgoing 1936 to Paris, ll. 284, 285.

5. RGASPI, f. 495, op. 184, d. 22, outgoing 1933 to Odessa, l. 96, coded dispatch of 27 September 1933.

6. RGASPI, f. 495, op. 184, d. 21, outgoing 1933, general directives, l. 96, coded dispatch of 22 December 1933.

7. RGASPI, f. 495, op. 184, d. 56, outgoing 1935, general directives, ll. 118, 119, coded dispatch of 8 December 1935. Stakhanovites were "hero workers" who over fulfilled their quotas.

8. RGASPI, f. 495, op. 73, d. 61, l. 8.

9. RGASPI, f. 495, op. 184, d. 77, outgoing 1936, general directives, ll. 290, 84–86. (General directives were distributed to all parties.)

10. RGASPI, f. 495, op. 184, d. 39, outgoing 1936 to Paris, l. 240 reverse, coded dispatch of 27 June 1936, ms.; RGASPI, f. 495, op. 184, d. 34, outgoing 1937 to New York, l. 202, coded dispatch of 7 July 1936, ms.; RGASPI, f. 495, op. 184, d. 73, outgoing 1936, general directives, l. 28.

11. RGASPI, f. 495, op. 184, d. 15, outgoing 1934 to Holland, "German," l. 104, coded dispatch of 23 December 1934; RGASPI, f. 495, op. 184, d. 73, outgoing 1936, general directives, ll. 28–29.

12. Kheifets's role as chief of Soviet intelligence operations in California and his involvement in atomic espionage are discussed in John Earl Haynes, Harvey Klehr, and Alexander Vassiliev, *Spies: The Rise and Fall of the KGB in America* (New Haven: Yale University Press, 2009).

13. Mask Material, N4833/S, No. 10. A copy of this cable is part of the Firsov collection at the Hoover Institution as well as the Mask collection, National Cryptologic Museum, Fort Meade, Maryland.

14. RGASPI, f. 495, op. 184, d. 55, outgoing, general directives, l. 154; d. 7, outgoing 1935 to Berlin, l. 84; d. 45, outgoing 1936 to Paris, l. 80. Boris Vasiliev, a head of the ECCI Organization Department, was arrested and executed by the NKVD in 1937.

15. RGASPI, f. 495, op. 184, d. 53, outgoing 1935 to South America, l. 26, coded dispatch of 11 June 1935; d. 54, outgoing 1935 to South America, l. 33, coded dispatch of 5 September 1935; d. 27, outgoing 1936 to New York, l. 136, coded dispatch of 5 December 1935; d. 34, outgoing 1936 to New York, l. 392, coded dispatch of 27 January 1937.

16. Paolo Spriano, *Storia del Partido communista italiano*, vol. 1: *Da Bordiga a Gramsci* (Turin: Giulio Einaudi Editore, 1967); RGASPI, f. 495, op. 184, d. 45, outgoing 1936 to Paris, ll. 158–156.

17. RGASPI, f. 495, op. 184, d. 21, outgoing 1936 to Spain (personal), l. 49 and l. 25, coded dispatch of 25 July 1936; RGASPI, f. 495, op. 184, d. 27, 1937, encrypted letters through the Central Committee, File No. 2 (incoming), l. 287, letter of 2 April 1937, received 17 May.

18. RGASPI, f. 495, op. 184, incoming registry (henceforth: inc. reg.) 15; special, outgoing 1937, ll. 84, 83; code for Pieck, 20.X.37.

19. RGASPI, f. 495, op. 127, d. 410, ll. 1–6, letter of 30 April 1934. The information bulletin *Ot bor'by za vlast'k vnutripartinnoi bor'be*, compiled by the ECCI apparat, 10 June 1934, states: "Miyamoto, Kisima, Akidzasa, Helmi, and others have promptly created 'Action Brigades' [the Red Lynching Brigades] and, through methods of terror, attempted to wipe out all their opponents simultaneously and to seize for themselves all power within the Party." RGASPI, f. 495, op. 127, d. 421, ll. 16–17.

20. RGASPI, f. 495, op. 30, d. 1070, ll. 71, 72, letter of 4 December 1935.

21. RGASPI, f. 495, op. 19, d. 680, l. 6, coded dispatch received in Moscow 4 June 1926.

22. RGASPI, f. 495, op. 184, d. 53, outgoing 1935 to South America, l. 22.

23. RGASPI, f. 495, op. 184, d. 21, outgoing 1935 to London, l. 24, coded dispatch of 29 January 1935.

24. RGASPI, f. 495, op. 184, d. 55, outgoing 1935, general directives, l. 201. Abramov moved to the Intelligence Directorate of the Red Army. He was arrested on 21 May 1937 and shot on 26 November 1937.

25. RGASPI, f. 495, op. 184, d. 45, outgoing 1936 to Paris, l. 23; d. 37, outgoing 1936 to New York, l. 4.

26. Melnikov was arrested on 25 May 1937 and was shot on 28 July 1938. RGASPI, f. 495, op. 184, d. 25, outgoing 1937 to Paris, l. 8.

27. Christopher Andrew, *Defend the Realm: The Authorized History of MI5* (New York: Alfred Knopf, 2009), pp. 175–185. Among the undiscovered hints was information on Melitta Norwood, who engaged in atomic espionage during World War 2. A set of the Mask material is maintained at the Mask collection, National Cryptologic Museum, Fort Meade, Maryland.

28. Nigel West, *Mask: MI5's Penetration of the Communist Party of Great Britain* (New York: Routledge, 2005), pp. 1–5.

29. See G. M. Adibekov, E. N. Shakhnazarova, and K. K. Shirinia, *Organizatsionnaya struktura Kominterna 1919–1943* (Moscow: ROSSPEN 1997).

30. Otto Wilhelm Kuusinen, Wilhelm Pieck, Palmiro Togliatti, Klement Gottwald, Dmitry Manuilsky, and André Marty served on the Secretariat of the ECCI. Wang Ming was a candidate member of the ECCI Secretariat. RGASPI, f. 495, op. 184, d. 13, outgoing 1935 to Spain, l. 120. These were the pseudonyms used by the leaders of the Comintern in the correspondence with the Spanish Communist Party in 1936. Ronald Radosh, Mary R. Habeck, and Grigory Sevostianov, *Spain Betrayed: The Soviet Union in the Spanish Civil War* (New Haven: Yale University Press, 2001), pp. 7–18; RGASPI, f. 495, op. 184, d. 45, outgoing 1936 to Paris, l. 80.

31. RGASPI, f. 546, op. 1, d. 388, l. 50.

32. RGASPI, f. 495, op. 184, d. 7, outgoing 1938 from Moscow to Kislovodsk, ll. 29, 27 ms.; 111 stood for Ercoli, 162 was Spain, and 195 was the Politburo. There were occasionally other recipients of messages in this cipher. On 26 September 1938, Dimitrov used it to communicate with two high-ranking members of the CP of Bulgaria. Georgi Dimitrov, *Dnevnik*, 9 March 1933–6 February 1949. Compilation. Translations, preface, footnotes and index: Dimitr Sirkov, Petko Boyev, Nikola Avreyski, and Ekaterine Kabakchiyeva (Sofia: St. Kliment Okhridski University Press, 1997), p. 140; Georgi Dimitroff, *Tagebücher 1933–1943*, ed. Bernhard H. Bayerlein; translated from the Russian and Bulgarian by Wladislaw Hedeler und Birgit Schliewenz (Berlin: Aufbau-Verlag, 2000), p. 186.

33. RGASPI, f. 495, op. 184, d. 8, outgoing 1938 to Moscow from Kislovodsk, l. 7, ms.; Dimitrov, *Dnevnik*, p. 140; Dimitroff, *Tagebücher*, pp. 185–186.

34. RGASPI, f. 495, op. 184, d. 7, outgoing 1938 from Moscow to Kislovodsk, l. 50, ms.

35. Dimitrov, *Dnevnik*, pp. 160, 191; Dimitroff, *Tagebücher*, pp. 225–226, 295. *Politburo TsK RKP(b)-VKP(b) i Komintern, 1919–1943: Dokumenty;* editorial board: G. M. Adibekov, K. M. Anderson, K. K. Shirinia (editor); compiled by G. M. Adibekov (editor), Zh. G. Adibekova, L. A. Rogovaya, and K. K. Shirinia (Moscow: ROSSPEN, 2004), pp. 770–771.

36. See Peter Huber, "Berta Zimmermann—eine Schweizer Kommunistin im Geheimapparatus der Komintern," in *Jahrbuch für Historische Kommunismusforschung* (1993), pp. 261–275; Peter Huber, *Stalins Schatten in die Schweiz. Schweizer Kommunisten in Moskau: Verteidiger und Gefangene der Komintern* (Zurich: Chronos Verlag, 1994), pp. 29, 33, 267–274. Platten-Zimmerman was arrested on 4 June 1937 and shot on 2 December.

37. RGASPI, f. 546, op. 1, d. 141, l. 15.

38. RGASPI, f. 546, op. 1, d. 388, ll. 49–87; d. 434, ll. 25–32; Chase, *Enemies*, pp. 244, 316.

39. Letter from Dimitrov and Manuilsky to Yezhov, Zhdanov, and Andreyev, 10 October 1937 (*Istorichesky arkhiv*, no. 1 [1992], p. 220); Chase, *Enemies*, p. 283. For details of the terror in the Comintern, see M. M. Panteleyev, "Repressy v Kominterne (1937–1938)," *Otechestvennaya istoriya*, no. 6 (1996): 161; Alexander Vatlin, "Kaderpolitik und Säuberungen in der Komintern," in *Terror: Stalinistische Parteisäuberungen 1936–1953*, ed. H. Weber and U. Mählert (Paderborn: Ferdinand Schöningh, 1998), pp. 33–119; Fridrick Firsov, "The Comintern and Stalin's Terror," in *Reflections on the Gulag: With a Documentary Appendix on the Italian Victims of Repression in the USSR*, ed. E. Dundovich, F. Gori, and E. Guercetti (Milan: Feltrinelli Editore, 2003), pp. 105–138.

40. The Cryptography Division was headed by Aleksandr Nikolaev, who sometimes used the pseudonym Rybakov.

41. Only those employees of the archive who selected files for readers had access to the card file of DIC employees, located in the archival storage facility where the Comintern archives documents are housed. The senior author had the opportunity to read through hundreds of cards containing the names, pseudonyms, and numbers of individuals

42. RGASPI, f. 546, op. 1, d. 378, l. 6; d. 410, l. 57; Chase, *Enemies*, p. 184.

43. RGASPI, f. 546, op. 1, d. 384, l. 55; d. 419, l. 88; op. 21, d. 66, l. 24; op. 1, d. 434, l. 29; op. 21, d. 30, l. 17; Petra Becker, ed., *In den Fängen des NKWD: Deutsche Opfer des stalinistischen Terrors in der UdSSR* (Berlin: Dietz Verlag, 1991), pp. 33, 52–53; Chase, *Enemies*, p. 313.

44. RGASPI, f. 546, op. 1, d. 417, l. 5; d. 408, l. 23; d. 419, l. 12; d. 416, l. 2.

45. RGASPI, f. 546, op. 1, d. 378, l. 75; d. 329, ll. 65, 33; d. 419, l. 12.

46. RGASPI, f. 546, op. 1, d. 358, l. 37.

47. RGASPI, f. 546, op. 1, d. 329, l. 108.

48. RGASPI, f. 546, op. 1, d. 329, l. 108; d. 378, l. 38; d. 408, ll. 1, 11; f. 495, op. 21, d. 52, l. 45; f. 546, op. 1, d. 384, l. 27.

49. Quoted in Philippe Robrieux, *Histoire intérieure du Parti communiste*, vol. 1 (Paris: Fayard, 1980), p. 391.

50. See L. S. Jeifets, *Latinskaya Amerika v orbite Kominterna (Opyt biograficheskogo slovaria)* (Moscow: ILA RAN, 2000), p. 162; R. S. Rose and Gordon D. Scott, *Johnny: A Spy's Life* (University Park, PA: Pennsylvania State University Press, 2010).

51. RGASPI, f. 495, op. 184, d. 54, outgoing to South America, l. 31, coded dispatch of 3 September 1935; d. 61, outgoing 1935 from South America, l. 48, sent 26 April 1935, received 13 May, encrypted 14 May; Waack, *Camaradas*, pp. 113, 360, 364.

52. RGASPI, f. 495, op. 184, d. 5, outgoing 1935 from Buenos Aires, l. 9, received from Rio, 19 December 1935, deciphered 19 December; d. 5, outgoing 1936 from Buenos Aires, l. 35, received from Rio, 7 January 1936, deciphered 7 January; Waack, *Camaradas*, pp. 247, 365.

53. See Jeifets, *Latinskaya Amerika*, p. 162.

54. RGASPI, f. 495, op. 184, d. 38, outgoing 1933 to Paris, l. 10, coded dispatch of 27 September 1933.

55. RGASPI, f. 495, op. 74, d. 398, l. 53; Panteleyev, "Repressy v Kominterne," p. 167. The senior author is deeply indebted to Yury Tsentsiper for permission to use excerpts from the case file on the investigation of his father, Arthur Khavkin (Walter).

56. RGASPI, f. 495, op. 184, d. 21, incoming 1936 from Spain, l. 181, sent 7 February 1936, received 7 February, deciphered 7 February. *Mundo Obrero* was the chief periodical of the Communist Party of Spain.

57. RGASPI, f. 495, op. 184, d. 38, incoming 1935 from Paris, l. 295, coded dispatch of 13 February 1936.

58. Quoted in Huber, *Stalins Schatten in die Schweiz*, pp. 400–401.

59. RGASPI, f. 495, op. 184, d. 24, outgoing 1937 to Paris, ll. 101–103, coded dispatch of 21 February 1937.

60. RGASPI, f. 17, op. 120, d. 297, l. 152; f. 495, op. 73, d. 69, l. 37.

61. RGASPI, f. 495, op. 184, d. 40, outgoing 1933 from New York, ll. 4, 4ob. Cipher message was sent 16 August 1933 and received 3 September.

62. RGASPI, f. 495, op. 184, d. 25, outgoing 1934 to New York, l. 34, coded dispatch of 8 May 1933; ibid, l. 17, coded dispatch of 11 March 1934; ibid, l. 167, coded dispatch of 20 December 1934; d. 28, outgoing 1935 to New York, l. 100, coded dispatch of 2 April 1935; d. 34, outgoing 1936 to New York, "Kraft," l. 442, coded dispatch of 5 January 1936. In 2012 values, $1,100 would be more than $18,000, while $3,000 would be nearly $50,000.

63. RGASPI, f. 495, op. 184, d. 28, outgoing 1935 to New York, l. 65, coded dispatch of 22 March 1935.

64. RGASPI, f. 495, op. 184, d. 33, 1936 file. See Klehr, Haynes, and Anderson, *The Soviet World*, pp. 44–47.

65. RGASPI, f. 495, op. 184, d. 34, outgoing to New York, "Kraft," l. 329, coded dispatch of 4 May 1936; d. 77, outgoing 1936 to New York, l. 273, coded dispatch of 11 April 1936.

66. RGASPI, f. 495, op. 184, d. 33, outgoing 1936 from New York, l. 375. Coded dispatch received 22 February 1936.

67. RGASPI, f. 495, op. 65a, d. 14458, ll. 39, 73, 83, 84–85, 98.

68. A report on Baker's life is found in RGASPI, f. 495, op. 74, d. 472; VKP(b), *Komintern i Kitay*, vol. 4, part 1, pp. 510–511, 714, 816–817, 823–824.

69. RGASPI, f. 495, op. 184, d. 34, outgoing 1936 to New York, "Kraft," l. 335, coded dispatch of 26 April 1936; op. 175, d. 291, l. 2. Harvey Klehr, John Earl Haynes, and Fridrikh Igorevich Firsov, *The Secret World of American Communism*; Russian documents translated by Timothy D. Sergay (New Haven: Yale University Press, 1995), p. 88.

70. RGASPI, f. 495, op. 184, d. 8, outgoing 1939 to New York, l. 42; Philip Jaffe, *The Rise and Fall of American Communism* (New York: Horizon Press, 1975), p. 40.

71. RGASPI, f. 495, op. 184, d. 8, outgoing 1939 to New York, l. 45; d. 8, incoming 1939 from New York, l. 42; d. 4, incoming 1940 from New York, l. 30, received 22 April, deciphered 29 April. John Earl Haynes and Harvey Klehr, *Venona: Decoding Soviet Espionage in America* (New Haven: Yale University Press, 1999), p. 71.

72. RGASPI, f. 495, op. 184, d. 4, incoming 1940 from New York, l. 7, sent 29 November 1939, received 5 February 1940; Klehr, Haynes, and Anderson, *The Soviet World*, p. 147.

73. RGASPI, f. 495, op. 184, d. 5, outgoing 1942 to New York, l. 29.

74. RGASPI, f. 495, op. 184, d. 8, outgoing 1939 to New York, l. 77, ms.; d. 15, outgoing 1940 to New York, l. 10; d. 4, incoming 1940 from New York, l. 30.

75. RGASPI, f. 495, op. 184, d. 15, outgoing 1940 to New York, l. 110, ms., handwriting of Sorkin (G. Z. Sorkin was a deputy to the chief of the ECCI's Communications Service). Klehr, Haynes, and Firsov, *The Secret World*, pp. 209–210.

76. RGASPI, f. 495, op. 184, d. 4, incoming 1940 from New York, l. 11, received 7 February 1940. We have cleaned up the decoded English text since it was very shakily translated.

77. RGASPI, f. 495, op. 184, d. 15, outgoing 1940 to New York, ll. 104, 103; RGASPI, f. 495, op. 184, d. 10, l. 34, outgoing 1943 to New York; *Komintern i Vtoraya Mirovaya Voyna*, edited, compiled, and introduced with commentaries by N. S. Lebedeva and M. M. Narinski (Moscow: Pamyatniki Istoricheskoy Mysli, 1998), vol. 2, p. 380.

CHAPTER 2. SUBVENTIONS

1. RGASPI, f. 495, op. 184, d. 8, outgoing 1935 to Vienna, "Wolf," l. 74. See Adibekov et al., eds., *Politburo TsK RKP(b)-VKP(b) i Komintern*, pp. 27, 28, 31–32, 38, 71, 82, 97–98, 121, 125–126, 131–132, 141–142, 166, 255, 261, 276, 281, 286, 297, 340–341, 394, 430, 506, 530, 575–576, 617, 619, 634, 637, 642–643, 670, 675, 686–687, 691, 693, 698, 703, 764–765, 770, 773, 782, 788, 798, 807–808, 810.

2. Adibekov et al., eds., *Politburo TsK RKP(b)-VKP(b) i Komintern*, pp. 132, 286, 770; RGASPI, f. 495, op. 82, d. 6, l. 5, annex to the minutes of the Budget Commission of the ECCI of 3 January 1922, l. 5; RGASPI, f. 495, op. 82, d. 12, annex to the minutes of the Budget Commission of 6 January 1925. Dollar values for 2012 calculated using the Federal Reserve Bank of Minneapolis "What is a dollar worth?" calculator. Http://www.minneapolisfed.org.

3. RGASPI, f. 495, op. 184, d. 38, outgoing 1933 to Paris, l. 10, coded dispatch of 27 September 1933; RGASPI, f. 495, op. 184, d. 39, outgoing 1935 to Paris, l. 84, coded dispatch of 21 April 1935; Robrieux, *Histoire intérieure*,

p. 398. The historical exchange rates of the franc and other currencies are drawn from Lawrence H. Officer, "Exchange Rates between the United States Dollar and Forty-one Currencies," *MeasuringWorth*, 2011. Http://www.measuringworth.com/exchangeglobal/.

4. RGASPI, f. 495, op. 184, d. 37, outgoing 1934 to Paris, ll. 4, 6; d. 42, outgoing 1935 to Paris, "Pascal," l. 442, coded dispatch of 2 January 1935; d. 35, outgoing 1935 to Paris, l. 21; d. 39, outgoing 1935 to Paris, l. 72; ibid., l. 29; d. 40, outgoing 1935 to Paris, l. 82; d. 35, outgoing 1935 to Paris, l. 29.

5. RGASPI, f. 495, op. 184, d. 47, outgoing 1936 to Paris, l. 236; d. 57, outgoing 1936 to Stockholm, l. 122; d. 31, outgoing 1936 to London, l. 19; d. 51, outgoing 1936 to Prague, "Roman," l. 227, coded dispatch of 11 August 1936.

6. RGASPI, f. 495, op. 184, d. 34, outgoing 1936 to New York, "Kraft," l. 111; d. 33, incoming 1936 from New York, l. 619, sent and received 19 October 1936.

7. RGASPI, f. 495, op. 184, d. 42, outgoing 1936 to Paris, "Pascal," ll. 67, 56; d. 43, outgoing 1936 to Paris, "Pascal," l. 331, coded dispatch of 29 March 1936.

8. RGASPI, f. 495, op. 184, d. 6, incoming 1939 from France, l. 36, coded dispatch of 29 January 1939; d. 14, outgoing 1939 to France, l. 58, ms., handwriting of Sorkin.

9. RGASPI, f. 495, op. 19, d. 348, l. 17, ms.; ibid., l. 25, official memorandum of 9 March 1928; d. 54, incoming 1933 from Shanghai, l. 130, received 13 September 1933.

10. RGASPI, f. 495, op. 184, d. 15, outgoing 1940 to New York, l. 42, handwriting of Sorkin, coded dispatch of 5 May 1940; ibid., l. 65, handwriting of Sorkin, coded dispatch of 24 July 1940; ibid., l. 70, handwriting of Sorkin, coded dispatch of 26 July 1940; d. 3, outgoing 1941 to the United States, ms., handwriting of Sorkin, coded dispatch of 26 May 1941; ibid., coded dispatch of 29 May 1941.

11. FBI summary of Nelson/Cooper [Zubilin] conversation, 22 October 1944, FBI Comintern Apparatus File, serial 3515. At the end of the 1960s, the senior author spoke several times with Anna Razumova, who had worked in the ECCI apparatus since 1927 and was a political assistant in Manuilsky's Secretariat in 1937. In spite of the fact that she had had to endure many years in prison and in concentration camps, she remained a diehard Communist. When asked what she would say about Pyatnitsky as leader of the Comintern, she responded: "I will tell you. Do you remember how Pyatnitsky used to carry the newspaper *Iskra* in suitcases with false bottoms? Yes, that's right. So imagine, in the 1920s and 1930s, when we in the Comintern transported materials and other things, he insisted that we do it like that. Even though times had changed, he remembered that method." Osip Pyatnitsky was a secretary of the ECCI in 1928–1935. He then worked in the CC of VKP(b), was arrested on 7 July 1937, and was shot on 29 July 1938.

12. Much is unclear in this material. Was Nadelman killed, or does the word "liquidated" mean something else? Immediately after the last sentence "Arno" wrote "Édouard again contacted him," which might suggest that Nadelman was not killed. However, in this lengthy dispatch, the author, "Arno," who is unidentified, referred twice to liquidating someone who is dangerous to the Communications Service. The first time, he mentioned a certain businessman, Berger, whom Walter had also hired. Arno declared, "At one time, the entire cashier's office was handed

over to this Berger (he often boasts that he had up to 3 million francs). He knew the exact addresses of our contacts, because he had gotten them for us, and he also knew who was going to see them. He knew all the addresses and what they were used for, and he controlled them. He knew all the areas of our work: passports, post, money, radio. Over the course of 1935 he was paid remuneration totaling 40 thousand francs. You can verify this with Abend. He cannot give any guarantee for our work and does not have anything to do with us, except that he can extort money from us. When we had the opportunity, we liquidated him; *Édouard again contacted him.*" Most likely, Nadelman was killed. RGASPI, f. 495, op. 184, d. 12, incoming 1937 from Paris, ll. 212–214, received 8 March 1937, deciphered 11 March.

13. RGASPI, f. 495, op. 184, d. 27, 1937. Encrypted letters through the Communications Service, File No. 2 (incoming), l. 257; d. 15, outgoing 1939 to France, l. 184, coded dispatch of 27 March 1939, ms.; d. 3, outgoing 1940 to France (Légros), l. 37, coded dispatch of 5 February 1940, ms., handwriting of Sorkin; d. 4, incoming 1940 from New York, l. 15, sent 17 November 1939, received 7 February 1940.

14. For details see Victor Loupan and Pierre Lorrain, *L'argente de Moscou: L'histoire la plus secrète du PCF;* preface by Branko Lazitch (Paris: Plon, 1994). See also *Komintern i ideya mirovoy revoliutsy: Dokumenty*, ed. Ya. S. Drabkin; compiled by Ya. S. Drabkin, L. G. Babichenko, and K. K. Shirinia (Moscow: Nauka, 1998), pp. 150–156, 170, 219, 228; Klehr, Haynes, and Anderson, *The Soviet World*, pp. 107–147; RGASPI, f. 495, op. 1, d. 1a, ll. 41, 11, minutes of the meeting of the Bureau of the ECCI of 25 October 1919; Klehr, Haynes, and Firsov, *The Secret World*, pp. 22–24.

15. RGASPI, f. 495, op. 73, d. 80, l. 1.

16. RGASPI, f. 495, op. 184, d. 24, outgoing 1937 to Paris, l. 184, coded dispatch of 22 March 1937, ms.

17. RGASPI, f. 495, op. 184, d. 13, incoming 1940 from China, l. 205, received 12 August 1940, deciphered 13 August; ibid., l. 334, sent 26 November 1940, received 27 November.

18. "Proekt secretnogo pis'ma TsK RCP(b) 9 sentiabria 1921," in V. I. Lenin, *Neizvestnye dokumenty, 1891–1922*; compiled by Yu. N Amiantov, Yu. A. Akhapkin, and V. N. Stepanov; ed. Yu. N. Amiantov, Yu. A. Akhapkin, and V. T. Loginov (Moscow: ROSSPEN, 1999), p. 470.

19. RGASPI, f. 495, op. 184, d. 14, outgoing 1939 to France, l. 17, handwriting of Sorkin, coded dispatch of 19 January 1939, ms.; ibid., l. 25, handwriting of Dimitrov, coded dispatch of 19 January 1939. Bruno Köhler was a member of the ECCI and a member of the Politburo of the CC of the Communist Party of Czechoslovakia. At that time he was a member of the foreign secretariat of that party in Paris.

20. RGASPI, f. 495, op. 184, d. 14, outgoing 1939 to France, l. 206, ms. In the archival copy some of the initial language Dimitrov used is crossed out and more euphemistic language is added. RGASPI, f. 495, op. 184, d. 37, outgoing 1936 to New York, l. 2.

21. RGASPI, f. 495, op. 184, d. 17, outgoing 1933 to London, l. 26.

22. RGASPI, f. 495, op. 184, d. 39, outgoing 1933 to Paris, l. 164, coded dispatch of 5 September 1933; d. 23, outgoing 1933 to Prague, l. 33, coded dispatch of 7 September 1933.

23. RGASPI, f. 495, op. 184, d. 16, outgoing 1934 to Spain, l. 25, coded dispatch of 15 May 1934; d. 20, outgoing 1934 to Copenhagen, "Peter," "Taube," "Pis'ma," "Il'za," l. 11, coded dispatch of 19 April 1934.

24. RGASPI, f. 495, op. 184, d. 42, incoming 1933 from New York, l. 145, sent 12 July 1933; d. 20, outgoing 1933 to New York, l. 190, coded dispatch of 21 July 1933; d. 42, incoming 1933 from New York, l. 132, sent 26 July 1933, received 27 July.

25. RGASPI, f. 495, op. 184, d. 38, outgoing 1934 from New York, l. 2, sent 10 January 1934, received 13 May.

26. RGASPI, f. 495, op. 184, d. 8, outgoing 1939 to New York, l. 76, coded dispatch of 16 December 1939, ms., handwriting of Sorkin; d. 2, outgoing 1942 to Sweden, l. 18, coded dispatch of 25 March 1942, ms.

27. RGASPI, f. 495, op. 184, d. 12, incoming 1937 from Paris, received 31 March 1937, deciphered 1 April.

28. RGASPI, f. 495, op. 184, d. 25, outgoing 1937 to Paris, l. 52, ms.

29. RGASPI, f. 495, op. 184, d. 7, outgoing 1938 to Kislovodsk, ll. 17–16, ms.; Dimitrov, *Dnevnik*, pp. 142, 163; Dimitroff, *Tagebücher*, pp. 190, 231; RGASPI, f. 495, op. 184, d. 3, outgoing 1940 to France, l. 161, coded dispatch of 27 November 1940, ms., handwriting of Sorkin. The $70,000 reserve established in 1938 had a 2012 value of $1,136,693.

30. RGASPI, f. 495, op. 184, d. 15, outgoing 1941 to New York, l. 111, ms., handwriting of Sorkin.

31. Adibekov et al., eds., *Politburo TsK RKP(b)-VKP(b) i Komintern*, pp. 798, 807–808; Dallin and Firsov, eds., *Dimitrov and Stalin, 1934–1943*, pp. 195–196; RGASPI, f. 495, op. 73, d. 196, l. 16, letter from Dimitrov to Andreyev, 6 July 1942.

32. RGASPI, f. 495, op. 73, d. 196, ll. 17–19, letter from Dimitrov to Andreyev, 10 July 1942.

33. RGASPI, f. 495, op. 73, d. 196, l. 23. Great Britain was commonly referred to as "England" in Comintern documents.

CHAPTER 3. THE POPULAR FRONT

1. Julian Jackson, *The Popular Front in France* (Cambridge: Cambridge University Press, 1988), 35.

2. See Jackson, *The Popular Front in France*.

3. RGASPI, f. 495, op. 184, d. 41, outgoing 1934 to Paris, l. 248 reverse. On the meeting, see Jackson, *The Popular Front in France*, p. 38.

4. Jackson, *The Popular Front in France*, 37.

5. RGASPI, f. 495, op. 184, d. 41, outgoing 1934 to Paris, ll. 215, 216.

6. RGASPI, f. 495, op. 184, d. 55, outgoing 1935, general directive, l. 201.

7. See Lars T. Lih, Oleg V. Naumov, and Oleg V. Khlevniuk, eds., *Stalin's Letters to Molotov 1925–1936* (New Haven: Yale University Press, 1995), p. 237; G. Dimitrov, *Nastuplenie fashizma i zadachi Kommunisticheckogo Internatsionala v bor'be za edinstvo rabochego klassa protiv fashizma: Doklad i zakliuchitel'noe slovo* (Moscow: Partizdat TsK VKP[b], 1935), p. 44.

8. *VII kongress Kommunisticheskogo Internatsionala i bor'ba protiv fashizma i voyny (Sbornik dokumentov)*, ed. K. K. Shirinia (Moscow: Politizdat, 1975), p. 373.

9. RGASPI, f. 495, op. 18, d. 1023, ll. 5, 16.

10. RGASPI, f. 495, op. 18, d. 1023, l. 144; d. 1024, l. 11; f. 495, op. 184, d. 44, outgoing 1935 to Paris, ll. 35–38, coded dispatch of 22 October 1935.

11. RGASPI, f. 495, op. 184, d. 19, outgoing 1935 to Kislovodsk, l. 14, coded dispatch of 26 October 1935; RGASPI, f. 495, op. 184, d. 20, incoming 1935 from Kislovodsk, Sukhumi, Novy Afon, Sochi, l. 14, coded dispatch of 28 October 1935.

12. RGASPI, f. 495, op. 184, d. 43, outgoing 1936 to Paris, "Pascal," ll. 163, 164.

13. RGASPI, f. 495, op. 184, d. 46, outgoing 1936 to Paris, l. 136.

14. RGASPI, f. 495, op. 18, d. 1086, l. 6.

15. RGASPI, f. 495, op. 184, d. 37, incoming 1936 from Paris, l. 481, coded dispatch of 12 May 1936; d. 43, outgoing 1936 to Paris, "Pascal," ll. 76, 76 reverse; d. 43, inc. reg. 15, outgoing 1937, special, l. 3, coded dispatch of 14 May 1936.

16. RGASPI, f. 495, op. 18, d. 1088, ll. 153, 154, 160.

17. RGASPI, f. 495, op. 184, inc. reg. 15, outgoing 1937 to Paris 1937, special, ll. 4–3, coded dispatch of 19 May 1936.

18. RGASPI, f. 495, op. 184, d. 39, outgoing 1936 to Paris, l. 171.

19. RGASPI, f. 495, op. 184, d. 40, outgoing 1936 to Paris, l. 164, coded dispatch of 3 December 1936, ms.; f. 495, op. 74, d. 510, l. 63; Loupan and Lorrain, *L'argente de Moscou*, pp. 190–191.

20. RGASPI, f. 495, op. 74, l. 65, letter of 11 December 1936; Loupan and Lorrain, *L'argente de Moscou*, pp. 190–191; Dimitrov, *Dnevnik*, p. 119; Dimitroff, *Tagebücher*, p. 139; Georgi Dimitrov, *The Diary of Georgi Dimitrov, 1933–1949*, ed. Ivo Banac; trans. Timothy D. Sergay, Jane T. Hedges, and Irina Faion (New Haven: Yale University Press, 2003), pp. 42, 43.

21. Dimitrov, *Dnevnik*, p. 132; Dimitroff, *Tagebücher*, p. 169. In the typewritten copy of Dimitrov's diary, Stalin's phrase, "The same is true for France," is missing (Central Party Archives [Sofia], f. 146, op. 2, ed. khr. 3, entry of 17 February 1938). The compilers of the Bulgarian edition cross-checked the handwritten original and the typewritten copy, so their edition contains some variations from the typewritten copy. The compilers of the German edition used the corrections made in the typewritten copy of the diary by the Bulgarian researchers. RGASPI, f. 495, op. 184, d. 1, outgoing 1938 to France, l. 34, coded dispatch of 11 March 1938.

22. RGASPI, f. 495, op. 184, d. 13, incoming 1938 from France, l. 47, received 13 March 1938, deciphered 13 March, ms.; ibid. ll. 49–50, sent 18 March 1938, received 19 March, deciphered 19 March, ms.; Dallin and Firsov, eds., *Dimitrov and Stalin, 1934–1943*, p. 38.

23. RGASPI, f. 495, op. 74, d. 517, l. 3, letter of 19 March 1938; op. 184, d. 1, outgoing 1938 to France, ll. 43–41, ms.; op. 74, d. 517, ll. 5–6, coded dispatch of 20 March 1938; Dallin and Firsov, eds., *Dimitrov and Stalin, 1934–1943*, pp. 36–38.

24. RGASPI, f. 495, op. 184, d. 13, incoming 1938 from France, l. 54, sent 23 March 1938, received 23 March, deciphered 23 March, ms.

25. RGASPI, f. 495, op. 74, d. 517, l. 7, ms., coded dispatch of 3 April 1938; op. 184, d. 1, outgoing 1938 to France, l. 55, ms.

26. RGASPI, f. 495, op. 184, d. 1, outgoing 1938 to France, l. 173, coded dispatch of 2 October.

27. RGASPI, f. 495, op. 184, d. 1, outgoing 1938 to France, l. 175; d. 9, outgoing 1938 from Kislovodsk, l. 36, coded dispatch of 5 October 1938. A slightly different text is found in Dimitrov, *Dnevnik*, p. 145; Dimitroff, *Tagebücher*, pp. 195–196.

28. RGASPI, f. 495, op. 74, d. 517, l. 39, letter of 20 April 1939; op. 18, d. 1278, l. 76; Dallin and Firsov, eds., *Dimitrov and Stalin, 1934–1943*, p. 43; Dimitrov, *Dnevnik*, p. 172; Dimitroff, *Tagebücher*, p. 252; Dimitrov, *The Diary of Georgi Dimitrov*, p. 105.

29. RGASPI, f. 495, op. 184, d. 8, outgoing 1938 to Moscow from Kislovodsk, l. 27, ms., coded dispatch of 28 September 1938, ms.; ibid., l. 26, coded dispatch of 28 September 1938, ms.

30. RGASPI, f. 495, op. 184, d. 9, outgoing 1938 from Kislovodsk, l. 5, received 19 September 1938, deciphered 19 September; ibid., 18–17, coded dispatch of 24 September 1938.

31. RGASPI, f. 495, op. 184, d. 7, outgoing 1938 from Moscow to Kislovodsk, l. 10, sent 26 September 1938, deciphered 26 September.

32. RGASPI, f. 495, op. 184, d. 8, outgoing 1938 from Moscow to Kislovodsk, l. 12, coded dispatch of 28 September 1938, ms.; d. 7, outgoing 1938 from Moscow to Kislovodsk, ll. 16–15, sent 29 September 1938, received 30 September, deciphered 30 September, ms.; Dimitrov, *Dnevnik*, p. 141; Dimitroff, *Tagebücher*, p. 187.

33. RGASPI, f. 495, op. 184, d. 8, outgoing 1938 to Moscow from Kislovodsk, l. 29, sent 29 September 1938, received 29 September, deciphered 29 September, ms.; d. 7, outgoing 1938 to Kislovodsk, l. 17, ms.; Dimitrov, *Dnevnik*, p. 142; Dimitroff, *Tagebücher*, p. 190.

34. RGASPI, f. 495, op. 184, d. 8, outgoing 1938 to Moscow, l. 331, coded dispatch of 30 September 1938, ms.

35. RGASPI, f. 495, op. 184, d. 7, outgoing 1938 from Moscow to Kislovodsk, l. 23, coded dispatch of 3 October 1938, ms.; d. 9, outgoing 1938 from Kislovodsk, l. 34, coded dispatch of 3 October 1938; Georgi Dimitrov, *Pis'ma 1905–1949* (Sofia: Izdatel'stvo na BKP, 1957), p. 362.

36. There are three versions of this text: the original coded telegram received from Togliatti, the coded message in Moskvin's code sent to Dimitrov in Kislovodsk, and the clear message Dimitrov wrote down in his diary. We have used the last, although Dimitrov decoded the message erroneously and had Togliatti criticizing the Czechoslovak Communists, not the French. RGASPI, f. 495, op. 184, d. 3, incoming 1938, special, from Spain, l. 123, received 14 October 1938; d. 7, outgoing 1938 from Moscow to Kislovodsk, ll. 38–36, sent 17 October, ll. 39–38, 37–36, ms.; Dimitrov, *Dnevnik*, p. 152; Dimitroff, *Tagebücher*, pp. 208–209.

37. RGASPI, f. 495, op. 184, d. 1, outgoing 1938 to France, ll. 195–194, ms.; Dimitrov, *Pis'ma 1905–1949*, pp. 369–370.

38. RGASPI, f. 495, op. 184, d. 8, outgoing 1938 to Moscow, ll. 59–54, ms.; d. 9, 1938, outgoing from Kislovodsk, ll. 46–45, sent 10 October 1938, received 11 October, deciphered 11 October; Dimitrov, *Dnevnik*, p. 149; Dimitroff, *Tagebücher*, p. 204.

39. RGASPI, f. 495, op. 184, d. 14, outgoing 1939 to France, l. 45; d. 8, outgoing 1939 to New York, l. 18; d. 4, outgoing 1939 to France, l. 12, coded dispatch of 4 June 1939, ms.

CHAPTER 4. THE SPANISH CIVIL WAR

1. RGASPI, f. 495, op. 184, d. 21, outgoing 1936 to Spain, l. 34 reverse; Ronald Radosh, Mary R. Habeck, and Grigory Nikolaevich Sevostianov, *Spain Betrayed: The Soviet Union in the Spanish Civil War* (New Haven: Yale University Press, 2001), p. 9.

2. RGASPI, f. 495, op. 184, inc. reg. 15, outgoing 1937, special, l. 28, coded dispatch of 20 July 1936; op. 74, d. 201, l. 2; op. 184, d. 21, incoming 1936 from Spain, l. 47, coded dispatch of 26 July 1936; Dallin and Firsov, eds., *Dimitrov and Stalin, 1934–1943*, p. 46; Adibekov et al., eds., *Politburo TsK RKP(b)-VKP(b) i Komintern*, p. 740.

3. RGASPI, f. 495, op. 184, d. 40, incoming 1936 from Paris, l. 66, coded dispatch of 1 September 1936.

4. Dimitrov, *Dnevnik*, p. 113; Dimitroff, *Tagebücher*, p. 127; Dimitrov, *The Diary of Georgi Dimitrov*, p. 28.

5. RGASPI, f. 495, op. 184, d. 20, incoming 1936 from Madrid, l. 20, coded dispatch of 4 September 1936.

6. Dimitrov, *Dnevnik*, p. 125; Dimitroff, *Tagebücher*, pp. 153–154; Dimitrov, *The Diary of Georgi Dimitrov*, p. 58.

7. RGASPI, f. 495, op. 184, inc. reg. 15, outgoing 1937, special, l. 77, coded dispatch of 14 March 1937.

8. RGASPI, f. 495, op. 184, d. 4, outgoing 1937 to Spain, special, l. 2, coded dispatch of 11 April 1937, ms.; op. 74, d. 201, l. 15; Dallin and Firsov, eds., *Dimitrov and Stalin, 1934–1943*, pp. 51, 55; RGASPI, f. 495, op. 74, d. 204, l. 27.

9. RGASPI, f. 495, op. 10a, d. 223, ll. 3–4, 17.

10. RGASPI, f. 495, op. 74, d. 201, l. 24.

11. RGASPI, f. 495, op. 74, d. 201, l. 23.

12. RGASPI, f. 495, op. 184, d. 3, outgoing 1936 to Kislovodsk, special, l. 17, coded dispatch of 17 November 1936, ms.

13. RGASPI, f. 495, op. 184, d. 47a, incoming 1936 from Kislovodsk, l. 13, coded dispatch of 18 November 1936, ms.

14. RGASPI, f. 495, op. 73, d. 48, l. 73. The Labour and Socialist International, sometimes called the Second International, was a loose federation of such non-Communist left parties as the British Labour Party, the exiled German Social Democratic Party, the Italian and French Socialist parties, and the Social Democratic parties of Scandinavia.

15. RGASPI, f. 495, op. 184, inc. reg. 15, outgoing 1937 to Paris, special, l. 80, ms.

16. RGASPI, f. 495, op. 184, d. 4, outgoing 1937 to Spain, special, l. 39, coded dispatch of 8 August 1937, ms., handwriting of Dimitrov.

17. RGASPI, f. 495, op. 10a, d. 219, ll. 62, 63. The report of 30 August 1937 was published (not in full) in Palmiro Togliatti, *Opere: A cura di Franco Andreucci e Paolo Spriano*, vol. 4, part 1, 1935–1944 (Rome: Riuniti, 1979), pp. 258–272.

18. RGASPI, f. 495, op. 184, d. 6, outgoing 1936 to Paris, special, l. 86, coded dispatch of 30 December 1936.

19. RGASPI, f. 495, op. 10a, d. 219, ll. 50–51, 54, 58–59.

20. RGASPI, f. 495, op. 74, d. 201, l. 26, coded dispatch of 4 September 1937.

21. RGASPI, f. 495, op. 184, d. 5, incoming 1937 from Spain, special, l. 96, sent 10 September 1937, received 10 September, deciphered 10 September, ms.

22. RGASPI, f. 495, op. 74, d. 212, ll. 56b, 56g. The report was published in Togliatti, *Opere*, vol. 4, part 1, 1935–1944, pp. 273–279. Dimitrov sent Ercoli's report to Stalin on 13 October 1937; RGASPI, f. 495, op. 74, d. 201, l. 36.

23. RGASPI, f. 495, op. 18, d. 1226, l. 1.

24. RGASPI, f. 495, op. 184, d. 5, incoming 1937 from Spain, special, l. 132, coded dispatch of 9 November 1937; Dimitrov, *Dnevnik*, p. 125; Dimitroff, *Tagebücher*, p. 154; Dimitrov, *The Diary of Georgi Dimitrov*, p. 59.

25. RGASPI, f. 495, op. 74, d. 201, l. 33; Dallin and Firsov, eds., *Dimitrov and Stalin, 1934–1943*, pp. 62–64.

26. RGASPI, f. 495, op. 18, d. 1224, l. 136; op. 10a, d. 219, l. 51; op. 74, d. 201, ll. 29, 31; op. 2, d. 257, l. 96; *Komintern i grazhdanskaya voyna v Ispany. Dokumenty*, ed. S. P. Pozharskaya (Moscow: Nauka, 2001), p. 300.

27. RGASPI, f. 495, op. 184, d. 5, incoming 1937 from Spain, special, ll. 120–121, sent 12 October 1937, received 12 October, deciphered 12 October, ms.; op. 74, d. 201, l. 35, letter of 13 October 1937.

28. RGASPI, f. 495, op. 184, d. 3, incoming 1938 from Spain, special, l. 12, coded dispatch of 17 February 1938.

29. RGASPI, f. 495, op. 184, d. 3, incoming 1938 from Spain, special, l. 18, sent 21 February 1938, received 23 February, deciphered 23 February. The term "rint" was not understood even by the cryptographer; possibly it referred to the anarcho-syndicalists, whose powerful trade union, the CNT, supported the Republic but refrained from direct participation in the government. They were referred to in Togliatti's subsequent cipher correspondence.

30. Dimitrov, *Dnevnik*, p. 132; Dimitroff, *Tagebücher*, pp. 168–169; Dimitrov, *The Diary of Georgi Dimitrov*, p. 73.

31. RGASPI, f. 495, op. 184, d. 3, incoming 1938 from Spain, special, l. 27, sent 14 March 1938, received 15 March, deciphered 15 March, ms.; ibid., l. 28, ms.

32. RGASPI, f. 495, op. 74, d. 216, ll. 3–4, coded dispatch sent 14 March 1938, received 15 March, deciphered 15 March, ms.; ibid., l. 28, ms.

33. RGASPI, f. 495, op. 74, d. 216, l. 2, letter of 19 March 1938.

34. RGASPI, f. 495, op. 184, d. 3, incoming 1938 from Spain, special, coded dispatch of 23 March 1938, ms.; d. 39, incoming 1938 from Spain, special, sent 30 March 1938, received 31 March, deciphered 31 March.

35. The report was published in Togliatti, *Opere*, vol. 4, part 1, 1935–1944, pp. 309–324. Dimitrov sent Ercoli's report to Stalin on 11 May 1938 (RGASPI, f. 495, op. 74, d. 216, l. 5); RGASPI, f. 495, op. 74, d. 212, l. 69.

36. RGASPI, f. 495, op. 74, d. 216, l. 14; telegram of 15 June 1938; op. 184, d. 3, incoming 1938 from Spain, special, ll. 82–81, sent 21 June 1938, received 22 June, deciphered 22 June; op. 74, d. 216, l. 21, letter of 22 June 1938; Dallin and Firsov, eds., *Dimitrov and Stalin, 1934–1943*, pp. 73, 75.

37. RGASPI, f. 495, op. 184, d. 3, incoming 1938 from Spain, special, l. 92, sent 22 July 1938, received 23 July, deciphered 23 July; ibid., incoming 1938 from Spain, special, l. 97.

38. RGASPI, f. 495, op. 74, d. 216, ll. 25–28; op. 18, d. 1252, ll. 16–18; Dallin and Firsov, eds., *Dimitrov and Stalin, 1934–1943*, pp. 77–78; Pozharskaya, ed., *Komintern i grazhdanskaya voyna v Ispany*, pp. 396–399.

39. Hugh Thomas, *The Spanish Civil War* (New York: Touchstone Books, 1986), p. 884; RGASPI, f. 495, op. 184, d. 3, incoming 1938 from Spain, special, ll. 144–143, received 19 November 1938, deciphered 19 November; d. 11, outgoing 1938 to New York, l. 47, coded dispatch of 20 November 1938, ms.; d. 1, outgoing 1938 to France, l. 203, coded dispatch of 20 November 1938.; ibid., outgoing 1938 to France, ll. 203, 204, coded dispatch of 20 November 1938.

40. RGASPI, f. 495, op. 184, d. 3, incoming 1938 from Spain, special, l. 135, coded dispatch of 29 October 1938; ibid., l. 149, sent 24 November 1938, received 26 November, deciphered 26 November.

41. RGASPI, f. 495, op. 184, d. 3, l. 128, sent 14 October 1938, received 15 October, deciphered 15 October; Thomas, *The Spanish Civil War*, p. 866; Pozharskaya, ed., *Komintern i grazhdanskaya voyna v Ispany*, p. 421.

42. RGASPI, f. 495, op. 184, d. 14, outgoing 1939 to France, l. 40, coded dispatch of 26 January 1939, ms.; ibid., l. 74, ms., coded dispatch of 27 January 1939.

43. RGASPI, f. 495, op. 184, d. 4, incoming 1939 from Spain, l. 13; d. 12, outgoing 1939 to Spain, l. 10, coded dispatch of 29 January 1939, ms.

44. RGASPI, f. 495, op. 184, d. 4, incoming 1939 from Spain, l. 23; Pozharskaya, ed., *Komintern i grazhdanskaya voyna v Ispany*, p. 446.

45. RGASPI, f. 495, op. 184, d. 4, incoming 1939 from Spain, l. 26, coded dispatch of 2 February 1939; ibid., l. 24, coded dispatch of 3 February 1939.

46. RGASPI, f. 495, op. 184, d. 14, outgoing 1939 to France, l. 62, coded dispatch of 8 February 1939; d. 4, incoming 1939 from Spain, l. 27, coded dispatch of 17 February 1939; Pozharskaya, ed., *Komintern i grazhdanskaya voyna v Ispany*, p. 451.

47. RGASPI, f. 495, op. 184, d. 4, l. 35, sent 27 February 1939, received 1 March, deciphered 4 March.

48. RGASPI, f. 495, op. 184, d. 4, incoming 1939 from Spain, l. 34, coded dispatch of 28 February 1939; ibid., l. 105, coded dispatch of 4 March 1939; Dimitrov, *Dnevnik*, p. 167; Dimitroff, *Tagebücher*, p. 242; RGASPI, f. 495, op. 184, d. 12, outgoing 1939 to Spain, l. 19, coded dispatch of 5 March 1939, ms.

49. RGASPI, f. 495, op. 184, d. 4, incoming 1939 from Spain, l. 37, coded dispatch of 6 March 1939; ibid., l. 38, coded dispatch of 6 March 1938; d. 14, outgoing 1939 to France, l. 105, coded dispatch of 7 March 1939, ms.; d. 12, outgoing 1939 to Spain, l. 23, coded dispatch of 7 March 1939, ms.; d. 6, incoming 1939 from France, l. 105, coded dispatch of 10 March 1939; d. 14, outgoing 1939 to France, l. 131, ms.; Pozharskaya, ed., *Komintern i grazhdanskaya voyna v Ispany*, p. 467.

50. RGASPI, f. 495, op. 74, d. 216, l. 55; d. 220, l. 33. The letter is published (not in full) in Togliatti, *Opere*, vol. 4, part 1, 1935–1944, pp. 325–332.

51. RGASPI, f. 495, op. 184, d. 3, outgoing to France, l. 113, ms., coded dispatch of 16 April 1940; ibid., l. 116, ms., coded dispatch of 21 April 1940; d. 9, incoming 1940 from France, ll. 110, 112, sent 22 April 1940, received 27 April; ibid., l. 124, received 11 May 1940; Bayerlein, Narinski, Studer, and Wolikow, eds., *Moscow-Paris-Berlin*, pp. 216–217.

52. Dimitrov, *Dnevnik*, p. 241; Dimitroff, *Tagebücher*, p. 404; Dimitrov, *The Diary of Georgi Dimitrov*, p. 182. Before Togliatti took the leadership, Antonio Gramsci had been the dominant figure in the Italian CP before his arrest by fascist authorities. Gramsci died in 1937.

CHAPTER 5. THE INTERNATIONAL BRIGADES IN SPAIN

1. E. H. Carr. *The Comintern and the Spanish Civil War*, ed. Tamara Deutscher (New York: Pantheon Books, 1984); Radosh, et al., *Spain Betrayed;* Stanley G. Payne, *The Spanish Civil War, the Soviet Union, and Communism* (New Haven: Yale University Press, 2004); R. Dan Richardson, *Comintern Army: The International Brigades and the Spanish Civil War* (Lexington: University Press of Kentucky, 1982).

2. RGASPI, f. 495, op. 184, d. 34, outgoing 1936 to New York, "Kraft," ll. 143–141; ibid., l. 132, coded dispatch of 18 August 1936; ibid., incoming 1936 from New York, l. 93, sent 31 August 1936, received 1 September; d. 2, outgoing 1937 to Spain, special, l. 6, coded dispatch of 29 October 1936.

3. RGASPI, f. 495, op. 184, d. 37, incoming 1936 from Paris, l. 3, coded dispatch of 17 August 1936; d. 39, incoming 1936 from Paris, l. 198, coded dispatch of 17 August 1936; d. 40, incoming 1936 from Paris, l. 67, sent 31 August 1936, received 31 August.

4. Dimitrov, *Dnevnik*, p. 112; Dimitroff, *Tagebücher*, p. 126; Dimitrov, *The Diary of Georgi Dimitrov*, p. 27; RGASPI, f. 495, op. 18, d. 1135, l. 2; *Kommunistichesky Internatsional: Kratky istorichesky ocherk*, ed. A. I. Sobolev et al. (Moscow: Politizdat, 1969), p. 460; RGASPI, f. 495, op. 184, d. 74, outgoing 1936, general directives, ll. 67, 66.

5. Pozharskaya, ed., *Komintern i grazhdanskaya voyna v Ispany*, p. 12.

6. RGASPI, f. 495, op. 184, d. 39, incoming 1936 from Paris, l. 127; d. 16, incoming 1936 from Paris, special, l. 44, coded dispatch of 18 October 1936; ibid., l. 7, coded dispatch of 18 October 1936.

7. RGASPI, f. 495, op. 184, d. 16, incoming 1936 from Paris, special, l. 16, ms.; d. 6, outgoing 1936 to Paris, special, l. 14, coded dispatch of 23 October 1936, ms.

8. RGASPI, f. 495, op. 184, d. 6, outgoing 1936 to Paris, special, l. 17, ms.; ibid., l. 24, coded dispatch of 6 November 1936, ms.

9. RGASPI, f. 495, op. 184, d. 16, incoming 1936 from Paris, special, l. 25, received 7 November 1936, deciphered 7 November; ibid., l. 32, received 13 November 1936, deciphered 13 November, ms.; d. 7, outgoing 1936 to Prague, special, l. 3, coded dispatch of unspecified day in November 1936, ms.; ibid., l. 5, coded dispatch of 28 November 1936, ms.; ibid., l. 6, coded dispatch of 20 December 1936, ms.

10. RGASPI, f. 495, op. 184, d. 6, outgoing 1936 to Paris, special, l. 30, ms.; d. 16, incoming 1936 from Paris, special, l. 48, sent 18 November 1936, received 25 November, deciphered 28 November, ms.; l. 40; ibid., l. 40, sent 21 November 1936, received 23 November, deciphered 23 November, ms.

11. RGASPI, f. 495, op. 184, d. 34, outgoing 1936 to New York, "Kraft," l. 74 reverse, coded dispatch of 26 October 1936, ms.; ibid., l. 64, coded dispatch of 10 November 1936, ms. The English translation of the coded dispatch mistakenly had "to urge Spanish Party" instead of "to urge Mexican Party." Ibid., l. 63, coded dispatch of 10 November 1936, ms.; d. 15, incoming 1936 from New York, special, l. 25, sent 17 December 1936, received 18 December, deciphered 18 December, ms.

12. RGASPI, f. 495, op. 184, d. 15, incoming 1936 from New York, special, l. 10, sent 18 November 1936, received 19 November, ms.; ibid., l. 13, received 20 November 1936; ibid., l. 17, sent 2 December 1936, received 2 December, deciphered 3 December, ms.

13. RGASPI, f. 495, op. 184, d. 15, l. 21 reverse, sent 2 December 1936, received 2 December, deciphered 3 December, ms.

14. RGASPI, f. 495, op. 184, d. 35, outgoing 1936 to New York, l. 27, ms.; d. 15, incoming 1936 from New York, special, l. 20, received 6 December 1936, deciphered 6 December, ms.; d. 5, outgoing 1936 to New York, special, l. 14, coded dispatch of 6 December 1936, ms.; d. 2, outgoing 1937 to Spain, special, l. 15, ms.

15. RGASPI, f. 495, op. 184, d. 5, outgoing 1936 to New York, special, l. 8, coded dispatch of 3 December 1936, ms.; d. 35, outgoing 1936 to New York, l. 15, coded dispatch of 13 December 1936, ms.

16. RGASPI, f. 495, op. 184, d. 15, incoming 1936 from New York, special, l. 26, sent 17 December 1936, received 18 December, ms.; d. 5, outgoing 1936 to New York, special, l. 15, coded dispatch of 20 December 1936, ms.

17. RGASPI, f. 495, op. 184, d. 5, outgoing 1936 to New York, ll. 17, 16, coded dispatch of 27 December 1936, ms.; 15, incoming 1936 from New York, special, l. 29, received 30 December 1936, ms.

18. RGASPI, f. 495, op. 184, d. 16, incoming 1936 from Paris, special, l. 74, sent 26 November 1936, received 27 November, ms.

19. RGASPI, f. 495, op. 184, d. 6, outgoing 1936 to Paris, special, l. 26, ms.; d. 13, incoming 1936 from Spain, special, l. 50, sent 7 December 1936, received 9 December, deciphered 9 December, ms.; op. 10a, d. 391, l. 96, letter of 10 December.

20. RGASPI, f. 495, op. 184, d. 5, outgoing 1936 to New York, special, l. 5, ms.

21. RGASPI, f. 495, op. 184, d. 2, outgoing 1937 to Spain, special, l. 10, ms.; d. 13, incoming 1936 from Spain, special, l. 35, coded dispatch of 29 November 1936, ms.; d. 5, outgoing 1936 to New York, special, l. 7, coded dispatch of 30 November 1936, ms.

22. RGASPI, f. 495, op. 184, d. 15, incoming 1936 from New York, special, l. 21 reverse, sent 11 December 1936, received 12 December, deciphered 13 December, ms.

23. RGASPI, f. 495, op. 184, d. 15, incoming 1936 from New York, special, ll. 24–24 reverse, sent 17 December 1936, received 18 December 1936, ms.

24. RGASPI, f. 495, op. 184, d. 13, incoming 1936 from Spain, special, l. 14, received 3 November 1936, deciphered 4 November.

25. RGASPI, f. 495, op. 184, d. 13, incoming 1936 from Spain, l. 23, sent 10 November 1936, received 24 November, deciphered 24 November; ibid., l. 30, sent 18 November 1936, received 25 November, deciphered 25 November; ibid., l. 42, sent 3 December 1936, received 4 December, deciphered 6 December; ibid., l. 49, sent 8 December 36, received 9 December, deciphered 9 December; ibid., l. 75, sent 25 December 1936, received 26 December, deciphered 27 December.

26. RGASPI, f. 495, op. 184, d. 2, outgoing 1937 to Spain, special, l. 8, coded dispatch of unspecified day November 1936, ms.; ibid., l. 4, coded dispatch of 29 October 1936.

27. Quoted in Pozharskaya, ed., *Komintern i grazhdanskaya voyna v Ispany*, p. 327.

28. RGASPI, f. 495, op. 184, d. 47a, incoming 1936 from Kislovodsk, l. 115, coded dispatch of 13 October 1936.

29. RGASPI, f. 495, op. 184, d. 13, incoming 1936 from Spain, special, l. 23, sent 10 November 1936, received 24 November, deciphered 24 November; d. 3, outgoing 1936 to Kislovodsk, special, l. 32, coded dispatch of 12 November 1936, ms.

30. RGASPI, f. 495, op. 184, d. 47a, incoming 1936 from Kislovodsk, l. 26, coded dispatch of 12 November 1936, ms.; *Izvestiia na Instituta po istory na BCP*, no. 15 (Sofia, 1966), p. 376. Lord George Byron, the famous English poet and a member of the House of Lords, went to Greece in 1824 to take part in the Greek people's struggle for national liberation from Turkish domination and died of a fever soon afterward.

31. Thomas, *The Spanish Civil War*, pp. 469, 566, 567.

32. RGASPI, f. 495, op. 184, d. 13, incoming 1936 from Spain, special, l. 37, sent 30 November 1936, received 3 December, deciphered 3 December, ms.

33. RGASPI, f. 495, op. 184, d. 2, outgoing 1937 to Spain, special, l. 13, coded dispatch of 1 December 1936, ms.; ibid., ll. 21, 20, coded dispatch of 13 December 1936, ms.

34. RGASPI, f. 495, op. 184, d. 13, incoming 1936 from Spain, special, sent 13 December 1936, received 14 December, deciphered 14 December, ms.; ibid., l. 64, sent 20 December 1936, received 23 December, deciphered 24 December; ibid., l. 58, coded dispatch of 19 December 1936, ms. The proposed decision was not carried out, and Kleber did not take part in the defense of Malaga.

35. RGASPI, f. 495, op. 184, d. 2, outgoing 1937 to Spain, special, l. 12, coded dispatch of 19 December 1936, ms.; d. 73, general directives, ll. 12, 12 reverse, coded dispatch of 26 December 1936.

36. See Walerij Brun-Zechowoj, *Manfred Stern—General Kleber: Die tragische Biographie eines Berufsrevolutionärs (1896–1954)* (Berlin: Trafo-Verl, Weisst, 2000).

37. Richardson, *Comintern Army*, pp. 51–52, 174–175; RGASPI, f. 495, op. 184, d. 13, incoming 1936 from Spain, special, l. 57, sent 17 December 1936, received 19 December, deciphered 19 December, ms.

38. RGASPI, f. 495, op. 184, d. 13, incoming 1936 from Spain, special, l. 60, coded dispatch of 18 December 1936; d. 2, l. 52, sent 17 December 1936, received 19 December, deciphered 19 December, ms.

39. RGASPI, f. 495, op. 184, d. 2, outgoing 1937 to Spain, special, l. 27, coded dispatch of 19 December 1936; ibid., l. 29, coded dispatch of 19 December 1936, ms.

40. RGASPI, f. 495, op. 184, d. 6, outgoing 1936 to Paris, special, l. 71, coded dispatch of 19 December 1936, ms.; d. 16, incoming 1936 from Paris, special, l. 59, sent 20 December 1936, received 31 December, deciphered 1 January 1937, ms.

41. RGASPI, f. 495, op. 184, d. 6, outgoing 1936 to Paris, special, l. 76, coded dispatch of 28 December 1936, ms.

42. RGASPI, f. 495, op. 74, d. 201, l. 10; Adibekov et al., eds., *Politburo TsK RKP(b)-VKP(b) i Komintern*, pp. 744–745.

43. Dimitrov, *Dnevnik*, p. 120; Dimitroff, *Tagebücher*, p. 143; RGASPI, f. 495, op. 184, d. 3, outgoing 1937 to Spain, special, l. 4, ms.

44. RGASPI, f. 495, op. 184, d. 8, outgoing 1937 to New York, special, ll. 3, 2, 1, ms.

45. RGASPI, f. 495, op. 184, d. 10, outgoing 1937 to Paris, special, ll. 2, 4, ms.

46. RGASPI, f. 495, op. 184, d. 4, incoming 1937 from Spain, special, ll. 9, 9 reverse, sent 6 January 1937, received 7–8 January, deciphered 8 January.

47. RGASPI, f. 495, op. 184, d. 4, l. 11, sent 7 January 1937, received 8 January, deciphered 8 January; Dimitrov, *Dnevnik*, p. 121; Dimitroff, *Tagebücher*, p. 144; RGASPI, f. 495, op. 184, d. 3, outgoing 1937 to Spain, special, ll. 5, 6, ms.; d. 10, outgoing 1937 to Paris, special, l. 6, ms.; d. 8, outgoing 1937 to New York, special, ll. 5, 6, ms.

48. RGASPI, f. 495, op. 184, d. 3, outgoing 1937 to Spain, special, l. 9, coded dispatch of 9 January 1937, ms.

49. RGASPI, f. 495, op. 184, d. 4, incoming 1937 from Spain, special, l. 12, sent 10 January 1937, received 11–12 January, deciphered 12 January; ibid., l. 23, sent 14 January 1937, received 16 January, deciphered 16 January.

50. RGASPI, f. 495, op. 184, d. 8, outgoing 1937 to New York, special, l. 16, coded dispatch of 15 January 1937, ms.; d. 34, outgoing 1936 to New York, "Kraft," l. 74 reverse, ms.; d. 8, outgoing 1937 to New York, special, l. 9, coded dispatch of 7 January 1937, ms.

51. RGASPI, f. 495, op. 184, d. 8, outgoing 1937 to New York, special, ll. 12, 13, coded dispatch of 13 January 1937, ms.; ibid., l. 21, coded dispatch of 23 January 1937, ms.

52. RGASPI, f. 495, op. 184, d. 7, incoming 1937 from New York, special, ll. 11, 12, 12 reverse, sent 21 January 1937, received 22 January, ms.; d. 8, outgoing 1937 to New York, special, l. 23, coded dispatch of 2 February 1937.

53. RGASPI, f. 495, op. 184, d. 10, outgoing 1937 to Paris, special, ll. 24, 18, 12, 9, coded dispatches of 9, 10, 26, and 29 January 1937, ms.; ibid., ll. 12, 28, coded dispatches of 27 January and 1 February 1937, ms.; d. 4, incoming 1937 from Spain, special, l. 64 reverse, sent 2 February 1937, received 3 February, deciphered 3 February; ibid., ll. 61, 61 reverse, sent 3 February 1937, received 5 February, deciphered 5 February.

54. RGASPI, f. 495, op. 184, d. 26, 1937, incoming encrypted letters through the Communications Service. File No. 1, l. 169.

55. RGASPI, f. 495, op. 184, d. 13, incoming 1937 from Paris, ll. 263, 263 reverse, sent 22 April 1937, received 5 May, deciphered 5 May.

56. RGASPI, f. 495, op. 74, d. 201, l. 31; op. 10a, d. 219, ll. 24, 25–26.

57. RGASPI, f. 495, op. 10a, ll. 28, 32–33.

58. RGASPI, f. 495, op. 18, d. 1224, ll. 97–98.

59. Quoted in Pozharskaya, ed., *Komintern i grazhdanskaya voyna v Ispany*, p. 299.

60. RGASPI, f. 495, op. 74, d. 201, l. 29, letter of 8 September 1937; ibid., l. 25, letter of 4 September; op. 18, d. 1224, l. 1; op. 74, d. 201, l. 33, letter of 16 September; op. 2, d. 257, l. 105; Dallin and Firsov, eds., *Dimitrov and Stalin, 1934–1943*, p. 71.

61. RGASPI, f. 495, op. 184, d. 9, outgoing 1937 to New York, special, l. 8, coded dispatch of 11 November 1937, ms.; op. 18, d. 1226, l. 1; op. 18, d. 1224, l. 51; op. 184, d. 5, incoming 1937 from Spain, special, l. 132, sent 9 November 1937, received 10 November, deciphered 10 November, ms.; ibid., l. 134, sent 12 November 1937, received 13 November, deciphered 13 November, ms.; d. 3, incoming 1938 from Spain, special, l. 18, sent 21 February 1938, received 23 February, deciphered 23 February. The message from Ercoli was signed by No. 27.

62. RGASPI, f. 495, op. 184, d. 3, l. 9, sent 11 February 1938, received 13 February, deciphered 13 February, ms. See Marklen Meshcheryakov, *Ispanskaya respublika i Komintern (Natsional'no-revoliutsionnaya voyna ispanskogo naroda i politika Kommunisticheskogo Internatsionala 1936–1939 gg.)* (Moscow: Mysl', 1981), pp. 167–168. The Non-Intervention Committee had been established by an international conference in 1936 led by Britain and France and other European nations that supported and signed an agreement to stop the flow of war materials to Spain. Germany, Italy, and the USSR, although signatories, ignored the agreement.

63. Dimitrov, *Dnevnik*, p. 133; Dimitroff, *Tagebücher*, p. 171; Dimitrov, *The Diary of Georgi Dimitrov*, p. 74; RGASPI, f. 495, op. 18, d. 1259, ll. 2, 3.

64. Dimitrov, *Dnevnik*, p. 133; Dimitroff, *Tagebücher*, p. 171; RGASPI, f. 495, op. 18, d. 1258, ll. 5–6.

65. RGASPI, f. 495, op. 184, d. 7, outgoing 1938 from Moscow to Kislovodsk, l. 14, ms.; Dimitrov, *Dnevnik*, p. 141; Dimitroff, *Tagebücher*, p. 188.

66. RGASPI, f. 495, op. 184, d. 4, incoming 1939 from Spain, l. 6, coded dispatch of 6 January 1939; d. 8, outgoing 1939 to New York, l. 1, coded dispatch of 11 January 1939.

67. RGASPI, f. 495, op. 184, d. 4, incoming 1939 from Spain, l. 6, coded dispatch of 8 January 1939; d. 11, outgoing 1939 to France, l. 19, coded dispatch of 11 January 1939.

68. RGASPI, f. 495, op. 184, d. 3, incoming 1938 from Spain, special, l. 130, sent 17 October 1938, received 19 October, deciphered 19 October; d. 7, outgoing 1938 from Moscow to Kislovodsk, l. 44, coded dispatch of 20 October 1938, ms.; Dimitrov, *Dnevnik*, p. 153; Dimitroff, *Tagebücher*, p. 211.

69. RGASPI, f. 495, op. 18, d. 1268, l. 25.

70. RGASPI, f. 495, op. 184, d. 16, outgoing 1939 to France, l. 21, coded dispatch of 2 June 1939, ms., handwriting of Sorkin; d. 8, outgoing 1939 to New York, l. 21, coded dispatch of 2 June 1939; op. 76, d. 22, l. 37.

71. RGASPI, f. 495, op. 76, d. 28, l. 8; op. 74, d. 541, l. 56, letter of 11 February 1939; f. 17, op. 162, d. 24, l. 104; f. 495, op. 184, d. 14, outgoing 1939 to France, l. 91, coded dispatch of 28 February 1939 ms., handwriting of Dimitrov; Adibekov et al., eds., *Politburo TsK RKP(b)-VKP(b) i Komintern*, pp. 772, 773.

72. RGASPI, f. 495, op. 184, d. 6, incoming 1939 from France, l. 73, coded dispatch of 24 February 1939; d. 4, incoming 1939 from Spain, l. 11, coded dispatch of 23 January 1939; d. 14, outgoing 1939 to France, l. 36, coded dispatch of 24 January 1939, ms.; ibid., l. 40, coded dispatch of 26 January 1939, ms.; op. 74, d. 216, l. 49, letter of 27 January 1939.

73. RGASPI, f. 495, op. 76, d. 22, ll. 37–38.

CHAPTER 6. THE COMINTERN AND THE TERROR

1. RGASPI, f. 495, op. 184, d. 55, outgoing 1935, general directives, l. 10; Chase, *Enemies*, p. 41.

2. RGASPI, f. 495, op. 184, d. 55, outgoing 1935, general directives, l. 78 reverse, coded dispatch of 18 August 1936.

3. RGASPI, f. 495, op. 184, d. 57, outgoing 1936 to Stockholm, l. 106 reverse; d. 31, outgoing 1936 to London, l. 4; d. 44, outgoing 1936 to Paris, l. 59 reverse; d. 34, outgoing 1936 to New York, l. 121.

4. RGASPI, f. 495, op. 184, d. 15, outgoing 1936, general directives, l. 61, coded dispatch of 21 August 1936; Chase, *Enemies*, pp. 147–148; RGASPI, f. 495, op. 184, d. 42, incoming 1936 from Paris, l. 118, coded dispatch of 1 September 1936.

5. RGASPI, f. 495, op. 184, d. 33, outgoing 1936 to Lithuania, l. 53; ibid., l. 46; ibid., l. 35; ibid., l. 33.

6. RGASPI, f. 495, op. 184, d. 33, outgoing 1936 to Lithuania, ll. 3–2 reverse, ms. The General Jewish Labor Bund of Lithuania, Poland, and Russia was established in 1907. It ceased to exist on the territory of Soviet Russia in 1921. The Jewish Bund in Lithuania and Poland was predominately Social Democratic in orientation.

7. RGASPI, f. 495, op. 184, d. 73, outgoing 1936, general directives, l. 4, coded dispatch of 30 December 1936; Chase, *Enemies*, p. 191.

8. RGASPI, f. 495, op. 184, d. 43, incoming 1936 from Paris, l. 174.

9. Dimitrov, *Dnevnik*, p. 119; Dimitroff, *Tagebücher*, p. 140; Dimitrov, *The Diary of Georgi Dimitrov, 1934–1949*, p. 44. The real name of the writer Maria Osten was Maria Gresshöner, a member of the CP of Germany since 1926. In June 1941 she was arrested by the NKVD and was shot on 8 August 1942 (Reinhard Müller, *Die Saüberung: Moskau 1936, Stenogramm einer geschlossenen Parteiversammlung* [Reinbek bei Hamburg: Rowohlt Taschenbuch Verlag, 1991], p. 233).

10. Quoted in Edward Radzinsky, *Stalin* (Moscow: Vagrius, 1997), pp. 376–377.

11. RGASPI, f. 495, op. 184, d. 19, outgoing, special, 1937, general directives, l. 7, coded dispatch of 17 January 1937, ms.; d. 23, outgoing 1937 to Paris, l. 72, coded dispatch of 21 January 1937, ms., handwriting of Ercoli; Chase, *Enemies*, p. 192.

12. RGASPI, f. 495, op. 184, d. 21, outgoing 1937 to Prague, l. 40, coded dispatch of 21 January 1937, ms., handwriting of Bronkowski.

13. RGASPI, f. 495, op. 184, d. 8, outgoing 1937 to Greece, l. 15, coded dispatch of 29 January 1937, ms. The message was signed by Wilhelm Pieck, leading German Communist and the ECCI secretary.

14. This episode was ignored by the official prosecutor and judges, who rigorously carried out the task of punishing the accused. But even modern-day neo-Stalinists usually pass over in silence this breakdown of Stalinist "justice." In the anthology *Stalin: V vospominaniyakh sovremennikov i documentakh epokhi* (compiled by M. Lobanov [Moscow, Novaya Kniga, 1995], 308–350), the pages from interrogations at the trial of Pyatakov and Radek, which refer to the meeting between Pyatakov and Trotsky, are cited as documents that reflect allegedly real events. However, one would hardly expect otherwise from an anthology for which the abstract states that Stalin emerges from the pages of this book as a "political figure and military commander, harsh and often merciless with his enemies, a wise ruler of an enormous country, which achieved unprecedented economic power under his leadership" (p. 4). Recently Western Stalin apologists have sought to resurrect Holtzman's claims about meeting Trotsky's son at the Hotel Bristol with a claim that a "Bristol Café" was located close to the Copenhagen Grand Hotel, and Holtzman simply confused the name of the café with that of the hotel. See Sven-Eric Holmström, "New Evidence Concerning the 'Hotel Bristol' Question in the First Moscow Trial of 1936," *Cultural Logic*, 2008, http://clogic.eserver.org/2008/Holmstrom.pdf.

15. RGASPI, f. 495, op. 184, d. 24, 1937, File No. 1, incoming correspondence through the Communications Service, l. 97, sent 29 January 1937, received 29 January, deciphered 29 January.

16. RGASPI, f. 495, op. 184, d. 12, incoming 1937 from Paris, l. 185, d. 26, 1937, l. 94, File No. 1, incoming encrypted letters through the Communications Service, received 2 March 1937, deciphered 3 March.

17. RGASPI, f. 495, op. 184, d. 23, outgoing 1937, general directives, l. 10, coded dispatch of 29 January 1937, ms.

18. RGASPI, f. 495, op. 156, d. 99, l. 151.

19. RGASPI, f. 495, op. 184, d. 16, outgoing 1937 to Lithuania 1937, l. 19, coded dispatch of 21 January 1937, ms.

20. RGASPI, f. 495, op. 184, d. 24, 1937, File No. 1, incoming encrypted correspondence through the Communications Service, l. 153, received 9 February 1937, deciphered 10 February; Chase, *Enemies*, pp. 205–206.

21. RGASPI, f. 495, op. 184, d. 24, 1937, l. 173, File No. 1, incoming encrypted correspondence through the Communications Service, received 14 February 1937, deciphered 14 February; Chase, *Enemies*, p. 206.

22. RGASPI, f. 495, op. 184, d. 24, 1937, l. 174, File No. 1, incoming encrypted correspondence through the Communications Service, received 14 February 1937, deciphered 14 February; Chase, *Enemies*, p. 206.

23. Dimitrov, *Dnevnik*, p. 122; Dimitroff, *Tagebücher*, p. 148; Dimitrov, *The Diary of Georgi Dimitrov*, p. 51; Grigory Sokolnikov (real name Gersh Brilliant), a member of the Bolshevik Party from 1905, was a long-time member of the Central Committee and Politburo and a high-ranking figure in the ECCI. He was arrested in 1936, sentenced to ten years' imprisonment in January 1937, and killed by fellow prisoners on 21 May. Without even mentioning the meeting between the leader of the Comintern and the German writer, William Chase mistakenly attributes these comments by Feuchtwanger, recorded by Dimitrov, as Dimitrov's own opinions. See Chase, *Enemies*, pp. 199–200, 205, 450.

24. Lion Feuchtwanger, *Moscow, 1937: My Visit Described for My Friends* (New York: Viking Press, 1937); Lion Feikhvanger, *Dva vzgliada iz-za rubezha: Perevody* (Moscow: Politizdat, 1990), p. 241.

25. RGASPI, f. 495, op. 2, d. 244, ll. 132, 135.

26. RGASPI, f. 495, op. 184, d. 19, outgoing 1937, general directives, ll. 12–15, ms., handwriting of Ercoli; Chase, *Enemies*, 203–204.

27. Dimitrov, *Dnevnik*, p. 123; Dimitroff, *Tagebücher*, p. 149; Dimitrov, *The Diary of Georgi Dimitrov*, p. 52.

28. RGASPI, f. 495, op. 73, d. 48, l. 66; op. 2, d. 245, ll. 53–54.

29. RGASPI, f. 495, op. 2, d. 245, l. 90.

30. RGASPI, f. 495, op. 2, d. 245, l. 92; Dimitrov, *Dnevnik*, pp. 129–130; Dimitroff, *Tagebücher*, pp. 163–164; Dimitrov, *The Diary of Georgi Dimitrov*, p. 67.

31. For more detailed information see F. I. Firsov and I. S. Jażborowska, "Komintern i Kommunisticheskaya partia Pol'shy," *Voprosy istory KPSS*, no. 11 (1988): 21–35, and no. 12 (1988): 40–55.

32. RGASPI, f. 495, op. 184, d. 11, outgoing 1937 to Paris, l. 17, ms.; ibid., l. 42, ms.; f. 17, op. 20, d. 297, l. 151.

33. Dimitrov, *Dnevnik*, pp. 127, 128; Dimitroff, *Tagebücher*, pp. 159, 160; Dimitrov, *The Diary of Georgi Dimitrov*, pp. 61, 62; RGASPI, f. 495, op. 184, d. 11, outgoing 1937 to Paris, l. 44, coded dispatch of 17 June 1937, ms.; d. 21, outgoing 1937 to Prague, l. 33, coded dispatch of 17 June 1937.

34. RGASPI, f. 495, op. 184, d. 11, outgoing 1937 to Paris, l. 60, ms.; ibid., l. 69, ms.

35. RGASPI, f. 495, op. 184, d. 11, outgoing 1937 to Paris, l. 72, coded dispatch of 21 July 1937, ms. Tadek was one of the pseudonyms of Efraim Goldstein, also known in the Comintern and the Polish CP by the party name Tadeusz Karłowski. He had been an employee of the ECCI apparatus from 1931 to 1936 and a member of Leński's political apparatus in Paris from 1936 to 1937.

36. RGASPI, f. 495, op. 184, d. 11, outgoing 1937 to Paris, l. 78, ms.

37. RGASPI, f. 495, op. 184, d. 4, outgoing 1937 to Spain, special, l. 32, ms., coded dispatch of 10 July 1937; ibid., l. 9, coded dispatch of 17 September 1937; d. 5, incoming 1937 from Spain, special, l. 67, coded dispatch received 29 July 1937, deciphered 29 July, ms.

38. Leon Morkowski (real name Leon Zandberg) and Aleksander Markowski (real name Aleksander Fornalski), both staff members of the Polish CP, were arrested by the NKVD and perished. RGASPI, f. 495, op. 74, d. 400, l. 77, letter of 14 August 1937.

39. Dimitrov's excerpts from these materials, which he titled "Polish cases," amounted to more than sixty pages of manuscript (RGASPI, op. 74, d. 411, ll. 1–62). Dimitrov's excerpts on the Leński case appear in Chase, *Enemies*, pp. 266–273.

40. RGASPI, f. 495, op. 74, d. 402, l. 2; Dallin and Firsov, eds., *Dimitrov and Stalin, 1934–1943*, p. 28; Adibekov et al., eds., *Politburo TsK RKP(b)-VKP(b) i Komintern*, pp. 758, 760.

41. RGASPI, f. 495, op. 2, d. 264, ll. 198, 202–205; *Tragedia Komunistycznej Partii Polski*, ed. Jarema Maciszewski (Warsaw: Książka i Wiedza, 1989), pp. 219–222.

42. On 9 August 1937 the Politburo of the CC of the VKP(b) decreed: "Confirm the order of the Narkomvnudel [people's commissar of internal affairs] of the USSR to eliminate Polish saboteur-espionage groups and POW organizations" (RGASPI, f. 17, op. 162, d. 21, l. 142). N. Petrov and A. Roginskii, "The 'Polish' Operation of the NKVD, 1937–38," in *Stalin's Terror: High Politics and Mass Repression in the Soviet Union*, ed. Barry McLoughlin and Kevin McDermott (New York: Palgrave Macmillan, 2002), pp. 153–172. See also Firsov and Jażborowska, "Komintern i Kommunisticheskaya partia Pol'shy."

43. RGASPI, f. 495, op. 184, d. 11, outgoing 1937 to Paris, l. 65, ms., with corrections by Dimitrov; f. 17, op. 20, d. 297, l. 168. The arrest and imprisonment in the Gulag of three American Communists, Lovett Fort-Whiteman (the CPUSA's leading black official in the late 1920s), Thomas Sgovio, and Joseph Sgovio, as well as the execution of hundreds of American and Canadian ethnic Finnish Communists (immigrants to Soviet Karelia) is discussed in Klehr, Haynes, and Firsov, *The Secret World*, pp. 215–251, and John Earl Haynes and Harvey Klehr, *In Denial: Historians, Communism, and Espionage* (San Francisco: Encounter Books, 2003), pp. 113–118, 235–247. The Sgovios, father and son, survived, but Fort-Whiteman died in the camps.

44. RGASPI, f. 495, op. 184, d. 26, outgoing 1935 to New York, l. 1, coded dispatch of 1 January 1935; Chase, *Enemies*, p. 39.

CHAPTER 7. THE COMINTERN AND THE CHINESE COMMUNIST PARTY

1. Materials from the ECCI's cipher correspondence with the Chinese Communist Party for 1931–1937 are published in Titarenko et al., eds., *VKP(b), Komintern i Kitay.*

2. Dimitrov, *Dnevnik*, p. 130; Dimitroff, *Tagebücher*, p. 164; Dimitrov, *The Diary of Georgi Dimitrov*, p. 68.

3. RGASPI, f. 495, op. 74, d. 294, l. 47.

4. RGASPI, f. 495, op. 74, d. 294, l. 50. Fang Lin was the pseudonym of Deng Fa, a candidate member of the Politburo of the CC of the CPCh.

5. RGASPI, f. 495, op. 10a, d. 409a, l. 62; ibid., l. 64;

6. RGASPI, f. 495, op. 184, d. 3, outgoing to China 1941 (Zheng Li), l. 24, ms.

7. RGASPI, f. 495, op. 74, d. 316, l. 12, letter of 15 September 1939; ibid., l. 10, letter of 29 January 1940; Dallin and Firsov, eds., *Dimitrov and Stalin, 1934–1943*, pp. 111–112; Dimitrov, *Dnevnik*, p. 190; Dimitroff, *Tagebücher*, p. 292; Dimitrov, *The Diary of Georgi Dimitrov*, p. 126. In this case Dimitrov extended the capitalized "You" to Beria.

8. RGASPI, f. 495, op. 74, d. 317, ll. 44, 49; op. 184, d. 2, outgoing 1940 to China, l. 17, coded dispatch of 17 March 1940, ms., handwriting of Dimitrov.

9. RGASPI, f. 495, op. 184, d. 13, incoming from China 1940, l. 175, coded dispatch of 7 November 1940; d. 2, outgoing 1940 to China, l. 88, coded dispatch of 16 November 1940, ms., handwriting of Dimitrov.

10. RGASPI, f. 495, op. 184, d. 13, incoming from China 1940, l. 200, directive of 7 November 1940; Dallin and Firsov, eds., *Dimitrov and Stalin, 1934–1943*, p. 132.

11. RGASPI, f. 495, op. 74, d. 317, ll. 69–70, letter of 23 November 1940; op. 184, d. 2, outgoing 1940 to China, ll. 95–94; coded dispatch of 26 November 1940, ms.; Dallin and Firsov, eds., *Dimitrov and Stalin, 1934–1943*, pp. 127–128.

12. RGASPI, f. 495, op. 184, d. 13, incoming 1940 from China, l. 229.

13. RGASPI, f. 495, op. 184, d. 2, outgoing 1940 to China, l. 96, ms., handwriting of Dimitrov; Dimitrov, *Dnevnik*, p. 206; Dimitroff, *Tagebücher*, p. 327; Dimitrov, *The Diary of Georgi Dimitrov*, p. 140; RGASPI, f. 495, op. 74, d. 317, l. 74, letter of 26 December 1940; op. 184, d. 2, outgoing 1940 to China, l. 113, ms., handwriting of Dimitrov, coded dispatch of 29 December 1940.

14. RGASPI, f. 495, op. 184, d. 4, incoming 1941 from China, l. 9; Dimitrov, *Dnevnik*, p. 210; Dimitroff, *Tagebücher*, pp. 335, 336; Dimitrov, *The Diary of Georgi Dimitrov*, p. 143.

15. Dimitrov, *Dnevnik*, pp. 210–211; Dimitroff, *Tagebücher*, pp. 336–337; Dimitrov, *The Diary of Georgi Dimitrov*, pp. 143–145; RGASPI, f. 495, op. 74, d. 317, l. 75; Dallin and Firsov, eds., *Dimitrov and Stalin, 1934–1943*, p. 135.

16. Dimitrov, *Dnevnik*, p. 214; Dimitroff, *Tagebücher*, p. 345; Dimitrov, *The Diary of Georgi Dimitrov*, p. 148; RGASPI, f. 495, op. 184, d. 4, incoming 1941 from China, ll. 36, 38; Dallin and Firsov, eds., *Dimitrov and Stalin, 1934–1943*, pp. 139–140.

17. RGASPI, f. 495, op. 184, d. 4, incoming from China 1941, l. 207, coded dispatch of 23 June 1941; ibid., l. 209, directive of 23 June 1941; Dallin and Firsov, eds., *Dimitrov and Stalin, 1934–1943*, p. 145.

18. Dimitrov, *Dnevnik*, pp. 238, 241; Dimitroff, *Tagebücher*, pp. 397, 405; Dimitrov, *The Diary of Georgi Dimitrov*, pp. 172, 183; RGASPI, f. 495, op. 184, d. 9, outgoing 1941, coded dispatch of 9 July 1941; Lebedeva and Narinski, *Komintern i Vtoraya Mirovaya Voyna*, vol. 2, p. 114; RGASPI, f. 495, op. 184, d. 4, incoming 1941 from China, l. 229; op. 74, d. 317, l. 81; Dallin and Firsov, eds., *Dimitrov and Stalin, 1934–1943*, p. 143.

19. RGASPI, f. 495, op. 184, d. 4, incoming 1941 from China, l. 235; ibid., ll. 241–240, coded dispatch of 25 July 1941; ibid., l. 240, handwriting of Dimitrov.

20. RGASPI, f. 495, op. 184, d. 3, incoming 1941 from China, l. 78, ms., handwriting of Dimitrov. Dimitrov wrote his text on the coded dispatch from Mao.

21. RGASPI, f. 495, op. 184, d. 3, incoming from China, l. 78, coded dispatch of 15 September 1941; Dallin and Firsov, eds., *Dimitrov and Stalin, 1934–1943*, p. 145.

22. RGASPI, f. 495, op. 74, d. 320, l. 37.

23. RGASPI, f. 495, op. 74, d. 317, ll. 85–86; Dallin and Firsov, eds., *Dimitrov and Stalin, 1934–1943*, p. 147; Lebedeva and Narinski, *Komintern i Vtoraya Mirovaya Voyna*, vol. 2, p. 169.

24. RGASPI, f. 495, op. 184, d. 15, incoming 1942 from China, ll. 146–145.

25. RGASPI, f. 495, op. 184, d. 17, outgoing 1942 to China, l. 51; *Kommunistichesky Internatsional i kitayskaya revolutsia: Dokumenty i materialy*, ed. M. L. Titarenko (Moscow: Nauka, 1986), pp. 291–292; Lebedeva and Narinski, *Komintern i Vtoraya Mirovaya Voyna*, vol. 2, p. 233.

26. RGASPI, f. 495, op. 184, d. 15, incoming 1943 from China, ll. 34–33, coded dispatch of 17 April 1943; ibid., l. 50, coded dispatch of 5 June 1943.

27. RGASPI, f. 495, op. 74, d. 342, ll. 50–51.

CHAPTER 8. THE NAZI-SOVIET PACT

1. RGASPI, f. 495, op. 184, d. 16, outgoing 1939 to France, ll. 111–109, coded dispatch of 22 August 1939, ms.; Bayerlein, Narinski, Studer, and Wolikow, eds., *Moscou-Paris-Berlin*, pp. 60–62.

2. Valery Kochik, *Razvedchiki i residenty GRU za predelami otchizny* (Moscow: Yauza, Eksmo, 2004), pp. 357, 359.

3. *Oglasheniyu podlezhit. SSSR-Germania 1939–1941: Dokumenty i materialy*, ed. and trans. Yuri Felshtinsky (Moscow: Moskovsky Rabochy), p. 71.

4. RGASPI, f. 495, op. 73, d. 67, ll. 44, 45–59; Lebedeva and Narinski, *Komintern i Vtoraya Mirovaya Voyna*, vol. 1, pp. 73–83.

5. RGASPI, f. 495, op. 74, d. 517, ll. 41–42; Dallin and Firsov, eds., *Dimitrov and Stalin, 1934–1943*, p. 150.

6. The draft outline of the conceptual framework, in its final form, was sent to Stalin, Molotov, and Zhdanov on 26 September, but subsequently this work was stopped.

7. RGASPI, f. 495, op. 18, d. 1302a, l. 57, ms.

8. RGASPI, f. 495, op. 18, d. 1302a, ll. 57, 59, ms.

9. RGASPI, f. 495, op. 184, d. 11, incoming 1939 from Bulgaria, l. 50, sent 5 September 1939, received 7 September, deciphered 7 September.

10. RGASPI, f. 495, op. 74, d. 517, l. 53; Lebedeva and Narinski, *Komintern i Vtoraya Mirovaya Voyna*, vol. 1, p. 88.

11. Dimitrov, *Dnevnik*, pp. 181–182; Dimitroff, *Tagebücher*, pp. 273–274; Dimitrov, *The Diary of Georgi Dimitrov*, pp. 115–116. Those seeking to mitigate the brutality of Stalin's remarks argue that the West could have had a deal with Stalin, noting that Dimitrov also recorded that Stalin said: "We preferred agreements with the so-called democratic countries and therefore conducted negotiations. But the English and the French wanted us for farmhands and at no cost! We, of course, would not go for being farmhands, still less for getting nothing in return." But this passes over what Stalin wanted "in return." Stalin asked for and got from Hitler acquiescence to Stalin's doing what he wished with half of Poland and all of Lithuania, Latvia, Estonia, and Finland, as well as annexing eastern Romania (Bessarabia). It is unrealistic to think that Western statesmen could have paid, or that their publics would have allowed them to pay, such a price.

12. RGASPI, f. 495, op. 184, d. 1292, ll. 47–48; d. 2, outgoing 1939 to Sweden, ll. 24–23; d. 10, outgoing 1939 to Holland, l. 23; d. 4, outgoing 1939 to France, ll. 35–34, ms.; d. 11, outgoing 1939 to Prague, l. 15; Lebedeva and Narinski, *Komintern i Vtoraya Mirovaya Voyna*, vol. 1, pp. 88–89; Bayerlein, Narinski, Studer, and Wolikow, eds., *Moscou-Paris-Berlin*, pp. 74–75.

13. RGASPI, f. 495, op. 184, d. 10, outgoing 1939 to Holland, l. 25, coded dispatch of 10 September 1939 ms., handwriting of Sorkin. The response from Goulooze on the situation with the leaders of the French Communist Party was received on 16 September.

14. RGASPI, f. 495, op. 184, d. 1, incoming 1939 from Holland, l. 41, sent 15 September 1939, received 16 September, deciphered 16 September.

15. RGASPI, f. 495, op. 184, d. 1, incoming 1939 from Holland, l. 38, sent 14 September 1939, received 16 September, deciphered 16 September; ibid., l. 52, sent 25 September 1939, received 26 September, deciphered 26 September; d. 13, incoming 1939 from Stockholm, l. 24, sent 17 September 1939, received 19 September, deciphered 19 September; d. 9, incoming 1939 from New York, l. 34, sent 14 September 1939, received 14 September, deciphered 14 September.

16. RGASPI, f. 495, op. 184, d. 2, outgoing 1939 to Sweden, l. 30, coded dispatch of 17 September 1939, ms.; op. 184, inc. reg. 17, outgoing 1939 to Sweden, l. 29; d. 10, outgoing 1939 to Holland, l. 31, coded dispatch of 17 September 1939, ms.; Bayerlein, Narinski, Studer, and Wolikow, eds., *Moscou-Paris-Berlin*, p. 76.

17. RGASPI, f. 495, op. 184, d. 4, outgoing 1940 to London, l. 5, coded dispatch of 4 February 1940; d. 1, incoming 1940 from London, l. 4, received 19 March 1940; d. 4, outgoing 1940 to England, l. 12, coded dispatch of 20 March 1940, ms., original in Dimitrov's handwriting; Bayerlein, Narinski, Studer, and Wolikow, eds., *Moscou-Paris-Berlin*, p. 154.

18. RGASPI, f. 495, op. 184, d. 4, outgoing 1939 to France, ll. 32, 31, coded dispatch of 4 September, 1939, ms., handwriting of Dimitrov; F. I. Firsov, "Arkhivy Kominterna i vneshnyaya politika SSSR v 1939–1941 gg.," *Novaya i noveyshaya istoria*, no. 6. (1992): 17.

19. RGASPI, f. 495, op. 184, d. 10, outgoing to Holland, l. 34, ms., handwriting of Dimitrov.

20. RGASPI, f. 495, op. 184, d. 5, incoming from France, "Jeannette," l. 5; Bayerlain, Narinski, Studer, and Wolikow, eds., *Moscou-Paris-Berlin*, pp. 107–108.

21. RGASPI, f. 495, op. 184, d. 4, outgoing 1939 to France, l. 66, ms.; d. 10, incoming from France, l. 73, sent 30 October 1939, received 1 November, deciphered 1 November.

22. RGASPI, f. 495, op. 184, d. 15, outgoing 1939 to France, l. 124, coded dispatch of 11 November 1939, ms., handwriting of Sorkin.

23. RGASPI, f. 495, op. 184, d. 10, outgoing 1939 to Holland, l. 131, ms., handwriting of Sorkin.

24. RGASPI, f. 495, op. 272, d. 8372.

25. RGASPI, f. 485, op. 74, d. 515, ll. 64–69, "O tt. Legro i Klemane."

26. *Pravda*, 29 September 1939; Felshtinsky, ed., *Oglasheniyu podlezhit*, p. 122.

27. Dimitrov, *Dnevnik*, p. 184; Dimitroff, *Tagebücher*, p. 279; Dimitrov, *The Diary of Georgi Dimitrov*, p. 120. The treaty with Estonia was signed on 28 September, with Latvia on 5 October, and with Lithuania on 10 October.

28. RGASPI, f. 495, op. 184, d. 6, outgoing 1940 to Lithuania, l. 2, coded dispatch of 17 June 1940, ms.; ibid., l. 6, coded dispatch of 3 July 1940, ms., handwriting of Dimitrov.

29. RGASPI, f. 495, op. 184, d. 10, outgoing 1939 to Holland, l. 43, ms., handwriting of Dimitrov.

30. RGASPI, f. 495, op. 184, d. 4, outgoing 1939 to France, ll. 48–47, ms., coded dispatch of 28 September 1939; Bayerlein, Narinski, Studer, and Wolikow, eds., *Moscou-Paris-Berlin*, pp. 80–81.

31. RGASPI, f. 495, op. 184, d. 4, outgoing 1939 to France, l. 53, coded dispatch of 29 September 1939, ms.; Bayerlein, Narinski, Studer, and Wolikow, eds., *Moscou-Paris-Berlin*, p. 84.

32. RGASPI, f. 495, op. 184, d. 8, outgoing 1939 to New York, ll. 60, 59–58; d. 2, outgoing 1939 to Sweden, l. 41; Bayerlein, Narinski, Studer, and Wolikow, eds., *Moscou-Paris-Berlin*, pp. 104–105.

33. RGASPI, f. 495, op. 184, d. 11, incoming 1939 from Bulgaria, l. 50, coded dispatch of 5 September 1939.

34. RGASPI, f. 495, op. 184, d. 7, outgoing 1939 to Bulgaria, ll. 36–34; coded dispatch of 11 October 1939.

35. RGASPI, f. 495, op. 184, d. 7, outgoing 1939 to Bulgaria, l. 42, coded dispatch of 3 November 1939.

36. RGASPI, f. 495, op. 184, d. 11, incoming 1939 from Bulgaria, l. 72, sent 15 November 1939, received 26 November, deciphered 26 November; d. 7, outgoing 1939 to Bulgaria, l. 53.

37. RGASPI, f. 495, op. 184, d. 11, outgoing to Bulgaria, l. 31, coded dispatch of 11 April 1940; RGASPI, f. 495, op. 184, d. 16, incoming 1940 from Bulgaria, l. 72, sent 22 April 1940, received 25 April.

38. RGASPI, f. 495, op. 184, d. 11, outgoing 1940 to Bulgaria, l. 49, coded dispatch of 7 May 1940, ms., handwriting of Kolarov; d. 16, incoming 1940 from Bulgaria, l. 94, sent 16 May 1940, received 19 May, deciphered 19 May.

39. RGASPI, f. 495, op. 74, d. 75, l. 3, letter of 22 May 1940; ibid., l. 2, letter of 22 May 1940; Lebedeva and Narinski, *Komintern i Vtoraya Mirovaya Voyna*, vol. 1, p. 343.

40. RGASPI, f. 495, op. 184, d. 16, incoming 1940 from Bulgaria, l. 109, sent 4 June 1940, received 7 June; d. 11, outgoing 1940 to Bulgaria, l. 62, coded dispatch of 25 June 1940.

41. RGASPI, f. 495, op. 184, d. 11, outgoing 1940 to Bulgaria, ll. 99–94.

42. RGASPI, f. 495, op. 184, d. 16, incoming 1940 from Bulgaria, l. 257, sent 1 October 1940, received 8 October; ibid., l. 262, received 11 October 1940; ibid., l. 272, received 19 October 1940.

43. RGASPI, f. 495, op. 184, d. 11, outgoing 1940 to Bulgaria, l. 108, coded dispatch of 15 November 1940, ms.

44. Dimitrov, *Dnevnik*, p. 203; Dimitroff, *Tagebücher*, p. 321; Dimitrov, *The Diary of Georgi Dimitrov*, pp. 136, 137.

45. Stalin opened secret negotiations with Nazi Germany seeking Soviet membership in the Tripartite Pact as soon as it was signed. Negotiations proceeded to the point of a formal Soviet proposal in late November 1940 for USSR membership in the Axis with the Soviets offering increased raw material aid to Germany in exchange for German confirmation of Soviet predominance over Finland, the signing of a Soviet-Bulgarian mutual assistance pact that included Soviet military bases in Bulgaria, Japanese renunciation of rights to northern Sakhalin, and German recognition of Soviet interests extending into Iran. Hitler, however, had already decided upon attacking the USSR, and nothing resulted from the negotiations. The negotiations are summarized in Aleksandr M. Nekrich, *Pariahs, Partners, Predators: German-Soviet Relations, 1922–1941*, ed. and trans. Gregory L. Freeze, with a foreword by Adam B. Ulam (New York: Columbia University Press, 1997), pp. 203–208, and Gerhard L. Weinberg, *A World at Arms: A Global History of World War II* (Cambridge: Cambridge University Press, 1994), pp. 199–201.

46. RGASPI, f. 495, op. 184, d. 11, outgoing 1940 to Bulgaria, l. 125, coded dispatch of 26 November 1940, ms., handwriting of Kolarov; op. 74, d. 75, l. 4, letter of 26 November 1940; Lebedeva and Narinski, *Komintern i Vtoraya Mirovaya Voyna*, vol. 1, p. 454.

47. RGASPI, f. 495, op. 184, d. 15, incoming 1940 from Bulgaria, l. 9, sent 27 November 1940, received 28 November, deciphered 28 November, ms.; ibid., l. 25, coded dispatch of 28 November 1940; ibid., l. 26, sent 29 November 1940, received 4 December; ibid., l. 24, coded dispatch of November 1940.

48. RGASPI, f. 495, op. 184, d. 11, outgoing 1940 to Bulgaria, l. 128, coded dispatch of 28 November 1940, ms., handwriting of Dimitrov; d. 15, incoming 1940 from Bulgaria, l. 22, sent 30 November 1940, received 3 December, deciphered 3 December; op. 74, d. 75, ll. 6, 5.

49. RGASPI, f. 495, op. 184, d. 11, outgoing 1940 to Bulgaria, l. 148, coded dispatch of 14 December 1940, ms.

50. Dimitrov, *Dnevnik*, pp. 208–209; Dimitroff, *Tagebücher*, pp. 332–333; Dimitrov, *The Diary of Georgi Dimitrov*, pp. 140–141.

51. Dimitrov, *Dnevnik*, p. 212; Dimitroff, *Tagebücher*, p. 339; RGASPI, f. 495, op. 10a, d. 430, ll. 8–9; Lebedeva and Narinski, *Komintern i Vtoraya Mirovaya Voyna*, vol. 1, p. 497.

52. Dimitrov, *Dnevnik*, p. 232; Dimitroff, *Tagebücher*, p. 385; Dimitrov, *The Diary of Georgi Dimitrov*, pp. 158–162.

53. RGASPI, f. 495, op. 184, d. 7, incoming 1939 from Prague, l. 18, sent 10 September 1939, received 13 September, deciphered 13 September.

54. RGASPI, f. 495, op. 184, d. 11, outgoing 1939 to Prague, l. 19, coded dispatch of 14 September 1939, ms.

55. RGASPI, f. 495, op. 184, d. 7, incoming 1939 from Prague, l. 32, sent 16 September 1939, received 28 September, deciphered 29 September; ibid., ll. 46–45, sent 31 October 1939, received 3 November, deciphered 4 November.

56. RGASPI, f. 495, op. 184, d. 11, outgoing 1939 to Prague, l. 26, coded dispatch of 16 October 1939, ms., handwriting of Gottwald; ibid., l. 28, coded dispatch of 21 October, ms., handwriting of Gottwald; d. 7, incoming 1939 from Prague, l. 70, coded dispatch of 13 December 1939, received 19 December, deciphered 19 December.

57. RGASPI, f. 495, op. 18, d. 1294, ll. 62a–69; d. 1296, ll. 153, 158; Lebedeva and Narinski, *Komintern i Vtoraya Mirovaya Voyna*, vol. 1, pp. 127–131.

58. RGASPI, f. 495, op. 18, d. 1296, ll. 151, 153.

59. RGASPI, f. 495, op. 184, d. 2, outgoing 1939 to Sweden, l. 81, ms., handwriting of Dimitrov; Bayerlein, Narinski, Studer, and Wolikow, eds., *Moscou-Paris-Berlin*, p. 128.

60. V. P. Smirnov, "Frantsuzskaya kommunisticheskaya partia i Komintern v 1939–1940 gg.: Novye arkhivnye materialy," *Novaya i noveyshaya istoria*, no. 1 (1994): 37.

61. RGASPI, f. 495, op. 184, d. 4, outgoing 1939 to France, l. 57, ms., handwriting of Dimitrov; d. 10, outgoing 1939 to Holland, ll. 65–64, ms.; d. 4, outgoing 1939 to France, l. 63, coded dispatch of 14 October 1939, ms.; Bayerlein, Narinski, Studer, and Wolikow, eds., *Moscou-Paris-Berlin*, pp. 97–98, 110–111. At the trial, which took place in the spring of 1940, the accused successfully rebutted charges of treason and espionage. But they were convicted of violating the decree banning the Communist Party and sentenced to five years' imprisonment.

62. RGASPI, f. 495, op. 73, d. 67, l. 78; Dallin and Firsov, eds., *Dimitrov and Stalin, 1934–1943*, p. 164.

63. Dimitrov, *Dnevnik*, p. 184; Dimitroff, *Tagebücher*, p. 279; Dimitrov, *The Diary of Georgi Dimitrov*, pp. 119–120.

64. *Pravda*, 7 October 1939; Felshtinsky, ed., *Oglasheniyu podlezhit*, p. 137.

65. *Pravda*, 30 November 1939; Felshtinsky, ed., *Oglasheniyu podlezhit*, p. 160.

66. RGASPI, f. 495, op. 184, d. 2, outgoing 1939 to Sweden, l. 56; d. 10, outgoing 1939 to Holland, l. 82, coded dispatch of 5 November 1939, ms., handwriting of Dimitrov; d. 8, outgoing 1939 to New York, l. 69, coded dispatch of 9 November 1939, ms., handwriting of Dimitrov.

67. RGASPI, f. 495, op. 184, d. 7, outgoing 1939 to Bulgaria, l. 50, coded dispatch of 17 November 1939, ms.; V. M. Molotov, "Doklad o vneshney politike Sovetskogo Soiuza na zasedany Verkhovnogo Soveta SSSR 31 oktiabria 1939 goda," *Kommunistichesky Internatsional*, nos. 8–9 (1939): 9, 11, 13; Felshtinsky, ed., *Oglasheniyu podlezhit*, pp. 149, 150, 152.

68. Dimitrov, *Dnevnik*, p. 185; Dimitroff, *Tagebücher*, p. 281; Dimitrov, *The Diary of Georgi Dimitrov*, p. 121

69. RGASPI, f. 495, op. 18, d. 1301, l. 100; Lebedeva and Narinski, *Komintern i Vtoraya Mirovaya Voyna*, vol. 1, p. 219.

70. RGASPI, f. 495, op. 18, d. 1301, l. 106; Lebedeva and Narinski, *Komintern i Vtoraya Mirovya Voyna*, vol. 1, p. 224; RGASPI, f. 495, op. 184, d. 1,

outgoing 1941 to Holland, coded dispatch of 21 January 1941, ms.; op. 74, d. 155, l. 3.

71. RGASPI, f. 495, op. 74, d. 50, ll. 5, 11.

72. RGASPI, f. 495, op. 184, d. 4, outgoing 1940 to London, l. 1, coded dispatch of 3 January 1940, ms., handwriting of Dimitrov; Bayerlein, Narinski, Studer, and Wolikow, eds., *Moscou-Paris-Berlin*, p. 143; *Daily Worker* (London), 30 December 1939; RGASPI, f. 495, op. 74, d. 50, l. 7, letter of 3 January 1940; d. 140, l. 31.

73. RGASPI, f. 495, op. 184, d. 4, outgoing 1940 to London, ll. 10, 11; d. 3, outgoing 1940 to France (Légros), l. 60, coded dispatch of 5 March 1940; Bayerlein, Narinski, Studer, and Wolikow, eds., *Moscou-Paris-Berlin*, p. 170; RGASPI, f. 495, op. 184, d. 1, incoming 1940 from London, l. 5, received 24 March 1940.

74. Quoted in Felshtinsky, ed., *Oglasheniyu podlezhit*, pp. 179, 180.

75. RGASPI, f. 495, op. 184, d. 9, outgoing 1940 to Stockholm, l. 52; op. 18, d. 1319, l. 117; Lebedeva and Narinski, *Komintern i Vtoraya Mirovaya Voyna*, vol. 1, p. 331.

76. RGASPI, f. 495, op. 184, d. 9, outgoing 1940 to Stockholm, l. 53.

77. RGASPI, f. 495, op. 184, d. 9, outgoing 1940 to Stockholm, l. 67, coded dispatch of 22 April 1940, ms., handwriting of Dimitrov; d. 3, outgoing 1940 to France (Légros), l. 118, coded dispatch of 22 April 1940, ms.

78. RGASPI, f. 495, op. 184, d. 1, outgoing 1940 to Holland, ll. 52–51, coded dispatch of 8 June 1940, ms., handwriting of Sorkin; ibid., l. 46, coded dispatch of 21 May 1940, ms., handwriting of Dimitrov; Lebedeva and Narinski, *Komintern i Vtoraya Mirovaya Voyna*, vol. 1, pp. 356–357.

79. RGASPI, f. 495, op. 184, d. 8, incoming 1941 from France, l. 71, sent 21 March 1941, received 24 March, deciphered 24 March. See also V. P. Smirnov, "Vtoraya Mirovaya Voyna i Komintern, 1939–1941 gg. (Po arkhivnym dokumentam)," *Novaya i noveshaya istoria*, no. 3 (1996): 28.

80. RGASPI, f. 495, op. 10a, d. 90, ll. 52–54; Lebedeva and Narinski, *Komintern i Vtoraya Mirovaya Voyna*, vol. 1, p. 401; RGASPI, f. 495, op. 74, d. 518, l. 40; Dallin and Firsov, eds., *Dimitrov and Stalin, 1934–1943*, p. 177; Central Party Archives (Sofia), f. 146, ed. khr. 426, l. 1. For the text of the directive see Lebedeva and Narinski, *Komintern i Vtoraya Mirovaya Voyna*, vol. 1, pp. 408–411.

81. RGASPI, f. 495, op. 184, d. 8, outgoing 1940 to Belgium, ll. 27, 26, coded dispatch of 6 August 1940, ms.; op. 74, d. 516, l. 93, ms., handwriting of Stepanov. The initial translation, containing inaccuracies, is published in Lebedeva and Narinski, *Komintern i Vtoraya Mirovaya Voyna*, vol. 1, pp. 421–422; op. 184, d. 10, incoming 1940 from Belgium, coded dispatch of 4 September 1940; Bayerlein, Narinski, Studer, and Wolikow, eds., *Moscou-Paris-Berlin*, pp. 277–278, 296–298.

82. RGASPI, f. 517, op. 1, d. 1916, l. 4; op. 74, d. 518, l. 45, letter of 13 September 1940.

83. RGASPI, f. 495, op. 18, d. 1321, ll. 59, 68, 69, 71; Lebedeva and Narinski, *Komintern i Vtoraya Mirovaya Voyna*, vol. 1, pp. 349–351; Bayerlein, Narinski, Studer, and Wolikow, eds., *Moscou-Paris-Berlin*, p. 232; RGASPI, f. 495, op. 184, d. 9, outgoing 1940 to Stockholm, l. 96, coded dispatch of 28 May 1940, ms.

84. RGASPI, f. 495, op. 74, d. 518, ll. 21–22, letter of 10 June 1940.

85. Bundesarchiv Koblenz, R.58 732, l. 7. The document was kindly provided to the senior author by Ryszard Nazarewicz.

86. RGASPI, f. 495, op. 184, d. 2, outgoing 1939 to Sweden, ll. 78, 78 reverse, coded dispatch of 4 December 1939, ms., handwriting of Dimitrov; ibid., ll. 87, 87 reverse, coded dispatch of 11 December 1939, ms.; Lebedeva and Narinski, *Komintern i Vtoraya Mirovaya Voyna*, vol. 1, pp. 201–202, 204; Bayerlein, Narinski, Studer, and Wolikow, eds., *Moscou-Paris-Berlin*, pp. 130–131. The Soviets even gave the fictitious Finnish Democratic Republic a small military force by clothing Finnish-speaking Red Army soldiers from Soviet Karelia in rebadged Polish army uniforms recently captured in the conquest of eastern Poland. This incident is discussed in the memoir of one of the ethnic Finns assigned to the ersatz army. Kaarlo Tuomi, *Spy Lost: Caught between the KGB and the FBI* (New York: Enigma Books, 2013).

87. RGASPI, f. 495, op. 184, d. 7, incoming 1939 from Prague, l. 68, sent 13 December 1939, received 19 December, deciphered 19 December.

88. RGASPI, f. 495, op. 184, d. 2, outgoing 1939 to Sweden, l. 100, coded dispatch of 28 December 1939, ms., handwriting of Sorkin. Anglo-French intervention also offered the Allies the possibility of taking control of Swedish iron ore fields that were supplying Nazi Germany.

89. RGASPI, f. 495, op. 184, d. 15, outgoing 1940 to New York, ll. 8, 8 reverse, coded dispatch of 16 February 1940, ms., handwriting of Dimitrov; d. 8, outgoing 1939 to New York, l. 79, coded dispatch of 31 December 1939, ms., handwriting of Sorkin; Lebedeva and Narinski, *Komintern i Vtoraya Mirovaya Voyna*, vol. 1, p. 309.

90. RGASPI, f. 495, op. 18, d. 1317, l. 206, coded dispatch of 18 March 1940; op. 184, d. 3, outgoing 1940 to France (Légros), ll. 74, 75; Bayerlein, Narinski, Studer, and Wolikow, eds., *Moscou-Paris-Berlin*, p. 176; Lebedeva and Narinski, *Komintern i Vtoraya Mirovaya Voyna*, vol. 1, pp. 308, 309.

91. Quoted in *Komintern i Finlandia, 1919–1934: Dokumenty*, ed. N. S. Lebedeva, K. Rentola, and T. Saarela (Moscow: Nauka, 2003), pp. 309, 310.

92. RGASPI, f. 495, op. 18, d. 1321, l. 19; op. 184, d. 9, outgoing 1940 to Stockholm, l. 126, coded dispatch of 29 June 1940, ms.; ibid., l. 129, coded dispatch of 4 July 1940, ms.; Bayerlein, Narinski, Studer, and Wolikow, eds., *Moscou-Paris-Berlin*, pp. 246, 254.

93. RGASPI, f. 495, op. 184, d. 5, outgoing 1940 to Yugoslavia, ll. 13–12; coded dispatch of 3 July 1940; Lebedeva and Narinski, *Komintern i Vtoraya Mirovyaa Voyna*, vol. 1, pp. 376–384; Bayerlein, Narinski, Studer, and Wolikow, eds., *Moscou-Paris-Berlin*, pp. 252–253.

94. RGASPI, f. 495, op. 184, d. 3, outgoing 1940 to France (Légros), l. 143, coded dispatch of 13 September 1940, ms., handwriting of Ercoli. In this message Ercoli uses the pseudonym Alfredo; Bayerlein, Narinski, Studer, and Wolikow, eds., *Moscou-Paris-Berlin*, pp. 266, 302; RGASPI, f. 495, op. 74, d. 518, l. 41; op. 18, d. 1322, l. 107; op. 184, d. 8, outgoing 1940 to Belgium, l. 3, ms., coded dispatch of 19 July 1940; Dallin and Firsov, eds., *Dimitrov and Stalin, 1934–1943*, p. 178; Lebedeva and Narinski, *Komintern i Vtoraya Mirovaya Voyna*, vol. 1, p. 395.

95. RGASPI, f. 495, op. 184, d. 9, outgoing 1940 to Stockholm, l. 157, coded dispatch of 3 September 1940, ms.; d. 15, outgoing 1941 to New York, l. 90, coded dispatch of 6 September 1940, ms.; d. 5, outgoing 1940 to Yugoslavia, l. 30, coded dispatch of 6 September 1940, ms.

96. RGASPI, f. 495, op. 184, d. 5, outgoing 1941 to France, coded dispatch of 4 January 1941. The text of the dispatch has "22 February," apparently an error made while deciphering the document.

97. RGASPI, f. 495, op. 74, d. 522, ll. 1–3, ms., handwriting of Stepanov; Bayerlein, Narinski, Studer, and Wolikow, eds., *Moscou-Paris-Berlin*, pp. 371–373; V. P. Smirnov, "Nachalo frantsuzskogo dvizhenia soprotivlenia: Novye dannye," *Novaya i noveyshaya istorya*, no. 2 (1999): 24. Thorez, conscripted into the French Army in 1939, deserted and secretly fled to Moscow. He was tried *in absentia* and sentenced to death. He did not return to France until late 1944, when he was pardoned by the French provisional government headed by Charles de Gaulle.

98. RGASPI, f. 495, op. 184, d. 8, incoming 1941 from France, l. 66, sent 15 March 1941, received 19 March, deciphered 19 March; op. 74, d. 522, l. 6, ms., handwriting of Stepanov; d. 8, incoming 1941 from France, l. 124; Lebedeva and Narinski, *Komintern i Vtoraya Mirovaya Voyna*, vol. 1, pp. 526–527; Bayerlein, Narinski, Studer, and Wolikow, eds., *Moscou-Paris-Berlin*, pp. 402–404, 411–412.

99. RGASPI, f. 495, op. 184, d. 3, outgoing 1941 to the United States, coded dispatch of 5 February 1941, ms.; ibid., coded dispatch of 7 February 1941, ms.

100. Dimitrov, *Dnevnik*, pp. 202–203; Dimitroff, *Tagebücher*, p. 320; Dimitrov, *The Diary of Georgi Dimitrov*, p. 136

101. Central Party Archives (Sofia), f. 146, op. 2, ed. khr. 430, ll. 2, 3.

102. Dimitrov, *Dnevnik*, p. 225; Dimitroff, *Tagebücher*, p. 370; Dimitrov, *The Diary of Georgi Dimitrov*, pp. 154–155.

103. RGASPI, f. 495, op. 73, d. 90, l. 16; RGASPI, f. 495, op. 18, d. 1330, ll. 226, 228, 229; Dimitrov, *Dnevnik*, p. 227; Dimitroff, *Tagebücher*, p. 373; Dimitrov, *The Diary of Georgi Dimitrov*, p. 155.

CHAPTER 9. THE COMINTERN, THE COMMUNIST PARTIES, AND THE GREAT PATRIOTIC WAR

1. Dimitrov, *Dnevnik*, pp. 235–236; Dimitroff, *Tagebücher*, pp. 392–393; Dimitrov, *The Diary of Georgi Dimitrov*, pp. 166–167; RGASPI, f. 495, op. 18, d. 1335, l. 3b; Lebedeva and Narinski, *Komintern i Vtoraya Mirovaya Voyna*, vol. 2, p. 94.

2. RGASPI, f. 495, op. 18, d. 1335, l. 1, coded dispatch of 22 June 1941; op. 184, d. 8, outgoing 1941 to Sweden, coded dispatch of 22 June 1941; d. 3, outgoing 1941 to the United States, coded dispatch of 22 June 1941, coded dispatch of 30 June 1941; op. 184, d. 4, outgoing 1941 to England, coded dispatch of 22 June 1941; d. 5, outgoing 1941 to France, coded dispatch of 22 June 1941; Lebedeva and Narinski, *Komintern i Vtoraya Mirovaya Voyna*, vol. 2, p. 97; Bayerlein, Narinski, Studer, and Wolikow, eds., *Moscou-Paris-Berlin*, pp. 437–438.

3. RGASPI, f. 495, op. 184, d. 8, outgoing 1941 to Sweden; op. 18, d. 1335, l. 14, coded dispatch of 24 June 1941; Lebedeva and Narinski, *Komintern i Vtoraya Mirovaya Voyna*, vol. 2, pp. 100, 102. The document published in this collection does not contain the correction made by Dimitrov. He replaced the word "fascist" by "capitalist" in the sentence that referred to the systems; RGASPI, f. 495, op. 184, d. 13, outgoing 1941 to France, l. 12, coded dispatch of 25 June 1941, ms.; Bayerlein, Narinski, Studer, and Wolikow, eds., *Moscou-Paris-Berlin*, p. 442.

4. Dimitrov, *Dnevnik*, p. 237; Dimitroff, *Tagebücher*, p. 396; Dimitrov, *The Diary of Georgi Dimitrov*, p. 171.

5. RGASPI, f. 495, op. 184, d. 11, outgoing 1941 to Yugoslavia, l. 19, ms., coded dispatch of 30 June 1941, ms.; Lebedeva and Narinski, *Komintern i Vtoraya Mirovaya Voyna*, vol. 2, p. 106.

6. RGASPI, f. 495, op. 184, d. 1, outgoing 1941 to Holland, coded dispatch of 30 June 1941, ms.; d. 5, outgoing 1941 to France, coded dispatch of 1 July 1941, ms.; Bayerlein, Narinski, Studer, and Wolikow, eds., *Moscou-Paris-Berlin*, p. 446.

7. RGASPI, f. 495, op. 184, d. 3, outgoing 1941 to the United States, l. 54, coded dispatch of 30 June 1941; ibid., l. 2, coded dispatch of 30 June 1941.

8. RGASPI, f. 495, op. 17, d. 112, l. 5, letter to Molotov of 1 July 1941; op. 73, d. 109, l. 5, coded dispatch of 7 July 1941 (sent to all parties); Lebedeva and Narinski, *Komintern i Vtoraya Mirovaya Voyna*, vol. 2, pp. 110, 114.

9. Dimitrov, *Dnevnik*, pp. 246, 253–254; Dimitroff, *Tagebücher*, pp. 416, 432; Dimitrov, *The Diary of Georgi Dimitrov*, p. 190.

10. RGASPI, f. 495, op. 184, d. 11, outgoing to Yugoslavia, l. 69, coded dispatch of 23 August 1941.

11. RGASPI, f. 495, op. 73, d. 141, ll. 9–10; Lebedeva and Narinski, *Komintern i Vtoraya Mirovaya Voyna*, vol. 2, pp. 194–195.

12. RGASPI, f. 495, op. 74, d. 109, l. 8; d. 255, ll. 12, 13.

13. RGASPI, f. 495, op. 184, d. 14, incoming 1942 to Ufa, l. 163, ms., handwriting of Sorkin; ibid., l. 107, ms., handwriting of Sorkin, coded dispatch of 14 March 1942.

14. RGASPI, f. 495, op. 73, d. 187, l. 7; letter of 23 January 1942; Lebedeva and Narinski, *Komintern i Vtoraya Mirovaya Voyna*, vol. 2, pp. 184–185.

15. RGASPI, f. 495, op. 74, d. 21, l. 27, letter of 31 August 1942; ibid., l. 31, letter of 20 September 1942; ibid., letter of 2 October 1942; Lebedeva and Narinski, *Komintern i Vtoraya Mirovaya Voyna*, vol. 2, p. 254.

16. RGASPI, f. 495, op. 74, d. 56, l. 57, letter of 3 March 1943; d. 484, l. 21, letter of 1 September 1942.

17. RGASPI, f. 495, op. 184, d. 7, incoming 1941 from Yugoslavia, l. 150, sent 28 July 1941, received 31 July, deciphered 31 July; ibid., l. 149, coded dispatch sent 23 July 1941, received 31 July, deciphered 31 July; d. 11, outgoing 1941 to Yugoslavia, coded dispatch of 1 August 1941.

18. RGASPI, f. 495, op. 184, d. 7, incoming 1941 from Yugoslavia, l. 152, coded dispatch of 1 August 1941; ibid., l. 153, coded dispatch of 4 August 1941

19. Quoted in Lebedeva and Narinski, *Komintern i Vtoraya Mirovaya Voyna*. vol. 2, p. 113.

20. RGASPI, f. 495, op. 184, d. 11, outgoing 1941 to Yugoslavia, coded dispatch of 4 July 1941, ms.; Lebedeva and Narinski, *Komintern i Vtoraya Mirovaya Voyna*, vol. 2, p. 113. The reference is to Stalin's address given on Moscow radio 3 July 1941.

21. RGASPI, f. 495, op. 184, d. 11, outgoing 1941 to Yugoslavia, coded dispatch of 9 July 1941, ms., handwriting of Dimitrov.

22. RGASPI, f. 495, op. 184, d. 7, incoming 1941 from Yugoslavia, ll. 165–164, coded dispatch of 24 September 1941.

23. RGASPI, f. 495, op. 184, d. 7, incoming 1941 from Yugoslavia, l. 165, coded dispatch of 24 September 1941. Rosa, who was also part of Kopinić's staff, added at the end of the radiogram, "I witnessed everything. In my view Vokshin is right. I believe that they want to deal with Vokshin, and possibly with me, because I know all of this. We have worked honestly and will continue to work in that way. Rosa."

24. RGASPI, f. 495, op. 184, d. 11, outgoing 1941 to Yugoslavia, l. 83, coded dispatch of 28 September 1941.

25. RGASPI, f. 495, op. 184, d. 5, outgoing 1943 to Yugoslavia, l. 7, coded dispatch of 10 February 1943; Dimitrov, *Dnevnik*, pp. 250, 267; Dimitroff, *Tagebücher*, pp. 425, 461; Dimitrov, *The Diary of Georgi Dimitrov*, pp. 193, 206; Lebedeva and Narinski, *Komintern i Vtoraya Mirovaya Voyna*, vol. 2, pp. 328–329.

26. RGASPI, f. 495, op. 184, d. 11, outgoing 1941 to Yugoslavia, l. 95, coded dispatch of 21 November 1941; ibid., l. 101, coded dispatch of 28 November 1941, ms.

27. RGASPI, f. 495, op. 74, d. 599, l. 13, coded dispatch of 2 December 1941; ibid., l. 15, coded dispatch of 4 December 1941; op. 184, d. 18, outgoing 1942 from Ufa, l. 43, coded dispatch of 15 January 1942; Lebedeva and Narinski, *Komintern i Vtoraya Mirovaya Voyna*, vol. 2, pp. 182–183; Dallin and Firsov, eds., *Dimitrov and Stalin, 1934–1943*, p. 215.

28. RGASPI, f. 495, op. 184, d. 5, incoming 1941–1942 from Ufa, l. 302, coded dispatch of 6 March 1942; d. 10, outgoing 1942 to Yugoslavia, l. 23, coded dispatch of 1 June 1942; Dimitrov, *Dnevnik*, pp. 313, 316; Dimitroff, *Tagebücher*, pp. 561, 568; Dimitrov, *The Diary of Georgi Dimitrov*, pp. 233, 234; Dallin and Firsov, eds., *Dimitrov and Stalin, 1934–1943*, pp. 217, 220, 221; Adibekov et al., eds., *Politburo TsK RKP(b)-VKP(b) i Komintern*, pp. 804, 806–807; Lebedeva and Narinski, *Komintern i Vtoraya Mirovaya Voyna*, vol. 2, pp. 221–222.

29. RGASPI, f. 495, op. 184, d. 10, outgoing 1942 to Yugoslavia, l. 23, ms., coded dispatch of 1 March 1942; d. 4, incoming 1942 from Yugoslavia, l. 67, received 25 March 1942.

30. RGASPI, f. 495, op. 184, d. 4, incoming 1942 from Yugoslavia, l. 104, received 17 April 1942; ibid., l. 179, received 8 June 1942.

31. Dimitrov, *Dnevnik*, p. 339; Dimitroff, *Tagebücher*, p. 617; RGASPI, f. 495, op. 184, d. 11, incoming 1942 from Yugoslavia, ll. 8–7.

32. RGASPI, f. 495, op. 184, d. 10, outgoing 1943 to Yugoslavia, l. 15; Lebedeva and Narinski, *Komintern i Vtoraya Mirovaya Voyna*, vol. 2, pp. 341–342.

33. RGASPI, f. 495, op. 277, d. 19, incoming 1943 from Yugoslavia, ll. 187–185; coded dispatch of 7 April 1943.

34. RGASPI, f. 495, op. 184, d. 20, incoming 1943 from Yugoslavia, l. 32, received 10 September 1943; d. 5, outgoing 1943 to Yugoslavia, l. 49, ms.; Lebedeva and Narinski, *Komintern i Vtoraya Mirovaya Voyna*, vol. 2, p. 399.

35. RGASPI, f. 495, op. 184, d. 11, outgoing 1941 to Yugoslavia, l. 53, ms., handwriting of Sorkin; ibid., l. 64, ms., handwriting of Sorkin, coded dispatch of 14 August 1941.

36. RGASPI, f. 495, op. 184, d. 5, incoming 1940 from Yugoslavia, l. 83, received 25 September 1940; Dimitrov, *Dnevnik*, p. 247; Dimitroff, *Tagebücher*,

p. 417; Dimitrov, *The Diary of Georgi Dimitrov*, p. 191; RGASPI, f. 495, op. 184, d. 11, outgoing 1941 to Yugoslavia, l. 68, coded dispatch of 23 August 1941.

37. RGASPI, f. 495, op. 184, d. 11, outgoing 1941 to Yugoslavia, l. 71, coded dispatch of 26 August 1941; op. 73, d. 124, l. 4, coded dispatch of 23 February 1942.

38. RGASPI, f. 495, op. 184, d. 10, outgoing 1942 to Yugoslavia, l. 72, coded dispatch of 29 June 1942.

39. RGASPI, f. 495, op. 184, d. 10, incoming 1942 from Yugoslavia, l. 114, sent 31 August 1942, received 1 September; ibid., l. 106, coded dispatch of 19 September 1942; ibid., l. 112, coded dispatch of 26 September 1942. No further information about Makhin or his fate could be located.

40. RGASPI, f. 495, op. 73, d. 141, l. 20; op. 184, d. 10, outgoing 1942 to Yugoslavia, l. 68, coded dispatch of 12 June 1942; d. 5, outgoing 1943 to Yugoslavia, l. 101, coded dispatch of 8 November 1943; d. 20, incoming 1943 from Yugoslavia, l. 218, received 12 November 1943.

41. RGASPI, f. 495, op. 184, d. 7, incoming 1941 from Yugoslavia, sent 20 September 1941, received 28 September, deciphered 28 September; ibid., l. 191, sent 3 October 1941, received 5 October, deciphered 5 October.

42. RGASPI, f. 495, op. 184, d. 11, outgoing 1941 to Yugoslavia, l. 50, coded dispatch of 2 July 1941; Lebedeva and Narinski, *Komintern i Vtoraya Mirovaya Voyna*, vol. 2, p. 112.

43. RGASPI, f. 495, op. 184, d. 10, incoming 1942 from Yugoslavia, l. 1, sent 27 July 1942, received 29 July; RGASPI, f. 495, op. 184, d. 10, outgoing 1942 to Yugoslavia, l. 133, coded dispatch of 10 December 1942.

44. RGASPI, f. 495, op. 184, d. 8, outgoing 1943 to Slovenia, l. 3; ibid., l. 11, coded dispatch of 23 March 1943; d. 16, incoming 1943 from Slovenia, l. 74, coded dispatch of 17 April 1943.

45. RGASPI, f. 495, op. 184, d. 16, incoming 1943 from Slovenia, l. 55, coded dispatch of 16 March 1943; d. 8, outgoing 1943 to Slovenia, l. 11, coded dispatch of 23 March 1943.

46. RGASPI, f. 495, op. 184, d. 19, incoming 1943 from Yugoslavia, l. 290, sent 7 June 1943, received 8 June, deciphered 8 June; ibid., incoming 1943 from Yugoslavia, ll. 295–294, received 25 June 1943.

47. RGASPI, f. 495, op. 184, d. 5, outgoing 1943 to Yugoslavia, l. 37, coded dispatch of 23 June 1943.

48. Dimitrov, *Dnevnik*, p. 248; Dimitroff, *Tagebücher*, p. 419; Dimitrov, *The Diary of Georgi Dimitrov*, p. 191.

49. RGASPI, f. 495, op. 184, d. 18, incoming 1942 from Poland, l. 39, sent 17 July 1942, received 18 July.

50. RGASPI, f. 495, op. 184, d. 3, outgoing 1942 to Poland, l. 16; d. 18, incoming 1942 from Poland, l. 60, sent 30 July 1942, received 31 July.

51. RGASPI, f. 495, op. 184, d. 3, outgoing 1942 to Poland, l. 35; ibid., l. 68, coded dispatch of 4 November 1942; Lebedeva and Narinski, *Komintern i Vtoraya Mirovaya Voyna*, vol. 2, p. 264.

52. RGASPI, f. 495, op. 184, d. 18, incoming 1942 from Poland, l. 176, sent 10 November 1942, received 12 November.

53. RGASPI, f. 495, op. 184, d. 18, ll. 97–96, sent 9 September 1942, received 11 September.

54. RGASPI, f. 495, op. 184, d. 3, outgoing 1942 to Poland, l. 67, coded dispatch of 31 October 1942; Lebedeva and Narinski, *Komintern i Vtoraya Mirovaya Voyna*, vol. 2, pp. 262–263.

55. RGASPI, f. 495, op. 184, d. 18, incoming 1942 from Poland, ll. 188–187, sent 21 November 1942, received 23 November. Anton Krajewski (real name Władysław Stein) was one of the founders of the Communist Party of Poland and a member of its Central Committee. In 1932 he became the head of the ECCI Personnel Department, and from 1935 he was a member of the Comintern ICC. On 26 May 1937 he was arrested by the NKVD and was executed.

56. RGASPI, f. 495, op. 184, d. 3, outgoing 1942 to Poland, l. 77, coded dispatch of 23 November 1942.

57. RGASPI, f. 495, op. 184, d. 18, incoming 1942 from Poland, l. 193; Lebedeva and Narinski, *Komintern i Vtoraya Mirovaya Voyna*, vol. 2, p. 277.

58. RGASPI, f. 495, op. 184, d. 3, outgoing 1942 to Poland, l. 84, coded dispatch of 5 December 1942; Lebedeva and Narinski, *Komintern i Vtoraya Mirovaya Voyna*, vol. 2, p. 184; RGASPI, f. 495, op. 184, d. 18, incoming 1942 from Poland, l. 196, sent 7 December 1942, received 7 December; ibid., l. 202, sent 17 December 1942, received 17 December.

59. RGASPI, f. 495, op. 184, d. 22, incoming 1943 from Poland, ll. 8–5; coded dispatch of 8 January 1943; Lebedeva and Narinski, *Komintern i Vtoraya Mirovaya Voyna*, vol. 2, pp. 308–309. Aleksander Kowalski, engaged in underground work in Poland from May 1942, was a member of the CC of the PWP. Teodor Duracz, a lawyer by profession, was a veteran Polish Communist.

60. RGASPI, f. 495, op. 184, d. 9, outgoing 1943 to Poland, l. 4, coded dispatch of 10 January 1943; Lebedeva and Narinski, *Komintern i Vtoraya Mirovaya Voyna*, vol. 2, p. 310; RGASPI, f. 495, op. 184, d. 22, incoming 1943 from Poland, l. 31, sent 17 January 1943, received 19 January; ibid., ll. 53–52, sent 29 January 1943, received 30 January.

61. RGASPI, f. 495, op. 184, d. 22, incoming 1943 from Poland, l. 333, received 14 June 1943; ibid., l. 38; op. 74, d. 425, l. 35, letter of 9 July 1943; Lebedeva and Narinski, *Komintern i Vtoraya Mirovaya Voyna*, vol. 2, pp. 383, 384.

62. RGASPI, f. 495, op. 184, d. 22, incoming 1943 from Poland, ll. 103–102, sent 18 February 1943, received 21 February.

63. RGASPI, f. 495, op. 184, d. 22, incoming 1943 from Poland, ll. 117–116, sent 24 February 1943, received 26 February; ibid., ll. 287–286; coded dispatch of 20 May 1943; ibid., l. 123, coded dispatch of 12 March 1943; d. 9, outgoing 1943 to Poland, l. 20, coded dispatch of 2 March 1943; Lebedeva and Narinski, *Komintern i Vtoraya Mirovaya Voyna*, vol. 2, p. 330.

64. RGASPI, f. 495, op. 184, d. 9, outgoing 1943 to Poland, ll. 47–46; coded dispatch of 2 April 1943; Lebedeva and Narinski, *Komintern i Vtoraya Mirovaya Voyna*, vol. 2, pp. 343–344.

65. RGASPI, f. 495, op. 184, d. 9, outgoing 1943 to Poland, l. 64, coded dispatch of 21 April 1943.

66. RGASPI, f. 495, op. 184, d. 22, incoming 1943 from Poland, l. 233, sent 22 April 1943, received 28 April; ibid., l. 224, coded dispatch of 27 April 1943; ibid., l. 225, coded dispatch of 27 April 1943; d. 9, outgoing 1943 to Poland, ll. 66–65; Lebedeva and Narinski, *Komintern i Vtoraya Mirovaya Voyna*, vol. 2, pp. 348–349.

67. RGASPI, f. 495, op. 184, d. 22, incoming 1943 from Poland, l. 289, coded dispatch of 22 May 1943; ibid., ll. 248–247, sent 5 May 1943, received 7 May; ibid., l. 348, sent 20 June 1943, received 22 June.

68. *Katyn'. Dokumenty ludobójstwa: Dokumenty i materialy archiwalne przekazane Polsce 14 października 1992 r.*, ed. Ewa Wosik (Warsaw: Instytut Studiów Politycznych Polskiej Akademii Nauk, 1992).

69. RGASPI, f. 495, op. 184, d. 18, ll. 141–140, sent 20 October 1942, received 22 October.

70. RGASPI, f. 495, op. 184, d. 22, incoming 1943 from Poland, l. 221, sent 21 April 1943, received 23 April; ibid., l. 223, sent 24 April 1943, received 26 April; ibid., l. 270, sent 14 May 1943, received 16 May.

71. RGASPI, f. 495, op. 184, d. 13, outgoing 1941 to France, l. 12, ms., coded dispatch of 25 June 1941; Bayerlein, Narinski, Studer, and Wolikow, eds., *Moscou-Paris-Berlin*, pp. 442, 458; Lebedeva and Narinski, *Komintern i Vtoraya Mirovaya Voyna*, vol. 2, p. 102

72. RGASPI, f. 495, op. 184, d. 5, outgoing 1941 to France, coded dispatch of 11 August 1941; d. 8, incoming 1941 from France l. 286, received 6 September 1941; d. 9, incoming 1941 from France, sent 9 December 1941, received 16 December; ibid., sent 14 December, received 23 December; Bayerlein, Narinski, Studer, and Wolikow, eds., *Moscou-Paris-Berlin*, pp. 468–470, 521–523, 527–528; Lebedeva and Narinski, *Komintern i Vtoraya Mirovaya Voyna*, vol. 2, pp. 142–143.

73. RGASPI, f. 495, op. 184, d. 9, incoming 1941 from France, sent 26 December 1941, received 31 December; ibid., sent 22 December 1941, received 27 December.

74. RGASPI, f. 495, op. 184, d. 8, outgoing 1942 to France, ll. 10, 8, coded dispatch of 10 February 1942; Lebedeva and Narinski, *Komintern i Vtoraya Mirovaya Voyna*, vol. 2, pp. 195–198.

75. RGASPI, f. 495, op. 184, d. 13, incoming 1942 from France, l. 12, sent 25 February 1942, received 4 March; d. 5, incoming 1941–1942 from Ufa, l. 331, received 19 March 1942; d. 13, incoming 1942 from France, l. 143, sent 13 August 1942, received 4 September; ibid., l. 96, sent 13 August 1942, received 7 September; ibid., l. 195, sent 29 November 1942, received 1 December; d. 15, incoming 1943 from France, ll. 190–189, sent 24 May 1943, received 31 May.

76. RGASPI, f. 495, op. 184, d. 8, outgoing 1942 to France, l. 151, coded dispatch of 25 December 1942; ibid., l. 108, coded dispatch of 31 December 1942; d. 14, outgoing 1943 to France, l. 70, coded dispatch of 15 September 1943 (Ivan Bolshakov's letter of 10 September 1943).

77. RGASPI, f. 495, op. 184, d. 14, outgoing 1943 to France, l. 62, coded dispatch of 6 October 1943, ms.; Kriegel and Courtois, *Eugen Fried*, pp. 389–390. Paul Langevin, a French physicist, was an active participant in the antifascist movement.

78. RGASPI, f. 495, op. 184, d. 18, outgoing 1942 from Ufa, l. 277, received 19 March 1942; d. 6, incoming 1942 from France, l. 88, received 26 March 1942; d. 4, incoming 1943 from France, l. 103, received 4 November 1943; Kriegel and Courtois, *Eugen Fried*, p. 394.

79. RGASPI, f. 495, op. 184, d. 6, incoming 1942 from France, l. 94, received 8 September 1942; ibid., l. 197, sent 21 September 1942, received 23 September; d. 15, incoming 1943 from France, l. 36, sent 29 January 1943, received 4 February.

80. RGASPI, f. 495, op. 184, d. 6, incoming 1942 from France, l. 111, sent 2 May 1942, received 6 May; d. 8, outgoing 1942 to France, l. 39, ms., handwriting of Dimitrov.

81. RGASPI, f. 495, op. 74, d. 528, ll. 1, 2, letter of 3 December 1942; Lebedeva and Narinski, *Komintern i Vtoraya Mirovaya Voyna*, vol. 2, pp. 270, 275; RGASPI, f. 495, op. 184, d. 4, outgoing 1942 to France, l. 238.

82. RGASPI, f. 495, op. 184, d. 8, outgoing 1942 to France, l. 105, coded dispatch of 31 December 1942; d. 15, incoming 1943 from France, ll. 110–109, sent 14 March 1943, received 24 March; ibid., ll. 176–172, sent 16 May 1943, received 22 May; d. 2, incoming 1943 from France, ll. 42–41, received 13 October 1943.

83. RGASPI, f. 495, op. 73, d. 124, l. 1, letter of 7 February 1942; ibid., ll. 7, 8, 11–14, coded dispatches of 28 February and 2, 4, 20, and 23 March 1942; op. 184, d. 14, incoming 1942, to Ufa, l. 111, ms., handwriting of Sorkin, coded dispatch of 8 February 1942.

84. RGASPI, f. 495, op. 184, d. 13, incoming 1942 from France, l. 2, sent 10 February 1942, received 11 February; d. 18, outgoing 1942 from Ufa, l. 178, coded dispatch of 20 February 1942.

85. RGASPI, f. 495, op. 184, d. 5, outgoing 1941 to France, coded dispatch of 14 December 1941, ms.; Fridrikh Firsov, "Die Komintern—Außenpolitisches Instrument des Stalin'schen Regimes," *Mittelweg 36*, no. 1 (2010): 88–89.

86. RGASPI, f. 495, op. 184, d. 5, incoming 1941–1942 from Ufa, l. 60, coded dispatch from Belgium of 22 December 1941; ibid., outgoing 1941 to France, coded dispatch of 14 December 1941, ms.; Kriegel and Courtois, *Eugen Fried*, p. 376; Valentin Tomin, *Bol'shoy shef Krasnoy kapelly* (Moscow: Eksmo, Yauza, 2005), pp. 52–53, 106, 151.

87. See Heinz Hohne, *Code-Word Direktor: The Story of the Red Orchestra* (New York: Ballantine Books, 1971). Wenzel had been a member of the Communist Party of Germany from 1923. After being arrested and tortured, he tried to commit suicide, then agreed to work for the Nazis but later escaped. In January 1945 he was sent to Moscow, arrested, and sentenced to ten years' imprisonment. He was freed in 1954, returned to Berlin, and died on 2 February 1969.

88. RGASPI, f. 495, op. 184, d. 8, outgoing 1942 to France, l. 63, coded dispatch of 1 September 1942; ibid., l. 63, coded dispatch of 9 September 1942.

89. RGASPI, f. 495, op. 184, d. 2, incoming 1942 from Holland, l. 89, sent 9 October 1942, received 12 October; ibid., l. 143, sent 15 November 1942, received 18 November; d. 6, outgoing 1942 to Holland, l. 127, coded dispatch of unspecified day in November 1942.

90. RGASPI, f. 495, op. 184, d. 13, incoming 1942 from France, l. 258, sent 22 December 1942, received 29 December.

91. Leopold Trepper, *Bol'shaya igra* (Moscow: Politizdat, 1990), p. 229. Translation from the French.

92. Sergei Poltorak, *Razvedchik Kent* (St Petersburg: Neva, 2003), p. 419; RGASPI, f. 495, op. 184, d. 15, incoming 1943 from France, l. 7, received 9 January 1943.

93. RGASPI, f. 495, op. 184, d. 14, outgoing 1943 to France, l. 8.

94. RGASPI, f. 495, op. 184, d. 14, outgoing 1943 to France, l. 11; ibid., l. 24, coded dispatch of 16 April 1943. Three days later a modification went out: "Urgently notify Michel that Leo requests to meet with him at Rueil Malmaison; he should arrive there by train after 14 h. [2 p.m.]" (ibid., l. 27, coded dispatch of 19 April 1943.) Trepper claims that details of these meetings were arranged via one of the German-controlled transmitters, but clearly it was the Comintern communications network being used.

95. RGASPI, f. 495, op. 184, d. 15, incoming 1943 from France, l. 184. According to Trepper, Michel was still at liberty in late 1943.

96. RGASPI, f. 495, op. 184, d. 6, incoming 1943 from France (through Belgium), l. 193, received 7 July 1943, deciphered 7 July; d. 15, incoming 1943 from France, l. 199, received 6 June 1943, deciphered 6 June; Kontra is an abbreviated form of the word *kontrrazvedka* (counterintelligence). Otto is Trepper, André is Leo Groosvogel, René is Hillel Katz, and Harry is Henry Robinson.

97. RGASPI, f. 495, op. 184, d. 15, incoming 1943 from France, l. 205, received 19 June 1943, deciphered 19 June.

98. RGASPI, f. 495, op. 184, d. 6, incoming 1943 from Belgium, l. 154, received 19 June 1943; Kriegel and Courtois, *Eugen Fried*, p. 389; RGASPI, f. 495, op. 184, d. 6, incoming 1943 from France (through Belgium), l. 193, received 7 July 1943, deciphered 7 July.

99. RGASPI, f. 495, op. 184, d. 6, incoming 1943 from France (through Belgium), l. 192, received 7 July 1943, deciphered 7 July. Henry Robinson was a senior Comintern official and Soviet intelligence agent. Arrested by the Gestapo in late December 1942, he was executed in 1944. Kent's real name was Anatoly Gurevich. A professional Soviet intelligence agent, he worked in Brussels from July 1939. He relocated to Marseilles in December 1941, where he was arrested by the Gestapo on 12 November 1942. While he cooperated with the Germans, he refused to name Soviet agents he had previously recruited. In April 1945 he convinced Gestapo officer Heinz Pannwitz, chief investigator of the Red Orchestra, and two of his assistants to surrender to the Red Army. After Gurevich arrived in Moscow, he was arrested and convicted for collaboration. He was freed in 1955, arrested again in 1958, released in 1960, and finally rehabilitated in 1991.

100. RGASPI, f. 495, op. 184, d. 14, outgoing 1943 to France, l. 49, coded dispatch of 12 July 1943, ms.; d. 4, incoming 1943 from France, l. 73, received 9 August 1943, deciphered 9 August.

101. RGASPI, f. 495, op. 184, d. 6, incoming 1943 from Belgium, l. 179; d. 14, outgoing 1943 to France, l. 58, coded dispatch of 20 August 1943, ms., handwriting of Dimitrov.

102. RGASPI, f. 495, op. 184, d. 4, incoming 1943 from France, l. 91, received 1 November 1943, deciphered 1 November; d. 14, outgoing 1943 to France, l. 75, coded dispatch of 22 November 1943.

103. RGASPI, f. 495, op. 184, d. 14, incoming 1941 from France, l. 172, sent 25 June 1941, received 30 June; Bayerlein, Narinski, Studer, and Wolikow, eds., *Moscou-Paris-Berlin*, p. 440; Kriegel and Courtois, *Eugen Fried*, p. 370; RGASPI, f. 495, op. 184, d. 14, incoming 1941 from France, l. 174, sent 29 June 1941, received 1 July; d. 5, outgoing 1941 to France, coded dispatch of 15 July 1941; ibid., l. 41, coded dispatch of 30 July 1941.

104. RGASPI, f. 495, op. 184, d. 6, incoming 1942 from France l. 70, coded dispatch of 20 February 1942; d. 11, outgoing 1942 to Belgium, l. 59, coded dispatch of 11 November 1942; Kriegel and Courtois, *Eugen Fried*, p. 378.

105. RGASPI, f. 495, op. 184, d. 6, incoming 1942 from France, l. 220, sent 19 November 1942, received 22 November; Kriegel and Courtois, *Eugen Fried*, p. 378; RGASPI, f. 495, op. 184, d. 6, incoming 1942 from France, l. 224; coded dispatch sent 21 November 1942, received 23 November; ibid., l. 20, sent 11 February 1943, received 18 February.

106. RGASPI, f. 495, op. 184, d. 6, incoming 1943 from Belgium, l. 166, coded dispatch received 8 July 1943; ibid., outgoing 1943 to Belgium, l. 18, coded dispatch of 10 July 1943.

107. RGASPI, f. 495, op. 184, d. 6, incoming 1943 from Belgium, l. 106, sent 6 May 1943, received 10 May, deciphered 10 May; ibid., outgoing 1943 to Belgium, coded dispatch of 13 May 1943; Kriegel and Courtois, *Eugen Fried*, p. 380.

108. RGASPI, f. 495, op. 184, d. 6, incoming 1943 from Belgium, l. 201, coded dispatch of 24 July 1943; ibid., l. 205, coded dispatch of 9 August 1943; ibid., outgoing 1943 to Belgium, ms., l. 20, coded dispatch of 9 August 1943; d. 14, l. 56, outgoing 1943 to France, coded dispatch of 10 August 1943, ms.; ibid., l. 60, ms.; d. 2, incoming 1943 from France, l. 37, sent 24 September 1943, received 28 September, deciphered 28 September; Kriegel and Courtois, *Eugen Fried*, p. 378, 387–389; Lebedeva and Narinski, *Komintern i Vtoraya Mirovaya Voyna*, vol. 2, p. 398; Branko Lazitch in collaboration with Milorad M. Drachkovitch, *The Biographical Dictionary of the Comintern, New, Revised, and Expanded Edition* (Stanford, CA: Hoover Institution, 1985), p. 125, reports that some ex-Communists believed Clément (Fried) had been executed by the party on orders from Moscow.

109. RGASPI, f. 495, op. 184, d. 1, outgoing 1941 to Holland, coded dispatch of 29 July 1941; ibid., coded dispatch of 2 September 1941, coded dispatch of 12 September 1941.

110. RGASPI, f. 495, op. 74, d. 170, l. 3, letter of 3 August 1943; op. 184, d. 6, outgoing 1942 to Holland, l. 80, coded dispatch of unspecified day in November 1942, ms.; ibid., l. 122, coded dispatch of 10 November 1942; d. 13, incoming 1943 from Holland, l. 51, sent 4 March 1943, received 6 March, deciphered 6 March; *The Rote Kapelle: The CIA's History of Soviet Intelligence and Espionage Networks in Western Europe, 1936–1945* (Washington, D.C.: University Publications of America, 1979), p. 71.

111. RGASPI, f. 495, op. 184, d. 2, incoming 1942 from Holland, sent 18 December 1941, received 30 December.

112. RGASPI, f. 495, op. 184, d. 5, outgoing 1941 to France, coded dispatch of 16 September 1941, ms., handwriting of Sorkin.

113. RGASPI, f. 495, op. 184, d. 1, outgoing 1941 to Holland, coded dispatch of unspecified day in July 1941, ms., handwriting of Pieck.

114. RGASPI, f. 495, op. 184, d. 2, outgoing 1941 to Holland, coded dispatch of 29 December 1941; d. 1, incoming 1941 from Holland, l. 72, sent 30 March 1942, received 31 March; Lebedeva and Narinski, *Komintern i Vtoraya Mirovaya Voyna*, vol. 2, p. 170.

115. RGASPI, f. 495, op. 184, d. 6, outgoing 1942 to Holland, ll. 61–62, coded dispatch of 27 June 1942; ibid., l. 14, coded dispatch of 1 May 1942, ms., handwriting of Dimitrov.

116. RGASPI, f. 495, op. 184, d. 13, incoming 1943 from Holland, l. 13, sent 19 January 1943, received 25 January; d. 2, outgoing 1943 to Holland, l. 11, ms., coded dispatch of 20 February 1943; d. 13, incoming 1943 from Holland, l. 40, sent 21 February 1943, received 23 February; ibid., l. 43., received 27 February 1943, deciphered 27 February; d. 2, outgoing 1943 to Holland, l. 12, coded dispatch of 2 March 1943; ibid., l. 16, coded dispatch of 2 March 1943, ms.

117. *Gestapo-Berichte über den antifaschistischen Widerstanskampf der KPD 1933 bis 1945. Band 1. Anfang 1933 bis August 1939*, ed. Margot Pikarski and Elke Warning (Berlin: Dietz Verlag, 1989), p. 66; RGASPI, f. 495, op. 184, d. 14, outgoing 1943 to France, l. 26, coded dispatch of 14 April 1943, ms. Knöchel was executed in 1944.

118. RGASPI, f. 495, op. 184, d. 13, incoming 1943 from Holland, l. 125a, coded dispatch of 1 May 1943, ms., handwriting of Sorkin; d. 2, outgoing 1943 to Holland, l. 60, coded dispatch of 20 May 1943.

119. RGASPI, f. 495, op. 184, d. 6, outgoing 1943 to Belgium, l. 19, ms.; op. 74, d. 170, l. 32; Kriegel and Courtois, *Eugen Fried*, p. 384.

120. RGASPI, f. 495, op. 73, d. 112, ll. 7–8, coded dispatch of 9 July 1941.

121. RGASPI, f. 495, op. 74, d. 84, l. 5.

122. Dimitrov, *Dnevnik*, p. 243; Dimitroff, *Tagebücher*, p. 409; Dimitrov, *The Diary of Georgi Dimitrov*, p. 187; Trendafila Angelova, *Georgi Dimitrov i bor'ba Bolgarskoy kommunisticheskoy party za obyedineniye demokraticheskikh sil protiv fashizma i voyny, za pobedu sotsialisticheskoy revoliutsy v Bolgary (1934–1944 gg.) in Georgi Dimitrov—vydayushchiysiya deyatel' kommunisticheskogo dvizhenia* (Moscow: Politizdat, 1972), p. 504; RGASPI, f. 495, op. 184, d. 13, incoming 1941 from Bulgaria, sent 12 August 1941; ibid., sent 12 August 1941, received 16 August.

123. RGASPI, f. 495, op. 184, d. 5, incoming 1941–1942 from Ufa, ms.; op. 74, d. 85, ll. 7–9, coded dispatch of 20 January 1942; op. 184, d. 18, outgoing 1941–1942 from Ufa, l. 249, coded dispatch of 10 March 1942; Lebedeva and Narinski, *Komintern i Vtoraya Mirovaya Voyna*, vol. 2, pp. 187–190, 202–203.

124. RGASPI, f. 495, op. 74, d. 90, l. 8.

125. RGASPI, f. 495, op. 74, d. 84, l. 16, letter of 15 April 1942.

126. Dimitrov, *Dnevnik*, p. 286; Dimitroff, *Tagebücher*, pp. 504–505.

127. RGASPI, f. 495, op. 184, d. 8, outgoing 1941 to Sweden, coded dispatch of 13 July 1941; ibid., l. 45, coded dispatch of 21 September 1941.

128. RGASPI, f. 495, op. 73, d. 141, l. 8; Lebedeva and Narinski, *Komintern i Vtoraya Mirovaya Voyna*, vol. 2, p. 171; RGASPI, f. 495, op. 184, d. 2, outgoing 1942 to Sweden, l. 47, coded dispatch of 9 September 1942; ibid., l. 53, coded dispatch of 30 September 1942.

129. RGASPI, f. 495, op. 184, d. 17, outgoing 1943 to Sweden, l. 8, coded dispatch of 20 March 1943; Lebedeva and Narinski, *Komintern i Vtoraya Mirovaya Voyna*, vol. 2, pp. 340–341.

130. RGASPI, f. 495, op. 184, d. 13, outgoing 1942 to Denmark, l. 3, coded dispatch of 7 September 1942. Larsen had been a member of the Communist Party of Denmark since 1921, its chairman since 1932. Arrested by the Germans in November 1942, he was a concentration camp prisoner until liberation in 1945. In 1958 he was expelled from the Communist Party of Denmark.

131. RGASPI, f. 495, op. 184, d. 13, outgoing to Denmark, l. 6, coded dispatch of 21 September 1942.

132. RGASPI, f. 495, op. 184, d. 5, outgoing 1942 to New York, l. 11, ms., handwriting of Sorkin.

133. RGASPI, f. 495, op. 184, d. 19, incoming 1942 from the United States, l. 48, sent 10 April 1942, received 14 April.

134. RGASPI, f. 495, op. 74, d. 484, l. 31, letter of 13 May 1942; Klehr, Haynes, and Firsov, *The Secret World*, p. 262.

135. RGASPI, f. 495, op. 184, d. 5, outgoing 1942 to New York, l. 24, coded dispatch of 14 May 1942.

136. RGASPI, f. 495, op. 74, d. 484, ll. 14–15; Fitin's letter of 1 June 1942; Klehr, Haynes, and Firsov, *The Secret World*, pp. 260–280.

137. RGASPI, f. 495, op. 184, d. 5, outgoing 1942 to New York, l. 28, coded dispatch of 5 June 1942. The involvement of International Brigades veterans, the CPUSA's covert arm, and the American OSS and negative reaction of the Comintern and Soviet intelligence to the interaction was discussed earlier in Klehr, Haynes, and Firsov, *The Secret World*, pp. 259–276.

CHAPTER 10. DISSOLUTION OF THE COMMUNIST INTERNATIONAL

1. Dimitrov, *Dnevnik*, p. 227; Dimitrov *Tagebücher*, p. 374; Dimitrov, *The Diary of Georgi Dimitrov*, p. 155.

2. Dimitrov, *Dnevnik*, p. 228; Dimitroff, *Tagebücher*, p. 375; Dimitrov, *The Diary of Georgi Dimitrov*, pp. 162–164.

3. RGASPI, f. 495, op. 73, d. 165, l. 20, letter of 20 February 1943; *Pravda*, 22 February 1943; Dimitrov, *Dnevnik*, p. 365; Dimitroff, *Tagebücher*, p. 652; Dimitrov, *The Diary of Georgi Dimitrov*, p. 261.

4. Dimitrov, *Dnevnik*, p. 372; Dimitroff, *Tagebücher*, p. 688; Dimitrov, *The Diary of Georgi Dimitrov*, p. 270.

5. RGASPI, f. 495, op. 73, d. 174, l. 1; Dallin and Firsov, eds., *Dimitrov and Stalin, 1934–1943*, p. 229; Dimitrov, *Dnevnik*, p. 372; Dimitroff, *Tagebücher*, p. 679; Dimitrov, *The Diary of Georgi Dimitrov*, p. 271

6. Dimitrov, *The Diary of Georgi Dimitrov*, pp. 271–273.

7. RGASPI, f. 495, op. 73, d. 174, l. 55; Dallin and Firsov, eds., *Dimitrov and Stalin 1934–1943*, p. 250; Lebedeva and Narinski, *Komintern i Vtoraya Mirovaya Voyna*, vol. 2, p. 368; Dimitrov, *Dnevnik*, p. 374; Dimitroff, *Tagebücher*, p. 694; Dimitrov, *The Diary of Georgi Dimitrov*, pp. 273–274.

8. Dimitrov, *Dnevnik*, p. 374; Dimitroff, *Tagebücher*, p. 694; Dimitrov, *The Diary of Georgi Dimitrov*, p. 274.

9. RGASPI, f. 495, op. 184, d. 5, outgoing 1943 to Yugoslavia, l. 31; d. 2, outgoing 1943 to Holland, l. 59; d. 14, outgoing 1943 to France, l. 37, ms.; Lebedeva and Narinski, *Komintern i Vtoraya Mirovaya Voyna*, vol. 2, p. 370.

10. Dimitrov, *Dnevnik*, p. 375; Dimitroff, *Tagebücher*, pp. 694–695; Dimitrov, *The Diary of Georgi Dimitrov*, pp. 275–276.

11. Dimitrov, *The Diary of Georgi Dimitrov*, pp. 276–277.

12. Dimitrov, *The Diary of Georgi Dimitrov*, pp. 277–280

13. RGASPI, f. 495, op. 73, d. 174, l. 57, letter of 31 May 1943; Dallin and Firsov, eds., *Dimitrov and Stalin, 1934–1943*, pp. 251–252; RGASPI, f. 495,

op. 184, d. 15, incoming 1943 from France, l. 215, sent 15 June 1943, received 21 June, deciphered 21 June; ibid., l. 252, received 12 June, deciphered 12 June.

14. Dimitrov, *The Diary of Georgi Dimitrov*, pp. 277–278.

15. RGASPI, f. 495, op. 184, d. 5, outgoing 1943 to Yugoslavia, l. 36, coded dispatch of 4 June 1943; Kriegel and Courtois, *Eugen Fried*, pp. 383–384; Lebedeva and Narinski, *Komintern i Vtoraya Mirovaya Voyna*, vol. 2, pp. 375–376.

16. RGASPI, f. 495, op. 184, d. 22, incoming 1943 from Poland, l. 333, sent 12 June 1943, received 14 June. The fate of the three Lipski brothers, all senior members of the prewar Polish Communist Party, is discussed above in chapter 9.

17. The Soviet origin of the Duclos article is documented in Klehr, Haynes, and Anderson, *The Soviet World*, pp. 91–106.

18. See I. V. Stalin, *O Velikoy Otechestvennoy voyne Sovetskogo Soiuza* (Moscow: Gospolitizdat, 1951), pp. 107–108. Referring to the contents of the decree of the ECCI Presidium, the works of Soviet historians assert that the reasons for the disbandment of the Comintern were the maturity and independence of the Communist parties and the impossibility of running their activities from a single center in wartime conditions. The senior author of this book also previously shared this opinion.

19. RGASPI, f. 495, op. 184, d. 15, outgoing 1943 to China, l. 24, coded dispatch of 10 June 1943; Dallin and Firsov, eds., *Dimitrov and Stalin, 1934–1943*, p. 255.

Conclusion

1. The Brooklyn Bridge was one of the oldest and for many years the longest cable suspension bridge in the United States. Joseph R. Starobin, *American Communism in Crisis, 1943–1957* (Cambridge, MA: Harvard University Press, 1972), p. 262.

2. Starobin, *American Communism in Crisis*, p. 223. Starobin was referring specifically to the CPUSA.

Index

Abetz, Otto, 171, 172
Abraham Lincoln Brigade, 235
Abramov, Alexander, 15, 18, 19, 21, 26
Aftenposten, 118
Alpari, Julius, 118
Anarcho-syndicalists, 264n29
Anderson, Kyrill, 3
Andreyev, Andrei, 43, 186
Antifascist Assembly for the People's Liberation of Yugoslavia (AVNOYu), 196–197
Anti-Imperialist League, 45–46
Anti-Semitism. *See* Jewish persecution
Anti-Soviet United Trotskyist-Zinovievite Center, 112
Antwerp dockers' strike, 8
Argentine Communist Party, money disbursement to, 42
Asencio, José, 96
Asnos, Leonardo (Peterson), 89
Austrian Communist Party: foreign bureau in USSR, 240; money disbursement to, 38, 40
Azaña, Manuel, 68, 77

Baker, Rudy, 176; background of, 34; clandestine contact to CPUSA, 20, 34–35; coded message transmission of, 36, 37; money transmission of, 41, 42–43
Baltic states: and Nazi-Soviet Pact, 141; Sovietization of, 151
Bamatter, Sigi, 26
Barron, Victor Allen, 28, 29
Bayerlein, Bernhard H., 3
Bedacht, Max, 46, 188
Belgian Communist Party, 8; antifascist mobilization of, 225–227; and anti-Trotskyite campaign, 113; and German resistance to Nazis, 228; money disbursement to, 39; and Nazi occupiers, 171; Nazi-Soviet Pact policy directives to, 153; Nazi-Soviet Pact response of, 144
Belgium, Nazi invasion of, 168
Bell, Thomas, 44
Beneš, Edvard, 161, 162
Benz, Irina (Rosa Gartman), 25
Beria, Lavrenty, 130, 135, 205, 208, 240
Berzin, Jan, 41
Bessarabia, 141
Bielewski (Jan Paszyn), 126
Blagoeva, Stella, 150
Blum, Léon, 57, 58, 59, 60, 62, 66
Blum, Rudolf. *See* Baker, Rudy
Bogomolov, Alexander, 216–217
Bolshakov, Ivan, 242
Bolshevik Revolution: anniversary of, 8–9; campaign against opponents of, 111–123
Bonnet, Georges (French foreign minister), 64
Boris, Tsar of Bulgaria, 156, 159, 231, 232
Brazilian Communist Party: Comintern files on, 15; money disbursement to, 42; uprising of, 28–29

Britain: decryption project in, 3, 19–20; Free French (Gaullists) in, 180; in Munich Agreement, 63; and Soviet-Finnish War, 175; Soviet intelligence in, 191; and Yugoslav invasion, 182; Yugoslav military mission of, 195–196
British Communist Party: decryption of messages, 19–20; International Brigade recruitment of, 88; and London manifesto, 167–168; money disbursement to, 40, 45; Nazi-Soviet Pact policy directives to, 147, 152–153; Nazi-Soviet Pact response of, 143
British Government Code and Cipher School (GC&GS), 19
Browder, Earl, 1, 37, 67, 176, 181; and Comintern contacts in U.S., 32, 34, 35; and dissolution of Comintern, 243; military aid to International Brigades, 91; and money disbursement, 32–33, 46, 47; and radio transmission, 35, 36; recruitment for International Brigades, 86, 88, 90, 100, 101; resettlement of International Brigades volunteers, 107, 109
Brunfaut, Fernand, 113
Bukharin, Nikolai, 2, 111
Bukharinists, 111
Bulgaria: pro-Nazi policy in, 231, 232–233; -Soviet pact proposal, 155–156, 157, 158–159, 278n45; in Tripartite Pact, 157–158
Bulgarian Communist Party, 201; antifascist mobilization of, 231–233; foreign bureau in USSR, 240; money disbursement to, 40, 49; Nazi-Soviet Pact policy directives to, 153–160; Nazi-Soviet Pact response of, 144

Cachin, Marcel, 65, 215, 216
Cadras, Félix, 215
Campbell, John, 148
Canadian Communist Party, 186
Catelas, Jean, 171
Chamberlain, Neville, 63, 64, 153, 161
Chambers, Whittaker, 188
Checa, Pedro, 75, 76, 83, 104
Chetniks (Serbian resistance movement), 194–195, 196, 200
Chiang Kai-shek, 128, 131–132, 133, 134, 135, 137, 138, 139
Chilean Communist Party, money disbursement to, 42
Chinese Communist Party: Comintern files of, 14; defeat of KMT, 139; military aid to, 133–134; money disbursement to, 44, 49, 129, 135; and resettlement of International Brigade volunteers, 108; Special Region, 128, 129, 130, 133, 134; in United Front against Japanese threat, 128–139
Chinese Nationalist Party (Kuomintang): defeat of, 139; in United Front against Japanese threat, 128–139
Cichowski, Kazimierz, 125, 126
Cipher correspondence: amount of, 14; breaches of security, 16, 18–19; British decryption of, 3, 19–20; code names for Comintern leaders, 15–16, 17, 21; communications apparatus for, 13–14, 20–21; content of, 1–2, 7; encryption methods, 14–17; headquarters copy of, 23; Moskvin code, 21–22; and Paris communications center, 29–31; publication of, 3; transmission methods, 17–18, 27–29, 35–36
Čižinski, Josip. See Gorkić, Milan
Clément. *See* Fried, Eugen
Coded communications. *See* Cipher correspondence
Code names, 15–16, 17, 21
Codevilla, Carlo (Mario), 15–16
Codovilla, Vittorio (Luis Medina), 69, 70, 73, 75, 86, 89, 91, 95, 97, 101, 104, 148
Comintern: budget of, 38–39, 43–44, 49–50; coded communications of (*see* Cipher correspondence); control over Communist parties, 246–247; dissolution of, 5, 238–244, 249, 293n18; European orientation of, 5–6; foreign representatives of, 13, 32–33; historiography of, 251n4; and intelligence services (*see* Intelligence services-Comintern cooperation); international public persona of, 11–12; mission of, 245, 246; money disbursements to Communist parties (*see* Money disbursements); and Nazi-Soviet Pact (*see* Nazi-Soviet Pact: on Comintern policy directives); operatives' lifestyle and risks, 12–14; Platform and Program of, 8; and Popular Front in France (*see* Popular Front); propaganda campaigns of, 8–11; publications of, 13; public pronouncements of, 247–248; and purges (*see* Purges; Purges of Comintern); scope of activities, 4–5; secrecy of, 187; as Soviet institution, 7, 8, 187, 245; and Spanish Republic (*see* International Brigades; Spanish Republic); Third

Period line of, 51–52, 53; in wartime (*see* World War II; World War II, post-Soviet invasion). *See also* Dimitrov, Georgi; *specific Communist parties*
Comintern archives: employee card file, 255n41; example of cipher document, 1–2; importance of, 4–5; and openness policy, 2–3; Opis 184 of, 5, 20; roadblocks to access, 3–4; secrecy about cipher documents, 2; transfer to Central Committee, 240
Communications center: European, 147, 148–150; in Paris, 19, 29–31, 39, 40, 47
Communications Service (CS), 13–14; purge of, 23–24, 30, 34; training in Lenin School, 20. *See also* Cipher correspondence
Communist International. *See* Comintern
Communist International magazine, 164, 168
Communist parties. *See specific parties* (e.g., United States Communist Party)
Condor Legion, 95
Constitution, Soviet, and propaganda campaign, 10–11
Cordier, 225
Couriers, 18, 28, 30, 33, 35–36, 40–41, 42, 43
Croatian Communist militia (Ustashe), 192–193, 198, 199
Cryptography Division, 21; purges in, 24–26
Czechoslovak Communist Party, 22; anti-Fascist position of, 160–161; Comintern files on, 14; and evacuation of International Brigades volunteers, 108; foreign bureau in USSR, 240; money disbursement to, 39, 40; Nazi-Soviet pact policy directives to, 161–162; and Popular Front, 65–66; recruitment of International Brigades, 88; and Soviet-Finnish War, 175
Czechoslovakia: and Munich Agreement, 63–64, 160; Nazi occupation of, 64, 160

Daily Worker, 148
Daladier, Édouard, 52, 54, 62–63, 64, 142, 143–144, 161
Dallidet, Arthur, 215
Daniel, Berta (Lore), 25
Danish Communist Party: Comintern files on, 14; Nazi-Soviet Pact policy directives to, 169
Darkness at Noon (Koestler), 8
David, Fritz, 113
Davies, Joseph, 244
DeGaulle, Charles, 180, 181, 216–217
De Graaf, Johann, 28, 29
Dekanozov, Vladimir, 151
Denmark: Nazi invasion of, 168–169, 174. *See also* Danish Communist Party
Dennis, Eugene (Tim Ryan), 236
Department of International Communications (DIC), 13–14, 15, 20–21, 29. *See also* Communications Service
Deutsch, Julius, 97, 98
Díaz, José, 66, 69, 70, 73, 84, 89, 93, 95, 97
Dimitrov, Georgi, 10, 12, 133; antifascist mobilization directives of, 185–186, 213, 214, 216, 225–227, 229, 230, 232, 233; budgetary requests of, 43, 49, 50; and Bulgarian Communist Party, 153, 160, 232, 233; and Bulgarian-Soviet pact proposal, 156, 157, 158–159; and Chinese United Front against Japan, 129, 130–131, 132–133, 134, 135–136, 137–138; coded dispatches of, 21; code names of, 15; and communication center in Europe, 148–149; correspondence with Stalin, 252n6; and dissolution of Comintern, 238, 239–240, 241–242, 243, 244; and Dutch Communist Party, 230–231; and French Communist Party, 171–173, 213, 214, 216; and French Popular Front, 55, 56–57, 58, 60; and Intelligence services, 188–189, 190–191, 227–228, 229, 233–235; and International Brigades, 94, 103, 105, 106, 107, 108, 109, 110; and Italian Communist Party communications, 201–202; on Italian Communist Party platform, 178; and London manifesto, 167; and money disbursements, 41, 44, 45, 47, 48, 129; and Moskvin code, 21–22; and Munich crisis of 1938, 64; and National Front, 216, 217; national liberation directive of, 180–181, 182–183; Nazi-Soviet Pact policy directives of, 142, 144–145, 146–148, 151, 160, 164, 165, 169, 170, 173; and Polish Communist Party, 124, 125, 126; and Polish Workers' Party, 204–205, 206, 207, 210, 211, 212; and purges of Comintern, 22–23, 24, 25; and radio transmission, 36; and Red Orchestra espionage network, 218, 219, 220–221, 222, 223–224; rise of, 53; on *Short Course* dissemination in China, 130; and

Dimitrov (*conti ...*)
Soviet-Finnish War, 176; and Spanish Republican government, 69, 70, 71–72, 73–74, 75, 77, 79, 80, 83, 93; Stalin's input in orders and directives of, 246; and Swedish Communist Party, 233–235; and Tito's partisans, 192, 194–195, 196–199, 202–203; and Trotskyite campaign, 115–116, 118, 121, 122; and U.S. Communist Party, 33, 37, 66–67, 235–237; workers' conference plan of, 64–66, 67
Dimitrov Secretariat, 4
Diplomatic mail, coded messages in, 17–18
Diplomatic missions, money transmission through, 41, 42
Dollfuss, Engelbert, 52
Dübi, Lydia (Pascal), 19, 30–32, 47
Duclos, Jacques, 243; and Belgium Communist Party, 225, 227; and Free French (Gaullists), 180, 216–217; and French Communist Party, 213, 214, 215–216; and French Popular Front, 58; and Nazi occupiers, 171; and Red Orchestra espionage network, 219, 221, 222, 223, 224; and Spanish Communist Party, 70, 73
Ducracz, Teodor, 208
Durutti Column, 73
Dutch Communist Party: antifascist mobilization of, 186, 227–228; communications with Comintern, 150; Nazi destruction of, 230–231; Nazi-Soviet Pact policy directives to, 147–148, 170
Dutt, Rajani Palme, 148

Eisenberg, 40
Encryption methods, 14–15
Ercoli. *See* Togliatti, Palmiro
Estonia: and Nazi-Soviet Pact, 141; Sovietization of, 151
Evelyn, Taylor, 41
Ewert, Arthur, 15, 29

Fang Lin, 129
Federal Security Service (FSB), 3
Feldman, Jenny, 40
Feldman, Simon, 40
Feuchtwanger, Lion, 115–116, 121, 272n23
Financial allocations. *See* Money disbursements
Finder, Pawel, 203, 207, 209, 210, 211, 212–213, 243
Finland: and Nazi-Soviet Pact, 141; Soviet invasion of, 174–177
Finnish Communist Party: foreign bureau in USSR, 240; money disbursement to, 49; suppression of, 177
Finnish Communists in U.S., and Soviet-Finnish War, 176
Finnish Communists in USSR, purge of, 127
Finnish Democratic Republic, 174–175, 176, 281n86
Finnish White Guards, 176
Firsov, Fridrikh I., 2, 3, 5, 6
Fisher, Louis, 102
Fitin, Pavel, 188, 190, 191, 200, 227–228, 231, 232, 233, 236, 242
Flieg, Leo (Karl), 31
Florin, Wilhelm, 126
Foissin, Robert, 172
Fornalska, Malgorzata, 207, 208
Fort-Whiteman, Lovett, 273n43
Foster, William, 235
France: defeat of, 156, 173; Free French movement (Gaullists), 180–181, 185, 216–217; internment of International Brigade volunteers in, 108, 110; Laval government, 54, 55; in Munich Agreement, 62, 63–64, 66; and Nationalist Spain, 80; right wing forces in, 52; and Soviet-Finnish War, 175; -Soviet pact, 55, 59; Spanish Communist refugees in, 84; workers-peasant group in, 163–164. *See also* French Communist Party; Popular Front (France)
Franco, Francisco, 78, 80, 82, 83, 85; German/Italian aid to, 95, 94, 106
Free French movement (Gaullists), 180–181, 185, 216–217
French Communist Party, 18, 30; antifascist mobilization of, 186, 213–215, 225; banning of, 163; Comintern files on, 14; foreign bureau in USSR, 240; and Free French movement (Gaullists), 180–181, 185, 216–217; and International Brigades, 87–88, 98, 100, 102; and Jewish persecution, campaign against, 179–180; and London manifesto, 167–168; money disbursement to, 39, 41, 49; and Nazi occupiers, 171–173, 215–216; Nazi-Soviet Pact policy directives to, 142–143, 147, 152, 170; and Red Orchestra (Rote Kappelle) espionage network, 218; telegram communications of, 27–28; underground, 213–214, 220. *See also* Popular Front (France)

Fried, Eugen (Clément): antifascist mobilization operations of, 22, 186, 225–227, 228; and communications center in Europe, 148, 149, 150; death of, 227; as French Communist Party representative, 53, 54, 56, 58, 152; and Goulooze, 231; and International Brigades, 87, 88, 98; on Nazi occupation, 171, 172; and Red Orchestra espionage network, 219, 223, 224

Galagan, A.L., 221
Gallo (Luigi Longo), 97
Garibaldi Battalion, 98
Gartman, Rosa (Irina Benz), 25
Gaullists. *See* Free French movement
General Workers' Union (UGT), Spain, 68
Gennis, Anna, 25
Gerish, Grigory, purge of, 26–27
German Communist Party: and anti-Nazi resistance, 228–230; foreign bureau in USSR, 240; on imperialist war, 173; and London manifesto, 167–168; money disbursement to, 39, 40, 47, 48, 49; and Nazi rise to power, 51–52; Nazi-Soviet Pact policy directives to, 162–163, 166–167, 173–174; Nazi-Soviet Pact response of, 143; political platform of, 166, 173; in Trotskyite show trials, 113–114
Germany. *See* Nazi Germany
Gerö, Ernö, 56
Giral, José, 69–70
Golikov, Fillip, 132, 137, 188
Gomułka, Władysław, 207
Gorbachev, Mikhail, 2
Göring, Hermann, 17
Gorkić, Milan (Josip Čižinski), 103, 127
Gottwald, Klement, 37, 65, 88, 108, 161, 162
Goulooze, Daan: antifascist mobilization operations of, 186, 227, 230–231; arrest of, 231; and European communications center, 148, 150; and German anti-Nazi resistance, 228, 229; on Jewish persecution, 179; Nazi-Soviet Pact policy directive to, 147; and Red Orchestra espionage network, 220
Gramsci, Antonio, 15, 265n52
Great Terror. *See* Purges; Purges of Comintern
Greece, German invasion of, 182, 183
Greek Communist Party, 117
Grenier, Fernand, 217
GRU (Main Intelligence Directorate), 29, 187, 198, 202, 221–222, 223
Grżegorżewski, Marcin. *See* Grżelszak, Franciszek
Grżelszak, Franciszek (Marcin Grżegorżewski), 125, 126
Guangxi clique, 133
Gurevich, Anatoly (Victor Sukulov, Kent), 223, 289n99

Hanse Leichtmetall, 200
Hansmann, Elly, 229–230
Hathaway, Clarence, 40
Haynes, John, 3, 6
Hernández, Tomás Jesús, 76, 94
Herriot, Édouard, 163, 164
Hess, Rudolf, 117, 118, 121, 122
Hitler, Adolf, 51, 52, 63, 64, 212
Holtzman, Edward, 118
Hoover Institution on War, Revolution, and Peace, 5
L' Humanité, 117, 171, 215
Hungarian Communist Party: foreign bureau in USSR, 240; money disbursement to, 40, 49
Hurley, Patrick, 138–139

Ibárruri, Dolores, 48, 66, 76, 84, 95
Illner, Arthur, 229
Ilyichev, Ivan, 198, 205, 208, 221, 223, 232, 242
Imperialist war, 146–148, 152, 154, 161–162, 163, 166, 169, 173, 182
Institute of Marxism-Leninism, 2
Intelligence services-Comintern cooperation: common mission and techniques in, 187–188; and dissolution of Comintern, 242; and Dutch Communist Party, 227–228; and intelligence channels for communications, 190–191, 233; and Katyn Massacre, 211–212; in money transmission, 41–42; and Polish Worker's Party, 204–206; in recruitment of agents, 189–190; and Red Orchestra espionage network, 217–225; and Swedish Communist Party, 233–235; and Tito's partisans, 198–200; during World War II, 188–191, 237, 248–249
International Brigades, 16, 74; casualty rate for, 99, 104; collective leadership of, 97–98; French Communist Party relations with, 98; heroic reputation of, 85; Kleber's command, 93, 94, 95–97;

International Brigades (*conti . . .*)
Marty's leadership of, 73, 75–76, 91, 92, 97, 98; military aid to, 90–92; morale and discipline problems in, 92–94, 99, 103–104; negative attitude toward in Spain, 100, 101; recruitment of volunteers, 86–90, 99–102, 105; training of, 92, 97, 99; transportation of, 102–103; veterans in OSS, 235–236, 292n137; withdrawal of, 106–110
International Lenin School, 19, 20, 34
International London Committee on Non-Intervention in the Affairs of Spain, 106
International Red Aid (MOPR), 30, 39, 44–45
Invisible ink, 18
Irish Communist Party, 45
Irujo y Ollo, Manuel de (Minister of Justice), 76, 77
Italian Communist Party, 15; anti-fascist messages of, 178–179; and antifascist National Front, 216; foreign bureau in USSR, 240; money disbursement to, 39, 40; platform of, 178–179; Togliatti's leadership of, 84, 179; wartime communications with, 201–202, 225
Italy: aid to Nationalist Spain, 94–95, 106; in Tripartite Pact, 157–158

Jacquemote, Joseph, 113
Janson, Anna, 25
Janson, Karl (Charles Scott), 25
Japan: Chinese United Front against, 128–129, 130–131, 132, 135–136; Soviet intelligence in, 190; in Tripartite Pact, 157–158
Japanese Communist Party, 64; coded messages of, 16–17
Jewish persecution: in occupied countries, 179–180, 231; Warsaw ghetto liquidation, 212–213
Jezierska, Helena (Romana Wolf), 124, 126
Jòźwiak, Franciszek, 207–208
Just war directive, 182–183

Kaartinen, Onni, 176
Kaganovich, Lazar, 70
Kalganov, Major General, 137
Kalinin, Mikhail, 241
Kamenev, Lev, 113
Kardelj, Edvard (Birk), 201, 202
Karelian Autonomous Soviet Socialist Republic, 176
Karelo-Finnish Soviet Socialist Republic, 176–177
Katyn Massacre, 211–212
Khavkin, Arthur (Siegfried Walter), 29–30, 39, 42, 256n55
Kheifets, Gregory, 12
Kirov, Sergei, assassination of, 111, 112
Kislenko, 137
Kleber, Emilio (Manfred Stern), 93, 94, 95–97
Klehr, Harvey, 3, 6
Knöchel, Wilhelm, 229, 230
Knorin, Wilhelm, 53
Kochkina-Leenman, Praskovia, 26
Koestler, Arthur, 8
Komarova, Eugenia, 25
Komarova, Maria, 32
Könen, Wilhelm, 167
Kong Sing, 129
Kopinić, Iosip (Vokshin), 192, 193–194, 198, 200, 201
Kousnetsov, Peter, 227–228
Kowalski, Aleksander, 208, 286n59
Kuczynski, Jürgen, 190
Kun, Béla, 53
Kuomintang (Chinese Nationalist Party): defeat of, 139; in United Front against Japanese threat, 128–139
Kuusinen, Otto, 22, 126, 175

Laborde, Hernán, 107–108
Labour and Socialist International, 73, 263n14
Lager, Karl, 48, 147, 233
Langevin, Paul, 215
Largo Caballero, Francisco (Caballero, Spaak), 69, 70, 71–72, 93, 96, 101
Larsen, Axel, 234–235
Latin American Communist parties: antifascist mobilization of, 186; and International Brigades, 88–89, 109; money disbursement to, 32; Nazi-Soviet Pact directives to, 153; radio transmissions to, 36–37
Latvia: and Nazi-Soviet Pact, 141; Sovietization of, 151
Latvian (Lettish) Federation of the Socialist Party, 25
Laval, Pierre, 54, 55
League of Nations, 107, 175
Lenin, Vladimir: anniversary of death, 9; leadership struggle after death of, 111; and money disbursement to foreign parties, 45

Lenin School. *See* International Lenin School
Leński, Julian, 124, 125, 126
Linderot, Sven, 109, 148, 233, 234
Lipski, Antoni, 124, 126, 209
Lipski, Leon, 209–210, 243
Lipski, Ludwik, 209
Lithuania, Sovietization of, 151
Lithuanian Communist Party: Nazi-Soviet Pact policy directives to, 151; and Trotskyite campaign, 114–115, 119–120
Litvakov, Isiah, 40
London manifesto, 167–168
Longo, Luigi (Gallo), 97
Lore (Berta Daniel), 25
Los Rios Irruti, Fernando de, 89, 91, 101
Lovestone, Jay, 246
Lozovsky, Alexander, 8
Lubienecki, Jan (Ignacy Rylski), 124, 125, 126
Lubyanka Prison, 13, 127
Lurje, Moses and Nathan, 113
Luxemburg, Nazi invasion of, 168
Luxemburg Communist Party, money disbursement to, 39, 40

Macciaci, Filippo, 190
Mailing of coded dispatches, 18, 27
Makarov, Mikhail, 218, 219
Makhin, Fyodor, 199–200
Malenkov, Georgi, 135, 186, 239
Manuilsky, Dmitry, 8, 15, 21, 22, 24, 33, 77, 80, 125, 126, 198, 207, 216; on Bulgarian-Soviet pact proposal, 159; on Chinese United Front, 130; and dissolution of Comintern, 239, 241, 242; and French Popular Front, 53, 55, 56, 64; and International Brigades, 89, 91, 93, 94, 101, 105, 110; and Nazi-Soviet Pact policy directives, 142, 144, 167, 173
Manuilsky Secretariat, 4
Mao Zedong, 128, 131–132, 133, 134–135, 136, 137, 138, 139
Markowski, Aleksander, 273n38
Marty, André, 37; breach of cipher secrecy, 16; in CPUSA leadership selection, 33; on dissolution of International Brigades, 100, 101; and evacuation of International Brigades, 106, 107; and French Communist Party under Nazi occupiers, 179, 180–181, 213, 216; on French Popular Front, 56; and Kleber, 95, 96; leadership of International Brigades, 73, 75–76, 86, 91, 92, 97, 98, 102; meeting with Soviet leaders, 70
Marx, Karl, 127, 242, 246
Mask (British decryption project), 19–20
Massola, Umberto (Quinto), 201–202
Medina, Luis (Vittorio Codovilla), 69, 70, 73, 75, 86, 89, 91, 97, 101, 104, 148
Medina (Comintern representative), 1, 16, 30–31
Melnikov, Boris (B. Müller), 19
Meretskov, Kyrill, 132
Merkulov, Vsevolod, 209, 242
Mexican Communist Party: and evacuation of International Brigade volunteers, 107–108; money disbursement to, 42
MI5, and Mask decryptions, 19, 20
MI6, informer for, 28
Mihailović, Draža, 194, 195, 196, 200
Mije, Antonio Garcio, 93–94
Mikhelson-Manuilov, Solomon: money transmission by, 40, 46; purge threat to, 33–34; U.S. operations of, 32–33, 35
Mikoyan, Anastas, 240
Minor, Robert, 90, 107, 235
Mirton (Soviet intelligence operative), 41–42, 176
Mission to Moscow (Davies), 244
Mołojec, Bolesław, 203, 207, 208, 209
Mołojec, Zygmunt, 209
Molotov, Vyacheslav, 70, 77, 80, 132, 135, 142, 143, 151, 205, 208, 209, 216; and Bulgarian pact proposal, 156, 157, 158, 159; dissolution of Comintern, 239, 240, 241, 243; on national independence struggle, 182; on Nazi invasion of neutral countries, 169, 174; Nazi-Soviet Pact policy directives of, 165–166; wartime policy directives of, 186
Money disbursements: accountability requirements for, 38, 44–46; to Chinese Communist Party, 44, 49, 129, 135; currency of, 44; documentary evidence of, 46–48; jewels and precious metals, 43; from Paris communications center, 30, 39, 40, 47; from reserve funds in France and Sweden, 48; size of allocations, 39–40; to Spanish Communist Party, 16, 30–31, 46, 48; transmission methods, 30, 40–43; to U.S. Communist Party, 32–33, 39, 40, 46, 47; during wartime, 48–49
Montenegro, Communist uprising in, 191, 192
MOPR (International Red Aid), 30, 39, 44–45

Morkowski, Leon, 273n38
Morrison, William, 20
Moscow-Paris-Berlin: Coded Telegrams of the Comintern 1939–1941, 3–4
Moskvin, Mikhail. *See* Trilliser, Meer
Moskvin code, 21–22, 108
Moussier, Juliette, 221, 222, 223
Munich Agreement, 62, 63–65, 66, 160
Münzenberg, Willi, 21, 26, 45–46, 115
Mussolini, Benito, 1, 67, 84, 201, 216

Nadelman, 42, 258–259n12
National Confederation of Labor (CNT), Spain, 68
Nazi Germany: anti-Nazi resistance in, 228–230; on Comintern policy directives, 174; Czech occupation, 64, 160; Greek-Yugoslav occupation, 182; Jewish persecution in occupied countries, 179–180; Munich Agreement, 63–64; neutral countries invaded by, 168–169; and peace negotiations, 226; Polish occupation, 141–142, 203; and Red Orchestra espionage network, 220, 221, 222–223; Soviet invasion, 135, 184, 239; in Spanish Civil War, 94–95, 106; and Third Period line, 51–52; in Tripartite Pact, 157–158, 278m45; Warsaw Ghetto liquidation, 212–213
Nazi-Soviet Pact, 245; anti-fascist policy changed by, 143–144, 145–148, 161, 248; Communist parties' response to, 142–144, 248; impact on U.S. Communist Party, 37; and Polish dismemberment, 141–142, 145; signing of, 140, 150–151; spheres of influence under, 141, 151; Stalin's motives in, 248, 276n11
Nazi-Soviet Pact, Comintern policy directives on: to British Communist Party, 147, 152–153; to Bulgarian Communist Party, 153–160; communication channel for, 147, 148–150; to Czechoslovak Communist Party, 160–162; to French Communist Party, 142–143, 147, 152, 170; to German Communist Party, 162–163, 166–167, 173–174; imperialist/unjust war rationale of, 146–148, 152, 161–162, 163, 166, 169; and initial response, 140–141; and Jewish persecution, 179–180; to Lithuanian Communist Party, 151; London manifesto violation of, 167–168; from Molotov's speeches, 165–166; and national independence struggle, 146, 179, 180–181, 182–183; to occupied countries' Communist parties, 169–173, 179, 182; and peace issue, 164–165; shift in policy, 178–183
Negrín, Juan, 25, 72, 74, 76–77, 78, 80, 81, 82, 83, 107
Nelson, Steve, 42
Nenni, Pietro, 74, 97, 98
Netherlands: Jewish persecution in, 179, 231; Nazi occupation of, 168, 170, 179. *See also* Dutch Communist Party
Nicoletti, Mario (Giuseppe Di Vittorio), 92, 95
Nin, Andrés, 81
NKGB, 242
NKVD, 12, 13, 21, 34; in Great Terror, 24, 111, 123, 127; in Katyn Massacre, 211–212; money transmission by, 41; wartime operations of, 187, 188, 190, 191, 209, 227–228; and Yugoslav partisans, 199, 200
Non-Intervention Committee, 270n62
Norway, Nazi invasion of, 168
Norwegian Communist Party: money disbursement to, 40, 41; and Nazi occupiers, 171; Nazi-Soviet Pact policy directives to, 170; and Trotskyite campaign, 118
Novaković, Ljubo, 196
Nowotko, Marceli, 203, 204, 205, 206–207, 212
Ny Dag, 173, 178

Obest (Polish underground operative), 206–207
Office of Strategic Services (OSS), International Brigade veterans in, 235–236
OGPU, 21, 188
Olberg, Valentin, 113
Oshants, Louis, 40
OSS (Office of Strategic Services), 235–236
Osten, Maria, 116
Ott (German intelligence agent), 200

Paivio, Karl, 176
Panfilov, Aleksei, 137
Pannwitz, Heinz, 289n99
Pan-Pacific Trade Union Secretariat, 20, 35
Parallel Anti-Soviet Trotskyist Center, 116–117
Paris communications center, 19, 29–31, 39, 40, 47

Partisans: of Polish Workers' Party, 204, 212; in Yugoslavia, 191–192, 194–195, 196–197, 198–200
Pascal (Lydia Dübi), 19, 30–32, 47
Paszyn, Jan (Bielewski), 126
Pauriol, Fernand, 218, 222, 224
Pavelić, Ante, 198
Payne, G. Lyman, 33
People's Guard, 204
People's Militia, Spain, 93
Péri, Gabriel, 149, 215
Peters, J., 20, 35, 188
Pieck, Wilhelm, 12, 16, 125, 126, 162, 167, 179
Piłsudski, Józef, 123, 126
Platten, Fritz, 23
Platten-Zimmerman, Berta, 23
Poland: government in exile, 203, 210–211; Katyn Massacre, 211–212; Nazi-Soviet division of, 141–142, 145, 203; Warsaw ghetto liquidation, 212–213. *See also* Polish Communist Party; Polish Workers' Party
Poles in USSR, purge of, 126–127
Polish Communist Party: money disbursement to, 46, 49; murder of Nowotko, 207; purges of, 64, 123–126, 248; Soviet dissolution of, 126–127, 203; and Trotskyite campaign, 116–117
Polish Military Organization (POW), 123, 126
Polish Workers' Party (PWP): founding of, 203–204; intelligence operations of, 204–206; and Katyn Massacre directive, 211–212; partisans of, 204, 212; and Polish government in exile, 210–211; sabotage operations of, 205, 206; violence against members of, 206–210
Pollitt, Harry, 40, 45, 88, 148, 191
Popular Front (France), 14, 30; collapse of Popular Front government, 60, 62–63; Communist Party's nonparticipation in government, 55–59, 60–62, 63; election victory of 1936, 57; formation of, 52–55; and Munich crisis of 1938, 62, 63–65, 66; and Spanish Republic, 60; workers' conference proposal, 64–65
Popular Front (Spain). *See* Spanish Republic
Poskrebyshev, Alexander, 134
POUM (Workers' Party of Marxist Unification), Spain, 68, 75, 76, 81
Pravda, 11, 117, 165, 239
Prestes, Louis Carlos, 28
Prieto, Indalecio, 70, 77, 79, 94
Prisoner of war camps, 226
Próchniak, Edward, 124, 125, 126
Profintern, 8, 34; Pan-Pacific Trade Union Secretariat, 20, 35
Purges, 248; of foreign communists in USSR, 127, 273n43; of Gorkić, 127; of International Brigade veterans, 83; of Kleber, 97; of Poles in USSR, 126–127; of Polish Communist Party, 64, 123–126; Trotskyite campaign, 33, 111–123, 271n14; of Yezhov, 23, 33
Purges of Comintern, 248; in Communications Service, 24, 30, 34; cryptographers, 24–26; foreign representatives, 30–32, 33–34; of Gerish, 26–27; of Trilliser (Moskvin), 22–23; Trilliser's role in, 21
Pyatakov, Georgi, 30, 112, 113, 117, 118, 119, 122, 271n14
Pyatnitsky, Osip, 21, 41, 53, 188, 258n11
Pyatnitsky Secretariat, 4

Questions of Leninism, 179

Racamond, Julien, 54
Radek, Karl, 112, 113, 117, 118, 119, 121, 271n14
Radiograms, 215
Radio transmissions, 1, 18, 28–29, 35, 36–37, 218
Rakovsky, Christian, 112, 113
Razumova, Anna, 258n11
Red Orchestra (Rote Kappelle) espionage network, 217–225
Relecom, Xavier, 88, 147
Republican Union Party, Spain, 68
Ribbentrop, Joachim von, 140, 141, 143, 150, 151, 165, 168
Richter, Emma, 40
Roasio, Antonio (Silvati), 178–179
Robinson, Henry, 223, 289n99
Romanian Communist Party: foreign bureau in USSR, 240; money disbursement to, 40, 46, 49
Roosevelt, Franklin D., 67, 138, 244
Rosenberg, Marcel, 93
Rote Kappelle (Red Orchestra) espionage network, 217–225
Rudé pravo, 117
Rundschau, 118
Russian Center for the Preservation and Study of Documents of Contemporary History, 2
Rwal, Gustav, 125, 126
Ryan, Tim (Eugene Dennis), 236
Rylski, Ignacy. *See* Lubienecki, Jan

Sanjurjo, José, 85
Scott, Charles (Karl Janson), 25
"Secret writing," 36
Sedov, Lev, 118
Semard, Pierre, 215
Serbian resistance movement (Chetniks), 194–195, 196, 200
Sgovio, Joseph, 273n43
Sgovio, Thomas, 273n43
Shcherbakov, Alexander, 186, 209, 242
Short Course of the History of the VKB(b), 80–81, 130
Sikorski, Władysław, 203, 207, 210
Skulski, Stefan, 124, 125, 126
Slovenian Communist Party, 201
Šmeral, Bohumir, 73, 116
Smirnova, Nadezhda, 26
Socialist Workers' Party (PSOE), Spain, 68, 70
Sokolnikov, Grigori, 121, 272n23
Sorge, Richard, 190
Sorkin, G.Z., 190, 198, 218
Soviet-Finnish War of 1939–1940, 174–177
The Soviet World of American Communism (Klehr and Haynes), 3
Sozial Demokraten, 118
Spanish Communist Party, 16, 25; conflict within Popular Front, 71, 72, 74–75, 77–78, 81, 82; foreign bureau in USSR, 240; and International Brigades, 104–105; money disbursement to, 16, 30–31, 46, 48, 49; participation in Popular Front, 68–71, 78; policy proposals of, 78–79; and Trotskyite campaign, 115
Spanish Nationalists, German/Italian aid to, 94–95, 106
Spanish Republic: Caballero government, 70–72, 93, 101; Comintern delegation to, 72–76; Communist Party participation in Popular Front, 68–71, 78; Communist Party policy proposals, 78–79; defeat of, 83–84; divisions within Popular Front, 71, 72, 74–75, 77–78, 81, 82; military coup in, 60, 83; and military retreat, 71, 77, 78, 80, 81–82; Negrín government, 73, 74, 76–77, 78, 80, 81, 82, 107; political formations of Popular Front, 68; and Soviet aid, 79–80, 81–82, 85. *See also* International Brigades
Special Region, China, 128, 129, 130, 133, 134
Springhall, Douglas, 147, 167, 168
Srebrenjak, Ivan (Anton), 198–199
Stalin, Joseph, 205, 208, 209, 213; and antifascist mobilization directives, 185–186, 225, 226, 228, 232; and Bulgarian mutual assistance pact proposal, 157, 158; and Chinese United Front against Japan, 129, 130, 131, 132–133, 134, 135; Comintern propaganda on behalf of, 9–10, 246; Comintern transmission of desires of, 246; and Davies meeting, 244; dissolution of Comintern, 238, 239–240, 241, 242, 243–244, 249; and French/Italian National Fronts, 216, 217; and French Popular Front, 55, 60, 61–62; on German invasion, 184; and International Brigades, 99, 105; Katyn massacre role of, 212; in leadership struggle, 111; and national independence directive, 182–183; in Nazi-Soviet Pact, 248, 276n11; Nazi-Soviet Pact policy directives of, 142, 145, 164–165; on peace issue, 164–165; shift to antifascist policy, 180; *Short Course* history of, 80–81, 130; and Spanish Popular Front, 69, 70, 72, 73, 74, 77–78, 79; and Spanish Republican aid, 80; Tripartite Pact membership sought by, 157–158, 248, 278n45; and Trotskyite purges, 114, 121, 122, 123, 271n14
Stepanov, Ivan, 71, 72, 73, 75, 125
Stern, Manfred (Emilio Kleber), 93, 94, 95–97
Stewart, Bob, 20
Strand, Evelina, 40
Stuchevskaia, Sofia, 28, 29
Stuchevsky, Pavel (Leon-Jules Vallée), 15, 28, 29
Suitcases, false-bottomed, 30, 42, 258n11
Sukharev, Konstantin, 34
Sukulov, Victor (Kent). *See* Gurevich, Anatoly
Swedish Communist Party, 22; intelligence directives to, 233–235; money disbursement to, 41; Nazi-Soviet Pact policy directives to, 147–148, 153, 173; and Soviet-Finnish War, 175–176
Swiss Communist Party, 23, 67, 153, 226
Switz, Robert Gordon, 217

Tadek, Jan, 124, 125, 126
Tehran Declaration, 243
Telegram communications, 16, 18, 27–28, 35
Terror. *See* Purges; Purges of Comintern

Thälmann, Ernst (Fritz), 17
Thälmann, Rosa, 17
Thälmann Defense Committee, 17, 39
Third Period line, 51–52, 53
Thorez, Maurice, 1, 21, 73, 82, 149, 238; and European communications, 150; and French Communist Party under Nazi occupiers, 172, 179, 180–181, 213, 215, 216; and French Popular Front, 53, 54, 55, 56, 58, 59, 62, 65; and International Brigades, 86, 87, 89, 98, 109; on Munich agreement, 66
Timoshenko, Semyon, 132, 133, 135
Tito, Josip (Walter), 186; and British mission, 195–196; Comintern relations with, 196–197; and Croatian nationalism, 193; Italian Communist Party communications of, 201; partisan army of, 191, 192, 194, 195, 202–203; and Soviet intelligence, 198–200
Togliatti, Palmiro (Ercoli), 21, 25, 37, 70, 148, 238; on aid to Spanish Republic, 79–80, 81–82; and antifascist National Front, 216; background of, 72; delegation to Spanish Republic, 72–76; departure from Spain, 83; French imprisonment of, 84; and French Popular Front, 54, 60–61; on International Brigades, 103–104, 105, 106, 107, 108, 110; internment of, 149; leadership of Italian Communist Party, 84, 179; on Munich Agreement, 66; *Short Course* translation by, 80–81; Spanish Republic reports of, 74–76, 78, 79, 81–82, 103–104; and Trotskyite show trials, 118–119
Trachtenberg, Alexander, 40, 42, 47
Trautenberg-Nikolaeva, Elena, 26
Tréand, Maurice (Légros), 41, 45, 48; and European communications, 149, 150; and French Communist Party under Nazi occupation, 171
Treasure Island, as codebook for Mask decryptions, 20
Trepper, Leopold: arrest of, 220, 222; background of, 217; espionage network of, 217–225; loyalty of, 224
Trilliser, Meer (Mikhail Moskvin), 33, 43, 48, 64, 67, 126; code of, 21–22; and Comintern purges, 21; and intelligence services, 188; and money disbursement, 31; purge of, 22–23; withdrawal of International Brigades volunteers, 107, 108
Tripartite Pact, 157–158, 248, 278n45
Trotsky, Leon, 2, 27, 107, 111, 112, 271n14
Trotskyites, campaign against, 33, 111–123
Tuominen, Arvo, 177

Ulbricht, Walter, 167–168
United States Communist Party (CPUSA), 1, 20; antifascist mobilization of, 186; Comintern demand for Democratic Front, 66–67; Comintern files on, 14; Comintern representatives to, 32–35; communication methods with, 35–37; Gerish in, 26; International Brigades recruitment in, 88, 89, 90, 100, 102; money disbursements to, 32–33, 39, 40, 46, 47; OSS cooperation with, 235–237, 292n137; and Soviet-Finnish War, 176; and Voorhis Act, 37; withdrawal from Comintern, 37, 235, 238
Uribe, Vicente, 94
Uritsky, Semyon, 91
Ustache (Croatian militia), 192–193, 198, 199

Vallée, Leon-Jules (Pavel Stuchevsky), 15, 28, 29
Vasilevsky, Alexander, 205
Vassart, Albert, 27–28
Versailles peace agreement, 143
Vichy France, 214, 218
Visson, Lynn, 6
Vittorio, Giuseppe Di (Mario Nicoletti), 92, 95
Vlasov, Andrei, 198
Vokshin (Iosip Kopinić), 192, 193–194, 198, 200, 201
Voorhis Act, 37
Voroshilov, Kliment, 70, 83, 99, 107, 135, 205
Vyshinsky, Andrei, 113, 118

Walecki, Henryk, 124, 126
Wałęsa, Lech, 212
Walter, Elena, 118–119
Walter, Siegfried (Arthur Khavkin), 29–30, 39, 42, 256n55
Wang Jiaxiang (Zheng Li), 129
Wang Jingwei, 138
Wang Ming, 129
Warsaw ghetto, liquidation of, 212–213
Wehner, Herbert, 229
Die Welt, 49–50
Wenzel, Johann, 219, 288n87
White Guards, 111; Finnish, 176

Winter War of 1939–1940 (Soviet-Finnish), 174–177
Wolf, Romana (Helena Jezierska), 124, 126
Wolff, Milton, 235, 236
Workers' Party of Marxist Unification (POUM), Spain, 68, 75, 76, 81
World War II: Free French movement (Gaullists), 180–181, 185, 216–217; Greece/Yugoslavia invasion, 182; as imperialist struggle during Nazi-Soviet Pact, 146–148, 152, 154, 161–162, 163, 166, 169, 173, 182, 184; intelligence services-Comintern cooperation during, 188–191, 237, 248–249; Italian entry into, 178; Jewish persecution in occupied countries, 179–180, 231; occupation of neutral countries, 168–169; outbreak of, 160; Soviet invasion, 135, 184, 239. *See also* Nazi-Soviet Pact; Nazi-Soviet Pact, Comintern policy directives on
World War II, post-Soviet invasion: and antifascist mobilization policy, 184–187, 191; and Belgian Communist Party, 225–227; and Bulgarian Communist Party, 231–233; and Dutch Communist Party, 186, 227–228, 230–231; and French Communist Party, 213–216, 225; and German resistance to Nazis, 228–230; and Italian Communist Party, 201–202, 225; Katyn Massacre, 211–212; in Poland (*see* Polish Workers' Party); Red Orchestra (Rote Kappelle) espionage network, 217–225; and Swedish Communist Party, 233–235; Warsaw ghetto liquidation, 212–213; and Yugoslav partisans, 191–192, 194, 198–200, 202–203

Yale University Press, 3, 6
Yefremov, Konstantin (Pascal), 219, 220, 223
Yeltsin, Boris, 212
Ye Ting, 134
Yezhov, Nikolai, 22, 23, 33, 124, 248
Yugoslav Communist Party, 178; antifascist mobilization of, 186; Comintern relations with, 196–198; and intelligence services, 189; and International Brigades volunteers, 102–103; and just war directive, 182–183; money disbursement to, 40; partisan army of, 191–192, 194–195, 198–200, 202–203; purge of Gorkić, 127
Yugoslavia: AVNOYu government, 196–197; British military mission to, 195–196; Croatian collaborationist regime, 192–194, 198; German invasion of, 182; Serbian resistance (Chetniks), 194–195, 200. *See also* Yugoslav Communist Party

Zarubin, Vasily (Cooper), 42
Zhdanov, Andrei, 132, 135, 142, 144, 145, 164, 182, 239
Zhou Enlai, 44, 130, 131
Zhukov, Georgy, 192
Zinoviev, Grigory, 2, 112–113, 116

Books in the Annals of Communism Series

The Diary of Georgi Dimitrov, 1933–1949, introduced and edited by Ivo Banac

Dimitrov and Stalin, 1934–1943: Letters from the Soviet Archives, edited by Alexander Dallin and Fridrikh I. Firsov

Enemies Within the Gates? The Comintern and the Stalinist Repression, 1934–1939, by William J. Chase

The Fall of the Romanovs: Political Dreams and Personal Struggles in a Time of Revolution, by Mark D. Steinberg and Vladimir M. Khrustalëv

Gulag Voices: An Anthology, edited by Anne Applebaum

The History of the Gulag: From Collectivization to the Great Terror, by Oleg V. Khlevniuk

Katyn: A Crime Without Punishment, edited by Anna M. Cienciala, Natalia S. Lebedeva, and Wojciech Materski

The KGB File of Andrei Sakharov, edited by Joshua Rubenstein and Alexander Gribanov

The Kirov Murder and Soviet History, by Matthew E. Lenoe

The Last Diary of Tsaritsa Alexandra, introduction by Robert K. Massie; edited by Vladimir A. Kozlov and Vladimir M. Khrustalëv

The Leningrad Blockade, 1941–1944: A New Documentary History from the Soviet Archives, by Richard Bidlack and Nikita Lomagin

The Road to Terror: Stalin and the Self-Destruction of the Bolsheviks, 1932–1939, by J. Arch Getty and Oleg V. Naumov

The Secret World of American Communism, by Harvey Klehr, John Earl Haynes, and Fridrikh I. Firsov

Secret Cables of the Comintern, 1933–1943, by Fridrikh I. Firsov, Harvey Klehr, and John Earl Haynes

Sedition: Everyday Resistance in the Soviet Union under Khrushchev and Brezhnev, edited by Vladimir A. Kozlov, Sheila Fitzpatrick, and Sergei V. Mironenko

Soviet Culture and Power, by Katerina Clark and Evgeny Dobrenko with Andrei Artizov and Oleg Naumov

The Soviet World of American Communism, by Harvey Klehr, John Earl Haynes, and Kyrill M. Anderson

Spain Betrayed: The Soviet Union in the Spanish Civil War, edited by Ronald Radosh, Mary R. Habeck, and G. N. Sevostianov

Stalinism as a Way of Life: A Narrative in Documents, edited by Lewis Siegelbaum and Andrei K. Sokolov

The Stalin-Kaganovich Correspondence, 1931–36, compiled and edited by R. W. Davies, Oleg V. Khlevniuk, E. A. Rees, Liudmila P. Kosheleva, and Larisa A. Rogovaya

Stalin's Letters to Molotov, 1925–1936, edited by Lars T. Lih, Oleg V. Naumov, and Oleg V. Khlevniuk

Stalin's Secret Pogrom: The Postwar Inquisition of the Soviet Jewish Anti-Fascist Committee, edited by Joshua Rubenstein and Vladimir P. Naumov

The Unknown Lenin: From the Secret Archive, edited by Richard Pipes

The Voice of the People: Letters from the Soviet Village, 1918–1932, by C. J. Storella and A. K. Sokolov

Voices of Revolution, 1917, by Mark D. Steinberg

The War Against the Peasantry, 1927–1930, edited by Lynne Viola, V. P. Danilov, N. A. Ivnitskii, and Denis Kozlov